A Hopi Social History

A HOPI SOCIAL HISTORY
Anthropological Perspectives on Sociocultural Persistence and Change

Scott Rushforth and Steadman Upham

 University of Texas Press, Austin

Copyright © 1992 by the University of Texas Press
All rights reserved
Printed in the United States of America

First Edition, 1992

Requests for permission to reproduce material from this work should
be sent to Permissions, University of Texas Press, Box 7819, Austin,
Texas 78713-7819.

⊗ The paper used in this publication meets the minimum requirements of American National Standard for Information Sciences—Per-
manence of Paper for Printed Library Materials, ANSI Z39.48-1984.

Library of Congress Cataloging-in-Publication Data

Rushforth, Scott.
   A Hopi social history / by Scott Rushforth and Steadman Upham. —
1st ed.
      p.   cm.
   Includes bibliographical references and index.
   ISBN 0-292-73066-7 (alk. paper). — ISBN 0-292-73067-5
(pbk. : alk. paper)
    1. Hopi Indians—History.   2. Hopi Indians—Social conditions.
I. Upham, Steadman. II. Title.
E99.H7R87   1992   91-30073
973'.04974—dc20   CIP

Contents

Figures

Tables

Preface

THIS BOOK is an outgrowth of long and stimulating discussions about sociocultural persistence and change that we have had over the last few years. The dialogue began as we read each others' research papers, books, and monographs and offered advice and criticism on work in preparation. Although our anthropological training and backgrounds are different (Rushforth is a cultural anthropologist; Upham is an archaeologist), we found common ground in the way we conceived of culture and society. We also discovered similarities in our views about how behavior and material culture can be identified, described, and used to construct explanations of sociocultural persistence and change.

Further, we found common ground in our interests in the prehistory, history, and ethnology of Southwestern Native American peoples. Rushforth has conducted most of his anthropological fieldwork among the Northern Athapaskan-speaking Bearlake Indians of Canada's Northwest Territories. His most recent work about Bearlake culture focuses on the persistence of fundamental values among these people. He has worked on linguistic projects among the Mescalero Apache of New Mexico who, along with other Apache and Navajo, also speak languages belonging to the Athapaskan language family. Upham has conducted most of his archaeological investigations in the American Southwest. He has written extensively about prehistoric and early historic Puebloan sociocultural systems. He has focused on the evolution of social and political institutions among these groups, but has also written about indigenous agricultural systems, prehistoric trade and exchange, and the effects on Native Americans of diseases that Europeans introduced during the colonial period.

In our discussions about sociocultural persistence and change we often referred to various prehistoric, historic, and ethnographic examples from the Southwest. We discovered that by concentrating on examples we were able to discuss more clearly and understand the explanatory arguments at issue. If, for instance, we were interested in the role of individual intentional behavior in sociocultural processes, it was useful to focus on an example such as the decline of traditional ritual practices in modern Hopi villages from 1909 to the present. According to one anthropologist (Whiteley 1988a), this ceremonial decline is partially the result of Hopi priests' conscious decisions to achieve this end. We found that attending to such specific cases made anthropological argumentation more transparent. It was easier to discuss the form of the explanation, evidential requirements, and connections among various ideas. This experience partially motivates our writing of this book. Our objective is to share that experience with the reader.

We thank Peter Whiteley for reading and commenting on an earlier draft of this book. His criticisms were extremely useful and the book is better because of his help. We also thank anonymous reviewers for the University of Texas Press who read our earlier manuscript. We benefited from their suggestions. Mistakes that remain are our own. We thank Theresa Hanley for helping us with the bibliography.

Part One
Persistence, Change, and History

1. Perspectives on Persistence and Change

IN THIS BOOK, we address numerous questions about sociocultural persistence and change. To begin, we consider how anthropologists describe and explain behavior, culture, and society for the groups they investigate. Because anthropology is the study of humankind, anthropologists are concerned about all features of the human condition. Since beliefs about humankind vary and there are so many components of the human condition, anthropologists approach their subject matter from widely divergent positions. Some view their discipline as akin to the hard sciences. These scholars seek objective explanations of facts about the real world and emphasize the necessity of formal observation, controlled investigation of empirical phenomena, and the need to avoid subjectivity in sociocultural description and explanation. Other anthropologists consider their studies to be similar to the interpretive sciences. They seek to discover, describe, interpret, and understand the meanings embedded in symbolic interaction. These scholars emphasize the role of mental phenomena in human existence, view reference to the nonobservable aspects of human life, such as beliefs and values, to be essential to almost any anthropological description or explanation, and stress the attendance of subjective factors in all scientific endeavors.

Despite such important differences within anthropology, the discipline is unified by a common concern with certain basic questions about individuals and social groups. Among the most crucial of such questions are those about human behavior. Why do people behave the way they do? Why do people from different societies often act in different ways? Why do patterns in the behavior of individuals and groups sometimes persist through time? Why do such patterns sometimes change? Anthropologists answer these and related questions in different ways. Cultural anthropologists like Rushforth frequently do so by providing ethnographic or cultural descriptions. These anthropologists assume that people behave the way they do, in part, because of their *culture;* because of the beliefs, knowledge, and values they acquire as members of a particular society. Since culture varies from group to group, so does behavior. When cultural systems persist, all other things being equal, patterns in behavior persist. When beliefs, knowledge, and values change, the associated behavioral patterns also change.

Social anthropologists often answer questions about behavior and patterns in behavior by referring to sociological constructs such as *social organization* and *social structure.* These anthropologists assume that people behave in specific ways because of the positions they occupy in systems of institutionalized social relationships. Real individuals come and go, but the system of social positions that those individuals occupy (and from which they acquire their rights, duties, and responsibilities) is reproduced and persists.

Archaeologists like Upham answer questions about individuals and social groups by analyzing *material culture,* the artifacts and other material residues that humans produce. Archaeologists describe, classify, and date all forms of material culture. They are, however, most interested in how such artifacts and material residues are associated and distributed on the landscape, and how the form and structure of these distributions change through time. Because material objects and their distributions reflect aspects of the cultural and behavioral systems in which they were made, used, and discarded, they are useful for studying the origin and development of such systems.

The concepts of culture and society are basic to anthropology. Because of their centrality, other fundamental questions emerge from and relate to these ideas. Questions about culture pertain to systems of belief, knowledge, and values. Why do different cultural systems possess certain traits and patterns? Why are there usually both similarities and differences in the cultural systems of different societies? Questions about society pertain to patterns of interaction among individuals in groups. What is the inherent nature of social interaction? Why are social interactions organized or structured the way they are? Why are social arrangements and institutions in different societies sometimes similar and sometimes different? We stress three points about these questions and their answers. First, they are logically separate from the more general questions and answers mentioned earlier. Explanations of individual and group behavior by explicit or implicit reference to culture or to social organization and structure are independent of explanations about the existence of specific knowledge, belief, and value systems or about the existence of specific social institutions and arrangements. An anthropologist might, for example, explain why a man "avoids" his mother-in-law by referring to that man's beliefs and values. The man might believe it inappropriate to speak, touch, maintain eye contact, eat with, or interact in any other way with her. These beliefs and values might be widely shared among the members of a social group, and the man might have acquired them by virtue of his membership in that society. Hence, the man's behavior is explained by reference to his (or his group's) culture and by his preference, disposition, or tendency to employ such beliefs and values in the organization of his own behavior. Patterns in the behavior of the group as a whole are thus explained by explicit or implicit reference to the social distribution of the relevant beliefs, values, and dispositions. This kind of explanation, however, does not itself explain *why* and *how* those cultural traits originated, developed, or presently exist in the society (Brown 1963: 92–98). Answers to these questions require a separate framework, possibly incorporating such variables as are mentioned in the next paragraph.

Second, questions about the existence of cultural and social systems are usually complex. Answers to them can vary tremendously. Such answers might refer to disparate variables. Answers to the question, "Why do men in the aforementioned society have beliefs and values that lead them to avoid their mothers-in-law?" might, for example, incorporate historical, cultural, social-structural, psychological, or biological factors, or a combination of some or even all of these variables. The men might have such beliefs because, for example: (1) the beliefs are part of a specific historical tradition, and the men acquired them from their parents and other members of previous generations; (2) the behavior associated with those beliefs communicates respect for one's in-laws, and such a message is somehow materially advantageous to the individual whose behavior is so interpreted; (3) the behavior "produced by" adherence to these beliefs provides for the reduction of conflict within the social group by minimizing contact between potentially contentious parties; (4) the behavior associated with this belief system prohibits contact between persons observing the incest taboo, between whom there may be incestuous desires; or (5) these beliefs and the associated behavior do all of these things and perhaps more.[1]

Third, differences in the answers anthropologists provide to such questions distinguish competing schools of thought in the discipline. Sociobiologists, for example, emphasize human biological variables in their explanations of cultural similarities and differences. Historical particularists give explanatory priority to the historic events that led to the emergence and development of specific cultural traits and configurations. Marxist anthropologists emphasize the forces and relations of production that give rise to other features of culture and society. Cultural ecologists stress the natural and social environments to which people must adapt (largely through cultural means) if they are to survive.

Finally, anthropologists also ask basic questions about continuity and change. Why do cultures (or aspects of cultures) and societies (or aspects of societies) sometimes persist, and why do they sometimes change through time? What are the bases for cultural and social continuity? What are the causes of cultural and social discontinuity, instability, and change? Again, these questions raise difficult issues, and their answers are often complex, changing significantly from one school of thought to the next. One anthropologist might suggest that the cultural traditions of some small-scale society persist because that group exists in essential *isolation*. Another might propose that a system of social arrangements persists because of stability in the *organization of production* of the society under investigation. One anthropologist might speculate that the social structure of a small-scale society changed because of *contact* with or the "influences" of a larger, sociopolitically dominant group. Another scholar might propose that the shared beliefs and values of some society changed because of shifts in the *environmental conditions* within which the group exists.

Our opinion about these and other similar explanatory claims is influenced by our beliefs about culture and society. We begin with the assumption that cultural systems are intrinsically related to social systems. We believe that people behave the way they do, in part, because of their beliefs, knowledge, and values, and that a significant portion of human action is intentional. Human action frequently results from decisions people make in pursuit of goals they establish in the contexts of their own cultural systems and traditions. We also believe that people have social-interactional constraints on their behavior. People belong to different social categories or groups within societies. Because of their social positions, people acquire beliefs and interests that can influence their intentional acts. People are sometimes constrained to behave in specific ways by the interpretations and responses of other members of their societies.

In our view, because culture and society are interrelated, the processes of cultural and social persistence and change are also connected. Hence, such processes must be investigated together. Returning to the hypothetical case presented earlier, we might answer questions about persistence or change in the behavior of men who avoid their mothers-in-law by referring to the cultural system upon which such behavior is based. We might, for example, document historical stability in the avoidance behavior of men in our hypothetical society and suggest that such stability occurs because the beliefs and values underlying the behavior persist. In this argument, the behavior persists because group members continue to believe certain things, and because they have an enduring tendency to act according to these beliefs. This approach assumes that forces leading to persistence of beliefs and values also lead to stability in associated behavior. Conversely, we might document behavioral innovation among the men who avoid their mothers-in-law and suggest that the patterned avoidance behavior changed because the original cultural system changed. That is, forces leading to the transformation of cultural systems are assumed to lead to changes in associated behavior. Through time, the men in our hypothetical society might learn new ways of interacting with their mothers-in-law. Within the context of such innovative behavioral options, they might attach a different meaning to avoidance. The original cultural system might therefore change. Hence, behavioral patterns associated with the original beliefs and values might also change. Why and how the men come to know and possibly prefer new ways of interacting with their mothers-in-law is, of course, a different question, requiring a different answer. We argue later in this book that six categories of variables and processes affect the persistence and change of any sociocultural system. These variables and processes are *demography, environment, culture contact, social structure, culture,* and *human agency and action.*

As stated, our general purpose in this book is to identify and characterize the answers to questions about sociocultural persistence and change raised in the preceding paragraphs. We are interested in anthropological views of the determinants and processes of persistence and change in both cultural (conceptual) and social (behavioral) systems. We are also interested, however, in the relationship between conceptual and behavioral systems. Our ultimate subject matter, then, is the variables and processes of sociocultural persistence and change as these are defined, analyzed, and employed in different types of anthropological explanations.[2] We are specifically concerned with the explanatory issues addressed (the "why" questions asked and answered) and the forms of argumentation that researchers from different anthropological schools of thought employ. In our discussions, we are especially interested in the critical variables that anthropologists incorporate (regardless of their subdisciplinary affiliation) in explanations of sociocultural persistence and change. Some anthropologists, for example, have considered selected *demographic variables* (pertaining to the size and density of human populations and changes in these conditions over time) crucial in their studies of sociocultural persistence and change. Our intention is to define the role of demographic (and other) variables in various explanations and to generalize about their significance in anthropological argumentation.

One useful way to organize a presentation of approaches to sociocultural persistence and change is by referring to various theoretical frameworks that have been significant in the history of anthropology (e.g., Bee 1974). Were we to employ this organization strategy, we might write chapters about unilineal evolutionism, historical particularism, British structural functionalism, French structuralism, acculturation theory, cultural ecology, Marxist anthropology, and practice theory. These are commonly identified schools of thought in the history of anthropology, and researchers from each of them have had important comments to make about sociocultural persistence and change. In each hypothetical chapter we would characterize one of the relevant historical schools according to its specific subject matter, explanatory goals, research methods, and standards of explanatory adequacy. We would illustrate our points using empirical studies that scholars working within the framework under consideration have undertaken. In a chapter about acculturation theory, for example, we would focus on what anthropologists from this school of thought have said about the significance of culture contact for sociocultural change (e.g., Herskovits 1938; Linton 1940; Barnett et al. 1954). In the discussion, we would review typologies of culture contact or contact situations, classifications of the possible results of culture contact, measurements of individual and group acculturation, and the way these have been employed in explanations of sociocultural persistence and change. We would illustrate our points using examples taken from different groups throughout the world.

Another effective way to organize a review of approaches to sociocultural persistence and change is to focus on the logical structure of explanatory arguments (e.g., Boudon 1986:9–22). Were we to employ this scheme, we would include, for example, chapters dealing with theories about universal trends and stages, conditional laws, social structures and functions, and the internal and external causes of change. In each of these chapters we would compare and contrast the claims that anthropologists from different scholarly traditions have made. In a hypothetical chapter on theories about universal trends and stages, for example, we would include discussions of "classic" unilinear evolutionism (Morgan 1877; White 1949, 1959) and more recent cross-cultural studies of societal types and evolutionary stages, such as those of Elman Service (1962) and Morton Fried (1967). A theme that unites these approaches is their concern for explaining the presence of certain sociocultural traits or the operation of particular sociocultural processes in a given "stage" of cultural evolution (Upham 1990). We would conclude this chapter by discussing the usefulness of such concepts in explanations of sociocultural persistence and change. We would confirm the similarities and differences in logical form among various explanatory models and illustrate our discussion using materials from many different societies. Our concluding chapter would include an evaluation of the approaches.

In this book, however, we proceed in a different manner. We construct our discussion of sociocultural persistence and change on the foundation of a historically ordered series of case studies taken from a single sociocultural system. We approach our subject matter in this way for three separate but related reasons. First, since anthropological explanations of sociocultural persistence and change are intended to account for observed facts about real cultures and societies, such explanations must be evaluated empirically. Case studies provide a useful means of relating explanatory arguments to the real world. In case studies, it is convenient to: (1) indicate precisely which features of a selected sociocultural system persisted and which changed over time, (2) consider different explanations for this persistence and change, and (3) evaluate the adequacy of the explanations. From the empirical foundation established by case studies, it is possible to move to a more theoretical level of analysis and discourse.

Second, we focus on a single sociocultural system because this approach allows for a more complete understanding of the *multiplicity of processes* that affect any sociocultural system through time. All cultures and societies are the products of many different events and processes. By looking at several of the events and processes that historically have shaped a specific sociocultural system, we can more clearly understand how and why that group came to possess its actual cultural and social characteristics. We can more clearly understand the *conjunctive nature* of the events and processes of sociocultural persistence and change. The form of any sociocultural system in the 1990s is the result not only of events and processes that have occurred during the twentieth century, but also of events and processes that occurred much earlier.[3] By focusing on a single group and discussing pivotal events over a long period, it is possible to describe more clearly the extent of sociocultural persistence and change in the system and determine the forces that operated to produce it. Had we opted to provide case studies from several different sociocultural systems, from different times, and from different parts of the world, such facts and understanding would be lost.

Third, there are not only theoretical reasons, but also archaeological and ethnographic motivations for concentrating on a single group. By doing so, our book about anthropological approaches to sociocultural persistence and change can simultaneously provide substantial information about a people outside the experience of most of its readers. For us, there is intrinsic merit in acquiring detailed knowledge about the history, culture, and society of any group. We believe that anthropologists inform not only by cross-cultural comparisons of broad similarities and differences among groups, but also by providing "thick" descriptions of individual sociocultural systems (Geertz 1973).

The Hopis of Northern Arizona

In this book, we concentrate on the culture and society of the Hopi Indians of northeastern Arizona, one of the best-known and most intensively studied groups in the American Southwest. The Hopis are Puebloan Indians. The majority of Hopis reside in different villages located on or near the Hopi Mesas, the southern extension of the Colorado Plateau's Black Mesa. The fingers of this extension are known as First, Second, and Third Mesa, respectively. The contemporary villages of Sichomovi, Walpi, Tewa Village (Hano), and Polacca are found at First Mesa. Second Mesa villages include Shongopavi, Shipaulovi, and Mishingnovi. The pueblos of Oraibi, Hotevilla, Bacavi, and Kykotsmovi (New Oraibi) are located at Third Mesa. Another Hopi village, Moenkopi, is located approximately forty miles northwest of the three Mesas, adjacent to the town of Tuba City, Arizona. Moenkopi originated in the 1870s as an Oraibi farming colony, is now split into Upper and Lower Moenkopi, and is, according to Hopi conceptions, part of Third Mesa. The location of contemporary Hopi villages is shown in Figure 1.

Other Puebloan peoples of Arizona and New Mexico include (1) the Zunis; (2) the Keres-speaking peoples of Acoma, Laguna, Cochiti, Santo Domingo, San Felipe, Santa Ana, and Zia; and (3) the Rio Grande Valley Tanoan-speaking peoples of Taos, Picuris, Sandia, Isleta, Santa Clara, San Juan, San Ildefonso, Nambe, Tesuque, Pojoaque, and Jemez. These peoples have been sedentary agriculturalists living in compact communities for many hundreds of years. The location of Puebloan peoples in Arizona and New Mexico is shown in Figure 2.

The Hopi language belongs to the Uto-Aztecan linguistic family, which also includes such diverse languages as Nahuatl (spoken by the Aztecs and their descendants in the Valley of Mexico), Pima and Papago (spoken by peoples from southern Arizona), and Shoshoni (spoken by Native Americans of the Great Basin) (Hale and Harris 1979; Steele 1979). These related, though separate and mutually unintelligible languages, share features of sound, structure, and meaning because they descended from a common parent language. At some distant point in

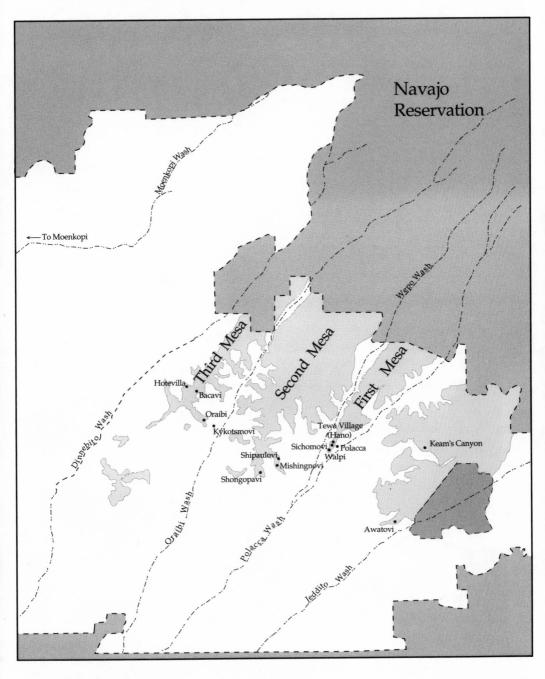

Figure 1. Northeastern Arizona and the Hopi Reservation

——————— 1882 Hopi Reservation

— — — — Present Hopi Reservation

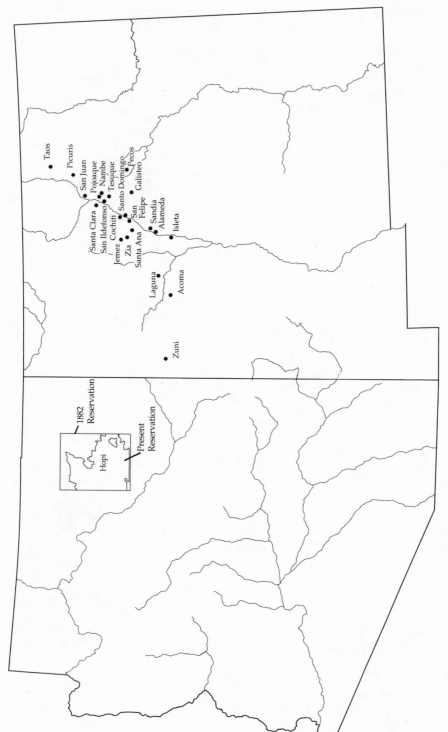

Figure 2. Puebloan Peoples of the American Southwest

time, the ancestors of today's speakers of the Uto-Aztecan languages belonged to a single speech community and spoke a common language (or set of closely related dialects). Through geographical and social separation over time, this common language diverged into today's Uto-Aztecan languages.

Other language families represented among the Puebloan Indians include Zuni, Keresan, and Tanoan. While the Hopi language is related to other Uto-Aztecan languages, Zuni and Keresan (which are unrelated to each other) have no apparent close relatives (Davis 1979). The former might, however, be remotely related to languages of the Penutian language family, which are spoken in California and Oregon (Newman 1964). Tanoan languages of the Rio Grande Valley (which are divided into three branches or subsets of related but mutually unintelligible languages: Tiwa, Tewa, and Towa) are distantly related to Kiowa. The latter language is spoken by the Plains tribe of the same name. The distribution of Uto-Aztecan and other Puebloan language families in Native North America is shown in Figure 3.

Hopi Social History

In this book, we characterize Hopi culture and society in different eras, beginning in prehistory and ending in contemporary times. We do not provide a complete history of the Hopi people, although we discuss several significant events and processes that affected the Hopis through the last five hundred years. Nor do we produce singularly comprehensive accounts of specific eras and events. Rather, we focus on a few important events and processes (which we describe using archaeological, historical, ethnohistorical, and ethnographic information) that have contributed to continuity and change in the Hopi sociocultural system. We thus use the Hopi case studies to begin our inquiry into anthropological explanations of sociocultural persistence and change. We then move to more theoretically oriented discussions later in the book.

We present our partial reconstruction of Hopi culture and society in Part Two. Part Two is organized into one introductory chapter (Chap. 2) and five case studies (Chaps. 3 through 7) extracted from different periods in Hopi prehistory and history. Chapter 2 provides archaeological and anthropological background information about Hopi prehistory, history, culture, and society. This background is necessary to understand the more detailed case studies. In Chapter 2, we introduce the term "Western Pueblo" and use it to discuss the prehistoric period in northern Arizona and central-western New Mexico. This term desig-

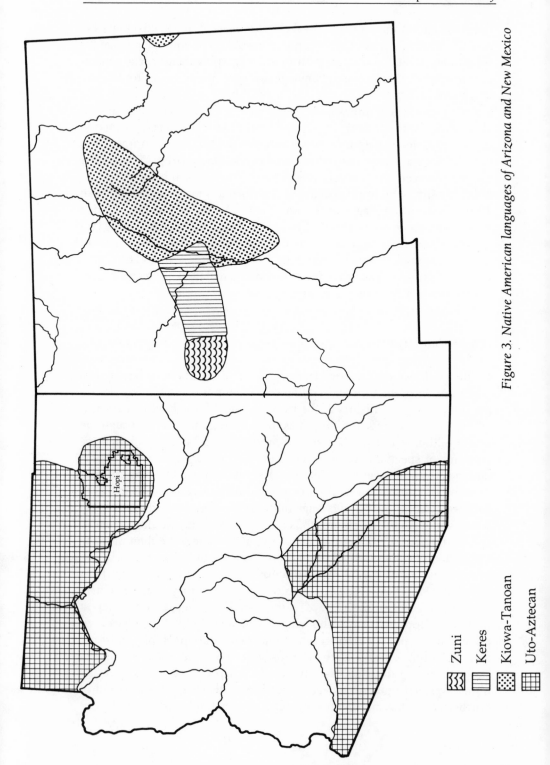

Figure 3. Native American languages of Arizona and New Mexico

Hopi

Zuni
Keres
Kiowa-Tanoan
Uto-Aztecan

nates the ancestors of contemporary Hopi people, but also the ancestors of Zuni and Acoma peoples (Eggan 1950). Also in Chapter 2, we describe Hopi culture and society from the "ethnographic present," the period of the late 1800s and early 1900s.

Following this introductory chapter, Upham presents our first case study (Chap. 3). It deals with Western Pueblo "abandonments" from A.D. 1450 to 1539. One of the first important observations that sixteenth-century Spanish explorers made about what is now Arizona and New Mexico pertained to the many abandoned villages and to regions that were seemingly devoid of population. These empty regions, or *despoblados* (as the Spanish referred to them), conjured up the mystery of lost civilizations and vanished peoples. Spanish narratives of this period reflect wonderment about an enigmatic history. Since that time, Pueblo abandonment has been a common topic in writings about Southwestern prehistory. More recently, the theme of abandonment has figured prominently in culture histories that archaeologists (especially those concerned with the prehistory of the Four Corners region and the San Juan Basin) have written. Archaeologists' explanations of regional abandonments have focused on drought-induced migrations, depopulation due to disease, raiding by predatory nomads, and a variety of other factors. In the first case study, Upham explores these issues and explanations. He then offers a different interpretation and explanation of Southwestern abandonments. Portions of this case study are based on Upham's paper "Adaptive Diversity and Southwestern Abandonments" (1984).

The second case study (Chap. 4) is also authored by Upham. It focuses on colonial contact, disease, and population decline in the Western Pueblo region from A.D. 1539 to 1680. One of the unintended consequences of European colonization of the Americas was the introduction of infectious diseases to which Native American populations had no immunity. The most devastating of these new diseases were the "crowd infections," smallpox, measles, and influenza. The rapid spread of these pathogens following Spanish contact caused dramatic population loss in the Americas (Dobyns 1966). In areas were the Spanish kept accurate records, such as the Valley of Mexico, census documents and other chronicles show that population declined by as much as 90 percent of precontact levels. In areas where records are poor or nonexistent, however, anthropologists and historical demographers have no way to assess the magnitude of population decline or the consequences of population loss on native sociocultural systems. The American Southwest is just such an area. In the second case study, Upham explores this issue and offers a new methodology for dealing with population loss due to disease. He then examines the efficacy of the method for explaining the demographic structure of the Western Pueblo region between A.D. 1539 and 1680. Aspects of this case study are drawn from Upham (1986).

Our third case study (Chap. 5) is written by Rushforth. It pertains to Hopi history from A.D. 1680 to 1880, during which time two major events occurred that affected Hopi culture and society. These events are the Pueblo Revolt of 1680 and the destruction of the Hopi pueblo of Awatovi by Hopi warriors from other pueblos between 1700 and 1701. The Pueblo Revolt refers to the overthrow of Spanish colonial tyranny by Pueblo Indians of New Mexico and Arizona, including the Hopis. Acting in concert under Northern Tewa leadership, Puebloan peoples successfully fought and expelled the Spanish from their territory. The destruction of Awatovi was a response by Hopi religious leaders to the reacceptance of Spanish priests after 1692 by the people of Awatovi. To ensure religious integrity, Hopis from other villages burned Awatovi, killed some of its people, and resettled the rest among the other Hopi pueblos. These two incidents were part of widespread Hopi resistance to foreign influence and domination during the eighteenth and nineteenth centuries. According to previous anthropological interpretations, this resistance contributed to Hopi sociocultural stability and persistence during that period.

The fourth case study (Chap. 6) is also written by Rushforth. It deals with the years 1880 to 1909 and focuses on an event in Hopi history that has received much anthropological attention. On the evening of September 7, 1906, 485 residents of Old Oraibi, a Hopi village of Third Mesa, either abandoned or were expelled from their homes and were forced to leave the pueblo. This event represented the disintegration of a village that had persisted for hundreds of years. The disintegration of Oraibi led directly to the establishment of three new and separate communities on Third Mesa. Subsequently, Hopi culture and society have persisted differentially in these villages. Our fourth case study explores the Oraibi split and examines different anthropological explanations for this event.

Our final case study (Chap. 7) is authored by Rushforth and focuses on events from 1910 to 1989. Among the important Hopi sociocultural changes discussed in Chapter 7 are: (1) an increase in population accompanied by shifts in residence patterns; (2) a shift in economic organization from subsistence agriculture to wage labor; (3) the widespread adoption of modern material culture; (4) a decline in relevance of some traditional features of social organization; (5) a decline in the significance of traditional religious institutions; and (6) a secularization of political organization. In Chapter 7, we attend to these changes and relate each to the overwhelming importance of the modern incorporation of Hopi culture and society into the American and world political economies.

A Digression Concerning Archaeological and Ethnographic Evidence

As noted, we structure our case studies around both prehistoric and historic events because detailed descriptions and analyses of such events and situations lend special insight into explanations of sociocultural persistence and change. Since case studies are central to our discussion, we must address two issues concerning the documentation, presentation, and interpretation of prehistoric and historic materials. The first issue concerns the data we employ in Chapters 3 through 7. The second pertains to the use of "ethnographic analogy" in the interpretation of both archaeological and historical materials.

First, because our case studies concern both prehistoric and historic periods, we document events and situations using different types of data. We support the prehistoric case studies primarily through archaeological data compiled during years of regional research and analysis. We also support these case studies (and the earliest historical case study) using obliquely recorded Spanish chronicles of conquest, as well as native oral traditions recorded in the nineteenth and twentieth centuries. We document later case studies by employing professional anthropological descriptions that trained ethnographers wrote after the turn of the twentieth century. We substantiate other case studies using the cold, hard numbers of the census taker.

The different data types we employ vary in their precision. In case studies about the prehistoric Western Pueblo, we rely on imprecise archaeological, early historical, and ethnohistorical data. Archaeological data are, by definition, imprecise because they are measures based on extinct, not "living," sociocultural systems. Spanish historic records, too, are inexact because they often were written as administrative records of contact, inventories of resources, or census lists of souls ripe for conversion to Christianity. Thus, the ethnohistories written from these data are also imprecise. Consequently, historical and ethnohistorical data sources may provide "facts" with strong biases. Hence, events and situations reconstructed using archaeological data, early historical documents, and ethnohistorical accounts are vague. Accordingly, caution must be used when identifying, describing, and explaining the associated processes of sociocultural persistence and change.

The data presented in Chapters 6 and 7, concerning the Oraibi split and modernization among the Hopis, contrast sharply with data used in descriptions of the prehistoric Western Pueblo. The Oraibi split is richly chronicled by historical sources that provide precise information (see Whiteley 1988a, 1988b). Eyewitness accounts, for example, specify exactly which individuals left and which remained at Old Oraibi on September 7, 1906. Since the split at Old Oraibi, more modern records of the Hopis also permit a relatively exact and accurate historical construction of sociocultural trends on the Hopi Reservation (which was established in 1882). Accurate figures are available from the 1980 U.S. census concerning everything from Hopi household income and education to the availability of indoor plumbing. Because these data are reasonably reliable, it is easier to reconstruct the events of sociocultural persistence and change for the modern period than for the prehistoric and early historic periods. Nevertheless, even in the modern era, room remains for differences of opinion concerning the description and explanation of sociocultural events and processes. Suichi Nagata suggests, for example, that the significance of nuclear family households among the Hopis increased during the twentieth century, at least at Moenkopi (1971). For Nagata, this sociocultural *change* requires explanation. On the other hand, Peter Whiteley suggests that household structure has not changed during these years, at least at Bacavi (1988a). According to him, Bacavi nuclear family households were common in the past and remain significant. For Whiteley, this sociocultural *persistence* requires explanation (see Chap. 7).

The second issue concerning our use of prehistoric and historic materials pertains to the appropriateness of "ethnographic analogy" in the interpretation of archaeological and historical records. In its widely used sense, ethnographic analogy entails the use of descriptions and explanations of "living" sociocultural systems and processes as heuristic devices to aid and structure the interpretation of archaeological data. Among those who advocate one form or another of ethnographic analogy, the principle of "uniformitarianism" is central (Sanders and Price 1968:221–222). For these archaeologists, most of what is known about the past is derived from observations and study of the present. If something is known about the past that is not directly observable today, that information must be derived deductively, using the comparative method based on observation and study of the present. For these archaeologists, though anthropologists may become students of prehistory, they remain prisoners of the present who evaluate and interpret reality based on their shared and idiosyncratic experiences. Knowledge of the past, then, is limited by understandings of present "reality."

Archaeologists have for decades used ethnographic analogy as a substitute for explaining sociocultural persistence and change among Western Pueblo peoples. In the 1880s and 1890s Adolf Bandelier, Jessie Walter Fewkes, and Frank Hamilton Cushing employed ethnographic analogy in the first systematic and semiprofessional observations made in the region. They assumed that "prehistoric cultures were broadly similar to the modern Pueblos" and, consequently, that "one could interpret prehistoric societies by direct analogy to the living peoples" (Longacre 1970a:2; Taylor 1954:561).

After the turn of the century, virtually all of the early efforts to establish chronologies for specific Southwestern regions began either at inhabited pueblos or at pueblos abandoned during periods of recorded history (e.g., Kidder 1915; Nelson 1914). These approaches to establishing chronological frameworks only made sense in light of existing native populations, their presumed link to long-abandoned sites, and the striking similarity between certain classes of material culture and artifacts found at prehistoric sites. During the 1930s and 1940s, the presumed link between modern and prehistoric Pueblo groups received additional impetus from two areas outside of archaeology, namely, the field of ethnology and legislative mandates from the Federal government. Some ethnologists working in the Southwest during the 1930s and 1940s argued that archaeologists could only interpret their data within frameworks provided by ethnographic field research (Hawley 1937; Steward 1937, 1938; Parsons 1940; Titiev 1944). At approximately the same time, the passage of the Indian Claims Act in 1946 set in motion a pattern of research with the explicit goal of establishing an unbroken chain of occupation from history to prehistory, thereby justifying Puebloan groups' claims to "ancestral" lands (see Chap. 7).

During the 1950s various studies employed the idea of occupational continuity that had been initially put forth by the land claims work. Much of this research was modeled after direct historical investigation. This approach was typified by interpretations that focused on the migrations of prehistoric populations to locations of their modern-day settlements (Wendorf and Reed 1955), efforts to establish the linguistic affiliation of prehistoric groups on the basis of ceramic distributions (Reed 1949),[4] and attempts to link modern groups of people with entire material assemblages from archaeological sites in particular regions (Reed 1948, 1955). Frequently, such research took an overtly descriptive, trait-oriented perspective.

The generation of archaeologists who began working in the Southwest during the 1960s brought with them a revised vision of the role ethnographic data could play in archaeological interpretation. Stimulated particularly by the writings of Lewis Binford (e.g., 1962, 1964), a school of archaeology emerged that advocated a positivist scientific philosophy, argued for the primacy of culture process over culture traits, and eschewed description for explanation. Many of these archaeologists followed deductive models of research and some suggested that a primary source of hypotheses was the sizable ethnographic literature that existed on Southwestern societies (e.g., Longacre 1964, 1970a, 1970b; Hill 1968, 1970). These researchers established for the first time in Southwestern archaeology the explicit goal of reconstructing prehistoric Pueblo social organization.

This renewed attention to ethnographic data resulted in several thoughtful suggestions of how such information could be employed most fruitfully in archaeological research (Binford 1967; Hill 1970; Dean 1970). Archaeologists gave little consideration, however, to the temporal character of the ethnographic observations that were to form the basis of hypothesis testing and interpretations. The "ethnographic present" is a concept familiar to most anthropologists, but one that has not been subjected to the critical examination it deserves. Exactly what is meant by this term? When archaeologists derive hypotheses from the ethnographic literature or use such literature to interpret prehistory, they make use of a wide variety of ethnographic work. Most often, ethnographic studies containing the "right" information are utilized to derive hypotheses or interpret data. Consequently, it is not unusual to find books, monographs, or articles on a single Pueblo group that were written years or decades apart cited in support of a particular interpretation. The "ethnographic present" for the Western Pueblo, for example, is actually a composite of ideas, observations, and information recorded over a span of nine decades. While this may not seem to present a serious problem to archaeologists who are accustomed to working with temporal periods from fifty to one hundred years, many significant factors affected the Pueblos between 1880 and 1960 (see Chaps. 6 and 7). Several anthropologists (Nagata 1970; Bradfield 1971; Dockstader 1979; Clemmer 1979; Whiteley 1988a, 1988b) have recorded the magnitude of these changes in detail and have shown that the loss of tribal autonomy, the imposition of federally sanctioned tribal governments, integration into a cash economy, and the individualization of social structure have had an enormous effect on virtually all aspects of Pueblo life (see Chap. 7). Nevertheless, some anthropologists have implied that Pueblo culture and social, political, and religious organizations were relatively unaffected by the pressures of the wider cultural milieu.

The opposite is more nearly true. Cultural systems do not exist in isolation, and it is naïve to suggest that the core of Puebloan organization has remained relatively unchanged since colonial times, let alone during the "ethnographic present." A body of literature is now accumulating that indicates it is precisely because the Pueblo were able to change and modify organizational structures that they were able to survive periods of successive domination (e.g., Plog 1978, 1983; Cordell and Plog 1979; Upham 1982, 1984, 1989; Upham, Lightfoot, and Jewett 1989). The "ethnographic present" archaeologists use as a source for hypotheses and a basis for interpretation of the Western Pueblo is nothing more than a blurred vision of a people in the throes of adjustment to a European-American socioeconomic system and the federal bureaucracy of the United States government. Ethnographers recorded sociocultural systems facing and responding to enormous social, political, and economic pressures.

In summary, the close allegiance between ethnology and archaeology has been both good and bad for interpretations of Southwestern prehistory. On the one hand, ethnologists have directed archaeologists' study toward the more dynamic aspects of extinct sociocultural systems. On the other hand, ethnologists have injected unwarranted notions about stability and conservatism in Pueblo social and political structure. The former occurred when archaeologists were most concerned with description. Consequently, the entreaties of ethnologists provided a structural alternative to the staid world of potsherds and architecture. The latter, however, had the effect of channeling research and interpretation toward a presumed, if not "known," end. The view of a prominent Southwestern ethnologist illustrates this point:

> The kinds of social structures found among the Pueblos today appear to be extremely old. Since conditions of life did not drastically change until recently, the Pueblos would appear to mirror the past rather well. The moves from subsistence farming to a credit system and then to a cash economy all came about in the second and third decades of this century. Hence *the old social structures were still functioning when the basic ethnographic studies of the Pueblos were made. It is not out of order, therefore, to suggest that probably all of the structures now found in the Pueblos existed in prehistoric times.* (Dozier 1970:209; emphasis added)

Most archaeologists and anthropologists acknowledge that change has occurred among the Pueblos. Nevertheless, some persist in aligning the organizational structure of prehistoric Pueblo societies with the model derived from the ethnographic present. As Cordell has pointed out, "the interpretive emphasis has been on continuity rather than on change" (1984:238). We might thus ask, "What types of changes would militate against using data from the ethnographic present to structure or interpret the past?" There are five categories of change that have occurred during the past five hundred years, rendering the ethnographic present a wholly suspect and inappropriate basis for understanding prehistory: demographic, economic, social, political, and religious change. We discuss such changes throughout this book.

Similar to the way that some archaeologists employ ethnographic analogy in their "readings" and "interpretations" of the archaeological record, historians and anthropologists often read and comprehend historical documents from some explicit or implicit, ethnographically based interpretive position. These scholars may have ethnographic biases or preconceptions that influence, if not determine, the alleged facts they derive from historical sources.[5] In the case of the Hopis, for example, anthropologists have sometimes interpreted Spanish documents as supporting a view of early Hopi culture and society that is virtually identical to what ethnographers found in the late nineteenth century. Some anthropologists suggest the documents establish that sixteenth-century Hopi society was egalitarian and that Hopi villages were autonomous or nearly autonomous political entities (Ellis and Colton 1974; Spicer 1962; Riley 1987). This description matches exactly how anthropologists described Hopis from the last half of the nineteenth and first half of the twentieth centuries. During the ethnographic present period, anthropologists found no class differences in access to economic resources among the Hopis. Further, each Hopi village was found to have its own, somewhat distinctive social, political, and religious organization. The villages from the three Hopi Mesas were seen to be united by a common language, culture, and ethnic identity, but not by coordinated tribal activities or functions (e.g., Titiev 1944). Thus, to the extent that Hopi culture in both the sixteenth and nineteenth centuries possessed these traits, significant sociopolitical *persistence* is indicated.

As noted, however, the interpretations of early and late historic Hopi culture and society are not necessarily independent. When ethnographers interpret historical documents, the frequently preferred result is to find historical *continuity* of cultural and social traits. The reason for this bias is that ethnographers can validate their ethnographic accounts through historical records (more precisely, through their interpretations of historical records). Their often implicit argument is that theirs is an accurate ethnographic description because similar cultural and social traits were documented in the past.

Not only do anthropologists use such arguments to add legitimacy to ethnographic descriptions, they also use them as a device to separate the culture and society being described from both literal and figurative contamination by the modern world. Anthropologists are often expected (both within and outside the discipline) to deal with "exotic" features (Keesing 1987, 1989) of non-Western, "experience-distant" cultures (Geertz 1976). If a group has been contacted and culturally influenced by the modern world, the distance that makes them interesting is diminished. Conversely, if cultural and social continuity between that group and the past is established through the use of historical records, it follows that the group has not been significantly affected by the modern world and that the desired distance has been maintained. Parenthetically, spatial distance as well as temporal distance is used to legitimate the "natural" and "pristine" character of cultures and societies. Traveling to distant and exotic places has been an important social, political, and academic part of American anthropology since Franz Boas's students first went to the field.

The significance of these issues to our case studies is established by considering Peter Whiteley's discussion of social stratification and leadership among the early historic Hopi (1988a:20ff.). As stated, anthropologists have interpreted Spanish documents as describing an egalitarian society with amorphous leadership and autonomous villages. Whiteley, however, points out that those same documents also frequently describe relatively formalized leadership patterns (e.g., "caciques" or "chiefs") and often attach some sort of political priority or centrality to the Third Mesa village of Oraibi, which is sometimes referred to as the Hopi "capital." If Oraibi was politically preeminent among the Hopi pueblos at the time of first contact with Europeans, Hopi villages were not then autonomous. Now, do such references represent untrained observers' misinterpretations of Hopi culture and society, as ethnographers seeking continuity sometimes suggest? Or do the Spanish documents provide an accurate description of the early Hopis, and did this sociocultural system undergo significant change by the time anthropologists formally described it? The answers to these questions depend on how one constructs the interpretations. The significance of these questions to a book about sociocultural persistence and change is self-evident. As we work through the case studies, we attempt to provide explicit answers to these and similar questions concerning Hopi culture and society. In our reconstruction, for example, the era between 1680 and 1880 was one of remarkable stability in Hopi culture and society. Nevertheless, particularly toward the end of this period, there was also significant and profound sociocultural change. Both processes require description and explanation.

In summary, in our presentation of the case studies, we employ different types of data with varying levels of precision. Because of this, we sometimes digress briefly to discuss our evidence for specific claims. We also try to avoid unwarranted ethnographic analogy in both anthropological and historical interpretation. Finally, we acknowledge a strong interpretive element in much of our social-historical reconstruction and address possible interpretive biases as they arise. As we work through our case studies, we make explicit many events and situations that are open to varying interpretations.

Our necessary preoccupation with evidence and the correct interpretation of events in Hopi social history should not mislead the reader. We are not merely anxious to provide an accurate *description* of Hopi sociocultural persistence and change. We are also interested in *explanations* of how and why some features of Hopi culture and society have persisted and how and why other features have changed. Accordingly, in the process of describing the relevant facts about Hopi culture and society, we define anthropologically important questions about sociocultural persistence and change that the case studies raise. We also describe how various anthropologists have explained what occurred. The split at Old Oraibi, for example, raises an obvious basic question about Hopi sociocultural persistence and change: What caused Oraibi, the longest continually inhabited settlement in North America north of Mexico, to divide? Anthropologists have answered this question in different ways. Mischa Titiev (1944) answered it by concentrating on *internal* socio-structural variables and claimed that the village divided, in part, because of an inherent weakness in Oraibi political organization. Richard M. Bradfield (1971) suggests that Oraibi divided because Oraibi Wash eroded. Oraibi Wash is an arroyo at the foot of Third Mesa that traditionally provided the pueblo's residents with water for their agricultural fields. Peter Whiteley (1988a) suggests that neither social-structural weaknesses nor loss of prime agricultural land due to erosion were the primary causes of the Oraibi division. For Whiteley, the split resulted from "deliberate acts" that Oraibi religious leaders undertook based on their interpretation of Hopi prophesy.

Anthropological Explanation

The Hopi materials of Part Two provide the groundwork upon which we build a discussion of anthropological approaches to sociocultural persistence and change in Part Three. In the case studies, we focus on various events in Hopi social history about which anthropologists have made explanatory claims. For most such explanations, we make explicit: (1) the object of explanation, that is, the features of Hopi culture or society anthropologists claim have persisted or changed through time; (2) the variables and processes incorporated in those accounts; and (3) the logical form of the explanations. From a discussion of the content and form of the Hopi explanations (in Part Two), we move to Part Three and more general considerations of anthropological arguments that employ the same kind of variables and refer to the same kind of processes. Consider, for example, the question, "What happened at Old Oraibi on September 7, 1906?" For Mischa Titiev, Hopi social structure changed. According to Titiev, Oraibi split because the community lacked strong leaders who could overcome the divisive tendencies of Hopi descent groups, when such tendencies were intensified by the external pressures of contact with European-Americans. In this explanation, Titiev gives priority to internal social-structural variables but acknowledges the effects of external contact between groups and such variables as personalities and personal loyalties. The kind of explanation Titiev provides makes reference (at least implicitly) to a set of necessary and sufficient conditions for the maintenance of social groups. He suggests that social institutions must exist that overcome the opposition between different descent groups that arises from the contrasting interests of individuals in those groups. If such institutions do not exist, or are inherently inadequate, then communities composed of multiple corporate descent units will divide and will fail to persist as social groups.

Analyses such as Titiev's provide an entry to discussions of other anthropological approaches to the study of sociocultural persistence and change and of the role of selected variables in those explanations. From a consideration of Titiev's explanation of the split at Old Oraibi we proceed to an evaluation of *internal (endogenous) social-structural variables* in explanations of sociocultural persistence and change. This requires consideration of structural-functionalism in anthropology (see Chap. 9). From Bradfield's explanation of the split, we proceed to a consideration of the role of *external (exogenous) environmental variables* (such as the erosion of arroyos) in sociocultural persistence and change (see Chap. 8). From the same explanation, we progress to a discussion of the significance of *population size and density* (in relation to the basic subsistence and economy of a society) for processes of sociocultural persistence and change (see Chap. 8). From Whiteley's account of the split, we advance to deliberate the role of *human agency and action* (involving *intentionality* and *meaning*) in sociocultural persistence and change (see Chap. 9). The different case studies, then, provide different points of entry to the theoretical discussions of Part Three.

In Chapter 10, "Explanation and Hopi Social History," we bring the book to an end by discussing what we have learned about sociocultural persistence and change in relation to Hopi social history. Among other things, we emphasize the complexity and multiplicity of the variables and processes that have affected the Hopi sociocultural system through the past five hundred years. Hopi culture and society of the twentieth century are different than they were before contact with the Spanish. Explaining such differences requires explanations for many different specific events. Hopi social history is the cumulative result of the outcomes of such events. Explanations of the events and outcomes require reference to many types of variables and processes.

Some Concepts and Definitions

To complete our introduction, we define several terms and concepts that we use throughout our discussion. Although there is nothing sacrosanct about the definitions we employ, and we sometimes employ them differently at various places in the book, it is advantageous to agree, for the moment, about their meaning. As we document in Chapters 8 and 9, other anthropologists interested in sociocultural persistence and change have sometimes used different definitions for these concepts.

We have previously introduced some of the most important concepts: culture, society, material culture, sociocultural system, sociocultural persistence, and sociocultural change. In this book, "culture" refers to conceptual frameworks of meaning and moral responsibility and to socially transmitted systems of belief, knowledge, and values.[6] There are three comments to make about this definition. First, it is distinct from the definition of culture that many other anthropologists use, including several of those whose analyses are reported in our case studies. Some of these anthropologists employ the term "culture" in a manner essentially synonymous with our term "sociocultural."

Second, our definition of culture is distinct from "human agency" and human "mental states." Agency refers to deliberate, goal-oriented human actions. Although cultural systems frequently provide individuals with the framework for their motivations and other mental states (which are a proper part of any explanation of intentional behavior), the former must be separated from the latter. Our reasons for this are discussed in Chapter 9.

Third, we also distinguish between culture as a conceptual framework for meaning and moral responsibility and "material culture." As stated earlier, we use the term "material culture" to denote the artifacts and material residues that human groups produce, the intentional and unintentional, tangible byproducts of human activity. Through the study of material culture, archaeologists attempt to discover features of past sociocultural activity.

We use the terms "social" and "society" to refer to the realm of human behavior. For us, human actions and interactions are "objective" phenomena (as is material culture) that must be distinguished from the conceptual systems that underlie them. As stated earlier, anthropologists are concerned with concrete behavior and objects, as well as the conceptual systems to which the latter are related. Nevertheless, these two ontological levels must be separated. We employ two other closely related terms, "social organization" and "social structure." The first is used to refer to "patterns for behavior" and entails reference to the ontological realm of culture, to the decision-oriented basis for the behavior of individuals in social groups. The latter refers to patterns in social relationships, behavior, and institutional arrangements. Social structure denotes empirical regularities in the behavior of individuals and groups and in the form(s) of social institutions (such as the family). As discussed in Chapters 9 and 10, we consider social structure to be real, supraindividual, and hierarchically structured in ways significant for the explanation of sociocultural persistence and change. We do, however, discuss other approaches to social structure.

The term "sociocultural" denotes objects, acts, or patterns of behavior that participate simultaneously in the cultural (conceptual) and the social (behavioral) realms. By this usage, we imply that human actions possess both cultural and social dimensions. Human actions are meaningful. They are communicative. We also imply by our use of this term that the cultural and social domains are inherently related. Humans behave the way they do, in part, because of their culture. From our perspective, much of human behavior is "considered action" (Fodor 1975; Rushforth 1985; Rushforth with Chisholm 1991). When people act, they often pursue goals deemed worthy within their own group and select from among options provided by their own cultural tradition. The phrase "sociocultural systems" emphasizes both the disjunction and the systematic conjunction of the conceptual and the behavioral. This idea is reflected by phrases like "the Hopi sociocultural system," which refers to the community of Hopi people sharing certain beliefs, knowledge, and values and interacting together through time. As noted earlier, many anthropologists and archaeologists use the term "culture" and phrases such as "the Hopi culture" in ways essentially synonymous with our use of the term "sociocultural," but without explicitly acknowledging the important distinctions made above. Further, the concept of material culture employed by archaeologists is logically related to the notion of sociocultural. The latter refers to the relationship of culture to human behavior. The former refers to the relationship of culture to the material products of human sociocultural activities. By material culture we mean, roughly, sociocultural materials.

"Sociocultural persistence and change" can be understood through the previously introduced ideas. Cultural persistence refers to stability over time in frameworks of meaning and moral responsibility and to continuity in systems of belief and values. Social persistence refers to similar stability in behavior and patterns in behavior. Sociocultural persistence, perforce, denotes stability through time in constellations of beliefs, values, and associated behavioral patterns. Sociocultural change refers to transformations in the content or form of conceptual systems and associated behavior.

With the issues, caveats, terms, and definitions identified in this chapter in mind, we turn to Chapter 2. In Chapter 2 we provide historical and ethnographic background to the Western Pueblo and the Hopis.

2. The Western Pueblo and the Hopis

The Prehistoric Western Pueblo

ANTHROPOLOGISTS AND ARCHAEOLOGISTS refer to the people of Hopi, Zuni, and Acoma as the Western Pueblo (Fig. 2). They do so not only because the contemporary settlements where these people live are the western-most pueblos, but also because these groups share common elements of culture and social organization.[1]

The earliest historical records of the Western Pueblo are from the Coronado Expedition of 1539–1540. Coronado and his men left Santa Barbara, Chihuahua, in 1539 in search of the fabled Seven Cities of Cibola. Fray Marcos de Niza, who had journeyed through the area a year earlier, reported that the province of Cibola (present-day Zuni) had seven "cities of gold." He said that each of the cities was occupied by a large population possessing enormous riches. So rich was this populace that Marcos de Niza claimed the cities' streets were paved with gold and the houses decorated with pieces of turquoise. After a lengthy journey across what is now Sonora and southeastern and central-eastern Arizona, the expedition reached Cibola. Instead of finding cities of gold and a wealthy populace, however, Coronado found small populations living in six (not seven) rude villages comprised of two- and three-story apartment-style structures made of rock and mud brick. Coronado and his men called these structures "pueblos" after the Spanish word for town. Spanish explorers also found this style of residential building throughout the central and northern Rio Grande Valley of present-day New Mexico. Because of the uniformity of this architectural style, the Indians who lived in the region came to be known to the Spanish as Pueblos, despite the evident cultural, linguistic, and ethnic diversity of the many different groups.

The Spanish reported finding six occupied villages at Zuni and a few thousand occupants. Coronado's attempts to gain information about the region were frustrated because Zunis had fled their villages and taken refuge in better-fortified settlements. Those few inhabitants who remained behind refused to divulge even the most rudimentary information about Zuni daily life or about other groups in the region. Consequently, Coronado was left to infer many of the details of social, political, and economic life at Zuni from what he saw in the half-empty villages and from what little cooperation he received from his Zuni hosts. The Zunis, however, did furnish Coronado with guides for the exploration of Tusayan province, today known as Hopi.

At Hopi, Don Pedro de Tovar, whom Coronado had dispatched to explore the region, encountered groups living under very similar conditions to those at Zuni. He reported finding relatively small populations living in seven villages grouped around four high mesas. Tovar, too, met resistance and was forced into brief battle with Hopis before gaining access to their settlements. The single village of Acoma, located well to the east of Hopi and Zuni, was also reported to have only a few thousand inhabitants. Nevertheless, the exaggerated claims of Marcos de Niza that motivated the Coronado expedition resulted in Spanish claims on Western Pueblo territory and a guaranteed Spanish presence in the future.

In addition to visiting each of the Western Pueblo villages, the Spanish reported seeing many groups of nomadic hunter-gatherers around the pueblos and in the open territory that separated Hopi, Zuni, and Acoma. The presence of hunter-gatherers around these pueblos was noted again in narratives of the 1580 and 1581 Espejo and Rodriguez-Chumascado expeditions. The Spanish referred to these latter groups of people generically as "wild and mountainous people," "*indios rayados,*" "*chichimecos,*" or "*Querechos.*" Thus, the Western Pueblo region appears to have been occupied by an amalgam of both sedentary pueblo dwellers and nomadic hunter-gatherers.

At the time of Spanish contact, the Western Pueblo were agriculturalists relying on maize, beans, and squash for much of their subsistence. They also grew cotton, and the Spanish commented on the extensive cotton fields at the base of the Hopi Mesas. The Western Pueblo, and especially the Hopi, practiced an extensive agricultural strategy, depending on the abundance and proper timing of rainfall to produce harvests from the many small fields they planted in different environmental zones. This agricultural strategy contrasted dramatically with what the Spanish saw along the Rio Grande, where the large village fields of the Eastern Pueblo were watered by elaborate, centrally controlled irrigation systems.

Other parts of the Western Pueblo diet were derived from hunting game and gathering edible wild plants in the local environment. People obtained other, less essential commodities through barter or trade with their neighbors. Low levels of trade linked Western Pueblo groups to populations residing outside the Western Pueblo zone of occupation. Buffalo hides and buffalo-hide clothing, for example, were described by the Spanish as characteristic modes of dress for Western Pueblo groups. Buffalo hides could only have been obtained by direct or indirect trade with native groups residing on the Great Plains to the east. In exchange for such goods, the Western Pueblo might have exchanged maize, pottery, or cotton mantas. By Spanish description, however, trade appears to have been infrequent and conducted in quite informal ways.

The Spanish were also impressed by the apparent relative lack of political leadership in Western Pueblo villages.[2] They noted, for example, that by comparison with the Mexican polities the Spanish had vanquished in the campaigns of the 1520s and 1530s, the Western Pueblo lacked centralized (pan-pueblo) political or military leadership. Instead, councils of elders vested with religious authority governed the individual Western Pueblo villages. The Spanish wrote of governors and war-chiefs who ruled either because of their age or force of personality. The Spanish also noted that villages appeared to be organized around membership in religious societies that met in special underground structures the Spanish called *estufas*. These *estufas* were the characteristic kivas, or special ceremonial rooms, of the Western Pueblo. Ritual and some social/civic activities take place in kivas.

The picture Spanish chroniclers provide of the early historic Western Pueblo contrasts sharply with what we now know about Western Pueblo prehistory, especially the three hundred years immediately preceding Coronado's visit. Based on years of pedestrian survey of the landscape, site excavations, and analyses of material culture, archaeologists reconstruct a prehistoric Western Pueblo sociocultural system that differs sharply from the early historic system. Prehistoric archaeological data from this region indicate, for example, a more densely populated landscape, the use of intensive systems of subsistence production, high levels of local and long-distance exchange, and the presence in some localities of social stratification and centralized political leadership.

Between A.D. 1250 and 1500, Western Pueblo populations occupied most of central and northern Arizona and central-western New Mexico. In contrast to the fourteen settlements that the Spanish found in 1540, nearly one hundred large villages were distributed over this Colorado Plateau region. Some of these settlements were large, having a thousand or more inhabitants. Other villages were smaller. They were, however, linked by elaborate trading relationships and the exchange of many different commodities over long distances. Today, archaeologists recon-

struct these trading relationships by analyzing the spectacularly decorated bichrome and polychrome pottery characteristic of the Pueblo
Southwest. Specialists produced certain types of this pottery in large
quantities, apparently for the express purpose of exchange (Graves
1978; Whittlesey 1978). Hopis, for example, produced their characteristic yellow-ware pottery in large quantities and traded it extensively over
the entire Southwest and beyond (Bishop et al. 1988).

The fourteenth-century spatial distribution of Western Pueblo settlements is of special interest because the geographical location of these
villages reveals details of past economic, social, and political organization. Archaeologists infer these details from quantitative spatial analyses. They use techniques developed in economic geography that permit
evaluation of settlement systems by positing different social and economic relationships between settlement size and settlement spacing
(Haggett 1966; Haggett and Chorley 1969; Hammond and McCullough
1974). During the three centuries prior to contact (and even before this
time), the Western Pueblo region settlement pattern was characterized
by "settlement clusters." Based on empirical studies of contemporary
settlement systems, economic geographers have shown that clustered
settlement distributions indicate a high level of integration and cooperation between the populations of proximate settlements. The Western
Pueblo settlement clusters each consisted of several large multistoried
pueblos (containing approximately fifty to a thousand rooms) whose
occupation spans averaged 120 to 150 years (Hantman 1984). As a result of such occupation spans, the configuration of settlement clusters
during this three-century period changed dramatically as various sites
were built, occupied, and abandoned. These changing configurations
also meant that the nature of cooperation and the structure of settlement integration during this period changed as well. The end of this
three-century period (A.D. 1350 to 1500) was both a time of regional
system formation (especially at Zuni) and, by A.D. 1500, a period of regional system collapse in much of the Western Pueblo region.

Among the interesting features of settlement organization across the
plateau and montane Southwest during this time was that the distance
between settlement clusters was strikingly regular (Upham 1982:117–
119; Upham and Reed 1989; Jewett 1989). Geographers suggest that
regularity in the spacing of settlement clusters indicates both regional
competition and integration. In the Western Pueblo case, competitive
economic relationships may have existed between settlement clusters,
suggesting that such clusters were articulated at regional scales (Upham
1982:73). Some archaeologists have taken umbrage at this conclusion
regarding Southwestern spatial organization. They claim that scholars

who postulate settlement clusters use an incomplete sample of settlements to support their position and neglect the zone of occupation below the Mogollon Rim (McGuire 1983). However, Jewett's recent analysis (1989) of the Mogollon Rim and Tonto Basin region, which also utilized the concept of settlement cluster, defines additional clusters in this area. More importantly, she confirms that these newly defined settlement clusters are regularly spaced at distances from fifty to seventy kilometers. Jewett also correlates her findings with Upham's analysis of the Western Pueblo region. She shows that settlement clusters both above and below the Mogollon Rim are, on the average, approximately fifty kilometers from the nearest neighboring settlement cluster. On the basis of these data, she concludes that decision-making "processes above and beyond the local level were operating to influence the location and distribution of large settlements across a wide region of the Southwest" (Jewett 1989:31).

Most of the archaeological analyses of fourteenth- and fifteenth-century regional settlement organization in the central and northern Southwest pertain to portions of the Colorado Plateaus in the Western Pueblo zone of occupation. Two notable exceptions to this are the study of the Piro by Earls (1987) and the study of the Rio Abajo by Marshall and Walt (1984).[3] We must realize, however, that the spatial organization of Western Pueblo settlements between A.D. 1350 and 1500 was but one segment of a much larger prehistoric system. Archaeologists have now conducted research in several additional central and northern New Mexican regions that permits a geographically more inclusive evaluation of the Western Pueblo settlement cluster model.

Based on predictions from Jewett's application of Upham's model of optimal settlement cluster spacing (fifty to seventy kilometers between immediately neighboring clusters), if an integrated and interdependent regional Southwestern settlement system existed during the 150 years prior to the Spanish arrival, settlement clusters should be found at regular intervals over central and northern New Mexico. Archaeologists have confirmed such predictions for several regions. Based on a model of equidistant spacing measured from Upham's Acoma settlement cluster (Upham 1982:64–75), similar clusters occur at fifty- to seventy-kilometer intervals in the following areas: Jemez Springs (Elliot 1982), Abiquiu-Chama (Beal 1987), Albuquerque (Schroeder 1972, 1979a), Taos (Schroeder 1972, 1979a), and Pecos-Galisteo (Cordell 1984, 1986; Kidder and Shepard 1936; Nelson 1914). Moving south from Albuquerque, additional settlement clusters occur at Quarai-Gran Quivira east of the Rio Grande (Hayes 1981) and on the Rio Puerco (of the east) west of the Rio Grande (Hibben 1975). Other settlement clusters are located

in the Gallinas Mountains (Cibola National Forest site files, n.d.), at Socorro (Schroeder 1972, 1979a), and on Chupadera Mesa (Beckett 1981;
Wiseman 1986).

This information is especially important when compared to the earliest Spanish descriptions of Western Pueblo settlement systems. The
Spanish described much of the Mogollon Rim country as a *despoblado*,
an uninhabited place or wilderness. Yet a few decades before their arrival, this region was the location of many large settlements. Further,
the inhabitants of these settlements appear to have had social and economic ties to other groups throughout the Southwest. The basis of these
inferences is a growing body of physico-chemical data that provides
mineral or molecular "fingerprints" for specific ceramic types. Archaeologists use such data to identify sites where different types of pottery were
manufactured. Such information is vital to the reconstruction of prehistoric trade routes. Using these data, archaeologists have postulated
the existence of social and economic ties between the populations of
widely separated localities that were linked, most obviously, by the exchange of highly distinctive pottery types. Archaeologists have also
demonstrated that many other commodities moved within these economic networks. Some scholars have used the information compiled on
traded pottery and other commodities to suggest that the social and economic links among Western Pueblo villages constituted formal "alliances" (Cordell and Plog 1979; Upham 1982; Plog 1985; Upham and
Reed 1989).

The differences archaeologists have identified between prehistoric
and early historic Western Pueblo subsistence systems are also significant. Historically known and ethnographically described Western
Pueblo groups practiced rainfall-dependent, extensive agriculture. As
noted, the key to success in this agricultural system is to "hedge your
bets" by planting crops in fields with different environmental characteristics (e.g., elevation, facing, soil type, and slope). The vagaries of rainfall, wind, insect infestation, and animal predation during the growing
season may result in the loss of crops in some fields. If people plant their
crops in fields that have different characteristics and that are located in
different places, however, the probability of their harvesting from at
least a few fields is increased. The success of this strategy is enhanced in
environments where rainfall is spatially and temporally variable and
where other conditions of climate vary with topography and elevation.
The central and northern Southwest exemplify such environments
(Hack 1942; Ford 1972; Plog 1978).

This strategy, which requires large amounts of land, was enormously
successful for some Western Pueblo groups (Hack 1942). Land require-

ments, however, limit the strategy's ability to sustain large populations. "Intensive" agricultural strategies are more suited to the productive requirements of large populations. Intensive agricultural strategies employ, for example, multicropping, irrigation, or the construction of soil- and water-control devices that slow surface runoff, enhance the absorption of moisture at root level, and prevent erosion. Such actions are labeled "intensive" because they increase the investment of human labor per unit of agricultural land. When successful, intensive agricultural systems also provide surplus production that people can store and use in times of need. Because the management of human labor is directly involved in the intensification of agricultural pursuits, intensive agricultural systems have long been the subject of anthropological interest. The evolution of such systems form the basis for some theories of political evolution (e.g., Wittfogel 1957; Sanders and Webster 1978).

During the fourteenth and fifteenth centuries, many Western Pueblo settlements had relatively intensive, rather than extensive, agricultural systems (Upham 1982). Prehistoric intensive agricultural systems commonly employed terraced hillside fields. Such systems often combined extensive terrace systems with groups of field houses that people used either for storage or for temporary residence and shelter during the growing season. Archaeologists also document waffle gardens, linear borders, check dams, and gravel or midden mulching of fields at settlements in the Western Pueblo area (Cordell and Upham 1983). Finally, irrigation agriculture may have been practiced at some settlements along the Little Colorado River, and on Silver Creek and Cottonwood Wash (Lightfoot 1984).

The labor investment in many of these intensive field systems was substantial, requiring community cooperation for construction and maintenance. Some archaeologists have hypothesized that more centralized political leadership developed not only to manage necessary labor, but also to allocate and redistribute resources either invested in or produced from the land. Such leaders might, for example, have controlled the food necessary to sustain work crews during construction or maintenance activities. They might also have controlled any surplus food produced from the intensive field systems (Cordell and Plog 1979; Upham 1982; Lightfoot 1984). Such a linkage might result in the usurpation of such resources for personal aggrandizement or for the creation of a "fund of power." In many societies, such economic privilege implies some form of social stratification, where birthright and blood relations supercede age, sex, and personal ability in determining one's standing in the community and establishing one's claim on resources. Some archaeologists have argued that fourteenth- and fifteenth-century Western Pueblo society had developed social stratification linked to the control of important economic resources and human labor (Upham 1982; Lightfoot 1984).

Southwestern archaeologists are increasingly willing to accept this postulate of prehistoric Western Pueblo social stratification because of the mounting supportive evidence for the differential distribution of wealth and luxury items within and between communities. Some burials from the period, for example, have large quantities of imported pottery, nonlocal turquoise jewelry, shell ornaments from the Gulf of Mexico, Gulf of California, and the Pacific Coast, quantities of pigments and minerals, copper bells, and Mexican macaws. Other burials from the same sites and same periods are completely devoid of such materials (Griffen 1967; Hohman 1982). In some cases, ostentatious burial treatment crosscuts age and sex lines, so a few infants and subadults are accorded the same elaborate treatment in death as some adults (Plog 1985). Anthropologists frequently associate such evidence with social hierarchy (Brown 1971).

Regardless of the exact degree of social stratification in Western Pueblo communities, some settlements likely had nascent social classes by the fourteenth century. This inference is supported by other social and economic developments linked to the intensification of agriculture, population aggregation, the development of long-distance exchange relationships, the formation of integrated settlement clusters, the articulation of those clusters throughout the Western Pueblo region via exchange, and the development of craft specialization.

As indicated, such developments and features contrast dramatically with Hopi, Zuni, and Acoma social formations from the early historic period. When compared to the previous three hundred years of Western Pueblo prehistory, in the sixteenth century these peoples were (1) significantly fewer; (2) farming more extensively (less intensively); (3) trading less with other groups; (4) less integrated among themselves and less connected to other sociocultural systems in the region; (5) politically less centralized; and (6) economically less stratified and more egalitarian.

Following Coronado's visit to the Western Pueblo, nearly four hundred years passed before anthropologists wrote the first systematic descriptions of Hopis, Zunis, and Keresans. During this lengthy period, Western Pueblo groups were subjected to colonial pressures from Spanish, Mexican, and European-American settlers. Nevertheless, more than their Eastern Pueblo counterparts, the Western Pueblo successfully resisted the permanent presence of the Spanish in their villages and zealously guarded their native belief systems from outsiders. Despite such resistance, European-introduced diseases (especially smallpox, measles, and influenza) entered Western Pueblo territory, and the resulting epidemics greatly affected native populations. As discussed in Chapters 4 and 5, epidemics during the first one hundred fifty years of this period and in the 1850s were especially severe and profoundly affected Hopi culture and society.

The Hopi Ethnographic Present

The late nineteenth and early twentieth centuries represent the Hopi ethnographic present. For most anthropologists, traditional, even "unchanging," Hopi culture and society are dated to this period because professional ethnographers began to work on the Hopi Mesas at that time. A reconstruction of Hopi culture and society from this period provides an intermediate reference point for gauging the nature and extent of sociocultural persistence and change that occurred during the five hundred years under consideration in this book. Comparing Hopi political organization from the ethnographic present period to the prehistoric and modern periods, for example, allows us to isolate the factors and processes of political change. In this case, demographic collapse probably contributed to the loss of formal, centralized political institutions from prehistoric times to the late eighteenth and early nineteenth centuries. Since then, contact between Hopis and the dominant American sociopolitical system (which imposed its own form of political organization on the Hopis) resulted in the Hopi adoption of more formal and centralized political organization after the 1930s than existed at the turn of the twentieth century.

When anthropologists wrote their first Hopi ethnographies, they recorded sociocultural details for a people whose population, according to these ethnographers and the available evidence, was approximately the same size as when the Spanish first arrived. The ethnographers also claimed that Hopis were living under approximately the same conditions as the Spanish had described some four centuries earlier. This apparent persistence, despite enormous colonizing pressure, has given contemporary anthropologists and historians the idea that Hopi culture and economic, social, political, and religious structures represent "survivals" of pre-Spanish traditional forms. These alleged survivals often form the foundation for interpretations of archaeological and historical records. We discussed the hazards of such potentially unwarranted ethnographic analogy in Chapter 1.

During the late 1800s and early 1900s Hopis were extensive maize, bean, and squash agriculturalists, relying on the hedge-your-bets system described earlier. Extralocal products acquired through trade or raiding and warfare contributed relatively little to the Hopi economy.[4] Moreover, local hunting and gathering provided only 5 to 10 percent of the Hopi's subsistence. A sedentary people, the Hopi continued to live in some six permanent, compact communities ranging in size from about 160 to 880 persons. The total Hopi population at this time was approximately 2,200.

Hopi villages were socially, politically, and religiously autonomous. The social structure of each village consisted of a set of hierarchically arranged, discrete organizational levels that were crosscut by horizontal ties of exogamy and membership in religious societies (Titiev 1944; Eggan 1950).[5] (In such "vertically" organized social structures, social groups or categories from one "level" are combined with like units to form more inclusive groups or categories at a "higher" level.) Among Hopis, the least inclusive organizational level, the smallest distinctive unit of Hopi society, was the household. Households consisted of a "co-residential matrilineal kindred" or "lineage segment" (a mature woman, her daughters, and, occasionally, her granddaughters) and the men who had married these women. Because of matrilocal postmarital residence rules, couples resided after marriage with the matrilineal kin of the wife in houses that the women owned as a lineage group. The closest social ties an individual had were to other members of his or her lineage who resided together in the same household. According to Titiev, ". . . in many ways, such as the inheritance of ceremonial offices, [the matrilineally extended household] is the most important social unit of all" (1944:58). The members of a household lived together, worked together, and usually pooled their resources. Nevertheless, there was no term in the Hopi language for households, they owned no ceremonies or ceremonial paraphernalia in their own right, and they were not recognized by Hopis as an independent kinship unit.

The next level of traditional Hopi social structure was occupied by unnamed matrilineages, exogamous descent groups formed by tracing descent ties to known female ancestors. Members of a given lineage included not only matrilineally related members of the same household, but also like-related individuals from other households. Phrased differently, lineages were matrilineally defined segments of larger, more inclusive clans. The significance of Hopi lineages derived from unequal or differential solidarity among the kin groups belonging to the same clan. Solidarity was greater within a lineage than between the lineages that together constituted a clan. Elsie Clews Parsons concurs with Robert Lowie (1929:330) when she suggests that the ceremonial offices and

privileges sometimes said to be owned or controlled by clans were actually possessed by a "maternal family or lineage in the clan" (1933:23;
also cited in Titiev 1944:46).

Clans occupied the next, more inclusive, level of traditional Hopi social structure. Clans were matrilineally defined descent groups whose
members traced ties to an unknown (fictive or stipulated) female an-
cestor. Clans were totemically named (based on events in mythological
migrations), exogamous, and, above all, corporate. Hopi clans owned or
controlled agricultural lands, religious ceremonies, religious items, and
clan houses (pace Lowie 1929; Parsons 1933; Whiteley 1985, 1986,
1988a). Clan houses were the symbolic "homes" of the original clan an-
cestress, the depository of the clan's sacred objects, the residence of the
clan's leaders, and the meeting place for clan members. According to
Titiev, corporate ownership by clans of land and ritual was the key to
their significance and made clans "the cornerstone of Hopi society"
(1944:58).

The final level in late-nineteenth to early-twentieth-century Hopi social structure was occupied by the phratry. Phratries were unnamed sets
of associated clans. Individuals from clans belonging to the same phratry used kinship terms with each other and extended to one another
certain ceremonial privileges. Phratries were also exogamous. The clans
constituting a phratry were not always thought to be related through
shared descent. Some were, but others were related through ties created
by shared experiences during the mythological migrations of clans to
their present locations (Eggan 1950:60–80; Whiteley 1988a:53–55).
H. R. Voth provides examples of Hopi myths about the emergence, migration, and settling of various clans in specific villages (1905a).

In this conventional view of Hopi social structure, the vertically organized system of household, lineage, clan, and phratry was crosscut by
exogamy and by individuals' memberships in religious societies and
kiva groups. Since Hopi descent groups were exogamous, such groups
were tied to each other by marriage alliances. Different members of the
Bear clan, for example, might be married to individuals from Rabbit,
Bow, Agave, and Badger clans. The Bear clan would, then, have alliances
with each of these other descent groups.

Hopi religious societies were voluntary organizations, "sodalities," responsible for the performance of a specific religious ceremony at a defi-
nite time of the year and in a particular kiva. Each Hopi village organized its own ceremonial cycle apart from the cycles of other pueblos.
According to Titiev and Eggan, a society's central ritual, along with the
religious objects used in its performance, were owned or controlled by a
specific clan. That clan also furnished the chief officers or priests of the

religious society. However, the "common" members of each religious society came from the other clans of a village. Therefore, each such ritual group crosscut memberships in and loyalties to the clans. At Oraibi in the late 1800s, for example, the Bear clan (or some segment of the Bear clan) controlled the *Soyal* ceremony. Bear clan controlled the sacred knowledge and objects used in performance of the *Soyal* and provided that society's chief priests. Nevertheless, other members of this religious society came from nearly all of the other clans represented in Oraibi at that time. In Titiev's view, such crosscutting loyalties helped to maintain solidarity in villages where primary loyalties belonged to otherwise autonomous clans (see Chap. 6).

Also linking persons from different descent groups were memberships in kiva groups. The latter were ritual associations responsible for the construction and upkeep of specific kivas within which religious ceremonies were held. Individuals became members of the kiva group responsible for the kiva within which they were initiated during tribal initiation ceremonies (Eggan 1950:96). Like the ceremonies themselves, kivas were controlled or owned by clans or clan segments. Titiev indicates that the leader of a clan (who was also the leader of his clan's ceremony) whose members built a kiva was frequently the chief of the kiva within which his society met (1944:104). Nevertheless, the clan controlling a kiva was not necessarily the same one that controlled a particular ceremony that was performed in that kiva. For example, at Oraibi before 1896, the *Soyal,* a ceremony owned by the Bear clan, was performed in the Blue Flute Kiva, which was controlled by the Spider clan. Like marriage and membership in religious societies, affiliation with a kiva group created loyalties to persons not belonging to one's own descent group.

In summary, a Hopi individual's primary rights, duties, responsibilities, and loyalties were to members of his or her household and matrilineage. An individual had similar, but less intense, duties and responsibilities to other members of his or her matrilineal clan and phratry. A person also had marriage ties to members of different descent groups and loyalties to the members of the religious sodalities and kiva groups to which he or she belonged. These ties crosscut the rights, duties, and obligations a person had to his or her household, lineage, clan, and phratry.

We previously introduced features of Hopi political organization from the period of the ethnographic present. Hopi villages during that period were essentially autonomous. There was no "national" or pan-Hopi political organization. There were few, if any, occasions when all of the leaders from different villages came together, and there was no tribal council (Titiev 1944:67). Chief priests of the religious societies provided local political leadership, and there was no real distinction between political and religious decision-making. Each village had a *kikmongwi,* or "Village Chief," who was also chief priest of the village's preeminent ceremony. At nineteenth-century Oraibi, for example, the *kikmongwi* was the head of the Bear clan and chief priest of the *Soyal* ceremony. Village chiefs were responsible for allocating civic duties and for the general peaceful maintenance of the village. Leaders of other religious societies assumed responsibility for the good behavior of a pueblo's citizens during the performance of their ceremonies. Each village also had a *qaletaqmongwi,* or "War Chief," who was responsible for enforcing internal social order and for dealing with external affairs, including threats to the safety of the pueblo. Whiteley contrasts the War Chief to the *kikmongwi* and suggests that in times of external stress the former is more important, while in times of harmony the latter is more important. Whiteley also suggests that an analogous contrast is to be found in some Hopi ceremonies that have both "outside chiefs" or "guardians" and "inside chiefs." War Chiefs are analogous to ceremonial outside chiefs, and Village Chiefs are analogous to the ceremonial inside chiefs (1988a:67).[6] The significance of these political traits becomes apparent when we discuss the disintegration of Oraibi in Chapter 6.

The most important Hopi religious institutions, as noted, were the ceremonial societies to which members of a village's different descent groups belonged. Religious sodalities controlled secret ritual knowledge, maintained vital religious paraphernalia, and performed ceremonies central to Hopi religion. Titiev provides more detail about these societies in the following passage:

> As a rule, the head man of a clan is the chief of his group's society and holds the most important object pertaining to the performance of his rites. This is a fetish (*tiponi*) consisting of an ear of corn, feathers, and a variety of outer wrappings. It is called the "mother" or the "heart" of a ceremony, and its possession marks a society's main leader. The *tiponi* is highly venerated, and when not in use it is secreted in *the* clan house in custody of the clan's head woman. Altar parts, netted gourds, and other paraphernalia are sometimes entrusted to secondary officials and may be stored in their clan houses. (1944:103)

As noted, most Hopi ceremonies were conducted in kivas that were independently controlled by different clans.

According to Titiev, the central concept of Hopi religion was the "belief in the continuity of life after death" (1944:107). Upon death, humans were transformed into spirits who occupied the Underworld (from which Hopis originally emerged in the mythological past). The "realm of the dead" mirrored the world of the living; spirits lived almost identically to people residing in the land of the living (Titiev 1944:107). These spirits were also equated in Hopi theology with both clouds and *katchinas* (Fewkes 1922:486; Titiev 1944:108). The latter term was, in addition, used to label the masked dancers who impersonated these ancestral spirits when they visited Hopi villages during the first half of each solar year. *Katchinas* had the power to assist people in various everyday activities, control rain and other weather, punish violators of secular and sacred rules, and act as connections between human beings and deities (Dockstader 1985:9). When deceased ancestors returned to Hopi pueblos in the form of clouds and *katchinas*, they brought rain and other benefits to the living.

The Hopi ceremonial cycle had two major divisions. The first was marked by the presence of *katchinas* and occurred from January to July. The latter was defined by their absence and occurred throughout the remainder of the year (Titiev 1944:109). When the *katchinas* were present, they were impersonated by masked dancers who were initiated members of the *katchina* society (which included all adult members of a pueblo). Ceremonies attended by masked *katchinas* included the *Powamu* (the tribal initiation ceremony, performed when the *katchinas* arrived) and the *Niman* (performed when the *katchinas* returned home). When the *katchinas* were absent (having returned to their home in the Underworld), ceremonies performed by the various societies included the Snake-Antelope ceremony, the *Wuwuchim* (the ceremonies of the four men's societies), and the *Soyal* ceremony (marking the winter solstice) (Frigout 1979:564–565). The dates of the ceremonies were determined by the lunar and solar calendars. The ceremonies had both private and public components (the former being performed in kivas). Most of them required smoking, singing, praying, and preparing altars as offerings to spirits and deities (Frigout 1979:570). Such activities created, acknowledged, and fulfilled reciprocal responsibilities between those in the land of the living and those in the Underworld. Such reciprocities and their relationship to subsistence activities and patterns in the natural world were pervasive elements of Hopi religion and "world view" (Hieb 1979:580).

Our preliminary sketch of Hopi culture and society from the ethnographic present is now complete, although we address key aspects of it and add significant details in later chapters. Before proceeding to our case studies, however, we must make two points about this description. First, there is substantial disagreement among anthropologists concerning the proper description of some features of Hopi culture and society. Most importantly, anthropologists often debate about Hopi social organization and structure. Peter Whiteley (1985, 1986, 1988a), in particular, criticizes the structural-functional approach dominating the writings of Titiev (1944) and Eggan (1950), upon which we relied heavily in our account of the ethnographic present. Whiteley suggests that Titiev and Eggan overemphasize the corporate clan and impose a model of social structure on the Hopi that is more appropriate for other parts of the world. According to Whiteley, corporate clans were not central to traditional Hopi social organization. Rather, there was great flexibility in Hopi social arrangements, with lineages being especially important. We address this issue in our historical case studies. We also discuss resilience in Hopi social arrangements when considering Western Pueblo abandonments in Chapter 3.

Second, there is a general anthropological tendency to reify sociocultural descriptions from the ethnographic present and to assume them to be accurate accounts of traditional, aboriginal, unchanging, and true culture. In reality, during the late 1800s and early 1900s (and before), important forces for sociocultural change operated among Hopis that greatly affected their culture and society. Hopis were, at that time, undergoing significant and rapid change. These forces and events are epitomized by circumstances at Oraibi pueblo. Accordingly, our case study pertaining to the ethnographic present period focuses almost exclusively on that village.

Summary

Events in Hopi prehistory and history raise a variety of questions about the nature of sociocultural persistence and change. Foremost among questions about the prehistoric period are those related to Western Pueblo demography. What type of social and economic processes account for the depopulation or abandonment of the Western Pueblo region? Did the Western Pueblo region experience a generalized abandonment? If far larger populations existed in the period immediately preceding Spanish contact, what happened to the inhabitants?

Other fundamental questions arise about the nature of sociocultural persistence and change among the historic Hopis. If the Western Pueblo experienced dramatic change in the decades preceding Spanish contact, why didn't Western Pueblo groups (specifically, Hopis) also change in response to the intense colonizing pressures of later Spanish, Hispanic, and European-American groups? As noted, sixteenth- and seventeenth-century Spanish reports and early anthropological descriptions of Hopi life in the late 1800s and early 1900s are similar. Is such agreement strong evidence of sociocultural persistence over more than four hundred years despite enormous pressures from culture contact, or are other interpretations possible? If Hopis have persisted relatively unchanged from the earliest contact period to the late nineteenth century, what sociocultural mechanisms allowed such persistence? Conversely, if another description is more accurate, why did early ethnographers assume the Western Pueblo were culturally static for so long a period?

Still other questions arise about stability and change among Hopis from the ethnographic present period to the modern era. If Hopi culture and society persisted remarkably unchanged since first contact with the Spanish until the ethnographic present, what factors operated during later years that led to dramatic social upheavals like the split of Oraibi in 1906?

Finally, to what extent is the description of Hopi culture and society from the ethnographic present valid in the late twentieth century? If Hopi society and culture changed substantially during the modern period (as we claim in Chapter 7), what mechanisms account for this transformation? Conversely, if features of the Hopi sociocultural system resisted change, what factors or processes account for this stability?

Part Two
A Hopi Social History

3. Regional Abandonments and the Western Pueblo (A.D. 1450–1539)

ARCHAEOLOGICAL DATA PAINT a remarkable picture of occupational continuity in the Western Pueblo region. Archaeologists demonstrate that humans have inhabited this stark and beautiful landscape of high mesas and expansive plains for more than 12,000 years. The evidence of human occupation in this area becomes more obvious during recent centuries because material remains of the late prehistoric period are more numerous, visible, and obtrusive than those of earlier times. A few pieces of chipped stone may constitute the only evidence of an archaeological site from several thousand years ago. In contrast, the typical Western Pueblo site immediately prior to A.D. 1539 and the beginning of recorded history contains the collapsed masonry walls and wooden roofs of houses and other structures. Because of such differences in sites, archaeologists ask different questions about human occupation and adaptation for different times. These questions often reflect both the strengths and limitations of archaeological data. In this case, the visibility and obtrusiveness of archaeological remains provide archaeologists with different perspectives of the past. Archaeologists have, for example, traditionally been concerned with questions about patterns of subsistence during the Paleo-Indian period (ca. 12,000 to 8,000 B.P.) because archaeological remains from this period lend themselves to the study of hunting practices.[1] For later prehistoric periods (A.D. 700–1538), archaeologists have been more concerned with settlement patterns, sedentism, and occupational continuity in the Western Pueblo region. As a result, archaeologists have widely discussed the issues of prehistoric colonization and abandonment. Of these two issues, archaeologists have attended more fully to the latter. Abandonments were first seriously discussed in print during the second decade of the twentieth century (Hewett, Henderson, and Robbins 1913; Huntington 1914; Gregory 1917; Nelson 1919). Since that time, abandonment has served as the centerpiece of numerous articles, and most archaeologists have accepted implicitly that abandonment is an important part of Southwestern prehistory.

In this case study, we present a new interpretation of Western Pueblo abandonment. We begin our analysis by discussing conventional archaeological descriptions and explanations of abandonment in the Southwest. We then introduce and examine the idea of "adaptive diversity." A few archaeologists have used this idea to denote the changing structure of past lifeways in a variety of world areas. Finally, we apply the concept of adaptive diversity to the problem of Western Pueblo abandonment.

Southwestern Abandonments

When archaeologists assert that a particular region was abandoned, they most frequently mean that occupancy of an area ceases because people die out or migrate (Cordell and Plog 1979:418). Accordingly, archaeologists usually associate abandonment with major occupational discontinuity in a region's history. We begin this case study by provisionally accepting the paradigmatic equation of abandonment with occupational discontinuity. The equation is logically valid, if not scientifically rigorous.

Early in the study of Southwestern prehistory, archaeologists assumed that only a single abandonment had occurred. This was a population exodus from the San Juan Basin during the twelfth and thirteenth centuries A.D. (Kidder 1924:340–342). However, further study led to the recognition that abandonment was more widespread than originally thought. Archaeologists have now shown that at least six Anasazi geographical subtraditions (Kayenta, Mesa Verde, Chaco, Rio Grande, Winslow, and Virgin) and at least six Mogollon subtraditions (San Simon, Forestdale, Cibola, Black River, Mimbres, and Jornada) have different developmental trajectories, distinct demographic trends, and, consequently, asynchronous settlement and abandonment records. In addition to these major Anasazi and Mogollon subtraditions, archaeologists have also developed numerous areally specific phase sequences to describe changes in material assemblages and adaptive patterns (e.g., Roberts 1930; Colton 1939; Lehmer 1948; Martin et al. 1952; Wheat 1955; Aikens 1966; Eddy 1966; Gumerman 1968, 1970; Gumerman and Skinner 1968; Lindsey 1969; Gumerman and Euler 1976). With the recognition of subtraditions and the proliferation of phase sequences in the plateau, montane, and desert regions of the Southwest, the number of abandonments has increased in direct proportion to the number of well-defined areas.

The earliest attempts to explain abandonment focused on variation in *climate* and on major episodes of *drought* (Hewett, Henderson, and Robbins 1913; Huntington 1914:33–34; Gregory 1917:131–132). Explanations based on a deteriorating climate were quickly rejected, however, for a hypothesis that postulated the presence of indigenous *predatory nomads* who raided the pueblos. Raiding and warfare allegedly made continued occupation of specific areas unfeasible (Nelson 1919; Kidder 1924: 340–342). Evidence cited for this hypothesis is usually inferential and cites the "defensive" character of Puebloan architecture. Some archaeologists, also noting the defensive character of pueblo architecture, have sought to explain abandonments in terms of inter-village strife and internecine *warfare* (e.g., Morris 1939:41–42; Martin, Quimby, and Collier 1947:146–149; Titiev 1944:96–99). Others have cited *overcrowding* and *poor sanitary conditions* as factors contributing to the spread of *epidemic diseases* (Colton 1936:337–343). Still others have made reference to the *overutilization of marginal lands* (Hawley 1934:78–80; Kelley 1952a:357 n.4) or to conditions of *population-resource imbalances* (Martin and Plog 1973:326–333). Finally, several archaeologists have returned to the climatic argument, suggesting that epochs of drought, erosion, and arroyo cutting made agriculture difficult and led to the movement of populations to more favorable, better watered areas (Bryan 1941:234–235; Hack 1942:76–80; Brew 1946:299–301; Reed 1946: 303; Schoenwetter and Dittert 1968; Euler et al. 1979).

Several summaries of the evidence for and against each of these hypotheses exist (e.g., Kelley 1952a; Jett 1964; Martin and Plog 1973). A perusal of these summaries suggests that none of the postulated explanations fully accounts for all of the prehistoric Southwestern occupational discontinuities. Because of this, Southwestern archaeologists have no clear consensus regarding either the physical evidence for or the processes involved in abandonments.

As noted, archaeologists frequently assume that two processes account for regional abandonments: depopulation and migration. Depopulation implies that apparent abandonments resulted from unusually high death rates, and that human populations were reduced in size from previous levels. Migration, on the other hand, suggests that some regional abandonments reflect group movements from one area to another. While either of these two processes could explain regional abandonments, neither is universally supported by the data.

Abandonments, Population Movement, and Depopulation

Postulated migrations fill the archaeological literature of the Southwest. For a long time, archaeologists believed that migration and diffusion could explain the sudden emergence, disappearance, or change of architectural styles, technology, and subsistence patterns in any region. While archaeologists now criticize hypotheses of migration and diffusion for their lack of explanatory power (Martin and Plog 1973; Adams, Van Gerven, and Levy 1978; Titiev 1944:97), population movements remain an implicit theme in Southwestern archaeology. Given the apparent number of suggested abandonments, the evidence for migration should be abundant.

Large-scale migrations involving the simultaneous exodus of people from many communities are historically uncommon (Adams, Van Gerven, and Levy 1978:489). Small-scale, or community-level, migrations are far more prevalent. Although postulated migrations are numerous, the criteria for identifying migrations (see Rouse 1958) in the Southwest have been applied in a less than rigorous fashion. As Reed pointed out some time ago (1958:7), a majority of the postulated Southwestern migrations, and especially those leading to the abandonment of regions, are based on nothing more substantial than the distribution of ceramic design traditions.

Migration is certainly one of the most visible processes, if not the most difficult to document, of those evident in the archaeological record. In the extreme, each time an archaeological site is recorded, it is the result of both a migration and an abandonment, even if Rouse's (1958) criteria for identifying migrations are rarely satisfied. In an innovative approach to the question of identifying population movements in the Southwest, Stephen Plog (1969) has employed statistical measures to assess whether emigrations from one area are detectable archaeologically as immigrations to another. He constructed population growth curves based on the number of dwelling units at tree-ring dated sites for several areas in the northern Southwest. He found that between A.D. 300 to 1700, only four migrations were possible, and these represented what might be considered small population movements (between twenty and fifty families each from the Upper Little Colorado, Tsegi Canyon, Canyon de Chelly, and Mesa Verde, all moving to the Hopi mesas ca. A.D. 1300). This result is surprising, given the high level of northern Southwestern population movement that some archaeologists postulate.

Other studies have also shown that archaeologists need not postulate

migration and diffusion to explain cultural developments or occupational discontinuities in specific areas (e.g., Fish, Pilles, and Fish 1980;
Weaver 1972; Hantman 1979; Upham and Rice 1980). These works indicate that populations often adapt locally to changing conditions, and
sudden increases or decreases in organizational complexity can be explained in relation to regional political or economic conditions. This
recognition makes it imperative for Southwestern archaeologists to resolve an apparent paradox. On the one hand, they have frequently referred to widespread migrations from particular regions. On the other
hand, they have been unable to muster the data necessary to document
or explain the dislocation and movement of populations.

Another process related to regional abandonments is depopulation,
which results when large segments of a population die from disease,
warfare, malnutrition, or other causes. Archaeologists and others have
previously discussed prehistoric depopulation without satisfactory resolution (Colton 1936; Morris 1939; Titiev 1944; Martin, Quimby, and
Collier 1947). The notion of demographic collapse has, however, recently returned in the writings of Cordell and Plog (1979:418).

> The notion of *abandonment* is a conceptual problem; it probably obscures a
> great diversity of behaviors that occurred during the period, including mi-
> gration, increased movement, and the death of some local groups. In re-
> sponse to the productive difficulties that were necessarily created by the
> use of intensive strategies in an area for which they were inappropriate, a
> demographic crash, though a very complex crash, ultimately occurred.

No single explanation of abandonments will suffice. Cordell and Plog
are correct that abandonment describes a diversity of behaviors. For example, there are currently no data to suggest that abandonments were accompanied by large numbers of deaths. The large burial populations from
Southwestern sites occupied just before the fifteenth-century abandonments (e.g., Nuvaqueotaka [Upham 1978], Grasshopper [Clark 1967;
Whittlesey 1978]) show no evidence that massive numbers of people
succumbed at any single time. The burials actually demonstrate the opposite. Dated burials are normally distributed throughout the occupation span of the sites. There are data from sites in the Southwest that do
suggest warfare (Chase 1976; Turner and Morris 1970), but the evidence
of violent death is not widespread enough to account for abandonment.

In summary, some Southwestern archaeologists have postulated numerous migrations to explain the abandonment of regions. While some
of these migrations may have occurred, existing data do not support

postulates of extensive prehistoric Southwestern migrations. Other archaeologists have claimed that abandonments actually represent episodes of regional depopulation. Again, data do not support such claims.

Adaptive Diversity in the Southwest

We suggest that it is not necessary to rely on either migration or regional depopulation to explain discontinuities in Southwestern regional
occupational histories. Instead, we argue that such discontinuities are
more parsimoniously accounted for by reference to adaptive diversity.
Cordell and Plog (1979) have broadly summarized problems that arise
when archaeologists use traditional categories and normative constructs
in their interpretations. One such construct, "phase sequences," exemplifies how an overreliance on these devices can diminish our capacity to describe and explain variability in the archaeological record. In
this section, we begin by addressing this issue. We then examine evidence for a sociocultural system in the prehistoric Western Pueblo region that is more complex than previously imagined. This sociocultural
system: (1) incorporates both sedentism and mobility in its subsistence-settlement organization; and (2) regionally integrates diverse and
autonomous sociocultural systems. In the next section, we return to the
issue of abandonments and demonstrate that the likely explanation of
this phenomenon lies not in demographic collapse or large migrations,
but in the diversity and resiliency of Southwestern adaptive strategies.

By archaeological standards, Southwestern prehistory is well known.
Archaeologists have well-defined phase sequences for most regions and
widely accepted chronologies to use interpretatively. Plog has, however,
recently questioned the accuracy of data archaeologists use to construct
Southwestern culture-historical sequences (1983). He notes that such
phase sequences are inherently normative because archaeologists construct them using the most characteristic and recognizable data from
particular regions during specific periods. Thus, we find the general divisions of the Anasazi or the Mogollon developmental sequence defined
using the most common house types, pottery types, and settlement
patterns.[2]

Plog also summarizes two recent studies dealing with this issue
(Adams 1980; Stuart and Gauthier 1981). These works focus on adaptive patterns (in sociocultural systems) and the way archaeologists have
described them. Stuart, Gauthier, and Adams dichotomize major evolutionary trends by opposing "power" and "efficiency" strategies (Stuart
and Gauthier 1981:10). By definition, cultural systems create a power

drive when they increase rates of population growth, production, and energy expenditure. Coloquially, such systems "pump up." They also "burn out." An efficient system is the opposite. Energy coming in and energy going out are more nearly equal. The efficiency drive is characterized by decreased rates of population growth, production, and energy expenditure. If efficiency and power represent two trajectories in cultural evolution, hunter-gatherers fall on the efficiency trajectory. Industrialized nation-states fall near the top of the power trajectory. Obviously, the majority of existing cultural systems fall somewhere between.

Anthropologists may criticize this binary view of cultural evolution as normative and simplistic. They might also criticize Adams, Stuart, and Gauthier for their largely metaphorical use of the terms, power and efficiency (which the latter borrow from biological ecology). Consequently, the concepts might lack logical, empirical, and theoretical force to explain human adaptive diversity. Nevertheless, power and efficiency provide an analytical framework suitable for identifying differences in adaptive strategies, both within and between regions. These concepts are useful in this context because they illustrate a serious problem in the way archaeologists have characterized prehistoric remains in the Southwest.

If we proceed with the metaphor, efficient sociocultural systems may be labeled "areally extensive." Such systems employ population self-regulating mechanisms (e.g., infanticide, postpartum sexual taboos, and population budding) to insure that available resources and population size remain in balance. As Wobst has pointed out (Wobst 1974), hunter-gatherers frequently maintain (through conscious and unconscious means) their local populations below the level at which they would deplete their resource base. Such homeostatic regulation allows some hunter-gatherer groups to survive during years when resources are scarce. The durability and resiliency of efficient sociocultural strategies is evidenced by the domination of hunting-gathering throughout most of human history. In contrast, power strategies are intensive and characterized by population growth. Such systems compensate for resource deficiencies through technological means and by increasing the energy investment in resource procurement. In some cases, the power drive is also characterized by the emergence of social stratification, productive specialization, elite political organizations, extensive local and regional exchange, and extralocal alliances. Obviously, there is a vast middle ground between these strategies. Although archaeologists only partially understand the evolutionary transformation of efficient systems to power systems, they have recently been concerned with the processes involved (e.g., Flannery 1972; Logan and Sanders 1976; Johnson

1978; Sanders and Webster 1978; Cordell and Plog 1979; Yoffee 1979; Blanton et al. 1981).

The concepts of power and efficiency are relevant to our present case study because of the way archaeologists have traditionally characterized Southwestern cultural developments. As Plog, Adams, Stuart, and Gauthier point out, archaeologists have usually focused on power drives as if such strategies were the expected, normal, and characteristic pattern in most areas and times. Because a power drive is far more likely to produce recognizable archaeological remains, groups relying on an efficient strategy may be less detectable in areas where power and efficiency are both characteristic. In areas co-occupied by sedentary agriculturalists and hunter-gatherers, the more durable and obtrusive material remains associated with sedentary occupations would be accepted as normal and characteristic, even though the hunter-gatherers might be more widespread and more numerous.

In the Southwest, archaeologists have always focused on power drives. Early investigators often dealt with the most visible of cultural remains (e.g., Chaco Canyon and Mesa Verde) or the most conspicuous developmental problems (e.g., transition in residence from pit houses to pueblos, development of maize agriculture, and abandonment). Today archaeological perspectives have changed, but the strong normative patterns characteristic of power drives still dominate research. This remains true even if archaeologists discuss power drives in a processual framework referring to agricultural intensification, population aggregation, social stratification, productive specialization, local and regional exchange, and leadership development. By approaching prehistory in this fashion, archaeologists imply that power driven societies constitute the exclusive adaptive strategy for any particular period. Consequently, archaeologists use such patterns to characterize cultural developments across broad regions (Adams 1980; Stuart and Gauthier 1981; Plog 1983). Such implications and procedures have, perhaps, obscured the true nature of abandonments and have prevented correct interpretations of occupational discontinuities. Because archaeologists have emphasized the obtrusive archaeological patterns associated with sedentism and agriculture (Schiffer, Sullivan, and Klinger 1978), they have not seen occupational discontinuity at puebloan sites except as depopulation and migration.

Archaeologists do recognize that adaptive diversity existed in the Southwest. Discussions of settlement-subsistence systems usually acknowledge that during some periods after the introduction of cultigens, particular groups may have relied on a central-based seasonal pattern of resource exploitation. In such an adaptive pattern, cultigens formed only a small part of the total diet. Groups were largely sedentary during the growing season, but highly mobile during the rest of the year. Archaeologists have identified this type of semisedentary pattern for the Basketmaker II occupation of Cedar Mesa (Matson and Lipe 1978), the Basketmaker and Pueblo periods on Black Mesa (Powell 1980), and many other areas in the Southwest (Schoenwetter and Dittert 1968; Euler and Chandler 1978; Lange 1979; Ward 1979). Nevertheless, archaeologists have assumed that this type of seasonal, semisedentary pattern was not widespread in the Southwest after A.D. 900.

The mixed subsistence strategy that includes part-time mobile hunting-gathering and part-time sedentary agriculture may represent an adaptation intermediate between full-time hunting-gathering and full-time agriculture. Archaeologists have, at least implicitly, used their understanding of this mixed strategy to interpret portions of Southwestern prehistory. The developmental sequence of Paleo-Indian big-game hunter → broad-spectrum hunter-gatherer → semi-sedentary part-time agriculturalist → sedentary agriculturalist is frequently repeated in the culture histories of different Southwest regions. Thus, archaeologists see Southwestern adaptive diversity serially, diachronically, or developmentally. This type of interpretation arbitrarily precludes the possibility that peoples following different adaptive strategies coexisted spatially and temporally. It also precludes the possibility that a single society employed a subsistence strategy that oscillated among full-time hunting-gathering, part-time hunting-gathering combined with part-time agriculture, and full-time agriculture. This complex mixed strategy would entail periods of relatively more efficiency and less power, and periods of less efficiency and more power.

Abandonment remains a significant conceptual problem because archaeologists have not yet appreciated the synchronic diversity of Southwestern adaptive strategies and the "resiliency" or flexibility of Southwestern settlement-subsistence patterns (see Cordell and Plog 1979: 410). We suggest now that abandonments do not necessarily represent demographic collapses or large-scale migrations. Occupational discontinuities more likely represent and reflect the adaptive diversity of prehistoric Southwestern groups. Such peoples probably employed adaptive strategies that varied between, and, in some cases, combined a variety of, different patterns. So, during some periods and in some areas, data suggest that: (1) the normative patterns characterized by obtrusive archaeological remains are mingled with the archaeological remains of groups relying on a much less intensive adaptive strategy;

and (2) during most of Southwestern prehistory after the Christian era, sedentary or semisedentary agriculturalist and hunter-gatherer groups were both common features of the landscape. Peoples following the two strategies lived in contiguous and overlapping territories. During some periods (those characterized by the archaeologically defined normative patterns), relatively more hunter-gatherers were assimilated into a sedentary lifestyle. During other periods (those often associated with abandonment), relatively more sedentary agriculturalists were forced into a pattern of hunting and gathering. It also seems likely that some of the environmental arguments advanced to account for periods of cultural change (e.g., Euler et al. 1979) apply to such shifts in adaptive patterns. Various cultural strategies (for example, agricultural intensification, as defined by Cordell and Plog, 1979:419) may have increased or decreased the margin of risk for sedentary agriculturalists and also contributed to these adaptive shifts.

If this kind of adaptive diversity is present in the Southwest, what data indicate that hunting-gathering and sedentary farming existed contemporaneously? The problem here is identifying (through material cultural remains) hunter-gatherer strategies during periods dominated by sedentary agriculturalists and during periods characterized by abandonment. This problem is particularly acute in areas where the most visible remains are those of sedentary agriculturalists, where the presumption is that a range of site types (habitation, limited activity, field house) is an expected pattern for a certain period of occupation. However, identifying archaeological remains of hunter-gatherer settlement-subsistence systems can even be difficult when such remains represent the only mode of settlement on the landscape. A good illustration of this latter problem can be found in those areas that ethnohistorically known groups like the Apache, Yavapai, Manso, and Suma occupied during the eighteenth and nineteenth centuries. In many instances, the precise territories of these groups are known, yet archaeologists have been unable, except in a few instances, to identify the sites they occupied.

Actually, archaeologists have collected the data needed to identify the type of adaptive diversity described above. Data pertaining to normative adaptive patterns might be most clearly understood in relation to the well-known architectural and ceramic sequences that have dominated Southwestern archaeology from the beginning of systematic investigations. Most, if not all of these sequences imply that a sedentary, agricultural adaptation was the characteristic pattern after A.D. 600. Archaeologists have, however, also collected site data far more characteristic of seasonally mobile settlement-subsistence systems. Archaeologists often assign such sites, which they most frequently identify as artifact scatters or limited-activity sites, a temporal and cultural affiliation based on the ceramic or diagnostic lithic material present. Archaeologists, however, often lack a clear understanding of the structural relationship of such sites to pertinent settlement-subsistence systems. If, for example, such sites contain ceramics that date to a specific time, archaeologists assign the sites to that period. The artifact scatters are assumed to relate to the cultural group that is presumed to have produced that pottery (and consequently to that group's settlement-subsistence pattern). If this is the case, then our expectations regarding the role of artifact scatters and limited-activity sites in a sedentary settlement pattern must be examined.

Sedentism, Mobility, and Limited Activity Sites

The idea that limited-activity sites are part of a sedentary settlement system has its roots in ethnographic studies of the modern Pueblo Indians. Archaeologists have reported different types of limited-activity sites (e.g., hunting stands, gathering camps, lithic quarry sites, and field houses). Are the limited-activity sites that archaeologists record structurally similar to the kind of sites that ethnographically known pueblo groups occupied on a temporary basis? The answer is yes, at least in some cases (e.g., Wilcox 1979). When artifact scatters exist in association with architectural features presumed to be the remains of field houses, or when they are proximate to arable land, archaeologists usually infer that the sites are in some way related to agricultural pursuits. However, most other kinds of limited-activity sites show no evidence of architectural features and are not associated with agriculturally suitable land. If such sites lack pottery and contain evidence of "Archaic style" projectile points, archaeologists routinely assign them to a preagricultural, mobile settlement-subsistence pattern. With the addition of ceramics to the material assemblages of these sites, however, limited-activity sites have become an extension of the sedentary agricultural pattern. We question the logic of this type of classifying and suggest there is currently no demonstrable theoretical basis for such assignments.

Among the difficult interpretive problems regarding limited-activity sites are those of determining whether they are: (1) auxiliary use areas for sedentary populations; (2) related to a mobile or seasonal pattern of resource exploitation; or (3) properly identified and classified. In some cases, limited-activity sites may be pit-house villages without visible surface manifestations (that is, surface depressions). In other cases, such sites may be habitation loci where ephemeral brush structures were constructed that cannot be identified archaeologically. Similarly, we do not know at present what the logistical requirements of sedentary populations of varying size were during particular periods. How many limited-activity sites are required for the average size site in the Southwest? Plog, Effland, and Green (1978) show that the average size of the Southwestern sites for all periods is 6.5 rooms; sites larger than 10 rooms are rare. What might be the formation rate of limited-activity sites over a decade of occupancy for the average size Southwestern site? For that matter, are limited-activity sites necessary logistical features of all sedentary adaptations, or are they primarily related to mobile settlement-subsistence systems?

The distributional expectations used to identify a mobile settlement-subsistence pattern are well known. In the Southwest, models of hunter-gatherer subsistence are exclusively related to the Archaic and derive from the definitions proposed by Irwin-Williams (1967, 1968a, 1968b) and Jennings (1957, 1964). In a more recent study, Biella and Chapman (1980) have expanded these original definitions. They propose three alternative models of Southwestern hunter-gatherer subsistence and settlement. They identify the logistical properties of mobile settlement-subsistence systems and focus on variation in demography, social structure, resource availability, settlement, and technology. A major feature of the original models, and of two of the models Biella and Chapman propose, is the existence of sites receiving only ephemeral use. These sites, called "logistical campsites" and "special-use sites," are occupied on a short-term basis and are the locations of task-specific behaviors (e.g., resource procurement, processing, and short-term camping). The third model that Biella and Chapman offer does not incorporate auxiliary locations. Rather, this model postulates the frequent movement of residential camps. Thus, the distributional expectations of a mobile settlement pattern in the Southwest generally require the existence of limited-activity sites. Archaeologically, such sites would be detected on the landscape as artifact scatters.

There are data that indicate great regional variation in the spatial distribution and artifact assemblages of limited-activity sites. We suggest that some of this variation is related to a largely unrecognized portion of the Southwest's prehistoric settlement history, the existence in many areas of mobile populations that were separate and distinct from the more sedentary groups archaeologists have used to define Southwestern culture-historical sequences.

We cannot completely resolve this issue at present because the available data are not of the necessary quality. We can, however, present data that partially support the patterning we postulate. These data imply human adaptive diversity in the Southwest and the existence of people who are, expressed colloquially, "in the cracks." These are "people without history" (Wolf 1982), people who, because of the unobtrusive character of their adaptation, have yet to be written into Southwestern prehistory.

Limited-Activity Sites: Functional Differences

If limited-activity sites or artifact scatters are often related to a mobile settlement-subsistence pattern, archaeologists might expect to find quantitative differences between the types of artifacts associated with these sites and those found at sites with architectural features. Very few studies have been undertaken on this problem. Stone has, however, examined the lithic assemblages from different kinds of sites in the Chevelon drainage (1975). She employed fuzzy-set theory to determine whether the lithic assemblages of artifact scatters differed significantly from those associated with sites that had structures (including field-house sites). Such differences were, in fact, identified. The differences that Stone found between artifact scatters and sites with structures imply that the range of activities carried out at the two categories of sites also differed significantly. McAllister and Plog (1979) achieved a similar result when they analyzed the assemblages of small sites in the Chevelon drainage. For sites in this region, they found site size to be a poor predictor of variation in ceramic, chipped-stone, and ground-stone assemblages. So, the diversity and quantity of artifacts present at a site were not related in any absolute way to site size. These studies indicate that there are functional differences between different categories of sites and that artifact scatters appear to be a functionally distinct category of sites.

The idea that limited-activity sites constitute a functionally distinct class suggests that the behavior associated with such sites is categorically different from the behavior that occurred at sites with structures. Archaeologists presume that many of these latter sites are associated with sedentary or semisedentary settlement patterns. Naturally, archaeologists can argue that artifact scatters are simply auxiliary use areas for small pueblo sites and that the observed functional differences result from the performances of subsistence-related activities not occurring at sites with structures. If this is the case, one might expect relative uniformity between regions where small pueblo sites exist in the ratio of limited-activity to habitation sites.

Limited-Activity Sites: Distributional Differences

Plog, Effland, and Green (1978) have examined the relationship between limited-activity sites and habitation sites, using site file information from the eight different regions. They found substantial variation in the ratio of habitation to limited-activity sites. In Elk Ridge, for example, only 36 percent of all recorded sites are limited-activity sites (122 of 346 sites). In contrast, 61.7 percent of recorded sites in the Chevelon drainage consist of limited-activity sites (340 of 551 sites). Other regions show marked variation in the quantity of limited-activity to habitation sites (compare, for example, the Mimbres Valley to Chevelon), but some of this observed variation most certainly relates to observer bias and to the lack of consistent recording techniques between regions. However, the variation between many regions is also an artifact of past settlement-subsistence systems and suggests that some peoples from some regions were highly mobile during some periods. At this point, we simply suggest that the indications of mobility may have referents substantially different from those Southwestern archaeologists have traditionally assumed.

In most regions and during most periods, limited-activity sites represent a significant portion of the data base. A planning study done on portions of the Apache-Sitgreaves Forest (Plog 1981:22), for example, projects that 49.8 percent of all cultural resources within a 3,200-square-kilometer area (8,870 of 17,797 sites) consist of such remains. In a finer-grained study, Plog (1974a) found dramatic differences in the number of limited-activity sites in two locations of the Upper Little Colorado region. Intensive survey of approximately 8 square kilometers in the Purcell-Larson locality, a drainage system of the Little Colorado River, resulted in the recording of only 40 such sites. By contrast, an intensive survey of nearly 13 square kilometers in the Hay Hollow Valley, several kilometers to the east, resulted in the identification of 183 limited-activity sites. Plog explains the resulting difference in density (5.0 versus 14.3 per square kilometer) by relating it to variation in the abundance and spacing of resources between the two localities. In the Hay Hollow locality, higher rates of mobility were apparently required to exploit critical resources in the valley. The indications of high mobility in Hay Hollow are particularly striking, since this area contains numerous large pueblos that archaeologists traditionally interpret as reflecting a sedentary agricultural adaptation (Longacre 1964; Hill 1970; Plog 1974b).

Limited-Activity Sites: Phase Sequences

The number of limited-activity sites in the Apache-Sitgreaves Forest approximates the number found in most parts of the northern Southwest. In peripheral areas, however, the relationship between data indicating sedentism and mobility is much different. The Jornada Mogollon exemplifies this. The Jornada Mogollon area encompasses the southeastern periphery of the American Southwest. Geographically, the area is delimited by the Sacramento Mountains on the east, the Mimbres Bolson on the west, the modern town of Socorro on the north, and the junction of the Rio Grande and Conchos Rivers on the south. The phase sequence developed for the region (Lehmer 1948) divided the Jornada culture area into two "branches." The northern end of the Caballo Mountains separates the northern from the southern branch. Only the southern branch is of concern in this discussion. Historically, various mobile and semisedentary groups that subsisted primarily through hunting and gathering inhabited the southern Jornada area. These groups included the Julimes, Cholomes, Sumas, Mansos, Janos (Kelley 1952a; 1952b), and, somewhat later, the Perrillo, or Mescalero Apache (Opler and Opler 1950; Schroeder 1973). Prehistorically, however, the culture-historical sequence developed for the Jornada area presupposes that sedentism and agriculture formed the characteristic pattern. Archaeologists suggest that mobility and hunting-gathering were not important strategies after approximately A.D. 1000 (Whalen 1977, 1978).

As originally defined by Lehmer (1948), the phase sequence for the southern Jornada Mogollon contains four divisions. The Hueco phase (A.D. 1 to 900) represents a time when Archaic hunter-gatherers were making the transition and adjustment to a settled, village way of life. This phase is either aceramic (lacking pottery) or associated with an infrequent use of plain Jornada Brown pottery. The following phase, Mesilla (A.D. 900 to 1100) is the early pit-house period. It is characterized by a growing reliance on agriculture and developing social and economic ties with groups occupying the Mimbres Valley to the west. The short-lived Dona Ana phase (A.D. 1100 to 1200) denotes the transition from pit-house to pueblo. The El Paso phase marks the full transition to above-ground adobe pueblos. Significantly, although he discusses other traits and artifacts, Lehmer uses architectural styles and ceramics as the sole diagnostic criteria for phase assignment.

In some respects, the Jornada-area phase sequence is identical to other Southwestern phase sequences that archaeologists have used for decades. However, for this area it is especially clear that the phase sequence defines a power drive that is uncharacteristic of the majority of archaeological data from the region. Archaeologists have, for example, recently completed several large surveys in the "heartland" of the Jornada culture area (Taylor and Brethauer 1980; Harkey 1981; Laumbach 1981a, 1981b, 1982; Bloch 1982; Brockman 1982; Duran 1982a, 1982b; J. Hilley 1982; Kirkpatrick and Duran 1982; G. Hilley 1983). In these surveys, archaeologists investigated a combined total of over 2,300 kilometers of linear transects between Hatch, New Mexico, and El Paso, Texas, on the margins of the Lower Rio Grande Valley, on the mesa top adjacent to the valley, and in immediately adjoining areas. Researchers recorded 492 archaeological sites, of which 190 (38.6 percent) were related to Jornada Mogollon occupation. Of these, 188 (98.9 percent) are lithic, ceramic and lithic, or lithic scatters. These sites show no evidence of permanent habitation. Actually, archaeologists positively identified only two permanent habitation sites. In addition, researchers were unable to assign 224 sites (45.5 percent) to a temporal period or cultural pattern, due to the absence of "diagnostic" materials.

Another project in the Jornada area heartland has also produced results that do not correspond to the pattern that Lehmer's original phase sequence suggests (Carmichael 1982). Carmichael's intensive survey of 991 square kilometers in the southern Tularosa Basin resulted in the discovery of 5,974 archaeological sites. Of these, Carmichael assigned 524 unambiguously to the Jornada Mogollon occupation. He classified only 85 (16.2 percent) as permanent habitation sites. The frequency of habitation to nonhabitation sites on this survey is remarkably low, since 86 percent of all sites Carmichael recorded (5,138 of 5,974) were artifact scatters, and he could not assign them a cultural affiliation or a date (because necessary diagnostic materials were absent). Hester obtained similar results from another large-scale survey in the Jornada area (1977).

The Jornada case illustrates the problem of defining a phase sequence based on the most obtrusive archaeological remains. This case also exemplifies the classificatory problems that arise when archaeologists attempt to fit data produced by different adaptive strategies into a single normative framework. In the southern Jornada area, data indicate that sedentary village life was not the most characteristic adaptive pattern for most periods. Instead, high rates of mobility seem far more representative. Although the surveys mentioned above did not examine areas in the flood plain of the Rio Grande Valley, site records indicate that very few permanent habitation sites ever existed in the area. The few villages that are known probably embody an important cultural development and may provide evidence for examining fundamental processual questions about population growth, agricultural intensification, exchange, and social stratification. However, defining a phase sequence on what appears to be less than 5 percent of the existing data and extending that phase sequence over a broad region is misleading. Such classificatory efforts hinder explanations of cultural variation and change.

As a class of sites, artifact clusters may have behavioral referents other than those related to the logistic activities of sedentary groups. Even assuming that artifact scatters represent peripheral features of an agriculturally centered adaptive strategy, is it reasonable to consider sedentism inherent to this strategy when between 50 percent and 90 percent of the data from some areas indicate mobility? The answer is probably no. We can be comfortable with sedentism and mobility only if we recognize that adaptive diversity characterized many areas of the Southwest after A.D. 600.

Adaptive Diversity and Abandonment

Oscillation between strategies based on sedentary agriculture and those emphasizing mobile hunting-gathering represents a serial change in subsistence and settlement systems between relatively more and relatively less intensive resource-extraction technologies. However, adaptive diversity as discussed here also relates to the interaction of groups relying on divergent adaptive strategies. Both hunting-gathering and agriculture appear to have been common in many Southwestern areas during many periods. Thus, puebloan abandonment does not require explanation as demographic collapse or regional migrations precipitated by drought, disease, Athapaskan intrusion, arroyo cutting, or erosion. Instead, the episodic adaptive shifts from hunting-gathering to agriculture to hunting-gathering again provides a more parsimonious explanation for abandonments.

Some data indicate that abandonments may be related to just such shifts. Kelley (1952a), for example, has described a situation in the La Junta area (at the junction of the Conchos River and the Rio Grande) between A.D. 1400 and 1600, where a variety of mobile hunting-gathering groups first assimilated a pattern that emphasized sedentism and reliance on agriculture, and then returned to a pattern of mobility.

Kelley argues that this change from mobility to sedentism was precipitated by short-term increases in rainfall. Such increased rainfall would decrease the risk associated with agriculture. With the return to drier conditions, along with the "consequent effects of nomadic pressure, intervillage rivalry, and intravillage feuding" (1952a:385), groups that had assimilated a sedentary pattern and reliance on agriculture returned to foraging. Kelley's analysis suggests that these adaptive shifts occurred repeatedly in the Lower Rio Grande and Conchos valleys during this two-hundred-year period.

Kelley raises another important issue (1952a, 1952b). This issue pertains to the way indigenous La Junta groups that had returned to hunting-gathering during the fifteenth century were assimilated by the Jumano and Cibolo. The latter had been dislodged by the Athapaskans from their territories on the southern Plains. As the Athapaskans expanded into the La Junta area during the seventeenth century, they, in turn, assimilated the Jumano and Cibolo (Kelley 1952a:384). So, the apparent ethnic identity of the indigenous groups occupying the Lower Rio Grande Valley was submerged first by the Jumano and Cibolo, who had been pushed from their territory on the southern Plains, and then by the Athapaskans.

The sociocultural dynamics of the situation Kelley describes have implications for understanding Southwestern Puebloan abandonments. The adaptive resiliency or flexibility exhibited in the Lower Rio Grande Valley during this time typify what Stuart and Gauthier (1981) describe as the oscillation between strategies based on power and those based on efficiency. Archaeologically, this kind of oscillation produces remains that are characteristic of a sedentary settlement pattern (villages), as well as an abundance of sites characteristic of a mobile settlement pattern (artifact scatters). The many limited-activity sites in some parts of the Southwest suggest that oscillation between sedentism and mobility was common. Prehistoric occupational discontinuities for sedentary groups may thus reflect similar adaptive changes. In other words, the oscillation between sedentism and mobility may be a valid model for large portions of the Southwest. The return to a mobile subsistence-settlement strategy may explain what archaeologists have traditionally characterized as abandonment (see Wimberly and Rogers 1977; Tainter 1981). The unrecognized portion of this equation, then, is the primary evidence for mobile groups in the Southwest following the abandonment of regions.

Documentary evidence from sixteenth-century Spanish explorations may provide the best information regarding the presence of mobile hunting-gathering groups in the Southwest. The Spanish entry followed closely on the generalized collapse of the large fourteenth- and fifteenth-century nucleated villages, that is, the collapse of what Upham has previously called the fourteenth-century regional system (Upham 1982). The first four Spanish expeditions of the period covered much of the Southwest. Although the narratives are of uneven quality and contain exaggerations, they suggest that hunter-gatherers inhabited sizable areas of the prehistoric Southwest.

Many archaeologists are fond of citing documentary evidence from the Coronado expedition describing the "*Gran Despoblado*," the area between Chichiticale and Cibola that was apparently uninhabited. According to Bolton (1949:32), Chichiticale refers to a large ruin located south of the Gila River at Eagle Pass, between the Pinaleno and Santa Teresa mountains, in Arizona. The area referred to as *despoblado* runs from immediately north of the Gila River in a direct line to the vicinity of St. John's, Arizona, a distance of some 150 kilometers. Although Marcos de Niza and members of the Coronado expedition describe this area as uninhabited, they only passed through the region. Despite the reference to this area as a *despoblado,* Marcos de Niza describes native groups that inhabited the region and provided him with food and other supplies during his passage (Riley 1987). In most other areas explored by the Spanish before A.D. 1600, they encountered mobile, non-Pueblo dwellers, whom they identified generically as Chichimecos, Jumanos, or Querechos.[3] Upham has shown that these groups could not have been Athapaskans (Upham 1982).

The number of mobile hunting-gathering groups the Spanish identify is striking. Numerous mobile groups were, for example, distributed continuously in the Conchos River and Rio Grande valleys between Santa Barbara, Chihuahua (site of embarkation for most expeditions after Coronado), and the Mesilla Valley, New Mexico, a distance of some 400 kilometers. The Spanish identified other such groups living near Acoma (Bolton 1930:183), Zuni (Hammond and Rey 1929:331), and Hopi (Hammond and Rey 1929:106–107). Thus, despite the claim that large areas of the Southwest were uninhabited, pueblo dwellers, hunter-gatherers, or both inhabited all regions the Spanish investigated.

Hunter-gatherer occupation of large areas of the northern Southwest may help to explain the rapid spread of Athapaskan-speaking peoples into this region during the seventeenth and eighteenth centuries. Traditional interpretations seeking to account for the Athapaskan spread assume that these people moved into unoccupied and, consequently, uncontested territory (Wilcox 1981). Curiously, Spanish narratives refer to an extremely large number of Apaches in the Southwest after A.D. 1600 (Forrestal 1954). Records document that Apaches lived in a variety of locations in sizable numbers. There are, however, no data indicating that these groups were moving across Puebloan territory in numbers large enough to account for their recorded distribution. So, the historically documented distribution of Apache groups, as well as the size of their populations, require an explanation that accounts for their massive intrusion through the Puebloan zone of settlement. At present, there are no data documenting such a movement. However, if Athapaskan groups like the Apache routinely assimilated indigenous hunter-gatherer populations, as they did in the La Junta region, then the large number of Apaches may simply reflect the amalgamation of indigenous and intrusive groups.

Conclusion

In this case study, we have suggested that many abandonments are reasonably conceived of as adaptive shifts from sedentary, agriculturally based power adaptations to more areally extensive and efficient hunting-gathering strategies. Others have made similar arguments for different areas (Wimberly and Rogers 1977; Stuart and Gauthier 1981; Tainter 1981), although they treat abandonments as an epiphenomenon. The important part of a return to more areally extensive and efficient strategies lies in the notion that such shifts appear to have been a relatively common adaptive response in the past. In addition, there are data suggesting that, during some periods and in some areas, different groups, some relying on strategies emphasizing sedentism and agriculture, some relying on mobility and hunting-gathering, coexisted, perhaps symbiotically. The recognition of serial and contemporaneous adaptive diversity in the Southwest is certainly not unique. Numerous ethnographic studies from other parts of the world document the interaction and symbiotic relationships between hunter-gatherers and other groups involved in diverse subsistence strategies (Gulliver 1955; Macquet 1961). In addition, various studies document adaptive shifts from relatively less intensive to relatively more intensive strategies (e.g., Leach 1954).

That previous explanations of Southwestern abandonment (positing demographic collapse or catastrophically induced migrations) have not withstood the test of one hundred years of archaeological investigation lends support to the position that the diversity of Southwestern adaptive patterns is linked to survival. The Southwest is a marginal environment for agriculture. Although the Southwestern archaeological record is filled with episodes of agricultural adaptation, discontinuities in the archaeological record indicate that over the long run very few have been successful. Given such marginality, it is unlikely that Southwestern groups would lock themselves into an irreversible position that mandated extinction when environmental or social conditions changed. Instead, it appears likely that, when conditions changed for the better or for the worse, prehistoric peoples responded by changing their mode of living.

4. Colonial Contact, Disease, and Population Decline in the Western Pueblo Region (A.D. 1540–1679)

WE ARGUE IN THE previous case study that some Southwestern regional abandonments may be explained using the concept of adaptive diversity. This idea focuses attention on the resilience or flexibility of Western Pueblo settlement and subsistence strategies. Such resilience is especially evident during the late periods of Southwestern prehistory, when, some archaeologists argue, so-called abandonments terminated occupation in much of the Western Pueblo region. As those archaeologists suggest, occupation of many large, multistoried pueblos in the region between the Verde Valley and Acoma ceased during the late fifteenth and early sixteenth centuries. When this highly obtrusive, compact settlement pattern ended, however, large segments of the population probably returned to a more extensive settlement and subsistence strategy, continued to occupy the area, and did not migrate to other regions. During this time, some groups probably returned to hunting-gathering, while others opted for more extensive, less intensive agricultural practices.

This kind of adaptive shift should not be surprising to archaeologists, since another profound adaptive shift occurred previously in the Western Pueblo region around A.D. 1275. During the thirteenth-century adaptive shift, many people came together in new social, political, and economic arrangements. Such arrangements resulted in large-scale population aggregation and the founding of large fourteenth-century communities across the Western Pueblo region. During the thirteenth-century shift, groups who were following more areally extensive settlement and subsistence strategies (defined by seasonal mobility and dispersed residence in small hamlets or residential units) adopted a new, areally intensive lifeway characterized by a greater reliance on agriculture and higher rates of sedentism (Cordell 1984; Cordell and Upham 1983). Consequently, the adaptive patterns described in Chapter 3 are not unique among the Western Pueblo. They appear as part of a broader long-term settlement and subsistence strategy in which groups aggregated and dispersed in response to different natural- and social-environmental conditions.

Two points emerge from Chapter 3 that are directly relevant to our present case study, which is about disease and depopulation in the Western Pueblo region at and immediately before European contact. First, late-prehistoric- and early-contact-period groups in the Western Pueblo region were not uniformly sedentary. Nor did all groups reside in communities built in the typical pueblo style. They were, instead, an amalgam of both sedentary pueblo-dwellers and indigenous hunter-gatherers. As noted, this amalgam is reflected in early Spanish narratives written before A.D. 1600 (Upham 1982:35–51, 1984, 1989). This population structure has implications for culture-historical reconstructions that focus on regional interactive ties and the amity-enmity relationships that characterized different Western Pueblo subregions. Riley describes the role that mobile hunting-gathering groups played in Southwestern trade and warfare in the sixteenth century (1987). On some occasions, hunter-gatherers acted as middlemen in trade. At other times during this period, they acted aggressively to disrupt peaceful interactions of all types.

Second, the Western Pueblo regional demographic structure area appears to have changed dramatically sometime before contact. We know that by A.D. 1300, interdependent regional settlement systems comprised of largely agriculturally based communities were present in the Western Pueblo area. These communities appear to have grown in size and influence in a relatively short period (ca. 25 years). They then flourished for at least another 125 years before disappearing (Cordell 1984). The demise of these communities, however, was not uniform. Some persisted for longer periods than others. In the southern portion of the Western Pueblo region, communities like Tuzigoot, Pinedale, and Showlow had major episodes of construction that appear to have begun between A.D. 1350 and 1385. People may have occupied these communities, and a few others, into the sixteenth century. Sixteenth-century dates are also known from a few large pueblos in the Western Pueblo region. Upham argues, for example, that Nuvakwewtaqa, an ancestral Hopi community founded between A.D. 1275 and 1300, was "abandoned" around A.D. 1525 (Upham and Bockley 1989:488). The occupations of many other communities in the region did not, however, continue into the sixteenth century. This differential persistence of major population centers in the Western Pueblo regional system, along with issues of adaptive diversity discussed in the previous case study, render discussions of regional "abandonments" problematic.

Archaeological data indicate that one hundred years before the Spanish entered the New World, the Western Pueblo regional system was flourishing. As a regional system, different types of interactive ties linked communities across the region and facilitated the exchange of goods, information, and, probably, people. However, no overarching, regional, sociopolitical organization bound the Western Pueblo communities together into a single polity. Rather, major organizational variability existed in these communities. Some appear to have been organized rather simply. Other communities appear to have been organized hierarchically, having complex sociopolitical structures, including managerial elites (Cordell and Plog 1979; Cordell 1984, Lightfoot 1984, Upham 1982; Upham and Lightfoot 1989).

Some anthropologists have objected to the use of the terms "hierarchy" and "elite" to characterize prehistoric Western Pueblo sociopolitical structures merely because the concepts stand in opposition to descriptions found in the anthropological literature from the ethnographic present. We discussed previously our criticisms of ethnographic analogy in archaeological interpretation (Chap. 1). Given our views, we find such criticisms of the use of "hierarchy" and "elite" to describe prehistoric Western Pueblo sociopolitical organizations weak. Given archaeological data supporting interpretations and descriptions other than those derived from ethnographic analogy, the former (data) must take precedence over the latter (analogy). As documented in other of our case studies (e.g., Chaps. 5 and 6), we believe that concepts like hierarchy and elite are appropriately and accurately applied to aspects of both prehistoric and historic Hopi sociopolitical structures. The original and preferred definition of the word "hierarchy" refers to a body of religious officials ordered by rank and jurisdiction. Hierarchical societies are thus related to or controlled by a religious hierarchy. Only secondarily does the term "hierarchy" refer to an authoritarian or stratified society. "Elite" refers to a segment or group that is regarded as socially superior and only secondarily to a minority group or stratum that exerts influence, authority, or decisive power. Thus, we find it ironic that some archaeologists have objected to using hierarchy and elite when referring to the prehistoric Western Pueblo. Descriptions of Western Pueblo groups from the ethnographic present frequently emphasize that religion and ceremonialism were key to social integration among these peoples (see Chap. 2).

We believe, however, that anthropologists may accurately apply these terms in all of their senses to at least some late-prehistoric-period Western Pueblo communities. The terms appropriately designate features of social, economic, and productive processes that converged during the fourteenth and fifteenth centuries in many of these communities. Several of the largest Western Pueblo communities, for example, were sustained by intensive agricultural systems that required substantial labor to construct and maintain. Productive specialization in the procurement of raw materials (e.g., obsidian and other lithics, pigments, and semi-precious stones) and in the manufacture of ceramics and, presumably, cotton mantas and garments, indicates a differentiation of labor within communities. Labor management is one aspect of decision-making that was probably incorporated into the sociopolitical hierarchy.

Labor differentiation is related to the likelihood of community-level specialization within the Western Pueblo regional system. Riley (1987) documents how different communities, like those of Hopis and Zunis, may have specialized in the production of certain commodities, the procurement of particular raw materials, or the distribution of goods. The earliest Spanish narratives document, for example, specialized production of cotton and cotton mantas at Hopi. People traded these products widely throughout the Southwest. Similarly, Zuni communities appear to have been transshipment points for a variety of different finished goods and raw materials that circulated in the regional system (Riley 1987:161–213). As Riley argues, perhaps one of the reasons that so many groups in the Greater Southwest knew about Cibola is that the communities of this region were central to the pan-regional exchange system that had developed.

Archaeological data indicate that other communities, like Kinnickinnick in the Anderson Mesa locality, may have been involved in the specialized procurement of obsidian from the Government Mountain area near Flagstaff. This obsidian was in demand throughout much of the Western Pueblo area and the inhabitants of Kinnickinnick, or the neighboring community of Nuvakwewtaqa, may have also been involved in the production and distribution of obsidian products (e.g., blanks and projectile points; see Brown 1982). Still other communities, like those of the Middle Little Colorado or the Pinedale-Snowflake area, appear to have specialized in the production of highly distinctive pottery that was widely traded throughout the Southwest (Lightfoot 1984). Such community specialization adds another dimension to labor management and decision-making. The organizational and managerial demands of this specialization make it even more likely that there were sociopolitical hierarchies in Western Pueblo communities of the fourteenth and fifteenth centuries.

In some of the late-prehistoric Western Pueblo communities, large amounts of storage space are localized around Great Kivas (Upham

1982:185–187). No direct evidence exists that people in the large sedentary communities used this storage space for food storage. Nevertheless, it is likely that people necessarily maintained large food reserves for use during the winter and to protect against bad agricultural years (Cordell and Upham 1983). Further, the few studies archaeologists have completed indicate that some of the large Western Pueblo communities did not have enough arable land in their immediate vicinity to support their large sedentary populations (Upham 1982:183–185). Consequently, some of these communities needed either to import large quantities of food or produce an animal surplus by intensively cropping the existing land.[1] In either case, people could have preserved the necessary extra food for one or more years in the storage rooms associated with their Great Kivas. Cross-cultural data suggest that community-level surplus production often requires some type of relatively formal allocation system (Harris 1959; Service 1962). Archaeologists have also argued that the direct association of storage spaces with Great Kivas indicates the presence of redistribution activities (e.g., Plog 1974; Lightfoot 1984). This argument is based on the assumption that activities associated with the Great Kivas performed some community-level integrative function. Thus, the allocation of food and other critical resources is another potential domain of decision-making that is likely to have been incorporated into the sociopolitical hierarchy.

All of the large late-prehistoric Western Pueblo communities were involved in regional and pan-regional exchange activities that connected them to other communities in the Greater Southwest and beyond. Riley describes such connections between Southwestern communities (1987:161–213). He also documents the incredible quantity and variety of goods and raw materials that moved through the "macro-regional economic system" that engulfed the Greater Southwest from the fourteenth through sixteenth centuries. The scope and complexity of this system make it likely that the management of regional productive and exchange activities was another domain of decision-making incorporated into the sociopolitical hierarchy.

We could cite other examples making likely the proposition that economic complexity within and between late-prehistoric Western Pueblo communities was associated with sociopolitical complexity and hierarchy. Decision-making within these communities was, in all probability, not based exclusively on group consensus. Rather, a few individuals possessing the necessary, legitimate authority and power probably made significant decisions that affected their communities. Some individuals might even have possessed enough power to make decisions affecting the entire regional system. Upham previously characterized decision-making among the late-prehistoric Western Pueblo communities in this way:

> Just as large, nucleated populations practicing intensive agriculture *require* more complex organizational forms than do smaller populations engaged in less-intensive systems of agriculture, agricultural productivity, [specialized production], and regional exchange *require* some form of management personnel to staff the decision-making organization. In the modern Western Pueblo, decisions pertaining to the use of community surpluses are made by the village chief, who belongs to a dominant clan that also furnishes individuals to fill other important leadership positions within the village. In the terminology of political anthropology, these individuals are the decision-making elite. (1982:120; emphasis added)

We suspect that decisions about community surpluses in the prehistoric period would likewise have required a decision-making elite operating within formal sociopolitical institutions. Because widespread regional exchange among the Western Pueblo did not exist when the classic ethnographies were written, prehistoric decision-making organization was probably different from that found in the modern Western Pueblos. Group consensus might have been important to "everyday" decision-making in prehistoric times. Nevertheless, relatively few powerful individuals probably made the truly important decisions about the organization and management of labor, the use of community surpluses, and the acquisition of nonlocal commodities. If such individuals controlled community surpluses and the acquisition of nonlocal goods, economic resources might have been concentrated in their hands. Political power would, thus, be transformed into economic power.

The decision-making structure described above appears to have developed during the late prehistoric period in the Western Pueblo region. Further, by virtue of their position in the sociopolitical hierarchy, leaders appear to have had at least some economic power and privilege. The overt manifestation of this economic control is found in late prehistoric burials from some of the Western Pueblo communities, where some individuals were accorded preferential treatment in death. These burials are diverse, rich in grave goods (e.g., highly decorated pottery, turquoise, jewelry, shell, pigments, and copper bells), and contrast with the vast majority of individual burials. Most people were interred with no or only a few such goods (Griffen 1967; Clark 1967; Hohman 1982; Plog 1985).[2] On the basis of such data, some researchers conclude that incipient social stratification is evident in some burial populations of the region (e.g., Hohman 1982; Plog 1985). Consequently, the type of social classes that Whiteley (1988a) and others describe for historic Hopi society appear to have precedent in the fourteenth- through sixteenth-century Western Pueblo system.

Why did this system collapse? Why were many of the great Western Pueblo communities unoccupied when Coronado entered the Southwest in A.D. 1540? The answers to these questions are complex. No single explanation is likely to answer both questions satisfactorily. Upham (1982:199–202) suggests that a kind of "systemic hypercoherence" (Flannery 1972) characterized the Western Pueblo regional system. The large sedentary communities that dotted the landscape were too interdependent, and the intensive agricultural and productive systems that sustained them could not be managed over the long term. He argues that populations from several of these communities dispersed and returned to more extensive settlement and subsistence strategies (Chap. 3).

It also appears, however, that several communities could have persisted into the sixteenth centuries. Numerous Hopi, Zuni, and Acoma villages were, for example, occupied in A.D. 1540. The organizational structure of these villages in the early sixteenth century before the arrival of Coronado was probably similar to what we described for the late prehistoric Western Pueblo regional system. Yet, the Spanish describe the Western Pueblo region in different terms than those suggested by the late-prehistoric archaeological record. In the remainder of this case study, we examine one process that possibly contributed to sociocultural change in the Western Pueblo region during this period.

Disease and the Possible Consequences of Epidemics for the Western Pueblo

For many decades anthropologists have operated under the assumption that Native peoples of the American Southwest were relatively unaffected by Spanish contact and later intrusions of Mexican and European-American populations. Despite the recorded occurrence of disease in census documents, anthropologists believed that smallpox, measles, influenza, and other European-introduced crowd infections reached the Southwest only during the last two hundred years. Consequently, anthropologists assumed that their estimates of contact-period populations and their reconstructions of various groups' social, political, and economic organization mirrored the past rather well.[3]

In this chapter, we elaborate on a growing list of arguments suggesting that these interpretations are incorrect. Specifically, we focus on two important and interrelated issues: (1) modeling the incidence and spread of disease, using data from the quantitative epidemiological literature concerned with smallpox; and (2) examining the effects of climate on the incidence and severity of epidemic smallpox. These two topics possibly appear to lack immediate connection to Southwestern prehistory. However, our discussion of these issues establishes the high probability that epidemic diseases like smallpox spread to the American Southwest before systematic, direct Spanish exploration of the region (between A.D. 1519 and 1598). Such epidemics and their associated high mortality have dramatic implications for Western Pueblo demographic, social, political, and economic structures.

Although we are primarily concerned in this chapter with the likelihood and probable sociocultural implications of an unrecorded, early-contact-period spread of smallpox to the Southwest, we feel that the relevant epidemiological data are of vital interest. For this reason, we begin our discussion in the realm of epidemiology. Following presentation of the disease model and a discussion of its implications, we examine how particular climatic conditions favor and inhibit the spread of smallpox. We then return to the Southwest and present a historical summary of the incidence of smallpox, focusing on the transgenerational demographic consequences of mortality due to disease. Finally, we attempt to correlate Southwestern climatic data with the optimal climatic conditions favoring the spread of smallpox. Although the arguments presented here are not conclusive, they establish the likelihood that epidemic smallpox spread to native Southwestern populations *before direct contact* with the Spanish.

Population Reconstructions, Epidemiological Models, and Disease

During the last half century, many anthropologists have attempted to reconstruct contact and precontact aboriginal population levels in the New World.[4] This enormous amount of research has spawned several controversies regarding the size of New World populations on the eve of contact and has raised numerous questions about the magnitude of depopulation that occurred because of European colonization. Foremost among these questions are those about the effects of European-introduced acute crowd infections (e.g., smallpox, measles, and influenza).

Many of these excursions into historical demography have used Spanish historical documents (particularly census and tribute lists) when attempting to reconstruct the size of aboriginal populations. Others have used archaeological data (e.g., mortuary and settlement data) or have derived various quantitative ratios and measures from cross-cultural studies that focus on the effects of European-introduced acute crowd infections in "virgin-soil" and unvaccinated populations. Given the amount of research that has taken place on this topic, it is surprising how little agreement exists regarding either the size of contact and precontact population levels or the effects of disease on native populations.

One potential answer to the interpretive morass that presently exists can be found in the quantitative epidemiological literature. We now present a disease model drawn from this literature. Our purpose is to show how one disease, smallpox, could have affected New World populations. We also have two more specific purposes. First, anthropologists have previously presented epidemiological models (e.g., Milner 1980; Ramenofsky 1982). To our knowledge, however, no anthropologist has attempted to use models to assess how the ecology of a particular disease might have actually affected virgin-soil populations. Some of these scholars have argued that the effects of diseases like smallpox on New World populations were devastating (e.g., Crosby 1972; Dobyns 1983). While this appears to be correct, most of these arguments have been based on textual information that report on the state and decline of aboriginal populations. These are, in effect, subjective readings of texts, the veracity of which is sometimes questionable.

Second, a quantitative epidemiological model that focuses on a single disease provides a basis for evaluating how the varying parameters of the disease (degree of infectivity, period of incubation, infectiousness, rates of morbidity and mortality) might affect completely susceptible host populations of differing size and spatial structure. This type of a model allows for the quantitative assessment of the impact of disease on virgin-soil populations.

The Disease Model

Deterministic models for general epidemics can be useful tools for analyzing the spread of European-introduced acute crowd infections in aboriginal New World populations. This is because the initial iteration of the model (that is, during the hypothetical initial spread of the infection) assumes that virtually 100 percent of a given population is susceptible to a particular disease. Although 100 percent susceptibility is relatively rare, the spread of some varieties of *Variola major* (smallpox) in

New World groups approximated that rate (Dixon 1962; Ramenofsky 1982). The assumption of 100 percent susceptibility can be seen in the initial set of differential equations

$$(1) \quad dx/dt = -Bxy$$
$$(2) \quad dy/dt = Bxy - y' \, y$$
$$(3) \quad dz/dt = y'y$$

where x is the number of susceptibles, y the number of infectives in circulation, z the number of removals, B the infection rate, y' the removal rate, and t a specified time interval (Bailey 1975, p. 82). Thus $x + y + z$ = all the members of a given community, while the differential equations describe changes in the values of x, y, and z.[5]

One of the major problems associated with using the equations for a general deterministic epidemic is to figure values for B, the infection rate. To make use of the various equations shown above, one must make certain simplifying assumptions. First, in determining various values for B one can assume that the infection rate, that is, the number of new cases appearing in a population during a particular interval, equals either the contact rate or some fraction of the contact rate. So, the contact rate parameter equals the number of susceptibles contacted by an infective (with contact being sufficiently great to permit transmission of the disease) per unit of population per unit of time. In cases with a fixed number of infectives, as in certain models, the contact rate can be figured simply as a function of the frequency of contact per unit of time. Thus, any infective coming in contact with a group of susceptibles will transmit the disease to the susceptibles, or to some portion thereof, making them infectives. We can further assume that these new infectives, after time interval t, will then transmit the disease to a new group of susceptibles at the same rate. Thus, the infection rate will be an ascending exponential curve, with the slope of the curve varying with the magnitude of person-to-person contact (Fig. 4).

Examination of Figure 4 reveals how quickly infection can spread in a susceptible host population, given even the smallest contact rate parameter. Of course, the curves represented in Figure 4 are slightly unrealistic, since, in most communities, individuals have a more or less confined circle of contacts, and rarely in a group of a specified size would all people contact n number of new individuals daily. Nevertheless, under certain nucleated settlement conditions, all individuals within a community of n size could be contacted within a short time.

Although the primary emphasis of most epidemiological models is to estimate the number of probable new cases of a disease before or during

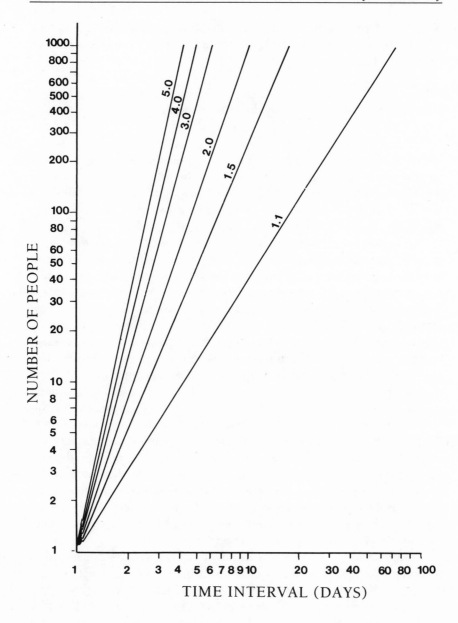

Figure 4. The Spread of Infection in a Completely Susceptible Host
Population of 1,000, Using Different Contact Parameters

the actual outbreak of an epidemic, equations do exist for calculating mortality rates for particular diseases. This class of equations is derived from vaccination models and, although some assumptions must be made, they provide a useful way of estimating average total and average daily mortality. To determine average mortality for varying values of B, we can solve for $D(n)$, the average number of deaths due to a given disease (Bailey 1975:366) where:

$$(4)\ D(n) = v\{1 + \frac{y'\ Bn}{w(y' - Bn)}\}$$

In this equation, v corresponds to the case mortality rate, y' to the mean infectious period before removal, B to the contact-rate parameter, w to the mean duration of the infectious period, and n to the total population at risk. Using this equation, it is possible to calculate average mortality for different levels of disease recognition and periods of infectiousness, while controlling for community size and estimated levels of face-to-face interaction.

Upham (1986) has presented a detailed consideration of the ecology of smallpox with particular attention to the infectivity of this disease and the varying rates of mortality associated with different varieties (Table 1). These data allow for the solution of equation (4) above for virgin-soil populations. Normally, solution of an equation such as this would require extensive knowledge about the effects of a particular disease on a given population and about patterns of community interaction. Fortunately, Becker (1979) has compiled just such information for the incidence of smallpox in the United States. Becker's data must be used cautiously since smallpox has not been a serious problem in the United States for at least one hundred years. Nevertheless, his data do set baseline parameters that can be extended to situations where modern health care practices, the tracing of infectives, and vaccination programs are not present. For our purposes, all parameters and assumptions of the model pertain to the first exposure to smallpox in a completely susceptible host population. The parameters and assumptions of the model are listed below. Becker's remarks (1979) are in quotes.

B = "This contact rate parameter is very community dependent. No estimate was available . . ." We have substituted a variety of contact rates, ranging from 1.5 to 5.0. The contact-rate parameter is an exponential measure.

y' = 2. "Although the period of infectiousness may be about three weeks, normal public health practices of contact tracing, early diagnosis, etc. considerably reduce the effective value of y'. The figure of $y' = 2$

Table 1. Variable Terminology Used to Describe the Manifestations of Variola Major

Researcher	Terms	Mortality
Beneson 1972	Ordinary type	30%
	Hemorrhagic type	100%
	Flat type	75% (vaccinated)
		96% (unvaccinated)
	Modified type	<5% (occurs only among vaccinated individuals)
Downie 1965	Classical smallpox	
	var. *purpura variolosa*	high mortality
	var. *Variola pustulosa*	
	haemorrhagica	high mortality
Van Rooyen and Rhodes 1948	Discrete smallpox	6%
	Confluent smallpox	45%
	Hemorrhagic smallpox	78%
	Purpuric smallpox	100%
Rhodes and Van Rooyen 1962	Discrete smallpox	10%
	Confluent smallpox	50%
	Hemorrhagic smallpox	>80%
	Secondary hemorrhagic smallpox	100%
Fenner and White 1976	Classical smallpox	15%
Christie 1980	Typical smallpox	variable
	Hypertoxic smallpox	
	var. hemorrhagic type	near 100%
	var. *purpura variolosa*	100%
	Modified smallpox	low
Dixon 1962	Fulminating smallpox	100%
	Malignant confluent smallpox	70%
	Malignant semi-confluent smallpox	23%
	Benign confluent smallpox	20%
	Benign semi-confluent smallpox	10%

corresponds to a mean infectious period before removal of 0.5 days."
We have assumed that in the first round of the disease in a virgin-soil
population, the mean period of infectiousness would correspond to the
total duration of the infectious period, or 26.75 days. To simplify the
equation, we have assumed that y' attains a maximum value of 100 for
each 25-day cycle.

$v = 10^{-1}$. "The case mortality rate (in the United States) is roughly 1
in 10." In attempting to derive values for v, we have used the relative conservative estimate of Crosby (1972), who suggests that mortality from
smallpox in an unvaccinated population is approximately 30 percent.

$w = 0.2$. "Based on the mean duration of the infectious period prior
to discovery being five days." In this equation, w is the decimal equivalent of y'. In other words, w attains a maximum value of 1.00 and corresponds to a mean duration of the infectious period of 25 days.

$n = 2 \times 10^8$. "Approximate population size of the U.S." We have used
a constant population size of 100,000 individuals for all solutions of the
equation.

Using the values noted above for virgin soil populations, Upham generated eight solutions to the equation, using different contact rate parameters and varying values of y' and w. The solutions appear in Table 2.
What is immediately apparent from the table is that slight variations in
the contact rate result in dramatically different projected daily case mortality rates. Although the projected total number of deaths will always
approximate 30 percent of the total population (since $v = .30$), the daily
mortality from smallpox varies from 1 to 4.2 percent of the total population. The impact of variation in projected daily case mortality has
enormous sociopolitical and economic implications for aboriginal populations, both in terms of immediate effects and long term, transgenerational impacts (see Lycett 1984).

Variola Major: *Nonhost Transmissibility and Aerial Convection*

Epidemiologists believe that smallpox is normally transmitted through
direct person-to-person contact. There are a good deal of data, however,
suggesting that aerial convection can and does occur under certain environmental conditions (Brachman 1970; Christie 1980:229–230; Morris et al. 1970; Thomas 1974; Wehrle et al. 1970). The possibility of
aerial convection is relevant to the present discussion since the transmission of the smallpox virus *without* direct person-to-person contact
has implications for the spread of this disease in virgin-soil populations.
The literature regarding the aerial convection of smallpox virus is equivo-

Table 2. Iterations of the Vaccination Model per 1,000 Population with an Estimated
30 Percent Case Mortality and Variable Contact Parameters

Infected People	Contact Parameter[a]	Standardized Contact Rate[b]	y'	Days to Contact 1,000	w	D(n)	Projected Average Deaths	Projected Daily Case Mortality
1,000	1.1	.015177	290	72.476574	2.90	.309591	310	4
1,000	1.5	.088046	68	17.036621	.68	.309052	309	18
1,000	2.0	.200687	40	9.965784	.40	.306107	306	31
1,000	2.5	.331617	30	7.538825	.30	.303668	303	40
1,000	3.0	.477121	25	6.287710	.25	.302541	303	48
1,000	3.5	.634746	22	5.514016	.22	.301906	302	55
1,000	4.0	.802747	20	4.982892	.20	.301500	302	61
1,000	4.5	.979819	18	4.592686	.18	.301232	301	66
1,000	5.0	1.164950	17	4.292030	.17	.301036	301	70

[a]The contact parameter is based on an exponential contact rate so that x infected individuals each contact the same number of individuals in the population who, in turn, spread the infection at the same rate. Thus, at a contact parameter of 5.0, a population of 1,000 would be contacted in 4.292030 days ($5^{4.292030}$).
[b]The standardized contact rate is derived by dividing the contact parameter by the time interval necessary to contact the total population at risk. In this case, the standardized contact rate = the contact parameter/days. The population at risk = 1,000.

cal regarding the distances over which the virus can be transported. Christie (1980) indicates that much of the evidence supporting the aerial convection of Variola virus is derived from the infection of individuals in hospitals. That is, individuals physically separated from the smallpox ward (in some cases, by as many as three floors), who had no contact with the infected individuals, became ill with smallpox. Two variables seem relevant under these conditions: (1) the absolute quantity of smallpox virus present in the atmosphere; and (2) the ambient conditions that favor the survival of the smallpox virus outside of the host. The former is related to the virulence of the virus and the number of infectives present at any place and time. The presence of individuals sick with smallpox in a closed environment like a hospital would contribute to the accumulation of the virus in the air. It has been demonstrated that airborne smallpox virus can be isolated from such an atmosphere (Thomas 1974). However, there are also known cases of smallpox infection that took place outside of a closed environment, spreading nearly a quarter of a mile in the open air from the original site of infection (Christie 1980:229).

While aerial convection is possible, there are probably limits on the distance the Variola virus can travel in the open air after release from an infected individual's respiratory tract. Remember, however, that viral release from the respiratory tract is only one aspect of infectivity from smallpox. The other, release from the skin, occurs when papules, pustules, and scabs are formed on the skin of an infected individual. Because the data on aerial convection suggest that Variola virus remains viable outside of the host for some time, the continued viability of the virus in scabs that have been sloughed from a host is potentially of great interest. The critical variables in this latter case would be environmental, since the concentrated nature of Variola virus in scabs provides a highly localized site for contamination and the subsequent spread of infection.

Some research has been directed at determining the optimal climatic conditions favoring the persistence of Variola virus outside a host (Downie and Dumbell 1947; Huq 1976; MacCallum and McDonald 1957; Mitra et al. 1974; Rogers 1926). All of the work, with the exception of Rogers' study (1926), began with smallpox virus isolated from the scabs of various patients. Rogers' study, on the other hand, focuses on the seasonal incidence of smallpox under different conditions of temperature and humidity. A more complete treatment of Rogers' work follows discussion of the data on nonhost transmissibility from scabs.

Variola virus is notoriously stable and durable. Although the virus completely loses infectivity at a temperature of 39° C (102.2° F [Downie 1965:936]) and can be killed in approximately ten minutes by moist heat at 60° C (140° F [Christie 1980:228]), there are data that suggest particular climatic conditions aid in the virus' survival. Much of the research that has been aimed at the survivability of the virus outside of a host stems from problems some countries have had with the importation of smallpox virus trapped in certain raw materials (particularly cotton) from areas where the disease is endemic. MacCallum and McDonald (1957) conducted experiments to determine how long Variola virus could survive in an infective state under different conditions of temperature and humidity. Their results are illuminating. They found that at temperatures of between 20° and 24° C (53.8° and 75.2° F) and at a relative humidity of approximately 55 percent Variola virus survived in a highly infectious state for at least 18 months. The virus continued to be viable at the end of this period, but the experiment was terminated. Downie and Dumbell (1947) obtained similar results, finding that Variola virus isolated from scabs survived for 417 days at 20° to 22° C (53.8° to 71.6° F) in an environment with a relative humidity of 35 to 65 percent.[6] These results have been augmented by the research of Huq (1976), who suggests that Variola virus remains infective for several weeks in ambient temperatures as high as 30° C (86° F) with a low relative humidity (ca. 25–30 percent), although 30° C would seem to be the upper limit of the virus' infectivity. He also indicates that under optimal climatic conditions Variola virus can remain infective for *several years.* Interestingly, Huq found that variation in temperature and humidity contributed to the loss of infectivity in the virus. So, in environments with stable temperatures between 22° to 30° C and with relative humidities between 25 and 55 percent, Variola virus remains stable and infective for several years. As temperature and humidity rise above 30° C and 55 percent respectively, Variola virus rapidly loses infectivity.

Unfortunately, laboratory research on the survivability of the smallpox virus has not been directed at determining the minimum temperature in which the virus can survive. Although there is no firm evidence, it would appear that 0° C represents the lower limit of survivability. As ambient moisture is frozen, the virus is presumably killed.

Several researchers have identified other modes of nonhost smallpox transmissibility. These include the spread of infection from handling the clothing and bedding of infectives, ingestion of the virus contained in contaminated food, and contact with animals from an infected environment. Flies that have contacted secretions from skin eruptions can also transmit smallpox. These data reinforce findings about the survivability of smallpox outside the host. The data have major implications for the spread of infection in totally susceptible host populations under aboriginal conditions.

Smallpox and the Environment

In 1926 Sir Leonard Rogers completed a remarkable study correlating climate with the incidence of smallpox in India. Rogers' specific intent was to investigate how particular climatic conditions affected variation in the death rate due to smallpox. At the time of Rogers' study, smallpox was endemic to most areas of the Indian subcontinent. Records charting the occurrence of smallpox indicated that epidemic spread of the disease followed a clear cyclical pattern. The pattern was, however, not obviously related to the introduction of new infectives into areas that were comparatively free of the disease. Instead, smallpox was occurring in endemic areas and appeared to be correlated with climatic conditions. Rogers' analysis revealed strong relationships between the increased incidence of smallpox, rainfall deficiencies, and specific conditions of absolute humidity (Rogers 1926:21–22). He portrayed these relationships graphically and also attempted to quantify the data using correlation coefficients. Although Rogers' analysis is one of the most complete and detailed of its kind, the periodicity of the data precluded him from specifying the precise relationships between epidemic smallpox and climatic conditions.

To resolve this problem and obtain data useful for predicting the ideal climatic conditions favoring the spread of smallpox, Upham performed two regression analyses (1986). The first, a standard least squares multiple linear regression, revealed several interesting relationships (Table 3). The analysis reveals time to be the most important of the variables. This result is expected since the climatic data as well as death rate are time-dependent variables. More important, however, the initial regression analysis shows that absolute humidity, Rogers' explanatory variable, is poorly correlated with the dependent variable. Mean temperature and relative humidity are much more highly correlated with death rate. Although absolute humidity is a composite variable that measures both temperature and relative humidity, the results of Upham's analysis do not completely support Rogers' conclusion.

Because of the obvious cyclical nature of Rogers' data and the problem of autocorrelation in the linear regression analysis (Durbin-Watson = 0.618117), Upham undertook another regression analysis in which

Table 3. Multiple Linear Regression on Rogers' Raw Data

Dependent variable: Death rate

Coefficient of determination: 0.372218
Multiple correlation coefficient: 0.610097
Estimated constant term: −4.71234
Standard error of estimate: 1.94949

Analysis of Variance for the Regression

Source of Variance	DF	Sum of Squares	Mean of Squares
Regression	5	175.762	35.1523
Residuals	78	296.439	3.8005
Total	83	472.201	

F Test: 9.24941, $p = .001$

Variable	Regression Coefficient	Standardized Coefficient	Correlation with Dependent
Month	−0.373610	−0.543967	−0.552864
Mean temp.	0.143567	0.548198	0.215949
Rainfall	−0.003336	−0.007937	−0.056590
Relative humidity	0.049340	0.331762	−0.149164
Absolute humidity	−4.980530	−0.455765	−0.004682

Durbin-Watson = 0.618117

the data from the seven Indian provinces were averaged, and periodic terms for the variable of time were added to the list of independent variables. This sinusoidal least squares model is derived from econometric forecasting models and is an accurate statistical approximation of time-dependent relationships between dependent (death rate) and independent variables (see Mendenhall and Reinmuth 1978:542). Averaging Rogers' data from the seven provinces has the effect of eliminating extreme high and low values for the climatic variables that result mainly from the differences in latitude between the weather recording stations. Results of the regression analysis are presented in Table 4.

The sinusoidal least squares model provides an excellent approximation of the relationships between the climatic measures and death rate. Significantly, absolute humidity is still relatively poorly correlated with

Table 4. Sinusoidal Least Squares Regression with Periodic Terms and Averaged Data

Dependent variable: Death rate

Coefficient of determination: 0.997626
Multiple correlation coefficient: 0.998812
Estimated constant term: −4.195690
Standard error of estimate: 0.146549

Analysis of Variance for the Regression

Source of Variance	DF	Sum of Squares	Mean of Squares
Regression	7	36.09070	5.15582
Residuals	4	0.08590	0.02147
Total	11	36.17660	

F Test: 240.065, p = .001

Variable	Regression Coefficient	Standardized Coefficient	Correlation with Dependent
Month	−0.019800	−0.039370	−0.718801
Mean temp.	0.102155	0.457918	0.316324
Rainfall	−0.368187	−0.890930	−0.300189
Relative humidity	0.175183	0.898977	−0.792864
Absolute humidity	−14.699400	−1.430240	−0.214501
Cosine	−4.222280	−1.719120	−0.529440
Sine	0.154838	0.063070	0.837536

Durbin-Watson = 2.81847

the dependent variable. Instead, the periodic model again indicates that the climatic variables of mean temperature and relative humidity are the strongest determinants of changes in the death rate due to smallpox. Further, mean temperature is positively correlated with changes in the death rate, and relative humidity is negatively correlated. Thus, an increase in the death rate would be correlated with increasing temperature and decreasing humidity. Finally, rainfall is negatively correlated with the dependent variable in the sinusoidal model. This parallels the inverse relationship between temperature and humidity.

These data indicate that the laboratory experiments noted earlier only partially account for the climatic conditions aiding in the survivability of the virus and, consequently, in the spread of epidemic smallpox. The laboratory experiments have only identified optimal conditions of temperature and humidity and have not accounted for either the interaction of climatic effects or the inverse relationship between mean temperature and relative humidity on the one hand, and increases or decreases in the death rate on the other.

Using the regression coefficients from the sinusoidal model, Upham has generated a series of estimates that portray the relationship between death rate from smallpox and mean temperature and relative humidity (see Table 5). He used only three variables from the regression analysis in computing these estimates: month, mean temperature, and relative humidity. The estimates confirm the inverse relationship between temperature and humidity, with maximum death rate occurring with maximum mean temperature and minimum relative humidity. Although the figures for estimated death rate are based on projections that are outside the parameter values of the regression equation, the low standard error of the estimate (0.146549) allows for this kind of extrapolation. The values for death rate are based on the projected number of deaths per 100,000 individuals. Remember that these data were compiled in an area where smallpox was endemic and where contact tracing and vaccination programs were not well organized. Because of this fact, the values should not be interpreted as direct measures. They should, instead, be considered as indices reflecting the types of climatic conditions that favor the spread of smallpox. In the seven Indian provinces, the mean annual death rate is 4.02 ± 2.38 and is correlated to a mean annual temperature of 77.5° F and a mean relative humidity of 67.3 percent. In other words, any values for death rate that exceed this mean and that are within the climatic parameters specified would suggest climatic situations that favor the spread of smallpox. To provide a conservative estimator, we can add the standard deviation to the mean death rate for the Indian provinces. Thus, death rates higher than 6.40 indicate the most favorable climatic conditions. Interpreted in this manner, relatively specific climatic conditions favoring the survivability of the smallpox virus can be specified.

In this brief treatment of epidemiological models, smallpox, and climate, we made two important points. First, we showed that by making certain assumptions about the infectivity and spread of smallpox, relatively detailed case mortality data can be obtained. Significantly, given a constant 30 percent case mortality rate in a hypothetical population of 100,000, the magnitude of *daily case mortality* is dependent on the contact-rate parameter. Because contact rates are exponential measures, the effects of the spread of infection have dramatically different consequences on populations of equal size. The implications of this result are important for understanding the effects of disease on contact-period

Table 5. Estimates of Death Rate Generated from the Sinusoidal Regression Analysis

Mean Annual Temperature °F	Mean Annual Relative Humidity (%)									
	10	20	30	40	50	60	70	80	90	100
10										
20										
30	7.84	**6.75**	5.67	4.58	3.50	2.41	1.33	.24	—	—
40	**8.54**	**7.46**	6.37	5.29	4.20	3.12	2.03	.94	—	—
50	**9.25**	**8.17**	**7.08**	5.99	4.91	3.82	2.74	1.65	.57	—
60	9.96	**8.87**	**7.79**	**6.70**	5.62	4.53	3.45	2.36	1.28	.19
70	**10.66**	**9.58**	**8.49**	**7.41**	6.32	5.24	4.15	3.07	1.98	.89
80	**11.37**	**10.28**	**9.19**	**8.11**	**7.03**	5.94	4.86	3.77	2.69	1.60
90										
100										

Loss of Infectivity at 32° F

Loss of Infectivity at 86° F

Note: Figures in **boldface** indicate optimal climatic conditions favoring the survivability of the smallpox virus.

Southwestern populations. An inescapable conclusion is that the structure of settlements and settlement patterns, a determining factor of community interaction levels, may have been the most important determinant of how severely a particular disease affected a given population. This also suggests that estimating mortality due to disease in the contact period must be undertaken on grouped data using similar kinds and sizes of settlements.

Second, the investigation of the clinical manifestations and infectivity of smallpox revealed that direct person-to-person contact is not required for the disease to spread. Aerial convection, flies, contaminated clothing and food, and even animals can transmit the disease with the same deadly result because the smallpox virus can survive for long periods outside of the host. Climatic conditions, in particular relative humidity and temperature, are the determining variables in the virus' survival. Through the use of regression analysis, relatively precise climatic conditions have been specified. As we turn now to the American Southwest, the data generated above can be used to assess how smallpox may have spread during the early contact period.

Smallpox and the American Southwest

We begin this section with the caveat that direct application of the disease model presented earlier in this chapter is not presently possible. Accurate demographic data and information on prehistoric Southwestern community interaction patterns are not available. Nevertheless, there are data on Southwestern contact history indicating that smallpox could have been transmitted to native populations prior to direct, face-to-face contact with the Spanish. Additional data suggest that Southwestern climatic conditions were ideal for the survival of Variola virus outside of the host. If the following scenario is correct, mortality rates generated by the disease model can be used to account for population loss among contact-period Southwestern peoples.

Like most other types of historical information, the evidence for epidemic smallpox in the American Southwest before A.D. 1800 is sketchy. Dobyns offers the most complete treatment to date about the New World spread of smallpox (1983). Although his work concerns the effects of various diseases on virgin-soil populations, he gives smallpox the most detailed treatment. One of Dobyns' most controversial assertions is that a hemispheric pandemic swept New World populations in the years between A.D. 1520 and 1524. The foundation of this pandemic, according to Dobyns, was smallpox, although other European-introduced diseases were also prominent.

Apart from Dobyns' assertion regarding the hemispheric pandemic, the evidence for the presence of smallpox in the Greater Southwest is remarkably poor before 1780. Although Dobyns argues that smallpox epidemics occurred in Sinaloa in 1592 to 1593 and again in 1602, it is unclear whether the disease in question was actually smallpox (see Dobyns 1983:28–29; Gibson 1964:449; and Sauer 1935). Thus, the first unequivocal Southwestern occurrence of epidemic smallpox was in 1780 to 1781 (Bancroft 1889:266; Stearn and Stearn 1945:48). This is fully 264 years after the Spanish had introduced the disease to the New World and 242 years after the Europeans first entered the Southwest. Following 1780 and until the beginning of the twentieth century, Southwestern smallpox epidemics occurred about every 18 years ($\pm$ 4.96) (Dobyns 1983:28–29). So, epidemics occurred about once every generation.

There is a remarkable discrepancy in the disease history of the American Southwest. In virtually every other New World region where Spanish contacted Native populations, smallpox epidemics followed such contact almost immediately. If we believe Spanish contact records, however, Southwestern Native peoples somehow escaped the effects of diseases like smallpox until well into the eighteenth century. This is highly unlikely. The first European contact with Southwestern groups occurred in 1539 (Marcos de Niza). The Spanish did not visit the Southwest between 1540 (Coronado) and 1581 (Rodriguez-Chumascado). Although there is no record of epidemics during this time, Southwestern populations were, presumably, no different from other New World groups in their lack of resistance to European diseases.

More importantly, potential disease vectors were introduced to the Southwest in 1540. Mexican Indians, presumably Tlaxcalans who accompanied the Coronado party in 1540, remained in the Southwest. The Spanish identified their descendants some forty years later (Riley 1974:30–32, 1988). Before their arrival in the Southwest, these Mexican Indians had been exposed to smallpox and other Old World diseases for nearly 20 years. Thus, although the evidence is purely inferential, the 40-year period unrepresented in Spanish documents would provide ample time for a smallpox epidemic to have occurred. If an epidemic occurred, one could expect population data related to mortality and annual rates of increase to provide clues.

In nearly all preindustrial societies, a disproportionate segment of the population is below the age of fifteen, producing an age pyramid with an extremely broad base. As Lycett points out (1984), the effects of epidemic disease on populations so structured is devastating due to the transgenerational reproductive consequences. For example, in a population where the mean life expectancy is forty years, that has an annual rate of increase of 2 percent, a birth rate of 4.33 percent, and a death rate of 2.33 percent, 41.1 percent of the population is under fifteen years of age and 74.5 percent of the population is under thirty-four (Shyrock et al. 1975:884). A 30 percent mortality rate due to epidemic smallpox would mean that a hypothetical population of 100,000 would suffer 22,350 of the 30,000 deaths in age categories that are reproductively viable, or would be reproductively viable if survival to maturity had occurred. In this circumstance, recovery to predisease population levels would not occur for roughly five generations (100 years), if the annual birth to population ratio was 0.099 and infant mortality was 50 percent. If infant mortality exceeded 60 percent, the population would never recover to predisease levels.

Southwestern Climate and Smallpox

As noted earlier in this chapter, the incidence and severity of smallpox is highly correlated with particular climatic conditions. Conditions favoring the survivability of the smallpox virus outside of the host include a mean annual relative humidity ranging from 10 to 50 percent, with mean annual temperatures between 32° and 86° F. Stable climatic conditions are also required. Annual fluctuations in temperature should not exceed 102.2° F or drop below 32° F. Fluctuations in relative humidity are less important, except when high relative humidity is coupled with elevated temperatures.

Table 6 presents generalized mean annual temperature and relative humidity data for various elevations in the Greater Southwest. Upham derived the data from a regression equation in which elevation was predicted on the basis of mean temperature and relative humidity. In the regression analysis, he used data from twenty-two weather stations at a variety of elevations in Arizona and New Mexico. Because no data were available for climatic conditions below 32° latitude, predictions are uncertain for areas south of the international boundary. Nevertheless, the data broadly characterize climatic conditions at varying elevations for much of the Greater Southwest.

Table 6 shows that Southwestern mean annual temperature and relative humidity fall within the optimal range favoring smallpox virus survivability outside a host. For elevations between sea level and 6,000 feet, Southwestern mean temperature and relative humidity is "ideal." These

Table 6. Generalized Climatic Data by Elevation for the Southwest

Elevation (ft.)	Mean Annual Temperature	Mean Annual Humidity
Sea level	74.0	30.7
200	73.3	30.9
400	72.5	31.2
600	71.7	31.5
800	70.9	31.8
1,000	70.2	32.1
1,500	68.4	32.7
2,000	66.5	33.4
2,500	64.6	34.1
3,000	62.7	34.9
3,500	60.8	35.6
4,000	58.9	36.3
4,500	57.0	37.0
5,000	55.1	37.7
5,500	53.2	38.4
6,000	51.4	39.1
6,500	49.5	39.8
7,000	47.6	40.5
7,500	45.7	41.2
8,000	43.8	41.9
8,500	41.9	42.6
	error = 2.4 degrees	error = 1.6%

data do not, however, show the variation in mean temperature and relative humidity. Such variation is critical to the virus' survival. An examination of monthly mean temperature data for the region indicate that, for elevations below 1,500 feet, there are usually three months with temperatures that exceed 86° F. Similarly, elevations above 7,000 feet are likely to have an average of three months with temperatures below 32° F. In other words, Southwestern areas between about 2,000 and 6,000 feet provide the most stable climatic conditions for smallpox. Daily fluctuations in summer and winter temperatures, particularly at the lowest and highest elevations in this range, may hinder the virus' survival.

These data suggest that once the smallpox virus entered the Southwest, climatic conditions would favor its survival. They also indicate that modes of disease transmission other than direct person-to-person contact probably occurred. Aerial convection, flies, garments, food, and animals could all contribute to the spread of epidemic smallpox among completely susceptible Southwestern host populations. If climatic conditions in the Southwest are so favorable for smallpox, why didn't the disease become endemic to the area? The answer to this question must lie in the size of the reserve population following smallpox's initial introduction and spread. Small numbers of susceptibles following an epidemic may have effectively limited the extent to which the disease could become entrenched in the population.

A Probable Scenario

The data presented in this chapter suggest that contact-period Southwestern conditions favored the spread of epidemic smallpox. Such conditions included the presence of a completely susceptible host population, the introduction of potential disease vectors, and an ideal climate. Because of the presence of these conditions, despite lacking corroborating historical texts for the occurrence of smallpox in the Southwest before 1780, we offer a likely scenario for the spread of this disease to Southwestern groups.

Either the hemispheric pandemic Dobyns describes or another early, more localized epidemic probably affected Southwestern Native peoples. Snow and Starna (1984) and Snow and Lamphear (1988) have taken a dissenting position on the hemispheric character of this event, based on their study of populations in the Mohawk Valley, New York. We believe, however, that climatic conditions in the Northeast may have prevented the spread of smallpox to this region. The data presented here would suggest that the "pandemic" to which Dobyns alludes or other epidemics may be restricted to those areas of the New World where climatic conditions favor survival of the Variola virus outside of the host. The repeated textual references to Southwestern epidemic smallpox after 1781 make it likely that this disease recurred after the initial pandemic. A plausible date for this recurrence is between Coronado's departure in 1541 and the Rodriguez-Chumascado expedition's arrival in 1581. Given the frequency of later Southwestern smallpox epidemics, at least one other epidemic probably occurred between the 1580s and 1780s.

These three postulated smallpox epidemics accord well with what we know about the size of Southwestern populations during this period. Elsewhere, Upham (1984) provides a revised Western Pueblo population estimate tied to a baseline date of 1520. The figures for the three groups of pueblos that he considered total 66,967 at that time (29,305 for the Hopi villages, 24,662 for the Zuni villages, and 13,000 for Acoma). Given a 30 percent mortality rate for each occurrence of smallpox, the spread of the initial epidemic in 1520 and another smallpox epidemic occurring in the 1541 to 1581 interval would result in a total remaining Western Pueblo population of approximately 32,813 (14,359 for Hopi, 12,084 for Zuni, and 6,370 for Acoma). These figures are close to what one would predict for these groups based on both Dobyns 20:1 depopulation ratio (Dobyns 1966; Upham 1982) and Ubelaker's esti-mate of a 91 percent decline among the Pueblos (1988).

Two friars made one of the first relatively reliable Western Pueblo population estimates. In 1745, the Catholic priests visited the Hopi Mesas and recorded 10,848 people living there (cited in Donaldson 1893). As discussed in Chapter 5, approximately 4,000 of these inhabi-tants were refugees from the Rio Grande pueblos in New Mexico. This means that approximately 7,500 Hopis were present. The postulated third unrecorded occurrence of smallpox after 1583, probably some-time in the 1600s and possibly related to one of the epidemics in Sinaloa that Dobyns cites, would leave a population at Hopi of 10,051. This fig-ure is within range of the two friars' estimate.

The above scenario is speculative. It is based only on the etiology of smallpox, inferential data regarding the spread of the disease, and plau-sible contact routes to the Southwest. Despite the hypothetical nature of our conclusions, the data are compelling. Minimally, anthropologists should attend more fully to the possibility of Southwestern population decline or collapse following Spanish contact.

Conclusion

Our consideration of smallpox has provided a largely inferential way to assess how this disease may have affected Southwestern populations during the contact period. We focused on disease and consequent popu-lation decimation for several reasons. First, and most important, is the widely held notion among anthropologists and archaeologists that Southwestern populations were extremely small during the proto-historic and early contact period. Elsewhere, Upham addresses why this idea persists and why it is wrong (Upham 1984, 1987). Second, the size of Southwestern native populations is directly related to the types of interpretations of sociopolitical and economic systems that are gener-ated. Ethnographic descriptions and interpretations of the Western Pueblo, for example, have all been based on the study of small, relatively autonomous groups that survived Spanish, Mexican, and European-American contact. Many of these descriptions and interpretations have been extended to the prehistoric period without considering the possible effects of disease and population reduction. We argue that the size and organizational complexity of Western Pueblo groups that anthropologists recorded in the ethnographic present are poor analogs when applied to groups from earlier periods.

The data presented in this chapter do not prove that Southwestern smallpox epidemics occurred prior to 1781. The data indicate, however, that conditions for the spread of smallpox were ideal at that time. Remember that between 1520 and 1581, the Spanish were only one of several potential disease vectors that could have transmitted smallpox to Southwestern populations. Riley (1980, 1987) describes the social, economic, and political ties among Greater Southwestern native populations between 1520 and 1650. Information, goods, and people were circulating throughout the Greater Southwest at that time. Given the infectivity of smallpox and the climatic conditions in the Southwest, the introduction of infection to one group could have resulted in widespread transmission of the pathogen. If this occurred before 1540 or between 1541 and 1598, historical documents would likely fail to record it. Consequently, model building coupled with archaeological research on sites dated to these intervals will provide the only information that might resolve the epidemic and population issues.

5. Hopi Resistance to Subjugation and Change (A.D. 1680–1879)

ANTHROPOLOGISTS OFTEN CHARACTERIZE Hopi history between 1680 and 1880 as a period of sociocultural stability and resistance to outside influence (Titiev 1944:3; Spicer 1962:208; Eggan 1970:vii; Dozier 1970:209; Dockstader 1979:524).[1] During this era, there were numerous expeditions to Hopi territory by Spanish, Mexican, and American explorers, missionaries, military personnel, and civilians. Throughout this time, outsiders sought to convert, subjugate, and exploit the Hopis, as Europeans were doing among many other Native American peoples. All of these efforts failed, however, because the Hopis passively and actively resisted them. This resistance is represented by Hopi participation in the Pueblo Revolt of 1680 and by their later destruction of Awatovi pueblo during the late fall of 1700 or early winter of 1701. The Pueblo Revolt of 1680 is the most famous example of historically documented political cooperation among the diverse Pueblo groups. Between 10 and 13 August of that year, Puebloan peoples responded to the repressive conditions of Spanish domination. They attacked Spanish military personnel, priests, and other colonists, killing many and driving the remainder south. As a result, Puebloan peoples were free from Spanish rule until Don Diego de Vargas and his troops reestablished control over the territory in 1692.

As noted, Hopis cooperated with other pueblos in the overthrow of Spanish authority. They, too, were free of colonial domination until de Vargas returned with his troops. At that time, leaders from all Hopi villages except Oraibi ostensibly acquiesced to de Vargas' demands. In the ensuing years, however, only Awatovi citizens actually resubmitted to Spanish and Catholic domination. The other Hopi pueblos passively or actively defied the outsiders. Because of the Awatovi resubmission, during the late fall of 1700 or early winter of 1701 Hopis from other villages destroyed much of that pueblo (including its Catholic mission). They also killed some of Awatovi's inhabitants and resettled the rest among other Hopi pueblos (Brew 1949). From that time until the late 1800s, Hopi religious and political leaders maintained control over their domain. During those years, they effectively resisted the intrusion of most foreign ideology.

In this chapter, we use the Pueblo Revolt and Awatovi's destruction to ground our discussion of Hopi sociocultural persistence and change from 1680 to 1880. We do so not only because these events represent a fascinating part of Hopi history, but also because they play a significant role in explaining later episodes of Hopi sociocultural persistence and change. We concur with other anthropologists that important features of Hopi culture and society probably persisted through the years under consideration. We also believe that significant changes occurred in the Hopi way of life from 1680 to 1880. The most consequential of these changes might have occurred after 1851 to 1853. At that time, a major smallpox epidemic devastated the Hopi population. Before proceeding with the description and analysis of this period, we return to certain points first raised in Chapter 1 about ethnographic analogy and the ethnographic interpretation of historical documents. The points we reiterate apply not only to the present, but also later case studies.

In Chapter 1, we cautioned against the uncritical use of ethnographic materials in the interpretation of archaeological remains. We then warned against the indiscriminate use of historical data to support ethnographic descriptions and, conversely, about the use of ethnographic descriptions to interpret historical texts. If historical documents are narrowly understood through the perspective of a particular ethnographic description, there is a strong possibility of incorrect analysis. As a result, the processes of sociocultural persistence or change might be incorrectly inferred. In this chapter, how we describe sociocultural persistence and change between 1680 and 1880 critically depends on our interpretation of material cultural remains and historical texts from this period. For example, given Titiev's (1944) description of Hopi political structure from the ethnographic present period (T_2, ca. 1880–1920), claims about the persistence or change of this pattern from earlier times (T_1, ca. 1680) depend on how political structure from the earlier period is described. If Hopi political institutions from T_1 and T_2 are thought to be different, change is indicated and must be explained. If such institutions from T_1 and T_2 are considered identical, persistence is entailed and requires explanation. More concretely, Titiev describes Hopi leadership from the ethnographic present as theocratic and "amorphous." He also stresses the autonomy of villages (see Chap. 2). If we understand early Spanish documents as descriptions of the same type of organization, we accept implicitly that this pattern has persisted. We must then explain why. If, on the other hand, we understand the same Spanish records to be describing more formal Hopi leadership structures and a pan-village organization with an Oraibi "capital," we assume implicitly that significant sociocultural change has taken place. We must then explain the transformation of Hopi political structure and organization. In sum, in this and later chapters, our interpretations of historical "facts" establish how we approach sociocultural persistence and change. Stated more strongly, our interpretations influence, if not determine for us, the sociocultural "events" that occurred among the Hopi during the period under consideration.

Thus, having alerted readers to the strong interpretive component of our analysis, we now proceed to our third case study. After a historical narrative, we interpret relevant events and review different anthropological explanations of the sociocultural processes that we uncover.

The Pueblo Revolt of 1680

As noted in Chapter 2, Spanish exploration of the American Southwest, including Hopi territory, was largely motivated by the search for souls, gold, and other treasures. Because of their quest for heathen souls and for riches of their own to support the Catholic Church, Spanish missionaries accompanied the earliest explorers and settled in the Southwest with the first colonists. From that time, the history of Spanish contact with Native American peoples along the Rio Grande Valley and west to the Hopi Mesas was one of subjugation and domination. The Spanish intended to expropriate Indian lands, resources, and labor and to obliterate all features of Native American culture and society.

The Spanish army was largely responsible for the accomplishment of this difficult task. Because of their superior military technology, based on horses and guns, the invaders were able to rapidly subdue and maintain control over the Pueblos. Diego Pérez de Luxán, a member of Antonio de Espejo's 1583 expedition, describes in his journal his party's initial confrontation with Hopis at Awatovi. His description of how the Spanish intimidated and coerced the Hopis by an extreme show of force is representative of much early contact between Spanish and Native Americans (see Brew 1949:7). Had the Hopis of Awatovi not capitulated, events probably would have gone far worse for them. Other historical accounts suggest that the Spanish frequently conquered Puebloan peoples through force.[2]

From the 1580s to the 1680s Hopis were primarily a tributary to the mainstream of Spanish colonial efforts among Puebloan Indians. Spanish presence was felt much more intensely along the Rio Grande. Because of the abundance of water and agricultural land, the majority of Spanish government personnel, missionaries, and colonists located there permanently. Because Hopis were distant from the New Mexican settlements and because their land lacked the agricultural potential of the Rio Grande Valley, Hopis were partially isolated from Spanish influences during this period. Nevertheless, Hopis became increasingly familiar with the Europeans through: (1) at least six major expeditions to their land by representatives of the Spanish government and military; (2) relatively frequent but unrecorded visits by other colonists; (3) many formal and informal Hopi visits to the Rio Grande; and (4) the establishment, after 1628, of permanent Catholic missions in different Hopi pueblos. From 1628 until 1680 there were, on the average, three active missions (at Awatovi, Oraibi, and Shongopavi) and about five friars present among the Hopi.

As among the Rio Grande pueblos, the experiences Hopis had with the Spanish after first contact were repressive and, as indicated, culminated with Hopi participation in the Pueblo Revolt of 1680. In 1599, for example, two Hopi men who were visiting Acoma became entangled in a Spanish net cast to catch and punish "rebels" among that people. Acoma men had apparently killed some soldiers. Each Acoma rebel was sentenced to have a foot cut off and to perform twenty years of hard labor. The Hopi men were sentenced to have their right hand cut off and to return home as a warning to other Hopis (Brew 1949:8).

In 1655 the Franciscan Father Salvador de Guerra found a unique way to punish an Oraibi man for his "act of idolatry." First, Guerra publicly beat him in the plaza, then took him inside the mission to administer another beating, and finally doused the Hopi with turpentine, set him afire, and burned him to death. A delegation of Hopis complained to officials in Santa Fe about this and other of Guerra's actions. Among other things, he had administered similar punishments to Hopis who did not provide him with enough cotton blankets. The Catholic Church disciplined their priest by forbidding him to perform mass for a short time and by removing him from Hopi territory (Scholes 1937:144–146; Spicer 1962:191; Whiteley 1988a:17).

At Awatovi, sometime between 1653 and 1656, Catholic Church officials accused and convicted a Hopi man of impersonating Friar Alonso de Posada while the latter, who was guardian of the Awatovi mission, was away from the pueblo (Scholes 1937:146–147). This event might be an example of behavior often associated nowadays with Hopi ceremonial or sacred "clowns."[3] It is, perhaps, the first recorded example of a joking imitation of "whitemen" along the lines that Keith H. Basso later described for the Western Apache (1979). Apparently, the Spanish were not amused.

Earlier at Awatovi, when the main Catholic church was constructed (ca. 1630), its altars were placed immediately on top of an Awatovi kiva that the priests filled with sand (Montgomery, Smith, and Brew 1949: 64–66). The practice of physically placing significant ritual objects on top of similar objects from "pagan" religions was widespread in the Catholic Church during this period (Montgomery, Smith, and Brew 1949:265–272). By doing so, the Spanish intended to symbolically establish religious and political dominance. Catholic priests also practiced such "superpositioning" of sacred objects at the other Hopi pueblos.

Throughout this period Spaniards expropriated Pueblo lands, resources, and labor and made every attempt to abolish traditional Puebloan ways of life. Harsh physical punishments and forced labor were the usual punishments for Indians who broke the new rules that the Spanish colonialists imposed. Puebloan religious and ceremonial life was selected for extermination, and the strongest punishments were reserved for recalcitrants who chose to follow their own religious beliefs and customs. Ironically, Spanish colonialists did not always present a unified front to the pueblos. The lay government in Santa Fe often fought with the Franciscans about authority over the Indians and over rights to Indian labor and tribute. In 1659 López de Mendizábal became Governor. Apparently to undermine the priests and promote his own self-interest, Mendizábal encouraged the pueblos to hold traditional ceremonial dances. For these and other actions Mendizábal was placed on trial, during which he died in 1664 (Dockstader 1985:163–164). Such inconsistency, perhaps, added to the turmoil the Indians faced (Sando 1979: 194–195).

Within this context, many Native Americans began to hate the foreigners and their institutions. After eighty years of subjugation, Puebloan peoples united to overthrow their oppressors. During August of 1680, following a plan that Tewa and Northern Tiwa leaders had developed, Puebloan peoples either killed or evicted the priests and other foreigners from their pueblos, confronted the Governor in Santa Fe, and forced him and his support personnel to leave New Mexico. Twenty-one of the thirty-three Franciscan friars in the territory were killed, along with approximately four hundred Spanish soldiers and civilians (Sando 1979:198).

Hopis attacked the Spanish priests present at the Hopi Mesas. The revolt, as it occurred at Oraibi, is recorded in Hopi oral history and reported by H. R. Voth (1905a).[4] The Hopi account begins with a description of the Spanish at Oraibi in the earliest years. It continues by discussing conditions at Oraibi under Spanish control. It describes: (1) the work Hopis were required to perform for the priests (the text mentions building Spanish dwellings and churches, hauling water, making cisterns, and hauling logs); (2) the ineffectiveness of the Spanish religion for bringing clouds and rain; (3) the suppression by the priests of Hopi religion; and (4) the general denigration by the priests of all Hopis and Hopi customs, including the chastity of Hopi women. The text then describes how Oraibi men met to consider their situation. After much debate, the Badger clan volunteered to eliminate the priest. They went to the mission, killed the priest, and threw his body off the mesa. Men from other Hopi villages then did the same to the priests in their pueblos. Hopis then destroyed the missions (Voth 1905a).

The Spanish did not immediately return to Oraibi or any other Hopi village because of the events occurring simultaneously in New Mexico. After the revolt, Hopis used materials from the Spanish churches to build new kivas. They also used church bells in some of their ceremonies. The Hopis thus employed their own form of "superposition" to reestablish their own religion's predominance.

Reconquest and the Destruction of Awatovi

Following the successful Pueblo Revolt of 1680, Hopis and other Native Americans were free of Spanish rule for only about twelve years. During this period, however, two significant events occurred among the Hopis. First, fearing eventual Spanish retaliation, hundreds (if not thousands) of Indians from the Rio Grande region left their homes and moved to the Hopi Mesas. Eventually, some of these people (and perhaps other refugees from the reconquest of New Mexico in 1692) built their own villages at Hopi. Northern Tewa established Hano pueblo on First Mesa. Sandia pueblo refugees (Southern Tiwa-speakers) apparently founded Payupki pueblo on Second Mesa (Brandt 1979:345). Other emigrants were probably absorbed into Hopi society. These Tanoan-speaking people from the Rio Grande brought with them their own distinct languages and cultures. Thus, Hopis experienced additional intimate contact with non-Hopi people.

The second major event of this period was the relocating of some Hopi pueblos between 1692 and 1699 (Brew 1949:20). Walpi was moved to the top of First Mesa.[5] Mishongnovi and Shongopovi were relocated at the top of Second Mesa. These relocations made it necessary for people to haul water from springs to their homes. The relocations also, however, made it easier to defend these villages from anticipated Spanish attacks.

Following various brutal but unsuccessful attempts by other military personnel (in 1681, 1688, and 1689), Don Diego de Vargas and his troops successfully reconquered all of Puebloan territory in 1692. In November of that year, de Vargas traveled to the Western Pueblo region to obtain Zuni and Hopi obedience and vassalage. Don Carlos de Siguenza y Góngora, who accompanied de Vargas, recorded the events at Antelope Mesa. He described how almost eight hundred Awatovi Hopis suddenly surrounded de Vargas and about twenty-five of his men as they approached Awatovi. The Spanish offered no resistance, and the Awatovi chief began to ride at de Vargas' side. In their conversation, de Vargas threatened the Awatovi chief with destruction of the pueblo, successfully intimidating the Awatovi chief. Hence, the Hopis laid down their arms and knelt to the Spanish. The latter entered the village and took possession of the town. Later, the Spanish left Awatovi, traveled a short distance, camped at a nearby spring, and coerced the Hopis to feed them. The next day, de Vargas and his people returned to Awatovi, reconsecrated the church, and baptized some infants (Góngora 1932: 80–88, quoted in Brew 1949:19).

Following the events of 20 November 1692, de Vargas, accompanied by the Awatovi chief, traveled to the other Hopi pueblos (excepting Oraibi). He obtained their submission by intimidation through displays of force. De Vargas went east with the Hopis' promise of compliance on 24 November.

The reconquest of 1692 did not mean that Native Americans completely accepted Spanish domination. Nor did it mean that the Rio Grande pueblos were pacified. Life with the Spanish remained tumultuous, and soon many more refugees escaped colonial tyranny by traveling to the Western Pueblo region. Nevertheless, reconquest among the Hopis resulted in relatively few immediate changes. Following de Vargas' visit of 1692, priests did not return at once, and they did not immediately reopen their Hopi missions. However, on 28 May 1700, Fray Juan de Garaycoechea and Fray Antonio Miranda arrived at the pueblo of Awatovi on Antelope Mesa and began proselytizing. After baptizing people at Awatovi, de Garaycoechea and Miranda notified the Hopi man, Don Francisco Espeleta, that they intended to travel to the other Hopi pueblos. Espeleta reacted strongly to this news. He went to Awatovi with approximately eight hundred Hopis, confronted the friars, and forbade them to leave that village. Hence, the friars continued to work at Awatovi and then returned to their missions requesting that the governor send troops to the Hopi Mesas (Hackett 1937:385–387; Brew 1949:22).

Before the Pueblo Revolt, Espeleta was trained by the Spanish priest, Joseph de Espeleta, from whom he (the Hopi man) took his name. Later in life, Espeleta probably helped orchestrate Hopi actions during the Pueblo Revolt. Afterward, he was instrumental in organizing Hopi resistance to the return of Catholicism. If, as still later historical records indicate, Espeleta became a leader or "cacique" of Oraibi, his time spent among the Spanish might constitute an example of the deliberate political intrigue that the Hopis sometimes practice.[6]

After the Spanish priests left Awatovi and returned to the east, disaster came to the village. Sometime at the end of 1700 or the beginning of 1701, men from other Hopi villages attacked Awatovi, burned many buildings (including kivas), killed many of the pueblo's men, and carried off many of the village's women and children.[7] Within a few short years, Awatovi was deserted and decaying. Fray Valverde, whose account was begun above, continues by attributing the attack to Espeleta and to "his people being infuriated because the Indians of the pueblo of Aquatubi had been reduced to our holy faith and the obedience of our king . . ." (Valverde in Hackett 1937:386).

Other details about the attack are recorded in Hopi oral history (e.g., Fewkes 1893; Voth 1905a:246–253, 254–255; Courlander 1971:175–184, 1982:55–60; James 1974:61–64). Although some of the specifics of the Hopi legends vary, many features of the accounts are shared. For example, all versions mention decadent and immoral conditions at Awatovi as the motivation for or the precipitating cause of the pueblo's destruction. Awatovi was destroyed because its citizens defiled traditional Hopi principles and ethical standards. In some narratives, as in the version that Harold Courlander recorded, the presence of Catholic priests accounts for the corruption at Awatovi. Because of their presence, "lawless people" roamed the streets, showed disrespect for traditional ways, taunted the old, pursued the women, and engaged in violence in the plazas (Courlander 1971:177–178). In all recorded versions, it is the Awatovi Village Chief, or *kikmongwi,* who initiated the destruction. He does this by approaching Village Chiefs from other pueblos with the proposal that they obliterate Awatovi, kill its men, and carry off its women and children. The Awatovi *kikmongwi* first approached the Village Chief of Walpi, who refused to cooperate. He then approached the Village Chief of Oraibi:

> . . . After they smoked for a while the Oraibi chief said, "You have had a long journey. What has brought you so far?"

The Awatovi chief said, "You are my friend. I need your help. My people are out of control. The Castilla missionaries have returned and they are preparing to stay forever. The village is in chaos. The young insult the old, women are raped, the shrines are desecrated. The ceremonies are ridiculed, contempt is shown for the kachinas, and the *kwitamuh* ['hooligans'] run wild. Thus the evil that followed us from the Lower World has torn us into pieces. Awatovi must be destroyed. Its people must be scattered and its houses razed to the ground." (Courlander 1971:179)

In the various accounts, the chief of Oraibi agreed to help the chief from Awatovi. They then returned to Walpi to enlist the support of that pueblo's War Chief. After doing so, the leaders from the three pueblos made plans to destroy Awatovi.

Some days later, a war party of men from Oraibi and Walpi (and perhaps other pueblos) approached Awatovi in the early morning. When they received the proper signal from the Awatovi chief, they attacked. They then entered the pueblo and trapped many Awatovi men in the kivas within which they were meeting. This was accomplished by pulling up the ladders that the Hopis used to gain access to the semisubterranean ceremonial structures. Next, the attackers burned the pueblo and killed many of its inhabitants. They also followed some Awatovi people out of the pueblo to the surrounding countryside to do so (Turner and Morris 1970). Finally, after arguing over surviving Awatovi women, the Walpi and Oraibi men killed some of the women and took the remainder, along with some children, to their own pueblos. Within a few years, Awatovi was abandoned, and its citizens were either dead or living in other villages. Although some people from Awatovi escaped (some of these took refuge among the Navajo), none ever returned to live at Awatovi.

From the time of Awatovi's destruction until the 1880s, a period of over 180 years, Hopis successfully resisted foreign encroachment and domination. Hopi religious and political leaders maintained relative autonomy for their people beyond the era of Spanish control, through the period of Mexican dominion, and into the age of European-American power. This independence was achieved, in part, because of the message (for Hopis and non-Hopis alike) contained in the destruction of Awatovi: "If you become a Christian and violate Hopi ethical standards, you will be destroyed." If Hopi traditions are accurate (or even if the stories are inaccurate but Hopis through time have accepted the legends), the events at Awatovi might have become a powerful symbol of cultural conservatism and a motivating force for cultural persistence. The Hopi religious elite might have used Awatovi as an important lesson to other Hopis who would abandon their traditional religion and way of life. Awatovi might also have sent a similar message to foreigners seeking power or influence over the Hopis. Peter Whiteley has also expressed this view:

> The symbolic import of the destruction of Awatovi over its reacceptance of the Franciscan church must have been powerful for Hopi and Spaniard alike. The fact that the Hopi were prepared to annihilate the male population of one of their own villages suggests an astonishingly intense form of cultural self-regulation in preference to direct confrontation with the external foe. It may be that this course of action was considered the most effective method of preserving independence with the least long-term cost. The Pueblos in general are known for stringent conservatism enforced by religious elites. Certainly, in the case of Awatovi, the devastating effects of deviation from cultural norms cannot have escaped the attention of any potential convert or any potential converter. (1988a:21)

From the Awatovi incident until 1716, at least three Spanish military expeditions entered the Western Pueblo region with intentions to punish the Hopis for their actions and to reclaim Hopi pueblos for the Spanish king. Hopis militarily resisted these expeditions. Each of the expeditions failed. Also during this period (to 1732), at least four groups of Catholic missionaries attempted to reenter the Hopi pueblos. Their efforts also failed (Brew 1979). Between 1741 (when Hopi territory was theoretically reassigned from the Franciscans to the Jesuits) and 1780, Catholic priests made at least six further attempts to proselytize among the Hopis, but the results were the same. Hopis would not capitulate to alien ideology any more than they would surrender to foreign military intimidation.

During this same period, many of the Rio Grande refugees who had sought safety in Hopi villages after the Pueblo Revolt of 1680 returned to their homes in New Mexico. Life under the Spanish was apparently settling down and the refugees seemingly longed for their homes. Further, the additional population in Hopi territory was beginning to put pressure on the productive capacity of the agricultural system.

In 1821, after more than two hundred years of Spanish colonial domination, the Puebloan peoples came under the authority of a new government, the Mexican Republic. Mexican rule, however, lasted for only twenty-five years. In 1846 the Mexican War broke out, and American General Stephen Watts Kearny occupied New Mexico. In 1848 the war ended, and the Pueblos came under European-American rule. In 1850 Hopis and the U.S. government met for the first time when a delegation of Hopi men visited in Santa Fe with James S. Calhoun, new Superintendent of Indian Affairs for the Territory of New Mexico.

Sometime between late 1851 and November of 1853, Hopis experienced a smallpox epidemic that was as devastating to them as were epidemics during the period of first contact (Donaldson 1893:28; Whiteley 1988a:32). Perhaps two-thirds of the Hopi people succumbed during this epidemic. This event, coupled with increasing contact with the dominant European-American society, forever changed Hopi culture and society.

During the ensuing years, Hopis became increasingly familiar with the European-Americans, as more and more of the latter moved West. In 1858 Jacob Hamblin, a Mormon missionary, first visited the Hopis. This visit began a long relationship between Hopis and Mormons, who had left the eastern United States to escape religious persecution. Between 1863 and 1864 Hopis witnessed U.S. military power when Kit Carson and the army rounded up Navajo people, marched them on the "Long Walk" to Bosque Redondo, and interned them in a concentration camp.

In the 1870s Mormons established themselves among the Hopis. With this foothold, a significant period of Hopi independence and resistance to foreign domination came to a close. In 1875 Mormons built a church at Moenkopi.

Around 1877 to 1880, the Hopi man, Loololma, became the Oraibi *kikmongwi,* Village Chief. This event marks the beginning of a historical period that we reconstruct in the next case study. Accordingly, we suspend our historical narrative until Chapter 6. We resume there by focusing on events at the Oraibi pueblo. Here, we turn to anthropological analyses of sociocultural persistence and change as represented in the incidents described in the previous sections of this chapter.

Explanations of Sociocultural Persistence and Change among the Hopi from 1680 to 1880

As noted, anthropologists often characterize the period of history under investigation here as one of sociocultural stability, of relatively insignificant change in Hopi culture and society. Many anthropologists suggest that Hopis maintained much of their own distinctive, traditional sociocultural system despite the pressures of contact. They associate such persistence with factors such as *geographical isolation* and *cultural conservatism* (e.g., Titiev 1944; Eggan 1970; Dockstader 1979).

We are now interested in several questions. Which features of Hopi culture and society persisted through the Spanish and Mexican periods and into the American era? Which features changed? What is the evidence for such persistence or change? How can such sociocultural stability and change be explained? We now endeavor to answer the first three of these questions together. Then we address the final question.

We begin our reflection on these issues by considering Hopi population.[8] From 1664 through 1851, the Hopi population remained relatively stable. The lowest point in Hopi population occurred at the beginning of this period, when Spanish priests counted 3,036 individuals. As discussed in Chapter 4, based on archaeological and historical records, analogy to other areas in the New World, and the retrodictions of disease models, there is every reason to believe that the Western Pueblo population (including the Hopi) was once far larger than it was in the seventeenth, eighteenth, and nineteenth centuries. Between 1520 and 1664, the Hopi population was reduced to less than one-quarter (perhaps even 10 percent) of what it had been in earlier, precontact times. Upham accounts for this decline primarily by reference to the probable effects of Western diseases like smallpox on virgin-soil Native American populations (Chap. 4). Nevertheless, after the massive reductions of the sixteenth and early seventeenth centuries, the size of Acoma, Zuni, and Hopi populations (together making up the Western Pueblo) was relatively constant. Following nadir in 1664, the Hopi population rose steadily until 1745, when, after subtracting for the number of Rio Grande refugees in Hopi territory, it numbered approximately 7,288. After some fluctuations, the Hopi population was approximately 6,720 in 1851. Estimates of Hopi population size for various years are contained in Figure 5.

From 1664 until 1851, the Hopi population averaged about 6,400 (plus or minus 25 percent) and was distributed among six villages (five, after Awatovi's destruction). Oraibi was the largest of the villages, containing perhaps as many as one-fourth or even one-third of the total Hopi population. The other pueblos were smaller, sharing roughly equally the remaining two-thirds to three-fourths of the total Hopi population.

As noted, the immigration of Rio Grande refugees after the Pueblo Revolt of 1682 added to the total number of people in Hopi territory. Precise figures are unavailable, but Bancroft estimated that approximately 4,000 Eastern Pueblo people migrated to Hopi lands (Whiteley 1988a:18). Apparently, 441 people from Sandia Pueblo returned to the Rio Grande in 1742, leaving about 3,559 Eastern Pueblo people in Hopi territory (Brew 1949:29). Brew also reports a Spanish priest's estimate of 10,848 for the total Hopi population in 1745 (1949:32–33). This

Figure 5. Hopi population, 1520–1989

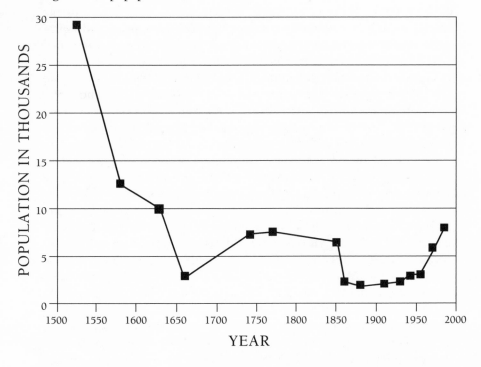

Date		Population	Reference
1.	1520	29,305	Upham 1982
2.	1582	12,000	Luxan 1929:39
3.	1604[a]	3,000	Whiteley 1988a:16
4.	1634	10,000	Benavides 1945
5.	1664	3,036	Scholes 1929:49
6.	1745	10,846	Brew 1949:33
7.	1775	7,497	Donaldson 1893:15
8.	1780[a]	2,450	Donaldson 1893:15
9.	1852	8,000	Donaldson 1893:15
10.	1853	6,720	Donaldson 1893:15
11.	1861	2,500	Donaldson 1893:15
12.	1865	3,000	Donaldson 1893:15
13.	1869	4,000	Donaldson 1893:15
14.	1874	1,950	Kunitz 1974:9
15.	1905	2,100	Kunitz 1974:9
16.	1930	2,752	Kunitz 1974:9
17.	1940	3,444	Kunitz 1974:9
18.	1950	3,528	Kunitz 1974:9
19.	1968	6,000	Kunitz 1974:9
20.	1980	8,000	U.S. Census

[a] Questionable estimates: 3 = based on estimates by counting houses after three hours at Oraibi; 8 = collected during harvest time, when most Hopis were in the fields.

number included the 3,559 Rio Grande refugees who remained after 1742. If Bancroft is correct (and he may have exaggerated), of the 10,848 total, 7,289 would have been Hopi. The same priests who provided the figure of 10,848 also estimate that 2,000 refugees returned with them to New Mexico later that year (although the passages containing this figure are ambiguous). Approximately 8,848 people would have remained in Hopi territory, of whom 7,289 were Hopi and 1,559 non-Hopi. Many of the latter were Tewa-speakers who settled at Hano pueblo. At any rate, we estimate that the Hopi population in 1745 was between 7,250 and 7,500.

Parenthetically, Brew attributes the return of many refugees to their homes along the Rio Grande to strain placed on economic resources. He suggests that stress placed on the Hopi agricultural system by the large population and by a possible drought in the mid-1700s caused many people to leave. For Brew, relations between the Eastern Puebloan peoples and their Hopi hosts possibly deteriorated in response to fighting over "fields and food." Such disputes made the former more willing to return to New Mexico (1949:32). Richard M. Bradfield (1971) uses similar arguments to account for social fissioning of the Oraibi pueblo in 1906.

If our reconstruction of the population figures provided in historical records are accurate, Hopis of 1664 to 1851 did not experience the catastrophic population loss characteristic of the preceding one hundred forty years (1520–1660). Between 1664 and 1851 Hopis apparently avoided the devastating epidemics that the Spanish carried to the Southwest. For us, this is a central "fact" about this period. We suggest below that population stability possibly contributed to Hopi sociocultural stability through these years. How did Hopis avoid such epidemics? The answer to this question is possibly that Hopis were sufficiently *isolated* from Spanish colonial and other disease-bearing populations that epidemic diseases affected them less during these years than most other Puebloan groups. Two factors conceivably contributed to this isolation. First, the Hopis were located far from the area of main colonial settlement along the Rio Grande. Because of this geographical isolation, Hopis had fewer direct interactions with potential disease carriers (whether Spanish or Native Americans in daily interaction with the colonialists). As noted, such anthropologists as Titiev and Spicer emphasize the importance of geographical isolation for Hopi sociocultural stability up to the ethnographic present period. These ethnologists do not, however, mention the contribution of such physical isolation to the avoidance of disease epidemics and population stability. Rather, they stress that isolation means fewer opportunities for the diffusion of cultural traits. This, in turn, means less culture change.

The second factor contributing to the Hopi isolation (thereby possibly allowing them to escape disastrous epidemics during this period) is the *deliberate activity* that the Hopi religious elite undertook to preserve their own religion and way of life. We refer here to the Pueblo Revolt of 1682, the destruction of Awatovi, and the armed resistance to Spanish military invasions. Detailed descriptions of the first two events and a report of the last events are provided above. Father Juan de Lezaún provides a reasonable summary of the years under consideration (cited in Brew 1949). According to de Lezaún, "the province of Moqui" (Hopi) was in continuous revolt until the 1860s and remained a refuge for Indians "tired of working for the governor and the alcolades mayores." He mentioned that continuous wars had reduced nine original pueblos to six. The priest then continued by recommending siege of the Hopi Mesas. The "continuous wars" de Lezaún mentioned are, no doubt, disputes between Hopis and Rio Grande refugees and, perhaps, between Hopis and Navajos, Utes, and Apaches. The abandoned pueblos probably represent the return of some people to New Mexico. Nevertheless, the important point is that Hopis "remained in revolt" and Spanish priests felt obliged to discuss ways of laying siege to the Hopi Mesas.

We hypothesize that there was an *unintended biological consequence* of Hopi efforts to politically resist the Spanish, eliminate Catholicism, and preserve their own religion. As an indirect result of these efforts, Hopis increased their biological isolation from the Spanish colonialists and from those Indian populations that were in close interaction with the Spanish along the Rio Grande. This isolation resulted in reduced transmission to the Hopis of contagious diseases from the Spanish and other affected groups. Hence, Hopi religiously motivated political acts increased their isolation and, because Hopis avoided epidemics, contributed to their preservation as a biological population. Hopi survival contributed to the persistence of Hopi culture and society.

If Hopis avoided major epidemics during this period, why didn't their population expand to its original limits? The probable answer is that they didn't avoid all epidemics, and that warfare and starvation continued to kill some Hopis even after the first hundred years of contact. Sporadic visits by Spanish, Mexican, and Puebloan peoples probably transmitted some diseases. The presence of warfare was noted above. During the same period, numerous droughts and crop failures were reported (Brew 1949:24–40). If some epidemics, wars, and crop failures occurred, population growth might have been precluded. Such factors

might have acted to maintain the number of Hopis within relatively nar-
row limits. Nevertheless, through whatever mechanisms, Hopi population size appears to have remained relatively stable between 1664
and 1851.

The end of Hopi population stability came in 1852. In 1851 the Hopi
population was 6,720 (Whipple 1855:13). In 1861 it was approximately 2,500. Sometime during the period from late 1851 to November,
1853 (hereafter represented as 1851–1853), another severe smallpox
epidemic devastated the Hopi. This epidemic reduced their population
to less than 40 percent of what it was the previous decade (Donaldson
1893:28; Whiteley 1988a:32). This population loss corresponded to
the arrival of European-Americans among the Hopis and a breakdown
of Hopi isolation. During the last half of the nineteenth century, the
Hopi population again remained relatively stable (epidemics once more
offsetting natural population growth rates), with Hopi population averaging about 2,800 people. This figure is less than half of what it had
averaged during the preceding two hundred years. The smallpox epidemic of 1851–1853, thus, resulted in a major demographic transformation of the Hopis. We later discuss the implications of this transformation for persistence and change in Hopi culture and society.

As Stephen J. Kunitz points out, only with the arrival of the twentieth
century and modern medical techniques were many epidemic and endemic diseases among the Hopi finally controlled. With the associated
decline in mortality, particularly among infants, and a continued high
birth rate, significant population growth began to occur after 1900
(Kunitz 1973). As a result, between 1900 and 1989 the Hopi population
almost quadrupled. It grew from approximately 2,100 in 1905 to over
8,000 people in 1990. We discuss the implications of these demographic
changes for Hopi sociocultural change and persistence in Chapter 7.

Returning to the question of sociocultural persistence and change between 1664 and 1880, the most obviously stable features of Hopi culture and society were the subsistence system and settlement pattern.
Despite acquiring many new items of material culture (e.g., stone and
wood-working tools [Brew 1979:520]) and some new domesticated
plants and animals (e.g., fruit trees, goats, and sheep), Hopis continued
to make their living by growing maize, beans, and squash, following the
extensive, hedge-your-bets agricultural strategy discussed in Chapter 2.
If changes occurred in the subsistence system, they were a slight increase in reliance on local agricultural foods and a corresponding decrease in the significance of extra local food products. Be this as it may,
there was general stability in the agricultural base of Hopi culture and
society during the two hundred years under consideration.

By the 1600s, trade appears to have been much less important than during the late prehistoric period (see Chaps. 2 and 3).[9] Trade was even less significant to Hopis in the 1880s than it had been in the 1600s. By the late nineteenth century, Hopis obtained less than 5 percent of their food from extra local sources. Further, Hopi clans possibly became less significant to economic organization through this period. This is addressed below.

The Hopi settlement pattern also remained relatively stable during this era. Hopis continued to occupy the mesa country that their ancestors had populated hundreds of years before. Hopi territory remained distinct from areas that other Native Americans controlled, at least until the 1870s.[10] Further, the size, location, and spatial arrangement of Hopi villages persisted with little modification. The exceptions to this were the destruction of Awatovi and the resettlement of Walpi on the top of First Mesa and of Mishongnovi and Shongopovi to the top of Second Mesa. As noted, Hopis relocated these villages anticipating Spanish retaliations after the Pueblo Revolt. At that same time, refugees from the Rio Grande constructed two non-Hopi villages in Hopi territory. One of these, Hano (Tewa Village), remains occupied today.

Persistence and change in Hopi social, political, and religious organization between 1680 and 1880 is less clear. Researchers' claims about what persisted and what changed depend on how they interpret historical records, that is, on how accurate and complete they feel historical descriptions of sociocultural phenomena to be. Since these interpretations vary, anthropologists' assertions about persistence and change are only more or less speculative.

In our view, many basic features of Hopi culture, social organization, and social structure likely persisted relatively unchanged throughout the period under consideration. Principles of matrilineal descent, for example, probably originated in Hopi prehistory and persisted throughout the historic era. We see no reason to assume that matrilineality is a recent innovation among the Hopis. Nevertheless, since early Spanish chroniclers did not adequately describe the Hopi descent system, the widely shared (and, in all probability, correct) view that Hopi matrilineality has great time depth remains tentative. Further, we suggest that the Hopi system of matrilineal clans was maintained *in some form* throughout this period. We do not claim, however, that all Hopi clans persisted. To the contrary, many clans died out (at least after 1851–1853), others merged to form larger groups, and still others divided into smaller descent groups (Parsons 1922; Lowie 1929; Titiev 1944). Nor do we claim that clans persisted as the idealized, corporate matrilineal descent groups that Titiev (1944), Eggan (1950), and others describe.

More specifically, we see at least three possibilities concerning the stability and persistence of Hopi clans through the years under consideration. We consider these possibilities in an order from least to most probable. First, the type of social organization and structure that early anthropologists describe for the ethnographic present (ca. 1880–1920) might have existed not only then, but also much earlier. It existed, perhaps, even before the first Spanish contact. If so, little change occurred during the intervening years. Such anthropologists as Titiev (1944), Eggan (1950), and Spicer (1962) have taken this position. Other anthropologists, however, have criticized this notion (e.g., Whiteley 1985, 1986, 1988a). Such persistence of Hopi social organization and structure (including the form of clans) might be accounted for by reference to isolation and cultural conservatism. Anthropologists like Titiev and Spicer would unambiguously associate changes in Hopi social organization with the modern era (see Titiev 1972). We consider this possibility unlikely.

Second, Hopi clans might have remained stable through much of the period from 1664 to about 1851, and then changed significantly between 1853 and 1880. At the beginning of this period, Hopi clans might have been similar to the groups that Titiev and Eggan describe. Perhaps they persisted in this form through most of the era under consideration and then changed, prior to the turn of the twentieth century. More specifically, Hopi clans from the 1700s to the mid-1800s might have been autonomous corporate groups controlling land and ritual. Access to and inheritance of resources then might have been based on strictly matrilineal descent principles. Such groups might have changed toward the end of this period, becoming more flexible, less autonomous, and less "corporate" after the 1850s. If this scenario is accurate, such persistence through 1851 might be explained by isolation and cultural conservatism. Change after 1851–1853 might be attributed to demographic collapse at that time.

Third, Hopi clans might never have been the rigid corporate groups portrayed in idealized anthropological descriptions. If this scenario is valid, as Whiteley has suggested (1985, 1986, 1988a), persistence and change of such groups must be discussed in different terms. Perhaps *flexibility and resilience,* rather than rigidity or immutability, has always characterized Hopi culture and society. Maybe Titiev, for example, attributed too much "structure" and stability to the Hopi cultural and social systems. If so, it might be that the *underlying* nature of Hopi social groupings changed insignificantly, if at all, during the period from 1680 to 1851, or even to 1880. If flexibility were inherent in the system (if, for example, Hopi society and culture were always able to accommodate descent groups with different patterns), the empirical configurations of groups like clans could have changed without fundamentally altering the organizational basis of Hopi social life. If this scenario is sound, Hopi sociocultural persistence might be explained not only by isolation and cultural conservatism, but also by the inherent resilience of the system. We return to these issues after discussing additional features of Hopi society and culture from the eighteenth and nineteenth centuries.

Titiev (1944), Eggan (1950), and others assert that Hopi society traditionally lacked significant social stratification. They portray the Hopis as egalitarian, with few differences in wealth. Whiteley agrees with this description insofar as it is restricted to *economic stratification.* He suggests, however, that Hopis were traditionally organized into two distinct classes based on the possession of or access to secret ritual knowledge (1988a). For Whiteley, this ideologically based stratification began to deteriorate after the split of Oraibi in 1906 (see Chap. 6). We are convinced by Whiteley's ethnographic description and by our belief in the presence of economically based social stratification in the prehistoric Western Pueblo that social stratification existed and persisted among the Hopis throughout the eighteenth and nineteenth centuries. Although wealth differences among Hopis were not recorded, early Spanish reporters consistently refer to Hopi leaders with the authority to determine the actions of entire pueblos. For us, this unambiguously signifies differences in individual power, and we see no obvious reason to believe that such differences were not based on the ritual knowledge that Whiteley and others have discussed (e.g., Brandt 1976; Upham 1982, 1989).

The presence of Hopi social stratification is tied to Hopi political and religious organization. During the ethnographic present period, Hopi religious leaders were also political leaders. The religious elite constituted the upper class of Hopi society. We assume that these general features of Hopi culture and society existed in the sixteenth century and that they persisted during the years under consideration. The religious basis for stratification and political organization probably persisted through this time. The "caciques" that the Spanish describe were most likely descent group leaders who, based on their secret ritual knowledge, were the principal chiefs or officers of ceremonies. If this scenario is valid, these features of the Hopi sociocultural system persisted even through the devastating epidemic of 1851–1853.

The suggestion that the cultural basis for leadership and stratification persisted between 1680 and 1880 does not imply that the precise association between descent groups, ceremonies, and religious and political leadership positions that Titiev, Eggan, and others have described also existed and persisted during these years. To the contrary, we see few reasons to believe in such persistence. We state our thinking about this issue after discussing Hopi religious persistence below.

Early Spanish descriptions also give credence to the belief that there were significant changes in Hopi political organization during the seventeenth, eighteenth, and nineteenth centuries. Village autonomy, for example, probably increased during these years. As noted, early Spanish documents frequently describe Oraibi as either the most important Hopi pueblo or as the Hopi "capital." This description of Oraibi was no longer valid when anthropologists worked during the ethnographic present period. Further, the importance of at least one type of traditional village leader, the War Chief, probably diminished during this time (Titiev 1944:65–66; Whiteley 1988a:66). As described in Chapter 2, the War Chief of a pueblo was responsible for maintaining discipline within his village and for leading warriors in defensive and offensive military actions. The Walpi War Chief, for example, helped lead the action against Awatovi. Titiev accounts for diminishment of the War Chief's authority by reference to the "abandonment of native warfare" (1944:66). The decreased significance of Hopi War Chiefs might also be associated with the increasing autonomy of Hopi villages throughout the years under consideration. Parenthetically, Whiteley suggests that anthropologists may have underestimated the importance of Hopi War Chiefs, especially at Oraibi, during the ethnographic present period (1988a:66). He points out that Titiev's primary consultant in the 1930s was the Oraibi *kikmongwi*. This person may have aggrandized the authority and power of individuals holding his office and denigrated the importance of individuals holding the office of War Chief. This bias would directly affect the historical accuracy of Titiev's ethnographic account. The possibility that this occurred reemphasizes the importance of interpretation to the ethnographic process.

Hopi religion also displayed significant cultural persistence between 1680 and 1880. There are few indications that the fundamental tenets of Hopi religion changed from first contact with the Spanish until the beginning of the twentieth century. Such religious persistence is central to anthropological descriptions of the Hopi as extremely culturally conservative. Nevertheless, Catholicism and the intrusion of non-Hopi Puebloan beliefs (including, possibly, the *katchinas* themselves) may have had some effect on Hopi religious ideology not reflected in the historical or ethnographic literature. Further, we see no reason to suggest that the Hopi ceremonial cycle was fundamentally altered in the years under consideration. Hopi religious societies probably continued to perform both public and private rituals based on mythologically expressed beliefs about the universe, with the intention of increasing community well-being and agricultural plenty. This sacred/secular dichotomy was the primary point of contention between Spanish priests and Hopi political leaders, who were priests themselves. The Pueblo Revolt of 1682 and the destruction of Awatovi during the fall of 1700 or winter of 1701 were largely about this issue. As indicated earlier, part of the Hopi motivation for participation in the Revolt was the proven ineffectiveness of Catholicism for bringing rain and ensuring plentiful crops.

On the other hand, we see no reason to assume that relationships between Hopi descent groups, ceremonies, religious societies, and political leadership were invariant during this period. We would be surprised if this were the case. Again, we see flexibility and resilience in the structural and organizational arrangements involving the above institutions and activities. We first discussed Hopi resilience when considering prehistoric Western Pueblo abandonments. We now return to this subject.

Flexibility in historic Hopi sociocultural arrangements is illustrated in many ways (see Parsons 1933:21ff.; Titiev 1944; Eggan 1950; Nagata 1970; Whiteley 1988a, 1988b). The specific clans and the number of clans represented in the different Hopi villages, for example, vary. Different clans (or clan segments) control different ceremonies and occupy different leadership positions in the various Hopi pueblos. The control by one descent group of a particular ceremony might be switched to another descent group if the first becomes too small or dies out. Ceremonies might be lost entirely under similar circumstances. Village leadership might be shared or rotated among the heads of various descent groups, or change from the head of one group to the chief of another group under similar demographic conditions.[11] A woman might even become *kikmongwi* of some village under the same circumstances, if eligible men refuse to assume this position of leadership, or under other novel circumstances (Nagata 1970:42–44). And members of a religious society might open up new avenues for recruitment if they find their number too small to cope with the demands of ceremonial life (Parsons 1922:297).

Other Hopi social arrangements also demonstrate flexibility. Our list merely illustrates Hopi resilience. In our view, potential Hopi flexibility is often realized in response to real-world demographic contingencies. Changing village and regional demography seems to elicit Hopi responses that both reflect and support institutional resilience. We raise the possibility that significant *change* in institutional arrangements occurred during these years, particularly after the demographic collapse of 1851–1853, despite significant *persistence* in the cultural basis for Hopi life.

One historical possibility will suffice to demonstrate our position.[12] In Titiev's discussion of the patterns and concepts of Hopi ceremonies, he raises the possibility that ". . . at one stage of Hopi cultural development the entire membership of a religious society was drawn from the proprietary clan" (1944:103).

We are curious about Titiev's hypothesis. It leads us to speculate that cross-clan membership in Hopi religious societies (and, perhaps, kiva groups) might have become more common and consequential after the Hopi population declined in 1851–1853 than it was earlier in Hopi history. We hypothesize that before the epidemic, control of and membership in Hopi religious societies might have been limited to or dominated by the members of single descent groups. When the Hopi population declined from an average of about 6,400 (between the years 1680 and 1851) to an average of about 2,800 (between the years 1861 and 1905), many Hopi descent groups might have died out or become so small that it was no longer possible for them to fulfill their religious responsibilities. In response, ceremony-controlling groups possibly allowed previously excluded persons from other descent groups to learn their society's secrets and to participate in their rituals. If so, ceremonial groups once dominated by individuals of the same descent category were transformed into religious sodalities with memberships defined independently of descent categories.

The historical scenario sketched in the preceding paragraph is frankly speculative. We offer, however, three items of ethnographic information as circumstantial evidence for the idea that religious societies might once have been more closely associated with descent groups. First, clans (or clan segments [see Parsons 1933:23; Whiteley 1985, 1986]) are said to own Hopi rituals. Descent groups possess and restrict access to the necessary religious paraphernalia and the secret knowledge requisite to the performance of specific ceremonies. Members of clans other than controlling clans are secondary (or common) members of Hopi religious societies. The distinction between central and peripheral members of societies could easily result from a loosening of the affiliation requirements in religious societies, that is, from an opening of membership to noncontrolling-clan individuals.

Second, the idiom of kinship and descent is used by Hopis to express relations among the members of religious societies from the ethnographic present (Titiev 1944; Eggan 1950; Whiteley 1988a). Such relationships suggest that religious societies are, at least metaphorically, viewed as kinds of kinship or descent groups and might reflect a period in Hopi history when this situation was actually the case.

The third item of circumstantial evidence is that Elsie Clews Parsons reported an apparent example from Shongopavi (Second Mesa) of an original extension of membership in a religious society to individuals who were nonmembers of the controlling clan:

> There are but three male members of the Kachina-Parrot clan, and their ceremonial obligations are heavy. A way out was found. The office of sing-ers Chief is made to rotate between the three men, each holding office for four years. As for the Agave society [controlled by the Katchina-Parrot clan at Shongopavi], sixteen years ago *it was decided to take men in from other clans* and to have the chief chosen by the members of the society to hold office for four years. The office has been filled four times. (Parsons 1922: 297; emphasis added)

Although the passage describing these events is ambiguous, we take Parsons to mean that membership in the Agave society at Shongopavi was once restricted to Katchina-Parrot clan members and that the three remaining members of the Agave society decided in 1906 to allow par-ticipation by individuals belonging to other clans.[13] We suggest that this situation might have arisen many times after the 1851–1853 smallpox epidemic killed thousands of Hopis. If so, patterns in Hopi institutional arrangements changed radically at that time. This change might also be associated with a general decline in the significance of clans as eco-nomic and political units. All three events may be the result of *demo-graphic collapse.* Following these changes in institutional arrangements, Hopis might have rationalized them through ideological reconstruc-tions. Parenthetically, Frigout (1979:575) lists Katchina, Sun, and Snow as controlling clans of the Shongopavi Agavi ceremony in the 1970s. Apparently, the relationship between descent groups and cere-monies continues to change at that pueblo.

We now offer a final item of circumstantial evidence that seems both to support and contradict our hypothesis. This item, again, shows the significance of interpretation to ethnographic analysis. In Hopi mythol-ogy, clans are viewed as autonomous migratory groups. After emerging from the Underworld, clans traveled as units, encountered objects or situations from which they took their totemic names, and eventually ar-rived at various villages where they now reside. Such clans were al-lowed to settle at specific locations based on their knowledge and per-formance of rituals beneficial to other clans in the village (see, e.g., Titiev 1944:61; Voth 1905a:24). In Hopi mythology, then, *clans* origi-nally performed rituals, not cross-clan religious sodalities. This "fact" seems to support the above scenario. Nevertheless, upon arrival at Oraibi (or other villages), clans were asked to participate in the rituals

of the original inhabitants of the village. This detail seems to imply significant time depth to crosscutting religious sodalities. Where the truth
lies, we can only guess. We point out, however, that Voth collected his
version of the Oraibi migration myth after the 1851–1853 demographic
collapse. As Richard Clemmer discusses in his consideration of the Hopi
"mythic process," Hopi readily adapt their mythology to incorporate and
reconstruct (our term) historic events (1978a:41–51). After contact
with Europeans, for example, Hopi mythology quickly incorporated the
emergence of non-Native Americans (Spanish, Anglos, and Mormons)
from the Underworld. With this mythological flexibility in mind, perhaps the 1905 reference to cross-clan participation in religious ceremonies represents the mythological incorporation of a post-1853 increase in the significance of this pattern of membership in religious
societies. Possibly, this reference represents an ideological accommodation to demographic and institutional reality. Whatever the truth, the
significance of interpretation in the reading of historical texts, myths, or
of texts with elements of both is apparent.

In summary, we suggest that the following events likely occurred
during the period under consideration in this chapter. First, certain features of Hopi culture and society such as matrilineal descent principles
and religious beliefs likely persisted from 1680, through the smallpox
epidemic of 1851–1853, to the 1880s. We see no obvious reason to believe that these and perhaps other components of Hopi belief systems
significantly changed during this period, even during the change in
scale of their society following 1851–1853. An exception to this perceived persistence might be changes in the basis for access to Hopi religious societies. Second, with the decrease in scale of Hopi society that
resulted from the smallpox epidemic of 1851–1853 came changes in
Hopi institutional arrangements. Whether such changes represent something new in Hopi society or are merely an example of continuing, inherent flexibility in Hopi social arrangements is a matter for discussion,
debate, and further research.

Anthropological explanations of Hopi sociocultural persistence and
change between 1680 and 1880 focus on several significant factors. We
discussed most of these in the preceding historical account. Anthropologists have frequently seen Hopi sociocultural stability and persistence
as a result of Hopi *isolation* from the effects of *culture contact*. Such isolation came, in large part, from the *geographical distance* between the
Hopi Mesas and the Rio Grande Valley in New Mexico. Hopis were far
from the locus of greatest interaction between Spanish colonialists and
other Puebloan Indians. In addition, Hopis themselves contributed to
their isolation through *deliberate political acts* such as the Pueblo Revolt,

the relocation of some villages to the tops of mesas, the destruction of Awatovi, and armed resistance to later Spanish expeditions to the Western Pueblo region. According to various anthropologists, such isolation had the effect of reducing culture contact, "outside influence," and the inevitable borrowing of cultural traits from external sources. Hence, Hopi culture and society persisted more strongly than would have otherwise been possible. Another possible effect of such isolation was the Hopis' partial avoidance of epidemic diseases between 1664 and 1851. This avoidance, perhaps, resulted in relative stability for the Hopi population. Such *continuity of scale* possibly resulted in Hopi social institutional stability until 1851–1853, when smallpox again ravaged these people. Without doubt, the loss of two-thirds of the Hopi population in 1851–1853 generated new and intense pressures for change in Hopi culture and society.

Factors other than isolation also contributed to stability in Hopi culture and society during the seventeenth, eighteenth, and nineteenth centuries. As noted, the material conditions of Hopi life were essentially constant. Hopi subsistence and settlement patterns remained relatively stable during these years. Further, with the possible exceptions of a decrease in extralocal trade and a diminishment of the corporate significance of clans and other descent groups, Hopi economic organization was stable throughout the years under consideration. Such stability in Hopi economic arrangements, or *infrastructure,* probably contributed to persistence in other aspects of Hopi culture and society. Stability in infrastructure possibly led to stability in Hopi social and ideological superstructure. Hopi political leaders were, for example, able to contribute to cultural and social isolation primarily because of the ideological power they possessed. Because religious leaders were also leaders of descent groups, their power was possibly based on their position in the Hopi economic structure. As leaders of descent groups, religious and political leaders theoretically controlled at least some agricultural lands. Perhaps these leaders were able to maintain their power and sustain their contribution to Hopi isolation and sociocultural persistence precisely because the organization of Hopi economic production persisted.

Finally, we also suggest that Hopi *cultural conservatism* contributed to sociocultural persistence through the period of 1680 to 1880. As noted, the significance of Hopi cultural conservatism resides primarily in the power of the religious elite to isolate Hopi culture and society from the outside world and to negatively sanction deviant behavior, such as that which occurred at Awatovi. Such power and its associated behavior might have had both intended and unintended consequences that contributed to the persistence of Hopi culture and society. The destruction of Awatovi, for example, resulted in the intended elimination of Catholicism from Awatovi and the reassertion of the supremacy of Hopi religion. As an unintended consequence, it contributed to Hopi isolation, helped these people avoid epidemics transmitted directly by Spanish colonialists, and contributed to Hopi population stability between 1680 and 1851.

Given the sources for sociocultural persistence in operation among the Hopi between 1680 and 1880 (isolation, stability of population, continuity in material conditions and the organization of production, cultural conservatism, and the power of the religious elite to direct behavior), how have anthropologists explained changes that occurred during these years? The answer lies in factors intimately related to the preceding list. For example, if isolation contributes to persistence, *culture contact* encourages change. Hopi borrowed many items of material and nonmaterial culture because of their contact with Europeans and with other, non-Hopi Native Americans, such as the Tewa-speaking people who moved to the Hopi Mesas after the Pueblo Revolt.

Further, if population stability helps account for persistence, *population instability,* such as that resulting from the 1851–1853 smallpox epidemic, helps to explain sociocultural change. The scale of Hopi society was changed because of this epidemic. Hence, Hopi social institutions exhibited either new or precedented flexibility in their interrelationships. Cross-clan societies possibly became more significant in Hopi social structure after 1851–1853. The fundamental tenets of Hopi ideology may have persisted through this devastation, but Hopi social arrangements appear to have undergone significant transformation.

Finally, if continuity in material conditions, organization of production, and ideological perspective contribute to sociocultural stability, changes in any of these factors might ramify throughout a sociocultural system and result in further transformation. After the epidemic of 1851–1853, such factors might have become increasingly influential among the Hopis. *Droughts* occurred that stressed their agricultural system. The Hopi organization of labor was altered because of population loss. The arrival of the European-Americans (including Mormons) initiated Hopi ideological disputes that challenged the religious elite's power and authority. We discuss these issues in the next chapter, which deals with Hopi history from 1880 to 1909.

6. Village Fission at Old Oraibi (A.D. 1880–1909)

FORCES FOR HOPI sociocultural change appear to have converged from 1880 to 1909 on Oraibi Pueblo at Third Mesa. Events that occurred there not only affected the organization and structure of life at Oraibi, but also at the other Hopi villages. Sociocultural processes operating at Oraibi during those years epitomize processes operating at all Hopi villages at the turn of the twentieth century. Accordingly, we focus Chapter 6 on Oraibi.

The most significant event of this period occurred on 6 and 7 September 1906, when approximately one-half of the men, women, and children of Oraibi either abandoned their homes or were expelled from the village by the other residents.[1] Anthropologists are interested in the Oraibi split not only for historical and ethnographic reasons, but also for theoretical ones. From a historical and ethnographic perspective, the split at Oraibi is significant because of its immediate and long-term consequences for Hopi culture and society. From a theoretical perspective, the Oraibi schism is important because it involved sociocultural units and processes that are significant in many different societies and that are central to many different theoretical orientations and analyses in anthropology. The split, for example, involved Hopi descent categories and groups and Hopi political factionalism. The split also involved the forces of demography, culture contact, and religious ideology affecting a small-scale sociocultural system. We begin this chapter by providing a historical narrative of Oraibi's disintegration. We then proceed to anthropological analyses of its causes and consequences.

The Oraibi Disintegration

Just prior to 1880, Oraibi acquired a new *kikmongwi*, or Village Chief. At that time, Loololma became head of the Bear clan following his father's death. Loololma's father, who was not a member of Bear clan in Hopi matrilineal society, acted as Village Chief and temporary head of the Soyal ceremony from about 1865 to about 1877 or 1880 because his son was too young during those years to assume his position as Bear clan leader (Titiev 1944:72). According to Titiev, "although Village chiefs should be from the Bear clan, it is not unusual for fathers or sons of Bear men to hold office under special circumstances . . ." (1944:72). The Bear clan leader is Oraibi's hereditary Village Chief because that descent group's ancestors founded the pueblo and because Bear clan controls the Soyal ceremony. The Soyal is a fundamental ritual of traditional Hopi society. The Bear clan leader is normally principal chief of the Soyal ceremony, although Loololma's brother apparently directed the Soyal for some years after their father's death. In addition, because their mythological ancestors founded the village, the Bear clan "owns" all land at the pueblo. Other clans obtained use-rights to agricultural fields from the original Bear clan inhabitants by virtue of their correct behavior and proper observance of useful ceremonies (Titiev 1944:61–63).[2]

Loololma took over the chieftainship of Oraibi in a social climate of marked antagonism toward the United States government, which had been unable or unwilling to provide aid during an extended drought and famine of the preceding decades. According to Titiev, Loololma's father held extreme anti-European-American views which Loololma adopted but then abandoned after he visited Washington D.C. early in the 1880s. When he returned from the east, Loololma had completely changed his attitude, "thus taking the first step towards the ultimate disintegration of the Hopi 'capital'" (Titiev 1944:72–73). Whiteley, however, disproves the details of Titiev's account of Loololma's conversion. Whiteley believes, based on unambiguous archival evidence, that Loololma did not visit Washington before 1890. Nevertheless, Frank Cushing mentioned that Loololma was leader of one of two political factions at Oraibi in 1882 or 1883. Whiteley concludes from this evidence that Loololma "favored a conciliatory stance toward the U.S. government eight years before his visit to Washington" (1988a:73). Hence, Loololma's visit to Washington was not the source of Oraibi factions.

As Whiteley's information suggests, well before Loololma visited Washington, he became leader of the "Friendly" or "Progressive" faction at Oraibi. This faction was so called because of its members' positive attitude toward the U.S. government and other representatives of the Western world. "Friendlies" were willing to learn from and adopt some of the ways of European-Americans. The "Hostile" or "Conservative" faction emerged in opposition to Loololma and the Friendlies. Members of the Hostile faction were antagonistic toward the U.S. Government, resisted any conciliation with its representatives, and opposed acceptance of or accommodation to anything foreign. During the next twenty or twenty-five years, these two factions and their leaders dominated the political scene at Oraibi. The factions and leaders influenced the nature and outcome of many different historic events. The Oraibi split, as discussed below, occurred along these factional lines. Friendlies expelled Hostiles from the village. In 1882, the U.S. government established the Hopi Reservation.

During the 1880's and 1890's factionalism at Oraibi intensified and focused on the issues of schooling and land. In 1887 a boarding school was built at Keam's Canyon, thirty-five miles from Oraibi. The Oraibi Hopis at first flatly refused to send their children there. Also in 1887, the U.S. Congress passed the General Allotment Act. The intention of the Dawes Act, as it is also known, was to end collective ownership of Indian lands and break up traditional tribal governments. The General Allotment Act allowed for a division of Indian lands into small, privately owned farms. It provided individuals, depending on their age and status, with provisional title to as many as 160 acres of land. The Dawes Act would free much Indian land for acquisition and use by the Euro-pean-Americans who were expanding westward. It would also, in the minds of some European-American church leaders (who lobbied for the Act) and some members of the U.S. Congress, facilitate transformation of pagan Indians into Christian Americans and common farmers. In 1890 Loololma and others visited Washington, D.C. The Commissioner of Indian Affairs arranged the trip. The Commissioner's intentions were to encourage Hopis to accept the allotment of land, the presence of Christian missionaries, and the education of their children in Western schools. Loololma returned to the Hopi Mesas supporting these programs. Around 1894 or 1895, Lomahongyoma, head of the Spider clan, began to lead the Hostile faction at Oraibi.

Unlike Loololma, most Oraibi Hopis resisted the Indian Affairs Commissioner's plans. Earlier in 1889 or 1890, for example, some Hopi men visited a Ghost Dance ceremony conducted among the Havasupai Indians. Some Hopis may also have participated at about this time in a Ghost Dance that a group of Paiute Indians sponsored. The Ghost Dance of 1889–1890 was a major religious revitalization movement among Native Americans. It promised a rejuvenated earth exclusively for Indian peoples. Deceased relatives would return from the dead, and the country would be rid of European-Americans. The Hopis, however, never adopted Ghost Dance ideology and never performed a Ghost Dance ritual in their own territory. Why this was so is discussed in the final section of this chapter.

In November of 1890, a meeting was held at Keam's Canyon between U.S. military and Office of Indian Affairs representatives. At this meeting, a quota system for the attendance of Hopi children in schools was established. The army was to implement and enforce the program. Whiteley suggests that this meeting marks the true beginning of direct U.S. intrusion into the Hopi factional dispute (1988a: 77). When Loololma supported the government program and identified members of the Hostile faction who opposed it, some of the Hostiles imprisoned him in a kiva. Federal troops eventually released Loololma.

In the spring of 1891, U.S. government surveyors arrived to map Hopi land for allotment. The Hostiles responded to this act by pulling up the surveyor's stakes. The government reacted by sending troops to Oraibi on 21 June 1891, to arrest Hostile leaders. When the troops arrived, they were met by armed Hostiles and by men impersonating Hopi deities. The Hopis then initiated a formal, ceremonial declaration of war against the United States (Fewkes 1902: 493–494; Parsons 1922: 275–276; Titiev 1944: 76–79). The troops did not comprehend the religious and political meaning of these events. Nevertheless, they left before fighting began and without resolving matters. In July the army returned in greater force. They then arrested and imprisoned at least nine of the Hostile leaders.

After the events of 1891, disputes between the two factions further intensified. Hostiles began openly questioning Loololma's right to be *kik-mongwi* and Lomahongyoma, head of the Spider clan and of the Hostile faction, claimed to be the legitimate Village Chief of Oraibi. This declaration resulted in further conflict in the ceremonial realm. Loololma responded to Lomahongyoma by claiming "ownership" of all Hopi lands and of the Soyal ceremony because he, not Lomahongyoma, was head of the Bear clan. The leader of the Spider clan responded by seizing a plot of ground in the Bear clan's ceremonial fields and by declaring the Blue Flute ceremony (which the Spider clan controlled) to be superior to the Soyal ceremony. This action challenged the religious basis for Bear clan leadership of Oraibi.

Through the mid-1890s, schooling and allotment continued to be central issues in Hopi disputes. A school was opened near Oraibi in 1892. Around thirty children attended regularly, but none of them were children of the Hostile faction. Concerning allotment, neither Friendlies nor Hostiles ever accepted individually owned lands. Even Loololma, leader of the Progressive faction, tacitly refused allotment by finding reason after reason to delay. In 1894 the U.S. government ended efforts to implement the allotment program. Also during this year, a dispute between the two factions over the use of land at Moenkopi, a farming colony of Oraibi at that time, led to the incarceration of nineteen Hostiles at the military prison at Alcatraz Island. They remained there until September, 1895 (Whiteley 1988a:87–88).

Through this period, members of the rival factions refused to participate in each other's ceremonies.[3] Members of one faction refused to participate in ceremonies directed by individuals belonging to the opposing faction. In 1896 Lomahongyoma refused to allow Loololma to perform the Soyal ceremony in the Blue Flute kiva, which the Spider clan controlled. This refusal violated Hopi religious tradition because Blue Flute kiva was "home" of the Soyal. Loololma had no alternative but to remove his sacred objects and take them to a new location, the Circle kiva. Following this action, Lomahongyoma began to perform his own version of the Soyal ceremony in the Blue Flute kiva, and other members of the Soyal religious society were forced to participate in one or the other of the Soyal ceremonies conducted each December. This religious or ritual cleavage (that leaders of the political factions fomented) intensified to the point where each group conducted its own complete ceremonial cycle each year. They did so until the final breakup of the pueblo in 1906.

In December of 1898 a severe smallpox epidemic struck the Hopis. On First and Second Mesas, 632 people were infected, and 159 of them died. The U.S. government responded by closing all schools, quarantining Oraibi with Indian police, and vaccinating four or five hundred people from Oraibi. The Hostiles refused vaccination and viewed the forced cleanup of clothing and housing to be yet another unwarranted intrusion by European-Americans into Hopi affairs.

In 1901 or 1902, Tawaqwaptiwa replaced Loololma as leader of the Friendlies and as Oraibi Village Chief. Tawaqwaptiwa was one of Loololma's sister's sons. About this same time, Yukioma gradually replaced Lomahongyoma as leader of the Hostiles. According to Titiev, the uncompromising character of these new leaders increased the ideological distance between the two factions and ended the possibility of compromise (1944:83). Loololma died sometime around 1904. Lomahongyoma died around 1919.

In January of 1906, members of a Hostile faction from Shongopavi, a pueblo on Second Mesa, refused to send their children to school. The U.S. government sent police to arrest the Shongopavi Hostile leaders. Some fighting occurred, and police made several arrests over the next few months. In March, approximately fifty-two Shongopavi Hostiles moved to Oraibi. They were ritually greeted by the Oraibi Hostile leaders, Lomahongyoma and Yukioma. Interactions between the two Oraibi factions became immeasurably worse. According to Whiteley, "Many

Hopis cite this influx from Second Mesa as the precipitating cause of the Oraibi split" (1988a:105).

During the summer of 1906, additional serious ceremonial interruptions occurred. Hostiles and Friendlies were no longer content to participate in their own separate ceremonies, but sought to challenge and disrupt those of the opposition. Members of the Friendly faction interfered with the Hostile faction's performance of their Niman ceremony (marking the return of *katchinas* to their home in the Underworld). Also, Hostiles postponed their Snake Dance several times, holding it just before Oraibi split. Titiev and Whiteley both feel that this postponement was related to the pueblo's disintegration. Hopis intended Oraibi to break up when they held the Snake Dance. They delayed the ceremony until the time was ripe.

And so we return to 6 and 7 September 1906. Tension at the pueblo had reached a peak, and leaders of the two factions undertook drastic actions to settle their conflicts once and for all. Titiev describes in detail the actual events of 6 and 7 September 1906. His account is based primarily on conversations in the 1930s with Tawaqwaptiwa, the Oraibi *kikmongwi*, a leader of the Friendly faction, and a central character in these events. Titiev's description of the actual split cannot be improved upon, and we encourage interested readers to review it (1944:85–86). Titiev describes how both sides held meetings on the evening of 6 September to make their plans. Both factions discussed the Friendlies' intention to expel Second Mesa Hostiles from Oraibi. Independently, both sides agreed there should be no violence. A U.S. government official arrived and warned that if violence occurred, troops would be sent in to "wipe out both sides." Finally, Friendlies decided to drive out the Second Mesa Hostiles and, if Oraibi Hostiles interfered, to drive out the latter as well. Oraibi Hostiles would be forced to go north to ". . . Kawestima, where the ancestors of the Spider clan had left the Spider Woman when they went to seek out the Bear clan's settlement at Oraibi" (Titiev 944:85). After breakfast, Friendlies ordered the Shongopavi Hostiles to leave Oraibi. The latter refused. When Friendlies began forcibly to evict some Shongopovi people, a scuffle broke out, Oraibi Hostiles came to their allies' aid, and general fighting erupted. The fighting lasted for several hours. Eventually, the two sides faced each other at the northern edge of the village. Yukioma, the Hostile leader, drew a line in the sand and said to Tawaqwaptiwa, "If your men . . . are strong enough to push us away from the village and to pass me over the line, it will be done. But if we pass you over the line, it will not be done, and we will have to live here" (Titiev 1944:86). A shoving match ensued, Yukioma was pushed over the line, and the decision was made. Hostiles gathered their belongings and left Oraibi. They made camp that night north of Oraibi at the present site of Hotevilla Pueblo. Following the disintegration of Oraibi, federal troops came, located the Hostile camp, and arrested both Third and Second Mesa leaders. On 3 and 4 November, federal troops returned the Second Mesa Hostiles who remained at Hotevilla to Shongopavi. Troops also seized eighty-two children at Hotevilla, who were then taken to boarding school. On 8 November the army returned approximately one hundred fifty Hostiles to Oraibi (Whiteley 1988b: 61). Although relations between returned Hostiles and Oraibi Friendlies were tense, the former remained in Oraibi for about three years. In November 1909, the returned Hostiles again left Oraibi and traveled to the present site of Bacavi, where they founded that pueblo.

The split immediately changed the lives of the 892 inhabitants of Oraibi who, taken together, represented approximately 42 percent of the total Hopi population (Titiev 1944; Hodge 1912). When Oraibi divided, approximately 20 percent of the total Hopi population was forced to relocate. By the standards of any society of whatever scale, resettlement of 20 percent of a population is significant. Those who left Oraibi were forced to start their lives over in a new location (albeit only a few miles distant), and their previously intimate social contacts with individuals remaining in Oraibi were forever diminished. By 1909 Oraibi had approximately 360 inhabitants. Between then and 1911, many more people had moved to Kykotsmovi (New Oraibi). Others moved to Moenkopi, near Tuba City. By 1911 the Oraibi population stood at approximately 220. This was approximately one-fourth of what it had been only five years earlier.

From a long-term perspective, the split is consequential because it led to the establishment of Bacavi, Hotevilla, and Kykotsmovi and to the expansion of Moenkopi. Until 1906, when Oraibi divided, the other villages of Third Mesa did not exist, and Moenkopi was primarily a farming colony of Oraibi. Before then, throughout all of contact history, people of Third Mesa had lived exclusively at the site of Oraibi. Since 1906, however, Third Mesa Hopis have resided in one or another of six small villages (including Upper and Lower Moenkopi). Each of these villages has experienced its own, slightly different version of Hopi history, and each has developed or reproduced its own subtly distinct version of Hopi society and culture (see Titiev 1944, 1972; Nagata 1970; Clemmer 1978a; Whiteley 1988a, 1988b).

How can the disruptive events at Oraibi be interpreted and understood? A pause for explanation is needed before returning to the historical narrative in Chapter 7, where we discuss Hopi sociocultural persistence and change in the twentieth century since the Oraibi disintegration.

Anthropological Analyses of the Oraibi Split

Anthropologists have offered at least four distinct explanations of the Oraibi fissioning. Among the variables figuring in these four explanations are: (1) population size, density, and pressure on resources; (2) mode of production and economic arrangements; (3) the environment and human ecology; (4) culture contact and acculturation; (5) social organization and structure; (6) political organization and factionalism; (7) individual interests; and (8) deliberate or intentional acts by individuals and groups of individuals. After considering the four explanations and the variables that they incorporate, we add a fifth explanation, integrating ideas from various of the other accounts, and suggesting that the Oraibi disintegration be classified as a "social movement." We then suggest that the split be explained using ideas developed to account for such phenomena.

Titiev provides the first explanation that we consider (1944). Taking all of Titiev's arguments together, he suggests that *internal social structural pressures and instabilities* (that were exacerbated by contact with European-American culture and society) led to the disintegration of the Oraibi pueblo. Titiev uses the term "disintegration" technically. Titiev intended that this term be understood in relation to its antithesis, the concept of "social integration." He intended to evoke the explanatory framework of structural-functional anthropology. Within this framework, the maintenance of social solidarity through time is of primary theoretical interest. Solidarity, based on shared interests and a commitment to shared beliefs and values, must be maintained for social systems or social structures to develop and persist. Social institutions (such as clans) are to be analyzed and understood in terms of the contribution they make to social solidarity.

Titiev's analysis of Oraibi disintegration is based on his view of Hopi social structure and social integration. For him, three features of the traditional social structure of Hopi villages, including Oraibi, were fundamental. The first feature was the vertical organization of Hopi matrilineal descent groups into households, lineages, clans, and phratries (1944: Chap. 4). In Titiev's view, Hopi clans were essentially autonomous and corporate, owning land, rituals, and kivas. The second feature was the horizontal organization of exogamy, religious societies, and kiva groups. As discussed in Chapters 2 and 5, the chief priests of religious sodalities were drawn from the descent group that "owned" a particular religious ceremony. The performance of the ceremony provided the organization's raison d'être. While such ceremonies and the associated religious paraphernalia were controlled by a particular descent group (matrilineal clan or matrilineage), common membership in the society that performed the ceremony was drawn from many descent groups throughout the pueblo. Further, one society's ceremony might be performed in a kiva controlled by a different descent group. For Titiev, such cross cutting memberships provided social integration of and solidarity within (not between) Hopi villages. To some extent, religious institutions counteracted the inherent divisive pressures created by the presence of autonomous, corporate descent groups. However, and this is the third significant feature of Hopi social structure, Hopi political organization, based on the religious sodalities, was "amorphous." It lacked powerful leadership positions and was inherently weaker than and could not withstand pressures generated by the opposing interests of corporate descent groups. For Titiev, "a Hopi pueblo is like an object with a thin outer shell which holds together a number of firm, distinct segments—should the shell be cracked, the segments would fall apart" (1944:69). The Oraibi split is, thus, to be understood within the context of the ever-present separatistic characteristics of Hopi clans and the inherent weakness of phratry and village ties. Titiev's propositions (sometimes implicit and sometimes explicit) begin with the suggestion that, as solidarity within social groups similar to clans increases, solidarity between these units decreases. Such solidarity is based on shared interests and values. If the interests of the members of a descent group are largely shared, and if those interests are distinct from or in opposition to those of other such units, there will be an inherent divisive tendency to any more inclusive social grouping of the two opposing groups. Traditional Hopi villages were weak because the clans were strong. What are the shared interests of Hopi clans? The answer for Titiev included ownership of land, ownership of ceremonies, access to political offices, relations with European-Americans after contact, and even the individual interests of descent-group leaders. For Titiev, factionalism that emerged in the political dispute over the influence of European-Americans may have been the split's casus belli, but the "separatistic quality" of clans already existed (1944:75). The causes of the split were largely sociological and internal. The presence of strong clans and weak political organization resulted in disintegration of the pueblo.

Richard M. Bradfield offers a second explanation of the Oraibi split. He begins his monograph, *The Changing Pattern of Hopi Agriculture,* by making explicit the questions he attempts to answer (1971:1): (1) Why do the Hopi establish their agricultural fields where they do? (2) What were the social and economic consequences of the dissection of the Oraibi Wash around the turn of the century? And, (3) What were the effects on Hopi agriculture of the introduction of draught animals and carts, and, later, of pickups and tractors? The second question concerns us here because Bradfield suggests that the Oraibi split was the most significant result of the erosion of Oraibi Wash below the pueblo. Although Bradfield modifies this view in a postscript to his monograph, we reserve discussion of his postscripted arguments until later.

Bradfield presents his explanation in a series of steps. The first step is to establish the "controlling" factors of Hopi *ak-chin* agriculture. Hopi territory is dominated by the geological contrast between the high mesas on which pueblos are built and the lower valleys dissected by permanent and impermanent watercourses along which agricultural fields are planted (see Fig. 6). *Ak-chin,* or agriculture practiced on the outwash fans of arroyos, is only one, but perhaps the most productive, form of the Hopi hedge-your-bets farming strategy discussed earlier. Hopis plant *ak-chin* fields at the point where a watercourse fans out because the water has reached more nearly level ground after having traveled down steeper areas at the immediate foot of a mesa. *Ak-chin* fields rely on direct rainfall and, more importantly, on the runoff that reaches them from higher ground by way of the watercourses in the valley.

The first set of controlling factors of *ak-chin* agriculture that Bradfield discusses are snowfall, frost, and summer rain (1971:2ff.). Snowfall and frost dictate the date of Hopi planting. *Ak-chin* fields must be planted while soil is still wet from winter snows, but after the threat of late spring frost has passed. Corn plants depend on the moisture retained from winter snows until the July and August rains arrive. During the summer, fields depend on direct rainfall and on runoff from rains higher on the mesas. Bradfield differentiates good from marginal agricultural fields by the amount of rainfall required to ensure adequate water during July and August. Marginal fields require a rainfall during these months of over three inches (1971:13). The second set of controlling factors for Hopi agriculture that Bradfield specifies are vegetation and soils (1971:13ff.). The type and amount of natural vegetation in an area indicate to Hopis whether or not to plant there. The kind and abundance of vegetation are dependent on the amount of moisture present, but also on the quality of soil.

The next step in Bradfield's analysis is to establish the productive potential of Hopi agriculture. He focuses on the relationship between Hopi agricultural productivity and Hopi village population. The productivity of any agricultural system depends on the acreage planted and the crop yield per acre. According to Bradfield's calculations, Hopi *ak-chin* fields yield approximately ten to twelve bushels of corn per year per acre. Hopi individuals need approximately twenty-four bushels of corn per year for consumption and reserve storage (1971:20–21). This level of

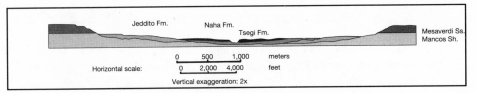

Hypothetical cross section of the Oraibi Valley (after Hack 1942:59)

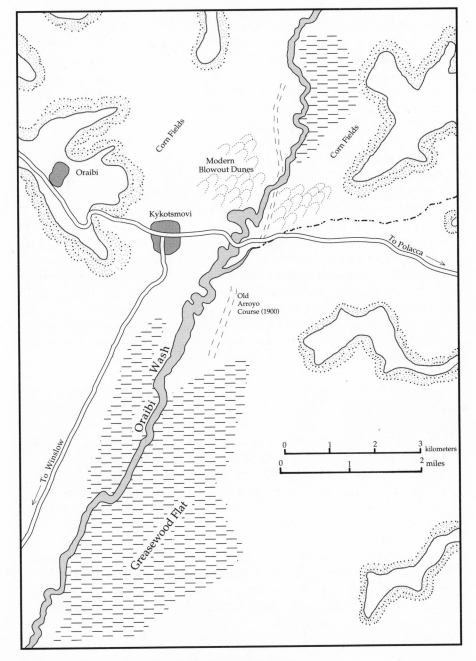

Figure 6. The Oraibi Valley (after Hack 1942:57)

productivity means that approximately 2 acres of corn fields are required per individual per year. After adding requirements for beans and
squash, Bradfield concludes that each Hopi requires 2.5 acres of cultivated fields per year.

Next, Bradfield establishes the amount of useful agricultural land
available to Oraibi people during the 1800s. He suggests that the best
agricultural lands available to the people of Oraibi were the fields on the
flood plain below the village and that the original clan lands of Oraibi
were the roughly 1,800 acres in the lower two-thirds of the valley. In
Bradfield's mind, this acreage was capable of supporting a population of
approximately 720 individuals (1971:22). According to Bradfield, with
the acquisition of burros (around 1865) to haul corn greater distances
after harvesting, approximately 600 acres in the upper two-thirds of the
valley became available for planting.[4] According to Bradfield, this expansion of agricultural fields after the technological innovation of burro
haulage went hand in hand with an increase in the Oraibi population. At
the turn of the century, approximately 2,400 acres were available to
support a population of approximately 880 people. Bradfield's figure is
almost identical to the actual population of Oraibi at that time.

The final step in Bradfield's explanation is to relate these data directly
to external events that affected the agricultural basis of Hopi society.
According to Bradfield, sometime between 1901 and 1906, the main
wash in lower Oraibi Valley became eroded to the point where flood-
water irrigation of the surrounding fields was impossible. The walls of
the arroyo were simply too high to allow irrigation. As a result, sometime during this period, approximately 800 acres of the best farm land
in the valley were lost. The agricultural system could no longer support
the Oraibi population. In Bradfield's interpretation, the Oraibi split was
related to economic events. For him, whatever other forces operated at
Oraibi to cause the split, ". . . the immediate, precipitating cause was
economic" (1971:23). He suggests that approximately one-third of the
best agricultural land was lost due to erosion, "the economic ground of
their leadership was undermined," and that this affected political and
religious organization (1971:23). Bradfield continues by discussing the
root causes of the wash's dissection and people's movements after the
Oraibi split. In his view, the dissection of Oraibi Wash can be traced to
general factors that caused or prohibited erosion. Most critical of these
were the state of vegetation in areas where water flowed. In Bradfield's
analysis, the vegetation in Oraibi Wash just before its dissection was depleted. This depletion did not result from human activities such as overgrazing or poor field management. Rather, it resulted from the prolonged and often severe drought at Third Mesa that lasted from 1865 to

1905. This drought was followed by a season or seasons of unusually high rainfall. Because of the depleted vegetation, the heavy rains critically eroded the wash. Again, additional agricultural lands were removed from the production basis of Oraibi society. When the critical fields could no longer be planted, the existing Oraibi population could no longer be sustained. Therefore, Oraibi split and its population was redistributed throughout Third Mesa and Moenkopi by local migrations.

Just before publishing his study, Bradfield discovered evidence that led him to modify the explanation he provides in the body of his monograph. Contrary to his earlier anecdotal testimony suggesting that the Oraibi Wash was dissected just before the Oraibi split, he found other evidence that the critical erosion did not occur until *after* the Hostiles left and founded Hotevilla. Accordingly, Bradfield offers an alternative account that is, nevertheless, closely related to his earlier explanatory arguments. Bradfield suggests in his alternate analysis that the extremely arid conditions of 1865 to 1905 still played a causal role in the split. He proposes that the drought during this period affected not only natural vegetation, but also domesticated plants. The productivity of agricultural fields was sharply reduced over a prolonged period. This reduction economically strained Oraibi, since the fields were not able to support the large human population. This economic stress, in turn, led to the intense dissension over land, ritual, and culture contact that Titiev documented. *Economically motivated dissension,* a failure in the productive basis of Oraibi society, caused the Oraibi split. This failure resulted from environmental, climatic, and other *external* factors beyond the understanding and control of the Oraibi leaders. The Oraibi split is thus to be understood in relation to the ecological and economic conditions within which Oraibi life operated.[5]

Richard Clemmer, in *Continuities of Hopi Culture Change* (1978a), provides a third explanation of the Oraibi split. In this study, Clemmer provides an ethnographic, historical, and political analysis of the twentieth-century "Hopi Traditionalist movement." Hopi Traditionalists of contemporary times frequently oppose change and modernization originating from or controlled by groups other than the Hopis themselves. According to Clemmer, contemporary Traditionalists seek self-determination, following a strategy based on ancestral Hopi social organization, culture, and history (1978a:70). He contrasts Traditionalists with the Hopi Tribal Council. The latter seeks self-determination, but follows a strategy closely allied with the European-American political-economic system. For Clemmer, the Hopi Traditionalist movement must be understood as a response to the nature of contact between Hopis and the U.S. government. Such contact has been dominated since the 1850s by the coercive attempts of European-Americans to change Hopi culture and society and by the subordinate political-economic position of Hopis. Within this context, the Traditionalist movement constitutes "directed resistance to contact and directed resistance to acculturation" (1978a:22). It is a kind of "revitalization movement."

The Oraibi split enters Clemmer's analysis as historical background for the contemporary Traditionalist movement. Traditionalists have historical and ideological roots among the Hostiles, who resisted foreign influence and domination at the turn of the twentieth century. Clemmer begins his explanation of the Oraibi split by asking whether it "was . . . largely a result of sociological factors peculiar to Hopi culture? Or was the American intrusion indeed the major cause of the conflict?" (1978a: 58). For Clemmer, sociological factors include not only the variables and forces that Titiev discussed, but also the type of "action designed in deliberation" that Krutz (1973) and Whiteley (1988a, 1988b) incorporate in their explanations of the split.[6] After emphasizing the uniqueness of the Oraibi split when compared to the formation of other new Hopi settlements, Clemmer answers his own question. He suggests that the Hopis knew how to solve population problems "without resorting to fabrication of a 20-year-long drama" (1978a:58). According to Clemmer, the split and establishment of Bacavi resulted from an "ideological, rather than a purely sociological situation." He suggests that the split resulted from tensions and conflicts caused by government interference in Hopi life. "(G)overnment interference in Hopi life . . . provided the immediate, ideological issue" (1978a:58). In Clemmer's view, U.S. intrusion into Hopi affairs, the role of European-Americans in "brewing the conflict," and a continuity of antagonistic events (e.g., arrests, imprisonments, forced schooling, and allotment) were the source of an ideological conflict that caused the split. Culture contact, associated tensions and pressures, and ideological disputes resulted in disintegration of the pueblo. If there was any "deliberateness" in the split (a suggestion to which we turn momentarily), "[it] resulted from ideological considerations as well as sociological ones, and it was the *ideological process* . . . brought on by the increasing pressures from the U.S. government" (1978a:77; emphasis added).

Peter Whiteley provides a fourth explanation of the disintegration of Oraibi in his books, *Deliberate Acts: Changing Hopi Culture Through the Oraibi Split* (1988a) and *Bacavi: Journey to Reed Springs* (1988b). In these works, Whiteley offers an analysis of the split that is based on or is compatible with the contemporary "ethnosociological" explanation his Hopi consultants provide. It is also compatible with explanations that various Hopi writers have offered (e.g., Nequatewa 1936; Sekaquaptewa

1972; Krutz 1973). He argues, supporting his case with a wealth of evidence, that the Hopi themselves know best what happened at Oraibi on 7 September 1906. Whiteley also suggests that previous anthropological explanations, such as those discussed above, are inadequate for one reason or another.

For Whiteley, the Oraibi split cannot be explained mechanically as the result of an inherently weak social structure, ecological/economic forces, or acculturative pressures. He rejects all forms of single-cause determinism and suggests, instead, that causes of the split are *multifaceted and complex*. According to Whiteley, some of the factors mentioned in earlier explanations played a role in the Oraibi split. Features of the environmental, economic, and political conditions at Oraibi before the split are accurately portrayed in the explanations of other anthropologists. The drought central to Bradfield's analysis, for example, was real. Oraibi's large population strained the agricultural system. Whiteley says that the Oraibi spring had slowed to a trickle by the time of the split. Disputes over land were occurring, but not necessarily between the autonomous, corporate clans that Titiev depicted. Culture contact had also stressed the Oraibi people. The issues of education and allotment were particularly disruptive. Further, the Hostile-Friendly political dispute reflected all these pressures. Real and bitter antagonism existed between people belonging to the different factions. Nevertheless, for Whiteley, ecological, economic, social-structural, historical, demographic, and political variables, taken individually or taken together, do not provide a sufficient explanation of the split. Nor can these factors alone account for events at Third Mesa after the disintegration of Oraibi (1988a:248ff.).

As implied by the title of his book, Whiteley explains the Oraibi split within a theoretical context that ascribes beliefs, values, and intentions to individual actors. Whiteley seeks to account for human behavior, in part, by reference to these phenomena. In this explanatory framework, people behave the way they do partly because they analyze (classify and interpret) situations in particular ways, pursue goals established for them by their cultural traditions, and expect their actions to have certain effects. Individuals make decisions and are capable of responding to events in a variety of different ways. The actions of individuals or groups, in turn, have specifiable intended and unintended consequences. In Whiteley's view, the disintegration of Oraibi was a deliberate act. Krutz shares this opinion (1973). Clemmer criticizes it (1978a).

More specifically, Whiteley suggests that Oraibi's religious and political leaders intentionally orchestrated the split. They did so based on their interpretations of specific events and on their desire to accomplish specific religious goals. According to Whiteley, Oraibi leaders at the time of the split interpreted events as satisfying the conditions specified by at least two Hopi prophesies. The first concerned *Pahaana,* an elder white brother character of Hopi mythology. *Pahaana* was to return to the Hopis during a period of decadence and corruption, having departed for the east after Hopi emergence into the present Fourth World. Some Hopis first interpreted fair-skinned European-Americans to represent *Pahaana.* Thus, they thought the prophesy was fulfilled. Eventually, however, because no outsider appeared with the requisite token of mythological connection, Hopis concluded that European-Americans did not qualify for the *Pahaana* role. Nevertheless, the conditions of social and religious deterioration that dominated Oraibi life around the turn of the century also played a role in a second prophesy. This prophesy concerned the fate of Oraibi and of the Hopi ritual order. In it, conditions of social decadence and ritual corruption were to signal the end of Oraibi. The pueblo was foreordained to be divided and eventually destroyed by an antagonistic, evicted group that would then return to their mythological homeland.

According to Whiteley, within the "ecological and social near-chaos" of the pueblo at the turn of the century, Oraibi leaders thought it necessary to take drastic steps. They interpreted events in the context of Hopi prophesy and thought it essential not only to end the symptoms of corruption (for example, tensions or disputes over water and land, overcrowding, ritual ineffectiveness, and the education of Hopi children by outsiders), but also to destroy the cause of the symptoms, the corrupted traditional ritual order. Hopi religious leaders resolved to accomplish both by orchestrating a political dispute over the acceptance or rejection of European-American customs and beliefs. They raised the temperature of the dispute through ritual competition, brought it to a boil by inviting the Second Mesa Hostiles to Oraibi, and precipitated an overflow by staging the pushing match that led immediately to the disintegration of the pueblo. Political factionalism was a tool of the Oraibi religious elite. It was the means they chose as the "necessary catalyst" for the destruction of the pueblo. They created and used the division between Hostiles and Friendlies to manipulate the class of unknowledgeable people (albeit for the latter's own good). By doing this, they sought to accomplish their secret religious ends (Whiteley 1988a:271). The split resulted from deliberate decisions made in the secret manner of Hopi "ritualized planning" (1988a:265ff.).[7]

Much of Whiteley's argumentation in his books and other writings can be interpreted as an effort to support his (and the Hopis') view of the Oraibi split. He dedicates part of this effort to presenting a revised, more accurate description of traditional Hopi sociopolitical structure and social stratification (1985, 1986, 1988a). Whiteley suggests, for example, that Third Mesa Hopis were not an egalitarian people, as Titiev (1944) and Eggan (1950) suggest. Rather, according to Whiteley, Oraibi was a class-based society within which a fundamental distinction was made, not between people of different economic standing, but between people who did and did not possess secret ritual knowledge and power (cf., Upham 1982, 1989). The former had the power to plan *secretly* the destiny of all Hopis. Through ritual planning, they had the power to control events in the world. Common Hopis lacked such power and capabilities. Further, they were often not informed by their leaders of the true meaning and intent of specific actions. For the Hopis, knowledge was power. Common Hopis lacked the former; hence, they also lacked the latter. Whiteley is interested in this class distinction at Oraibi because, for him to be correct that the Oraibi split resulted from Oraibi religious leaders' secret and deliberate decision-making, there had to have been a class of such individuals empowered to accomplish the act.

Whiteley is also concerned about accurately describing Hopi social structure. In his view, Hopi matrilineal clans were not the autonomous, land-holding, ceremony-controlling, corporate descent groups that Titiev and Eggan characterized. Entire clans did not control "clan lands" and "clan ceremonies" (along with the associated ritual knowledge, paraphernalia, and power). Rather, lineages or other clan segments controlled such phenomena. Clan segments normally controlled the inheritance of such "estates." The relationship of clans to land is consequential because Titiev and Bradfield have claimed that the Oraibi split was caused by or associated with disputes between clans over scarce agricultural land that they owned. According to Whiteley, neither the Bear clan nor any other clan actually "owned" land, since the Hopi deity *Masau'u* (or *Maasaw*) owns all Hopi land.[8] Clans have use or usufruct rights to land, rather than exclusive ownership. According to Whiteley (1985:368–372), the view of Oraibi clan lands must also be modified to include these additional points: (1) the concept of "clan lands" actually refers only to the "ritual/ceremonial fields" upon which corn is planted; (2) not all lands were inherited through the matrilineage or matrilineal clan (men might inherit from their fathers) and some land was individually owned; (3) clan land holdings varied from one descent group to another and not all clans possessed "clan land"; (4) "clan land was controlled by the leading family or lineage segment that controlled the particular ceremony for which the land was granted" (1985:370); (5) the concept of clan lands is largely "vestigial" at Third Mesa today, due primarily to the Oraibi split. The split entailed abolishment of the ceremonial structure to which ceremonial fields were linked. If Whiteley is correct that the split was not caused by disputes over land by corporate descent groups, it helps that such groups (probably) did not exist at Oraibi.

Whiteley also devotes part of his effort to documenting the complex history of political negotiations between Hopis and the Spanish, Mexican, and European-American peoples. The events surrounding these negotiations demonstrate that Hopi leaders understood complex political issues. Such leaders also showed an uncanny ability to confuse and manipulate representatives of foreign interests. Whiteley's argument that the split resulted from the machinations of a religious and political elite is indirectly supported by the circumstantial evidence that other Hopi leaders operated in similar ways at other times. Whiteley is also concerned with demonstrating that his view of the split is compatible with or based on Hopi "ethnosociological" analyses. If one purports to be explaining the actions of individuals in specific situations by describing their intentions, it helps that informed members of the society whose actions are being explained concur with the analysis.

Finally, Whiteley dedicates a good deal of his effort to describing and accounting for changes in Hopi culture and society at Third Mesa since the Oraibi split. In Whiteley's view, many of such changes can be explained by assuming that they stem from Hopi leaders' deliberate acts on 7 September 1906. We address this subject in Chapter 7.

Many of the points Whiteley makes about the Oraibi split appear meritorious. His analysis represents a significant contribution to our understanding of that historical incident. The evidence he marshals to support his interpretation is persuasive. Also, the role he assigns in his account to the intentional actions of Hopi leaders (to active interpretations and deliberate activities of human agents) corrects previous anthropological explanations. Those accounts tend to view Hopi behavior as mechanical, purely responsive, or merely the "enactment" of cultural principles. Nevertheless, his analysis is possibly subject to four separate but related criticisms. All these are potential problems of historical accounts that incorporate, interpret, reconstruct, or otherwise refer to the mental antecedents of human actions. The potential problems are shared by all explanations that refer to actors' mental states (including motivations) when accounting for the actors' behavior. First, in the language of phenomenology, descriptions of others' mental states (by anthropologists or anyone else) normally represent "constructs of the second degree." They are accounts of accounts. Such descriptions are, at best, idealized. Whiteley's account is actually a construct of the third degree. It is an account of his consultants' accounts of 1906 Oraibi leaders' accounts of their motivations in destroying the pueblo. Being this far removed (in time and reconstruction) from the Old Oraibi leaders' mental states introduces the possibility that Whiteley's third-degree construct, however accurate as a description of his consultants' accounts, is a less than accurate description of Friendly and Hostile leaders' mental states. As indicated above, however, Whiteley provides important circumstantial evidence for the validity of his reconstruction. Second, actors' accounts of their reasons for doing something are frequently not accurate descriptions of their antecedent mental states. Rather, such accounts often represent actors' secondary rationalizations and attempts to legitimate their actions (see Giddens 1976:81ff.). The reasons actors give for their actions may have little relation to their earlier intentions and motives. This claim is related to Clemmer's concept of the Hopi "mythic process." Clemmer might say that Whiteley is describing mythological rationalization, rather than antecedent mental states. Further, actors' accounts of their earlier intentions and motivations may represent "dissimulations." Such accounts may be active attempts to hide "real" intentions and motives (see Giddens 1984:4). Whiteley actually claims that Oraibi leaders' earlier accounts of the Oraibi split were dissimulations. Those accounts hid the leaders' religious motives by discursively referring to political factionalism. This dissimulation raises the possibility that Whiteley's consultants, intentionally or unintentionally, are doing the same. Finally, Whiteley's analysis might be criticized for attributing intentions and motivations to a class or group (the religious elite), rather than to single individuals. Doing so requires additional evidence that individuals constituting the group actually shared such intentions and motivations, possessed the power to act as a group, and exhibited solidarity in their collective actions. Again, as noted earlier, Whiteley devotes much attention to these features of his analysis.

Despite these possible criticisms of Whiteley's analysis, we proceed for the remainder of this chapter with the working assumption that his account is valid. We suggest that the next logical question to ask about the split at Oraibi concerns the origins of religious leaders' mental states. Why did they come to be in a mental state that led them to undertake their drastic actions? Rather than focusing exclusively on the unique history of Third Mesa, can we seek general explanatory arguments to explain such mental states? By doing so, can we account for the events that occurred at Oraibi in 1906? We suggest that the intentional acts of Hopi leaders in 1906 can be placed in a wider explanatory context that provides a more general explanation and that sheds further light on the meaning of actions that the Hopi religious elite undertook. By doing so, it is possible to take advantage of generalizations that other scholars have provided when dealing with different historic events. The events at Oraibi may be shown to have implications for the understanding of sociocultural persistence and change.

Our proposal, based partly on Clemmer's and Whiteley's work, is that the Oraibi split can be comprehended as a "revitalization," "millinarian," "nativistic," or "transformative social movement."[9] To support this view, we begin by discussing such movements apart from the Oraibi case. Then we return to the Hopis and determine if the Oraibi split is reasonably viewed from the explanatory perspective of social movements.

Anthony F. C. Wallace defines a revitalization movement "as a deliberate, organized, conscious effort by members of a society to construct a more satisfying culture" (1956:265). For Wallace, revitalization movements are a type of culture change. In such movements, individuals must perceive their culture to be "unsatisfactory" and "innovate" a new cultural system (1956:265).

David F. Aberle offers a definition of social movements that emphasizes two characteristics (1982:315–316). First, social movements are organized group efforts. Second, they seek change despite "resistance by other human beings." Social movements are different from individual or unorganized group efforts to cause change. They are also different from attempts to change that occur without conscious, active or passive resistance (1982:315–316).

For Aberle, religious movements are varieties of social movements. Aberle does not, however, pursue the latter apart from other types of the former. Instead, Aberle differentiates categories of social movements according to the locus of change sought (in the individual or supraindividual) and the amount of change sought (total or partial). In this typology, some social movements are "transformative . . . which aim at a total change in supra-individual systems" (1982:317). Others might be "redemptive . . . which aim at a total change in individuals" (1982:317). Concerning transformative movements, Aberle adds,

> Transformative movements consist of organized groups of people who actively seek, by whatever means, ritual or practical, a transformation of the socio-cultural, or indeed the natural order, including the socio-cultural—and this in their own lifetimes. Such movements involve a radical rejection of things as they are, and a perception of the enormous force necessary to make the shift from things as they are to things as they should be. (1982:318)

According to Aberle (1982:318–320), transformative social movements, despite variation, share several constants. Among such constants are those of (1) time perspective (people expect changes to be imminent and cataclysmic), (2) theory of history (people think that changes are destined to occur because of forces beyond human control), (3) leadership (charismatic leaders direct changes), and (4) disengagement (people endeavor to change by increasing social and spatial distance between themselves and members of a dominant society). Variation in transformative movements can involve (1) means (the methods people employ to accomplish change); (2) model (the nature of the new conditions people seek, which might be restorative of past conditions, imitative of the conditions of other groups, or innovative); (3) scope (the beneficiaries of changes); and (4) relationship to existing systems (the existing state of affairs might be destroyed or persist).

Within the time frame under consideration in this case study, several social movements occurred among native peoples of Western North America. The Ghost Dance of 1889 to 1890 and the Peyote Religion spread throughout the Southwest. South of the Hopis, Western Apaches participated in at least four religious revitalization movements between 1880 and 1920 (Kessel 1976). Participation in these movements was, however, largely restricted to the Apaches. To the north of the Hopis, Utes performed the modern or postreservation version of the Sun Dance after about 1890. Southern Utes probably learned about the Sun Dance by attending Northern Ute dances during the 1890s and first performed their own dance after the turn of the century, possibly in 1904 (Jorgensen 1972). Each of these social movements requires brief consideration.

The Ghost Dance of 1889 to 1890 is well known in anthropological and sociological literature (e.g., Mooney 1896; Lesser 1933; Spier 1935; Herskovits 1938; Hill 1944; Dobyns and Euler 1967; La Barre 1972; Carroll 1975; Thornton 1981, 1986). The Ghost Dance was a postreservation social transformational movement. Its ideology stressed that deceased Native Americans would return to a regenerated world and that, through some cataclysmic event, all other peoples would be destroyed. Indians, however, would be saved from this destruction and live an ideal existence. To facilitate these events, people participated in the Ghost Dance ritual, consisting of the dance and accompanying ceremonial activities. Following the rapid spread of the Ghost Dance from Nevada (it originated in the visions of a Paviasto Indian) to many tribes in the western and eastern United States, the Ghost Dance followed an equally rapid decline, since the imminent events it foretold did not occur.

The Peyote Religion is also well documented in the literature (e.g., La Barre 1938; Slotkin 1955, 1956; Opler 1940; Aberle 1982; Stewart 1987; Collins 1968). Lipan Apaches probably brought this pan-Indian religion to Native Americans north of Mexico sometime following the 1870s. It was first practiced in Oklahoma, but rapidly spread throughout much of the continent, including the American Southwest. This religion (which ideologically precludes whites) was based on the ritual consumption of peyote cactus. Peyote was the primary symbol of the church, a source of power, and the means through which Indians communicated with an all-powerful, transcendent god. This god was capable of providing gifts and good luck to followers of the religion who changed their lives by giving up alcohol, behaving more responsibly with their families, and abandoning other misguided actions. The Peyote Religion was redemptive, rather than transformative. The locus of change was in the soul of individuals, rather than in the social order (Aberle 1982).

At least three of the religious movements among Western Apaches of Arizona between 1880 and 1920 were ideologically similar to the Ghost Dance. Each of them emphasized rejuvenation of the world for Indian peoples and destruction of whites. These religious movements were transformative social movements. The other Western Apache religious movement (post 1920) emphasized curing and the religious protection of its followers.

The Ute Sun Dance Religion should not be confused with the older Plains Indian Sun Dance Religion (Jorgensen 1972). The newer one was historically based on the older, but was ideologically modified in fundamental ways to fit the postreservation context within which it spread to the west. The Plains Indian Sun Dance was focused on regeneration of the world, the acquisition of power for use in the pursuit of buffalo and in warfare, and the general welfare of the group whose members performed it. On the other hand, the Ute version was focused on the curing of illness and the acquisition of power to be used for the benefit of the Ute community and for the maintenance of community unity (Jorgensen 1972:17ff.). Similar to the Peyote Religion, the Ute Sun Dance can be classified as a redemptive movement. Individuals who danced to obtain power were encouraged to radically change their lives.

Anthropologists offer different explanations for social movements such as those that occurred among Native Americans from 1880 to 1920. They attempt to answer a variety of questions about these movements. An example of one such question is: Why did some groups who knew about the Ghost Dance adopt and perform it, while other groups that also knew about the dance rejected it? Scholars have answered this question by referring to (1) the nature of culture contact and level of acculturation for individual groups (Herskovits 1938), (2) the level of individual solidarity with or commitment to particular social groups (Carroll 1979), (3) the allotment of land under the General Allotment Act (Landsman 1979), and (4) the "demographic antecedents" of the dance (Thornton 1981, 1986). Researchers have offered similar explanations for the other social movements. Aberle (1982) and Jorgensen (1972), however, provide the most useful explanations of the relevant social movements. Aberle seeks to account for Navajo adoption of the Peyote Religion (1982). Jorgensen explains why the Utes initially borrowed and continue to perform the Sun Dance (1972). For these anthropologists, social movements must be understood within the context of the *political-economic forces* that create conditions necessary or sufficient for their generation. For instance, these anthropologists refer to conditions of *relative or absolute deprivation* and to how people respond in such situations, when they are politically and economically powerless to change their lives.

Aberle's concept of relative deprivation is defined "as a negative discrepancy between legitimate expectation and actuality, or between legitimate expectation and anticipated actuality, or both" (Aberle 1982: 323). According to Aberle, relative deprivation as an explanatory concept is based on three assumptions: (1) human wants are in principle unlimited, (2) legitimate expectations are defined by sociocultural systems, and (3) sociocultural change can disrupt such definitions (1982: 323). Aberle discusses four kinds of deprivation, deprivation in possession, status, behavior, and worth. In the introduction to the 1982 edition of *The Peyote Religion among the Navajo,* he adds a fifth, deprivation of power.[10]

For Aberle, social movements are, "almost by definition, associated with some notion of distress, deprivation, dysphoria, or discontent" (1982:322). They arise when a people's legitimate expectations are not being met and when drastic actions must be taken or extreme forces must be channelled in order to remedy the situation. Nevertheless, Aberle suggests that it is difficult to associate relative deprivation with social movements, because the former is only one element of a theory of the latter. "The other elements include the context of social relationships of the deprived group with others, and the deprived group's diagnosis of the source of its deprivations. And undoubtedly other elements are also crucial" (1982:329). He also defines the features of context that affect the relationship between relative deprivation and social movements: (1) the nature of power relationships between the groups, (2) the spatial segregation of the group in question, (3) the nature and extent of involvement of the group with the groups that are the source of the deprivations, and (4) other factors as well. He continues, "The question of the group's diagnosis of the source of deprivation, however, also is related to its conception of an appropriate solution" (1982:330).

For Jorgensen, an explanation of the origins and persistence of the Ute Sun Dance Religion does not require reference to relative deprivation. Rather, such an explanation must refer to the *absolute deprivation* of Utes from the time they were corralled on reservations until the present. For him, the Ute Sun Dance must be understood as a religious response to conditions of *political and economic powerlessness.* Through the Sun Dance movement, Utes sought supernatural power and spiritual redemption as an alternative to the secular power denied them.

With this background, we now return to the Oraibi split. We suggest this incident may be understood as a transformative social movement. The Oraibi split occurred within the same set of political-economic conditions that spawned the other social movements discussed above. That the Oraibi split can be thought of as a transformative social movement is established by using Aberle's definitions to interpret Whiteley's account of Oraibi leaders' actions. The split was a deliberate act intended to transform the social universe. It was cataclysmic and predestined, based on Hopi prophesy. Charismatic Hopi leaders directed it. Further, it was designed to separate socially at least one of the Hopi factions from contact with European-Americans. Relevant to this last point, Hopi Indian Agent Theodore H. Lemmon described *"Ka-weis-ti-ma"* (*Kawestima,* the Hostiles' mythological homeland, to which they were to return and re-establish their home after destroying Oraibi) as "a land where no white men are to be found, and away to the North" (Whiteley 1988b:59).

Establishing that the Oraibi split may be classified as a transformative social movement does not, however, constitute an explanation, or even an explanatory sketch. It remains to show how this classification contributes to a more complete understanding of the events that occurred. Our suggestion is that Oraibi people were subjected to the same political-economic conditions between 1880 and 1920 that led other groups to adopt the Ghost Dance, Sun Dance, Peyote Religion, or other religious movements. These conditions, which Whiteley descriptively summarizes in the phrase "ecological and social near-chaos," are also accurately characterized by the explanatory terms "relative" and "absolute deprivation," as Aberle and Jorgensen define them. Oraibi's religious elite interpreted events and circumstances from the perspective of their own cultural tradition and intentionally destroyed the village. The means that Oraibi leaders selected to transform their world differed from the ways that other Southwestern groups selected. However, the conditions that led to Oraibi leaders' actions and their desire for radical change were shared by other groups. As Aberle (1982:329) points out, relative deprivation is only one component of a theory of social movements. Other components are the context of social relationships and the group's diagnosis (cultural interpretation) of the source of deprivation.

We offer as partial evidence for this interpretation of the Oraibi split not only the timing of the event and the similarity of conditions among Hopi and other Native American groups participating in different social movements around the time of the split, but also the circumstantial evidence that Hopis knew of these social movements and investigated the possibility of participating in them to remedy their own problems. As noted earlier, some Hopis visited a Havasupai performance of the Ghost Dance in 1890, and others may have taken part in a Ghost Dance that Paiutes held at Grass Springs in 1889.[11] Hopis from all three Mesas probably knew about the Ghost Dance, although they never held a Ghost Dance in their territory and never participated as a group in that movement (Dobyns and Euler 1967). Hopis also knew about the Peyote Religion, but never adopted and practiced it (La Barre 1959; Stewart 1987). It is also likely that Hopis learned of the Sun Dance Religion from Southern Ute people around the turn of the century, but we find no evidence that they ever participated in this religious movement. Our suggestion is that Oraibi religious leaders, despite being aware of the Ghost Dance, the Peyote Religion, the Sun Dance Religion, and even the various Western Apache religious movements, selected other means to cope with the corrupt conditions at Oraibi. In Aberle's terms, they diagnosed the situation, investigated and rejected the other social movements, then proceeded to find their own solution within the framework of their own religious system. Hopi mythology concerning the destruction of Oraibi apparently provided the answer.

Why didn't Hopi participate in the Ghost Dance, the Sun Dance or the Peyote Religion if they experienced conditions of relative deprivation nearly identical to those experienced by groups who did participate in one or more of these movements? According to Mooney (1896), Hopis rejected the Ghost Dance because Hopi mythology is incompatible with Ghost Dance ideology. Similarly, according to W. W. Hill (1944), Navajos rejected the Ghost Dance because of their culturally established fear of ghosts. For us, differences in mythology or beliefs about ghosts are merely part of a more general context that conditioned acceptance or rejection of specific movements. Hopis, for example, differed in culture, social organization and social structure, population size and distribution, their continued occupation of traditional lands after the establishment of reservations, and in the specific kinds and magnitudes of changes from pre- to postreservation life. Since these specifics varied, the Hopi religious elite responded differently to conditions of relative deprivation. They did not use their power over uninformed Hopis to encourage participation in religious movements originating outside Hopi culture. They used their power to destroy Oraibi, as foretold in Hopi mythology.

In summary, we submit that ideas Aberle and others developed to account for social movements can be applied with advantage to the Oraibi split. By doing so, we suggest that Clemmer's and Whiteley's contributions to our understanding of this event may be integrated and placed in a more general explanatory framework. This framework refers to external forces that impinged on the Hopis between the 1850s and early 1900s. These forces created conditions of relative deprivation at Oraibi and the other pueblos. The empowered religious elite of Oraibi interpreted these conditions from an internal perspective. They then undertook a conscious effort to remedy the ills of Hopi society by destroying Oraibi.

Since the Oraibi split, many changes have occurred among the Hopis. Some of these changes have their origins in the events of 7 September 1906. We deal with the years 1910 to 1990 in the next chapter.

7. Accommodation to the Modern World (A.D. 1910–1990)

THE MOST CONSPICUOUS FACT about the modern Hopi socio-cultural system is its incorporation into the U.S. and world political economies. The geographical and social isolation that contributed to socio-cultural persistence throughout much of Hopi history decreased rapidly after 1900. Hopi contact with European-Americans moving into northern Arizona increased. The federal government invaded many areas of Hopi life. Modern technology came to First, Second, and Third Mesas. Political-economic subordination became a reservation reality. With such intrusions came a fundamental shift in the economic basis of Hopi culture and society. A subsistence economy grounded in maize agriculture was transformed into an underdeveloped cash economy based on wage labor supplemented by income from many other sources. Such economic changes ramified throughout Hopi culture and society. Economic changes resulted in or contributed to modifications in social groups, traditional religious institutions, and political organization.

In the first section of this chapter we conclude the historical narrative started in Chapter 3. We reinitiate the chronicle of Hopi history by discussing the establishment of new Hopi villages on Third Mesa following the split of Old Oraibi. After briefly considering events of the 1920s, we focus on Hopi experiences with the "Indian New Deal" of the 1930s. Events occurring during this time included federally initiated livestock reduction and federally sanctioned formation of the Hopi Tribal Council. We then examine the years of World War II and the federal government's efforts after the war to promote Hopi economic development. We finish by considering the Navajo-Hopi land dispute and energy development on the reservation since the 1970s.

The second section of this chapter concentrates on major twentieth-century changes in Hopi culture and society. We first summarize the changes and then examine various anthropological explanations of the changes. We conclude by stressing the significance to Hopis of their in-

corporation into the national and world political-economies. We al\
examine some of the federal government's intentional and unintention\
actions that contributed to this process.

Hopi History in the Twentieth Century

As noted in Chapter 6, the fissioning of Old Oraibi led to the establishment of three new villages on Third Mesa and to the expansion and independence from Oraibi of Moenkopi Pueblo. After the disruptive events
of 6 and 7 September 1906, Hostile refugees from Oraibi traveled approximately six miles north on Third Mesa to a location known for its
reliable water supply. The site where they camped eventually became
Hotevilla Pueblo. In October, federal troops came, located the Hostile
camp, and arrested both Third and Second Mesa leaders. The federal
government sent 17 men to jail in southern Arizona for one year and 11
to Carlisle Indian School in Pennsylvania for five years. The government
sentenced the remainder to ninety days of labor in Keams Canyon
(Whiteley 1988b:62). On 3 and 4 November the army returned the Second Mesa Hostiles who remained at Hotevilla to Shongopavi. Troops also
seized 82 children at Hotevilla and took them to boarding school. On
8 November the government returned 151 Hostiles to Oraibi (Whiteley
1988b:61). Among those the government returned were Lomahongyoma and Heevi'ima, two prominent Hostile leaders. Although interactions between the returned Hostiles and Oraibi Friendlies were apparently tense, the former remained in Oraibi for about three years. Most of
the Hostiles who remained at the site of their first camp following the
Oraibi split were women and children. The government forced them to
spend the winter living in rock and brush shelters and to fend for themselves under harsh conditions (Titiev 1944:93).

In October 1906, the government forced the Friendly leader and *kikmongwi,* Tawaquaptewa, and about 20 others to leave Oraibi to attend
the Sherman Institute in Riverside, California (Titiev 1944:93). When
Tawaquaptewa and the others returned in 1909, the *kikmongwi* was
bitter toward European-Americans. He sought actions that would ensure prophesies leading to the Oraibi split were fulfilled (Whiteley
1988a:226). His bitterness and actions probably contributed to later fissioning of the pueblo.

In 1910 the federal government again attempted to allot the Hopi
Reservation, intending to divide it into small parcels of individually
owned land. This program failed everywhere except Moenkopi because
of Hopi indifference and resistance and because of the special allotting

agent's incompetence (Whiteley 1988a:152). The government abandoned allotment in 1911. Two years earlier, approximately 127 of the Hostiles who had returned to Oraibi left that village again. This time they traveled to the present site of Bacavi, where they founded that pueblo, about one mile east of Hotevilla. Twelve Hopi clans were represented among the founders of Bacavi, along with a disproportionate number of the original Oraibi religious and political leaders (Whiteley 1988b:74ff.).

With the establishment of Bacavi, more than half of Oraibi's presplit population had relocated. Between 1909 and 1911, more people left Oraibi. They did so, apparently, because Tawaquaptewa wanted to drive from Oraibi anyone motivated to become Christian or adopt other foreign ways (Titiev 1944:94). Some of these people moved to another new pueblo at the foot of Third Mesa, Kykotsmovi or New Oraibi. Others moved to Moenkopi. Moenkopi originated in the latter part of the nineteenth century as an Oraibi farming colony, but became at least partially independent economically, socially, politically, and religiously in the years following the fissioning of its parent village. Eventually, Moenkopi itself split into two factions similar to those present in Oraibi in 1906. When these two factions became identified with different areas in the pueblo, Lower Moenkopi was differentiated from Upper Moenkopi. More "conservative" individuals often reside in Lower Moenkopi. They retain closer ties with Oraibi than do the more "progressive" people living in Upper Moenkopi (Nagata 1970:49ff.).

During the years between the establishment of the new pueblos on Third Mesa and 1928, Hopi contacts with the outside world increased dramatically. Many, if not most of these contacts were with representatives of the federal government. In most of these interactions, Hopi interests were subordinated to those of the dominant sociocultural system. Shuichi Nagata summarizes this era of Hopi history, especially as reflected at Moenkopi (1970:303–304). According to Nagata, the federal government during this period consciously set out to change Moenkopi and the other Hopi pueblos. The government's paternalistic intention was to assimilate Hopis into European-American society through allotment and off-reservation education. The government treated Hopis as agency employees' "wards" and "children" (Nagata 1970:303–304).

Some of the federal government's specific actions in these years are noteworthy. For example, the government frequently incarcerated Hopis far from their home for both real and imaginary offenses. Government employees forced children (and some adults) to attend boarding schools as far away as Riverside, California, and Carlisle, Pennsylvania, or as close as the newly constructed reservation day schools (Dockstader 1979:530). The government also provided Hopis with their largest and most stable source of cash income by providing wage work at or under the auspices of the Keams Canyon and Tuba City agencies (Whiteley 1988a:155; Nagata 1970:175ff., 303). If Hopis wanted cash, they usually worked for the government in construction, farming, agency service, or off-reservation gang labor. Since many of the opportunities for wage labor were located at or near these two "agency towns," people began to move to those communities (Nagata 1970:180).

The federal government also encouraged, either directly or indirectly, the development of Hopi consumerism during these years. It did so by licensing traders among the Hopis who, in turn, imported foreign goods and regulated Hopi spending by controlling credit (Nagata 1970:213–215). Their demand for foreign goods committed Hopis to some participation in the cash economy.

The federal government also brought modern medical facilities to the Hopis during the years following the Oraibi split. Doctors and nurses provided more and better health services. The government also built hospitals (at Keams Canyon, for example, in 1913). As mentioned in Chapter 5, the arrival of Western medicine along with new standards of sanitation contributed to the growth of the Hopi population during the twentieth century (Kunitz 1973).

During this same time, nongovernment personnel also escalated their activities near and among the Hopis. Missionaries expanded their operations and built new missions at various sites on the Mesas and at Moenkopi. European-American farmers, ranchers, and miners (including Mormons from Utah) moved in large numbers to the northern Arizona–northern New Mexico region. The communities they built and populated became points of increasing contact between Hopis and the larger American society. Among other things, Hopis sought part-time employment and began to shop for food and other items in such places as Gallup, New Mexico, and Flagstaff, Holbrook, Winslow, and Tuba City, Arizona. The railroad completed in 1881 tied most of these places to the larger U.S. political economy.

In 1924 the federal Congress granted Hopis and other Native Americans U.S. citizenship. In 1926 the Secretary of the Interior commissioned the Institute of Government Research in Washington, D.C., to determine the "state" of American Indian reservations. In 1928 the results of this study concerning Indian health, welfare, and education were released as *The Problem of Indian Administration,* the so-called Meriam Report (Meriam 1928). The findings were unequivocal. Conditions on reservations were devastatingly poor. Government policy, particularly allotment, had failed miserably, primarily because the government had not "appropriated enough funds" to hire enough qualified personnel to accomplish the necessary tasks (Meriam 1928:8). The Meriam Report concluded by recommending that new procedures for improving the Indian Service be implemented. Over the next years, many of the report's suggestions became government policy.

In 1933 John Collier became Commissioner of Indian Affairs and set out to change "Indian policy" in the United States. During the Great Depression, Hopis and other Native Americans were increasingly immersed in the national political economy through Collier's "Indian New Deal" policies. These were federal programs designed to solve problems of health, welfare, and education on American Indian reservations. Such efforts were part of the larger New Deal struggle to ease depressed conditions throughout the nation. Among the prominent features of the Indian New Deal were the Public Works Administration projects. These projects involved the construction of irrigation works, roads, and agency buildings. Such efforts provided Hopis with employment opportunities until World War II. During this period, the federal government became more influential than ever before as a source of cash for the Hopis. Whiteley estimates, for example, that 57 percent of Bacavi's income in 1935 came from federally funded work projects (1988a:160 citing Leathers 1937:68).

Two additional features of the Indian New Deal affected the Hopis and their later history. The first is the initiation of livestock reduction and range management among the Navajos and Hopis between 1933 and 1937. The second is passage of the Indian Reorganization Act of 1934. This Act led to establishment of the Hopi Tribal Council in 1935.

In 1933 Collier met for the first time with representatives of the Navajo Tribe to discuss the reduction of their sheep and goat herds. Navajo herds had grown from approximately 15,000 animals in 1868 (following Navajo incarceration at Fort Sumner) to approximately 1.5 million animals in 1915. By the latter date, increasing degradation of the range had become a major problem (Aberle 1983:642). Collier's intention was to convince Navajos of the seriousness of the issue and to persuade them to reduce voluntarily the size of their herds. According to Aberle, "the BIA's livestock reduction program initiated direct government intervention in the Navajo household economy and terminated an economy based primarily on Navajo production of Navajo goods" (1983:642). It had equal significance for the Hopis.

By 1936 the Bureau of Indian Affairs decided that voluntary reduction was not enough to save the range. Hence, the government began a program of forced reductions that began with the division of the Navajo and Hopi reservations into eighteen grazing districts. Among the Hopis, whose reservation is surrounded by the Navajo Reservation, and who were never as committed to animal husbandry as their Athapaskan-speaking neighbors, the political implications of overgrazing became apparent with this division. In 1882 approximately 2.5 million acres were designated for the Hopi Reservation "for the use and occupancy of the Moqui [Hopi] and such other Indians as the Secretary of the Interior may see fit to settle thereon" (Kammer 1980:27, quoting Chester A. Arthur's executive order establishing the Hopi Reservation). Between then and 1935, Navajos had expanded beyond the boundaries of their original reservation and into Hopi territory, while the Hopis themselves restricted most of their activities to within a short distance of their Mesas.[1] Reflecting this land-use pattern, in 1936 the federal government granted the Hopis exclusive use of Grazing District 6, consisting of 499,248 acres—or approximately one-fifth of the original 1882 reservation. The remaining acreage was designated for Navajo use. Many Navajo already occupied land within the 1882 boundary.

Hopis rigorously opposed their restriction to District 6. Collier assured them that their confinement was for grazing only and would not compromise their rights to the remainder of their original reservation (Kammer 1980:41). In 1941, in acknowledgment of some Hopi demands, the government slightly expanded District 6 to 631,194 acres.[2] The significance of these events and issues becomes apparent later in Hopi history, since they are related to the Navajo-Hopi land dispute that became a central political issue for both tribes in the 1970s and 1980s. They also played a role in the reestablishment of the Hopi Tribal Council in the 1950s because some Hopis saw the Council as a means to get their land back (Clemmer 1978a).

The second significant feature of the Indian New Deal was the Indian Reorganization Act of 1934 (IRA), also known as the Wheeler-Howard Act. Congress designed this legislation to correct problems on Indian reservations (as the Meriam Report had delineated such problems) by implementing a series of economic and political reforms. Economically, the act formally ended allotment, precluded the alienation of a tribe's land or shares in a tribal corporation other than to the tribe itself, authorized the Secretary of the Interior to restore certain Indian lands and to purchase other lands for Indian use, and established a revolving credit fund from which the Secretary of the Interior could make loans to tribal corporations. Politically, the act allowed tribes to form tribal governments after having adopted approved constitutions and bylaws, allowed tribes to hire their own lawyers, and permitted tribal councils formed under the IRA to negotiate with federal, state, and local governments (see Deloria and Lytle 1983:14). The IRA's general thrust was to de-centralize federal authority over Indian peoples. Nevertheless, the Sec-retary of Interior retained control over many aspects of Native Ameri-can lives. Most tribal governments operating in the 1980s, including the Hopi Tribal Council, do so under the auspices of the 1934 IRA.

For the Hopis, adopting a constitution modeled after the U.S. Consti-tution and forming a tribal council meant fundamental changes in po-litical organization. A political system that Titiev called a "theocracy" was replaced with a Western form of democracy. Politically independent villages lost some of their autonomy when united in a pan-village orga-nization. The first step in the process was to obtain Hopi approval of the IRA. This step was accomplished through a local referendum. Next, in 1936 Collier selected the anthropologist, Oliver La Farge, to write the "Constitutions and Bylaws of the Hopi Tribe." The Hopis voted on and adopted these in a constitutional referendum on 24 October. Signifi-cantly, the results of both referenda are open to question because there is reason to believe that fewer Hopis than required by law participated in the votes and that Collier fabricated statistics to ensure passage of the constitution and bylaws and the formation of a tribal council (Clemmer 1978a:60; 1978b:25).[3] Despite people's active and passive resistance (many Hopis, for example, refused to vote), the Hopi Tribal Council was established, and all villages except Oraibi and Hotevilla sent repre-sentatives. In 1937 villages from Second Mesa withdrew their represen-tatives because the Council tried to adopt an unacceptable legal code that the Department of the Interior had written. The Council operated until 1943, when the federal government disbanded it because of its in-effectiveness in dealing with livestock reduction (Clemmer 1978a:61).[4]

During World War II, two situations developed that affected the Hopis. First, the war forced reductions in funding necessary to federal projects initiated under the IRA. This cutback significantly decreased federal employment on the reservation and required many individuals to search for cash income from other sources (Nagata 1970:181). Sec-ond, the war led to a major increase in the off-reservation experience of Hopis. Several hundred Hopi men served in the military during the war, many provided alternate service as conscientious objectors, and hun-dreds of men and women were induced to leave the reservation to work at jobs necessary to the war effort (Kennard 1965:26; Nagata 1970:181; Dockstader 1979:531; Whiteley 1988a:160, 1988b:132). For many Hopis, this constituted their first sustained off-reservation residence and contact with non-Native Americans. After the war, many, if not most, of the people who had been away returned to their homes on the reserva-tion. Others, however, decided to continue living and working in places

like Winslow and Flagstaff, Arizona (Kennard 1965:26). Since that
time, a growing number of Hopis have resided and worked away from
the reservation. According to Nagata, the increasingly available alternative of off-reservation residence and employment was the main economic effect of the war (1970:309).

Socioeconomic conditions on the reservation after the war were difficult for the Hopis. Experience away from the Mesas increased people's
demand for cash. However, jobs were scarce and unemployment was
high, while standards of health, welfare, and education were low.
Within this social and economic environment, Congress enacted the
Navajo-Hopi Long Range Rehabilitation Project of 1950. This act appropriated approximately $90 million to be spent on the reservations be-
tween 1951 and 1962. Projects funded included the construction of
schools, housing, and hospitals, the development of irrigation works
and soil and water conservation, the construction and maintenance of
roads, the construction of sewer systems, and the provision of electricity (Kelly 1953:77–81). According to Nagata, the Long Range Program
significantly changed the economic structure of the Navajo and Hopi
reservations. Funds from this program were, however, usually spent for
the improvement of reservation infrastructure to encourage companies
from off the reservation to locate there and to hire Hopis. Funds were
rarely allocated for programs conducive to local capital accumulation
and locally controlled enterprises.

A series of projects were implemented at Moenkopi and Tuba City
during the 1950s that represent similar, though less intensive development throughout the reservation. Many of the projects at Moenkopi and
throughout the reservation were funded through the Long Range Program (Nagata 1970:182–186). To begin with, an unprecedented growth
in wage work occurred (many Hopis, for example, were employed in
construction labor). The government built roads connecting the reservations to places like Flagstaff, Arizona.[5] The government began to operate a post office. Dial telephone service was set up. An air strip, complete with air control tower, was constructed. The government built a
new school and a new hospital. They constructed new federal agency
buildings to house the Bureau of Indian Affairs. The number of federal
agencies dealing with the Hopis proliferated and expanded in size
through the addition of both Hopis and non-Native American personnel. These agencies became true bureaucracies. Finally, the government
encouraged Hopis through the Relocation Service Program (established
in 1948) to seek permanent employment and residence off the reservation in cities such as Los Angeles, Denver, San Francisco, and Chicago.

In 1951 the Hopi Tribal Council was reconstituted after having been defunct since 1943. According to Richard Clemmer, revival of the Council was intimately tied to Hopi concerns over land and must be understood in the context of the effects on Hopis of the establishment of Grazing District 6 and passage of the Indian Claims Commission Act in 1946 (1978a:62–64). The latter act established a federal commission to hear Indian groups' claims against the United States arising from the loss of tribal lands. When thought appropriate, compensation was to be made to Indian peoples for their losses (Clemmer 1978a:63–64). It was the government's desire to have every Indian group file a land claim through a formally constituted tribal authority so it could proceed as quickly as possible with settlement of claims. Having compensated people for their losses, the government intended to terminate the special status for Indian peoples in the United States (Clemmer 1978a:66). Hence, the Hopis were encouraged to reconstitute a tribal government. The government did not, however, want to provide them with an opportunity to get land back, but to settle for the lands the Hopis had already lost.

In 1955 the federal government recognized the new Hopi Tribal Council. In 1958 Congress passed legislation formally allowing the Hopi and Navajo tribes to sue each other over the final dispensation of the original 1882 reservation lands. Since the establishment of grazing districts in 1936 (and their reorganization in 1943) Hopis had mostly remained within the confines of District 6. Navajos had expanded their occupation of the remainder of the districts. In 1960, in a trial heard by a three-judge federal court, the Hopi tribe sued the Navajo tribe, claiming that the entire 1882 reservation belonged exclusively to them. The Navajo countered by claiming rights to all but District 6 (Kammer 1980:46). In 1962, in a decision that the U.S. Supreme Court upheld in 1963, the court found that the Hopi and Navajo tribes had joint and equal access to the 1882 reservation (excepting District 6, which was reserved exclusively for the Hopis) and that the court had no authority to partition this Joint Use Area. The division of the Joint Use Area between the two tribes was held to be a legislative matter coming under Congressional jurisdiction.

By 1974 legal, political, and public relations efforts deeply involved both tribes in the national political arena. These actions led to the Navajo and Hopi Land Settlement Act of 1974. This federal act directed that representatives of the two tribes, with the assistance of a federally appointed mediator, begin negotiations to resolve the dispute. If this failed, the federal district court in Arizona was to partition equally the Joint Use Area and to relocate families from either tribe who resided on land eventually given to the other group. The act also (1) provided funds for relocation and incentive bonuses to families who relocated;

(2) established a three-member Navajo and Hopi Indian Relocation Commission, the members of which were to be appointed by the Secretary of the Interior; (3) provided for livestock reduction in the Joint Use Area; and (4) directed the Bureau of Land Management to sell to the Navajo tribe as many as 250,000 acres for use in relocating families from the Joint Use Area (Kammer 1980:129–130).

In 1981, following failed negotiations between the two tribes, judicial partitioning of the land, and various attempts to amend the 1974 Resolution, the federal district court provided Congress with a plan for partitioning and relocation. Upon its acceptance, the federal government began to relocate families residing in the Joint Use Area. The majority of relocated families have been Navajo.

During the years of the Navajo-Hopi land dispute, other momentous events also took place. Most significantly, the Hopis participated in various economic development projects that the Tribal Council supported. In 1969, for example, Hopis invested approximately $1.6 million, which they had obtained from mineral leases, to construct a factory for the manufacture of B.V.D. undergarments. The factory operated until 1975 (Clemmer 1978a:69). More importantly, however, the Tribal Council participated in mineral development on the reservation. In 1961 the Secretary of the Interior authorized the Hopi Tribal Council to lease Hopi land. By 1963 the Council had signed $3 million in oil and gas exploration leases (Clemmer 1978b:27). In 1964 Peabody Coal Company signed a lease with the Navajo Tribe allowing for strip mining of 40,000 acres on the Navajo Reservation. In 1966 the Hopi Tribal Council signed a lease with Peabody allowing for strip mining of 25,000 acres in the Joint Use Area (Clemmer 1978b:17). They signed additional leases with Peabody to provide 38 billion gallons of water for processing the coal that would be burned at power plants.

Mining operations began on Black Mesa in 1970. The coal from the Navajo and Hopi reservations is used to generate electricity at the Page and Four Corners power plants. Electricity from Navajo and Hopi coal goes predominantly to southern California, Phoenix and Tucson, Arizona, and Las Vegas, Nevada. The tribes use revenue from the coal leases to support the activities of their tribal councils. In 1978 the Hopi Tribal Council received over $900,000 as a result of Peabody operations (Clemmer 1978b:32). Steady income from such leases is vital to the continuation of the Tribal Council. For this compensation, Hopis assume the costs of environmental degradation, the loss of water, and increased air pollution. Few Hopis have been employed in the Peabody Coal development.

In the 1990s, issues of land and water and of acceptance or rejection

of foreign influence remain central to the Hopis (Clemmer 1979; Whiteley 1988a). The latter issue is reflected by the continuing presence of
"traditional" and "progressive" political factions. Traditionalists have
ideological views similar to those of the earlier Hostiles. Progressives
have ideological ties to earlier Friendlies and contemporary political
bonds to the Hopi Tribal Council (Clemmer 1978a, 1978b, 1979;
Whiteley 1988a:233ff.). The two factions have opposed one another in
both formal and informal ways over a variety of issues, including acceptance of Western material culture, formation of the Tribal Council, development of mineral resources, and the relocation of Navajo from the
Joint Use Area. In each of these cases, Traditionalists have adopted the
culturally conservative position. Some of these issues are explored further in the next section of this chapter.

Sociocultural Persistence and Change

In this section, we summarize six examples of Hopi sociocultural
change between 1910 and 1990, along with anthropological discussions
of the processes involved. These changes or trends in the Hopi sociocultural system are (1) an increase in population, accompanied by expanded off-reservation residence and increased residence in reservation
"agency towns"; (2) a shift in the economic basis of society from subsistence agriculture to wage labor; (3) the adoption of many items of Western material culture; (4) a decline in the relevance of lineages, clans,
and phratries to the organization of social life, coupled with an increase
in the significance of nuclear family households; (5) a decline in the importance of the traditional religious system; and (6) a secularization of
political institutions.

As noted in Chapter 5, Hopi population has increased throughout
the twentieth century, although at different rates during different decades (Kunitz 1973). Population estimates for the Hopis as a whole are
provided in Figure 5. Population estimates for individual villages, including agency towns, are provided in Table 7.

According to Stephen Kunitz (1973:14), the establishment (and con-
traction) of the Hopi Reservation, the arrival and implementation of
Western medicine (with its effects on the birth and death rates), and
Hopi participation in the wage economy all affected Hopi demography.
In addition to general population growth among the Hopis, two signifi-
cant demographic trends emerged in the mid-twentieth century. The
first is movement off the reservation by a relatively large number of
Hopis. The second is the disproportionate growth of the "agency

Table 7. Twentieth-Century Hopi Population by Village[a]

Village	1900	1910	1930[j]	1940	1950	1960	1980[k]
Polacca[b]	20		787			530	667
Sichomovi	119		315				
Walpi	205		163				
Hano[c]	160		309		164	230	218
Mishongnovi	244		266				
Shongopavi	225		307				536
Shipaulovi	126		123				
Oraibi[d]	905	220	87		119		142
Hotevilla[e]	—		418				385
Bacavi[f]	—		127	143	141	145	237
Kykotsmovi[g]	—		355				477
Moenkopi[h]	200	182	388	409	500	597	654
Total[i]	2,204	2,100	3,645	3,444	3,528	5,176	8,000

[a]All the figures contained in this table are estimates; they should be evaluated accordingly.

[b]Polacca is an agency town founded at the east base of First Mesa in 1888. Some population figures are from Stanislawski (1979). Keams Canyon, another agency town near First Mesa, was founded in the late 1800s, and a school was built there in 1887. Stanislawski estimated the 1975 population of Keams Canyon to have been 252.

[c]Some population figures are from Stanislawski (1979). In the 1980s Tewa constituted perhaps one-third of the First Mesa population and one-tenth of the total Hopi population.

[d]Titiev estimated the Oraibi population in 1930 at 112 and in 1970 at about 130 (1972:327).

[e]Hotevilla is a Third Mesa village founded by "Hostiles" after the Oraibi split.

[f]Bacavi is a Third Mesa Village founded after the Oraibi split. Some population figures are from Whiteley (1988a:130–136). Whiteley's figure of 145 is for Bacavi in 1968.

[g]Kykotsmovi, New Oraibi, is an agency town founded at the foot of Third Mesa after the split of Old Oraibi.

[h]Moenkopi was originally an Oraibi farming colony near Tuba City. It expanded in 1909. Population figures are from Nagata (1970:224, 227).

[i]Some of the total figures are based on Kunitz (1974). Kunitz estimated the 1901 population at 1,841, the 1905 population at 2,100, the 1930 population at 2,752, and the 1934 population at 2,538. Dozier estimated the 1950 total Hopi population at 4,405 (1970). Nagata estimated the Hopi population in 1904 at 1,878, in 1912 at 2,272, in 1930 between 2,336 and 2,848, in 1932 at 3,647, in 1943 at 4,100, and in 1962 at 4,000 (1970:224). Before the 1930s less than 10 percent of the total Hopi population resided off the reservation. In the 1950s perhaps 20 percent of the total Hopi population resided off the reservation (see Whiteley 1988a: 133–134). In the 1960s the figure had risen to perhaps 25 percent; in the 1970s, to perhaps 30 percent (see Nagata 1970:226, 228). By the 1980s possibly 35 percent of the Hopi population resided off the reservation. Again, these figures should be taken as estimates.

[j]The 1930 figures are from Colton and Baxter (1932). Most of their figures are, undoubtedly, inflated.

[k]Some 1980 figures are estimated from U.S. Census data.

towns," Moenkopi, Kykotsmovi, Keams Canyon, and Polacca. As stated, off-reservation residence and employment became consequential among the Hopis only during and after World War II. Precise figures for Hopi off-reservation residence are lacking. The following data, however, partially demonstrate the trend. Before the war, less than 10 percent of the total Hopi population resided away from the reservation. In 1937, for example, less than 10 Bacavi people resided off the reservation.[6] That number represented less than 10 percent of the total Bacavi population. By 1950 the Bacavi figure had risen to almost 20 percent. In 1962 approximately 24 percent of the Hopi people lived off-reservation, and the number was increasing (Nagata 1970:226). In 1970 approximately 30 percent of Moenkopi families resided away from the reservation (Nagata 1970:228), and there were at least 761 Hopis living in Holbrook, Winslow, and Flagstaff, Arizona in 1971 (Kunitz 1973:13). These data indicate that over 10 percent of the total Hopi population at that time lived in these three cities alone. By 1980 the number of Bacavi residents who lived away from their pueblo had increased to 35.3 percent.

Education and employment are apparently the two most common Hopi motivations for off-reservation residence. People usually leave the pueblos to attend school or to work, either temporarily or permanently (Nagata 1970:187, 218; Whiteley 1988b:132). While away from the reservation, individuals encounter a way of life distinct from the one described earlier in this book. Hopis residing in Los Angeles, Denver, Albuquerque, or Washington, D.C., share much of their lifestyle with other people living and working in the urban centers of the United States. They have beliefs and values based not only on Hopi traditions, but also on their own education and experiences in the modern world. They are likely to be concerned with unemployment, crime, and nuclear proliferation. They are apt to root for the Los Angeles Lakers, Denver Broncos, Houston Astros, or other teams. This is not to say, however, that Hopis who become interested in global politics or professional sports must abandon their interests in, for example, the performance of traditional *katchina* dances on the reservation. To the contrary, there is no reason to expect them to do so.

As is true for other Native Americans who reside away from their homes, many Hopis eventually return to live on their reservation. Economic considerations, again, play a major role in such decisions. Individuals frequently move off the reservation to find work. If they are unable to find a well-paying job, if the work they find is temporary or unstable, if they become unemployed, or if the cost of living in the city becomes too high, people customarily return home. Jobs may pay less on and around the reservation, but living expenses are reduced, and a network of kin and friends is available for mutual support. There might also be certain satisfactions gained from working with and for other Hopis, rather than for a large business or multinational corporation.

Economic considerations are not the only motivation for returning to reside on the reservation. Nagata suggests that Hopis residing away from the reservation lose something of their Hopi identity (1971:132). If this loss of identity occurs and is assumed to be undesirable (as Hopis themselves suggest), and if people living in cities miss their association with and support from friends and relatives on the Mesas, there would be additional grounds for returning home. Such personal motivations are probably even more critical to some people than purely economic considerations.

The second additional trend in Hopi demography is the concentration of people in agency towns on the reservation. These are communities that grew up around schools, missions, trading posts, federal agencies, and tribal agencies that entered Hopi territory after the 1880s. At the turn of the twentieth century, these communities possessed few people. Polacca (located at the eastern foot of First Mesa), for example, was established in 1888 with the construction of the First Mesa day school. In 1900 Polacca had approximately 20 Hopi residents (Stanislawski 1979:590). By 1975 Polacca had approximately 800 Hopi residents, representing perhaps 40 or 50 percent of the First Mesa population and perhaps 10 percent of the total Hopi population. The growth of other agency towns is not as dramatic, but still impressive (see Table 7). If we conservatively assume (since precise figures are lacking) that the total number of Hopis is approximately 8,000, that 25 percent of this number resides away from the reservation (leaving 6,000 Hopis in Moenkopi and on the reservation), and that a total of 2,000 Hopis reside in the four agency towns (Moenkopi, Kykotsmovi, Keams Canyon, and Polacca), then approximately 33 percent of the Hopi Reservation population resides today in these relatively new communities.

The development of Hopi agency towns is significant because they are different socially and culturally from the other, older Hopi communities. Nagata agrees and argues that agency towns (our term) are larger (with populations of a thousand or more), have more ethnic diversity, more occupational diversity, more services and amenities, and a higher standard of living. He also suggests that Indians in agency towns are less subject to "psychological alienation" than those in off-reservation cities. For Nagata, agency towns represent "urbanization" on the reservation (1971:117).

Hopi agency towns are, thus, larger, more "modern" (having more paved roads, newer housing, and more service facilities), and more heterogeneous socially and ethnically. Such heterogeneity develops since non-Hopis living on the reservation are more likely to reside in agency towns than other places. Hopis from different pueblos are more likely to work and interact in communities such as Kykotsmovi than in one of the smaller pueblos on the Mesas. People who have resided away from the reservation are more apt to return to live in agency towns than in other Hopi villages. Further, Hopi agency towns are centers of economic and political power on the reservation. Jobs are highly concentrated in these communities since the federal and tribal governments continue to be among the largest employers on the reservation, and since nongovernment jobs, for example those in service industries, are also more numerous there. Political power is concentrated in agency towns because of the interrelated factors of disproportionate size, the concentration of economic power, and the presence of federal and tribal governments. Political decisions that affect Hopi lives (such as the signing of leases with Peabody Coal) are made by individuals living in agency towns. These people act as mediators between the Hopis and national or world political-economic powers. Many such individuals have been educated or have worked off the reservation and have returned to assume their new positions.

Spicer discusses the development of agency towns on reservations as a small scale "rural-urban" pattern (1962:468). Nagata concurs and, as indicated, pursues Spicer's analysis. For them, the relationship between an agency town such as Polacca and a pueblo like Walpi is analogous to the relationship between an urban center such as Phoenix and a rural area like that surrounding Snowflake, Arizona. We find merit in their descriptions and develop related ideas later by following the insight of Jorgensen (1971, 1972, 1978) in his use of "dependency theory." These ideas provide one means of understanding the twentieth-century development of socioeconomic conditions on the Hopi Reservation, including the expansion of agency towns.

The second major trend in Hopi culture and society during the twentieth century is a shift from an economy based on subsistence agriculture to one focused on wage labor (Titiev 1944, 1972; Beaglehole 1937; Eggan 1950; Bradfield 1971; Kennard 1965; Clemmer 1978a; Whiteley 1988a, 1988b). At the time of the Oraibi split, Hopis relied almost exclusively on locally produced agricultural products, most notably maize, beans, and squash. Either clans or clan segments (perhaps even individual families) controlled the agricultural lands (Titiev 1944; Eggan 1950; Whiteley 1985, 1986). A man usually worked either the fields of his own or of his wife's descent group. Agriculture was supplemented by sheep herding, trading, orchard husbandry, and, for some, temporary wage labor. Wage employment was frequently in construction or freighting for the government, missionaries, and traders.

During the years under consideration, the traditional subsistence economy was replaced by a cash economy centered on wage labor. For many, if not most, Hopis, agriculture is now a part-time activity. The amount of cultivated land at the Hopi Mesas has actually decreased despite the significant increase in population (Bradfield 1971:31ff.; Nagata 1970:120; Whiteley 1988a:139–141). Sheep herding is almost nonexistent in many pueblos, though it has been partially replaced by cattle ranching.[7] Peach and apricot orchards have declined. Hunting and the gathering of wild plants is now motivated by nonutilitarian considerations.

Today, people participate in many different capacities in the local wage labor economy, which is tied to the national and world economies. As noted, the commitment to this new economic system intensified with the Indian New Deal, World War II, and the Navajo-Hopi Long Range Rehabilitation Project of 1950. In the twenty-five-year period since these events (and continuing into the 1990s), increasing numbers of Hopis have sought wage employment either on or off the reservation. The search for employment has contributed significantly to the increase in off-reservation residence discussed earlier and to an increase in residential instability, as people relocate for economic reasons. An individual might, for example, move from Walpi to work in Flagstaff, return to Walpi for many different reasons, and then move to Kykotsmovi to work for the tribal government.

Either directly or indirectly, federal and tribal governments have always provided the most reservation jobs. In the 1930s, people worked on Public Works Administration projects. In the 1940s, people engaged in labor supportive of the war effort (primarily off-reservation). In the 1950s, people worked at jobs funded under the Long Range Program. Since then, federal and tribal bureaucracies have employed Hopis in jobs ranging from construction worker to tribal president, from economist to nurse, from police officer to lawyer. During this period, federal and tribal governments also have funded numerous projects such as road and housing construction. Private companies perform these jobs using some Hopi labor. Non-Hopis control the majority of these companies.

Through its profound involvement as a source of employment in the Hopi economy, the federal government has always exerted control over economic development on the reservation. When federal policy leads to an abundance of funds for domestic spending (as it did in the 1960s during President Johnson's administration), for example, employment on the reservation is relatively high. When federal policy leads to cuts in funds for domestic spending (as it did during President Reagan's tenure), unemployment on the reservation increases, and the economic state of reservation communities suffers. In either case, government actions originating far from the Hopi Mesas determine economic conditions on the reservation.

Similar federal power over the Hopi economy is reflected in other events in twentieth-century Hopi history, including livestock reduction, the establishment of the Hopi Tribal Council, the negotiation of mineral leases on the reservation, and the settlement of the Navajo-Hopi land dispute. We discuss the issue of control later in this chapter.

Anthropologists have focused on several interrelated processes in their explanations for the abandonment of subsistence agriculture (and other traditional economic activities) for participation in the modern cash economy. Bradfield, for example, discusses the marginality of the original economy because of the aridity of the northern Arizona environment (1971:31ff.). When agricultural fields were lost to erosion, there might have been impetus to replace farming activities with other gainful pursuits, such as wage labor for a government agency. Agricultural risk, then, might be a significant factor contributing to the rise of wage labor.[8] Nagata also mentions the Hopi desert environment as a factor contributing to peripheral Hopi participation in the developing U.S. economy in the early twentieth century (1970:212).

Other explanations to account for the shift in the economic basis of Hopi society are based on the breakdown of Hopi isolation and increasing contact with European-American society. Whiteley, for example, explains the decreasing significance of sheep herding (the second-most important economic activity in 1900) by reference to the difficulties that livestock reduction imposed, coupled with other economic forces (1988a:142–143). Nagata refers to the increased Hopi demand for Western goods that trading posts and stores in towns surrounding the reservation created. This demand committed Hopis to the pursuit of cash through wage labor (1970:213).

Arguments such as those in the preceding paragraph stress the importance of *culture contact* and *acculturation* in the process of economic change. Nagata goes further in his analysis of economic change in Moenkopi. He focuses on two sets of particularly consequential factors (1970:212–222). Nagata's second set of factors relates to Moenkopi's special relationship to Oraibi and to the Navajo, among whom Moenkopi people reside. We will not review them here. The first set of factors is notable since these factors also affect other Hopi communities. These are factors that make all Hopi communities marginal to (unintegrated with) the national economy and help perpetuate the traditional subsistence economy. Among the first set of factors are (1) isolation due to the desert environment, the lack of easily accessible mineral resources, the long distances to major towns, and a culturally different labor force; (2) the government's control of land capital, exclusion of outside capital, and failure to provide incentives for local capital accumulation; and (3) the Hopis' contact with the national consumer market. Pertaining to the last feature, Nagata suggests that the government fostered Hopi consumerism as a way to "civilize" them. Nevertheless, Hopis remained isolated from such mercantile markets because of low income, communication and transportation difficulties, market conditions, lack of stores, and the government's conscious control of reservation trading posts (Nagata 1970:212–213). For Nagata, *marginality* and *government control* emerge as central forces for Hopi economic persistence and change.

Clemmer's analysis of Hopi socioeconomic change is similar in some ways to Nagata's. He uses concepts such as "directed culture change" and the "metropolis-satellite" political-economic model to stress the "superordination and coercion" European-Americans employed in their contact relationships with Hopis (Clemmer 1978a:20–21). Directed culture change refers to contact situations within which (1) individuals from one society are subject to sanctions from another society; and (2) the sanctions applied by the latter are intended to change the culture and society of the former (see Spicer 1961:520–521; Clemmer 1978a:21). According to Clemmer, the federal government has acted to direct contact with Native Americans, including the Hopis, in many ways. The government has (1) used the constant threat of force to enforce its laws, (2) used compulsory education to control children, (3) applied its laws unilaterally, (4) given the Secretary of the Interior ultimate authority over "most Indian affairs," (5) subjected Indians to a foreign judicial system, (6) provided legal protection to European-American business interests in their dealings with Indians, (7) imposed a foreign political system on Indians, and (8) fostered missionary work (1978a:21). For Clemmer, the events of Hopi history provide concrete examples of his generalizations. Answers to questions about economic change must be provided by looking at the larger context in which they occur. The course of Hopi economic history in the twentieth century has been determined largely by the interests of the superordinate and coercive society. We return to the metropolis-satellite model later in this chapter.

The third major change in Hopi culture and society during the period under review is the adoption of innumerable items of modern material culture. Hopis have accepted many twentieth-century technological innovations. At the turn of this century, Hopi technology and material culture were similar to what they had been since the Spanish arrived with new tools, technology, and domesticated plants and animals. Perhaps the most notable addition up to 1900 was the horse and wagon, which revolutionized transportation. In 1909 only five Bacavi men owned wagons (Whiteley 1988b:133).

Since the turn of the century, Hopis have been as affected by modern technology as the rest of the world. Pickup trucks arrived in the 1930s and began to replace burros, horses, and wagons (Whiteley 1988b:133). In the 1950s (with the increased number of paved roads) cars and trucks became even more popular. Since then they have become an essential part of modern reservation life. According to Titiev, the most "drastic" changes in Hopi material culture have been the result of the new roads and cars (1972:336–337; also see Kennard 1965:27).

Other important technological innovations that Hopis have accepted include irrigation works, plows, tractors, modern housing, electricity, telephones, clocks, household appliances, and television sets (Kennard 1965; Nagata 1970; Titiev 1972; Whiteley 1988a, 1988b). There is nothing surprising in such changes in Hopi material culture. These changes mirror similar ones in the rest of the United States, although they customarily arrive and are adopted later on the Mesas than in Los Angeles and New York.

Two points, however, need to be made about Hopi acceptance of modern technology. First, Hopi "traditional" and "progressive" political factions have sometimes hotly debated such acceptance. On occasion, traditionalists have strongly disapproved of "modern conveniences" (like paved roads, electricity, and modern plumbing) in their villages. Clemmer documents one example of this opposition. At Hotevilla, in 1968, the majority of that pueblo's residents bitterly fought the extension of electric utilities to their village (1978a:73–77). According to Clemmer, such opposition is intimately tied to issues of "sovereignty and independence versus assimilation and dependence" (1978a:74). Whiteley concurs when he suggests that differences in lifestyle between traditional and progressive individuals is relative. He notes that Hotevilla lacks some (but not all) of the modern technology found at Bacavi. The difference between the two pueblos has not emerged, however, because Hotevilla individuals do not want modern conveniences. The difference stems from the latter's demand for "full individual control of these amenities . . ." (Whiteley 1988a:233). Local control is the issue.

The second point we make about Hopi endorsement of modern technology is that the demand for Western material culture played a role in Hopi commitment to participation in the wage labor economy. We discussed this relationship earlier.

   The fourth major trend in Hopi culture and society of the modern period is a decline in the significance of lineages, clans, and phratries. This decline is accompanied by an increase in the importance of nuclear families as residential and economic units. The import of this claim, however, varies depending on the descriptive and explanatory perspective of the anthropologists who have dealt with Hopi social organization and structure. As noted in earlier chapters, anthropologists disagree about the different categories, groups, and levels of Hopi social structure. For Titiev and Eggan, Hopi lineages and clans were discrete, corporate groups controlling both ceremonies and agricultural lands. Lineages and clans possessed an estate to which individuals had access by virtue of their descent-group memberships (Titiev 1944; Eggan 1950). According to Whiteley, "the conventional [anthropological] view of Hopi descent groups as solidary corporations reflects structural-functional theoretical bias," rather than being an accurate description of traditional Hopi social structure (1988a: 185; 1985, 1986).

   Whatever the truth in this matter, in the past, Hopi descent groups were more intimately associated with ceremonies and agricultural lands than they are in the latter part of the twentieth century (Nagata 1970: 94, 110–111, 244; Whiteley 1988a: 173, 185). With a decline of earlier subsistence patterns and ritual practices, the "functions" and "meanings," if not "corporateness" and "solidarity" of lineages, clans, and phratries have changed. At present, descent-group membership is significant primarily as a component of an individual's personal identity.[9] Descent-group membership is also significant because of its role in regulating marriage (clan and phratry exogamy persist), and because it provides individuals with a network of potential cooperators and supporters (Whiteley 1988a: 172ff.). However, contemporary Hopi lineages, clans, and phratries are not discrete, corporate economic groups possessing a common estate.

   According to Nagata, Whiteley, and others, changes in Hopi descent groups are related to some of the sociocultural changes discussed in this chapter. If Hopi lineages and clans are less intimately tied to land and ceremonies, it is partly because the economy and religious systems have changed. Economic changes are particularly important. Nagata suggests, for example, that the foundation of lineage solidarity (at Moenkopi) collapsed because of "participation in the cash economy through wage work," and because of government encouragement of individual land ownership (1970: 250). Participation in the cash economy discouraged cooperation among groups of kin larger than the nuclear family. Hence, the latter emerged as the primary corporate economic unit during the twentieth century (1970: 240–245, 299, 313). Although nuclear family households were probably important at other times and places among the Hopis (Whiteley 1988a:165–172), their significance has likely increased in the modern world as cash-earning activities became a primary concern of individual families. If so, modern economic conditions, including economically motivated residential instability and neo-locality, likely decreased the significance of larger descent groups and increased solidarity within nuclear family households.

The fifth fundamental change in Hopi culture and society during the twentieth century is the widespread decline in the importance of ancestral religious institutions. At most pueblos, the majority of ceremonies in the traditional ritual cycle have been abandoned (Nagata 1970:94, 240–244, 292–293; Titiev 1972:337ff.; Whiteley 1988a: 198ff.). In the 1980s, some pueblos performed only relatively secular *katchina* dances, and possibly only Shongopavi on Second Mesa performs a full, annual ceremonial cycle. Even Hotevilla, one of the most conservative villages, no longer performs some of the ceremonies. And, according to Titiev, the loss of ceremonies at Old Oraibi represents the most momentous change at that pueblo (1970:337). Further, at most pueblos membership in religious societies or sodalities has seriously declined (Nagata 1970:94, 292–293; Whiteley 1988a:195). Young people are being initiated into the religious groups responsible for Hopi health and welfare, including rain and agricultural plenty, far less frequently. As a result, the esoteric knowledge that Hopi priests traditionally possessed is being lost, as one generation fails to pass it on to the next. As noted in Chapters 2 and 6, such knowledge constituted the foundation of power for the Hopi religious and political elite (Whiteley 1988a; Upham 1982, 1989). As this knowledge erodes, the elite's power and authority deteriorates.

With this deterioration, distinctions between Hopi social classes also fail, since such differences are based on the possession of esoteric knowledge and the power to influence the course of events supernaturally, rather than on differential access to economic resources (Whiteley 1988a:65–69). Whiteley acknowledges that many twentieth-century Hopi changes, especially in the economic realm, result from the "acculturative" influences of European-American society.[10] He emphasizes, however, that other changes, especially pertaining to social structure, "derive from decline of the politico-religious system" (1988a:273):

> Disappearance of the higher-order societies entails the absence of a traditional system of offices and the perceived elimination of powerful supernatural forces that animated the meta-dynamics of all Hopi social action. The main component of *pavansinom* ["powerful people"] status was inher-

ited ritual knowledge and its attendant transformative power, the demise of which has left everyone nowadays *sukavungsinom* ["common people"]. In short, the Oraibi split as a social "revolution" effectively abolished the Third Mesa "class system."

Also associated with the loss of traditional religious institutions, knowledge, and power, and of the authority of traditional religious leaders is the decline of religiously based ethical standards that were fundamental to the organization of Hopi life. According to Whiteley, his consultants relate this directly to a decline in community solidarity (1988a: 273). As noted in Chapter 5, anthropologists have used the religious elite's power to enforce cultural conservatism as a partial explanation for sociocultural persistence among the Hopis. With the decline of the religious elite and of the ethical system that they enforced, cultural conservatism also waned (Eggan 1964:182; Titiev 1972:337–338). The decline of Hopi cultural conservatism, perhaps, contributes to other changes documented in this chapter.

The sixth major change in Hopi society and culture of the twentieth century is secularization of the political system. This change is closely related to the decline of older religious institutions. Traditional Hopi religious and political institutions were inseparable. Political leaders were the chief priests of villages. Political decision making was religious deliberation. This situation has changed in the twentieth century. Religious institutions and the power of religious leaders have declined. The federal government created the Hopi Tribal Council and supports its authority. Many, if not most, of the political actions now influencing Hopis' lives originate with that elected body. Tribal and federal enforcement agencies help to maintain social order.

Significant Hopi opposition remains, however, to secular leadership. Traditionalists frequently oppose progressive supporters of the Tribal Council on many political issues. Such issues often relate to village sovereignty, modernization, and land. Traditional pueblos (e.g., Hotevilla, Old Oraibi, Lower Moenkopi, and the three Second Mesa villages) have sometimes refused to send representatives to the Tribal Council. Traditional leaders have even tried to sue the Council in federal court over issues surrounding energy development (Clemmer 1978a, 1978b, 1979). Nevertheless, the secular Tribal Council is likely to remain central to modern Hopi politics, and there is little likelihood that earlier religious leadership will reemerge to dominate the political scene.

Explanations for the decline of Hopi religious institutions and the secularization of political organization are frequently embedded in more general explanations for sociocultural change, such as those that Nagata and Clemmer provide. Anthropologists have, for example, included reduced participation in ceremonies as one example of acculturation resulting from increased culture contact. This view is represented in Titiev's work. He suggests that Hopis in Old Oraibi participate less frequently in traditional ceremonies because their attention is directed "outward . . . , especially in such matters as jobs, shopping, and entertainment" (Titiev 1972:337). He accounts for this change in attention by referring to new roads and cars. For Titiev, the construction of roads, the breakdown of isolation, and culture contact led to a loss of interest in the old ceremonies. These factors led to a "marked indifference" of younger people in the perpetuation of old Hopi customs and beliefs (1972:337–342). When key priests died without having trained successors (because younger people were not interested in the rigors of traditional Hopi religious life), their knowledge was lost, and ceremonial life decayed as people became less willing to perform their duties. When the ceremonies ceased, their connection to political life also stopped. Further, according to Titiev, culture contact introduced Western technology and an expansion of human control over the world and everything in it. Since modern technology (for example, modern irrigation systems) "brought more . . . under human control, there has been less reliance on the supernatural" (1972:337–338). This process, in Titiev's explanation, contributed to the indifference of younger generations toward Hopi religion.

Whiteley provides a different analysis of the twentieth-century demise of Hopi religious/political institutions. For him, the key to understanding the present is in the past; in this case, in the Oraibi split. As discussed in Chapter 6, Whiteley views the split as a deliberate act perpetrated on common Hopis by their religious leaders. The latter intentionally divided the pueblo because of circumstances that, in their interpretation, fulfilled the conditions of Hopi prophesy. The prophesy demanded Oraibi's destruction. It also required termination of the traditional ritual system. In the twentieth century, Hopi ceremonies declined (at least at Oraibi and Bacavi) because earlier leaders had decided that they should. Religious leaders stopped performing ceremonies and ceased initiating successors deliberately. Culture contact was significant primarily because it contributed to conditions that the religious elite interpreted in a particular way. According to Whiteley, one reason to prefer his interpretation of the Oraibi split over anthropologists' explanations is that it also accounts for the decline of Hopi religious societies and ceremonies (1988a:275–277).

Hopi Political Economy

The above changes are related to Hopi incorporation into the national and international political economies. We turn, now, to this topic.

Political economists are often concerned with economic development and with the distribution of the costs and benefits of growth. They focus on the loci of control over resources and surpluses, because such control is considered central to economic developmental processes. Within political-economic analysis, there are two major schools of thought concerning economic development. The two schools are distinguished by their identification of and concentration on different loci of power and control. Marxist scholars concentrate on internal class structure and ideology as keys to understanding the control of surplus (hence, development) within any society. Dependency theorists focus on the exploitative external relationships between groups, societies, or nations (Frank 1967, 1979, 1984).

Earlier in this chapter, we referred to Clemmer's and Jorgensen's use of dependency theory and of the metropolis-satellite model to understand socioeconomic development and underdevelopment among Native Americans (Jorgensen 1971, 1972, 1978; Clemmer 1978a). In the metropolis-satellite model of economic development, which is based on the work of Paul Baran (1957) and André Gunder Frank (1967, 1979, 1984), metropolises are social spheres within which economic and political power are concentrated. Satellites are areas lacking in significant concentrations of either type of power. In Jorgensen's terms, both metropolises and satellites have "locus" and "nexus" (1978:3). Locus refers to the association of metropolises with urban areas and of satellites with rural areas. Nexus refers to the concentration or absence of political and economic power in these locations and to the political and economic relationships between areas of greater and lesser power. Other scholars use the terms "core" or "center," "periphery," and "semi-periphery" to denote similar concepts (e.g., Wallerstein 1974, 1980).

Metropolises, as centers for economic and political intercourse, have an exploitative relationship with their satellites. Metropolises exert monopolistic control over resources and surpluses. Hence, they also control development of such resources and surpluses. Metropolises develop economically and serve the interests of their ruling classes at the expense of satellites. Metropolises expropriate from satellites both capital and surpluses. Metropolises contribute to their own development by controlling development in satellites. They accomplish this in a variety of ways. A metropolis might simply expropriate (using military force, if needed) satellite land and resources as such land and resources become necessary to its growth and expansion. A metropolis might provide funds for satellite development that are designed to support its own expansion, rather than independence and growth of the satellite. Metropolises might provide money (perhaps in the form of tax incentives) to corporations for the extraction of raw materials from satellite land. Raw materials and the products (or energy) they provide, along with any profits generated, might flow to the metropolis, rather than remain in the satellite. Finally, a metropolis might establish legal and bureaucratic institutions to ensure control over and cooperation by its satellites. Individuals from the periphery who challenge metropolis control might be subject to external sanctions by the metropolis.

The metropolis-satellite model does not imply a simple two-member relationship. Rather, it represents "a whole chain of constellations of metropoles and satellites" (Frank 1984:101). Jorgensen says that the model denotes a "pyramidal structure of political and economic power positions (nexus), and these power positions comprise a discernible ordering in space (locus)" (1978:4). Within such a pyramid, any "unit" (e.g., city, state, or nation) may be defined by its political-economic relationship to the other units. Units with less political and economic power are satellite to those with greater power. Within this model, Flagstaff, Arizona, might simultaneously be satellite to Phoenix and metropolis to Polacca. While being satellite to Flagstaff, Polacca might be metropolis to other First Mesa villages.

As Jorgensen mentions, the metropolis-satellite model implies that metropolis development (through unequal exchanges with satellites) promotes the social, economic, and political underdevelopment of satellites. Underdevelopment is created because metropolises siphon off satellite resources and surpluses to promote their own growth. Hence, underdevelopment is generated by the same processes that lead to development. The survival of archaic institutions and traditions and low capital in peripheral groups does not, by itself, create underdevelopment.

We suggest, concurring with Clemmer (1978a, 1978b), that recent Hopi history and sociocultural change is profitably understood within the metropolis-satellite framework. Twentieth-century Hopi sociocultural change has not resulted simply from a breakdown in isolation, contact with European-American society, and acculturation. Rather, such change is the result of contact and exchange characterized by domination, exploitation, and internal colonialism. Phrased simply, the Hopis are satellite to the larger U.S. metropolis. Hopi land, resources, and labor have been systematically exploited, and their surpluses expropriated for the benefit of the dominant sociopolitical system. The Hopi economy is not a dual economy with a mixture of subsistence agriculture and wage labor, as Nagata suggests (1970). It is an underdeveloped satellite economy.

Expropriation of Hopi resources and the creation of Hopi dependency and underdevelopment have been largely accomplished through the federal government's intentional and unintentional activities. The federal government created the Hopi Reservation within the context of a general effort to confine the movements of Native Americans and free land for the European-American expansion westward. Federal agencies forced Hopi children to attend school with the goal of eliminating their native language, beliefs, and customs. The government forced livestock reduction and partitioning of the reservation. Hopis opposed both of these programs for economic and cultural reasons. Within the framework of the IRA, federal agencies coerced and cajoled the Hopis into accepting a form of political organization permissible to the U.S. government, but damaging to the position and authority of traditional leaders. Federal agencies disbanded the Council when it failed to implement effectively the externally imposed plan of livestock reduction.[11] The government later encouraged re-formation of the Council to settle land claims, achieve termination of the special legal status afforded Hopis, and provide a tribal body legally able (according to federal law) to sign leases permitting the extraction from Hopi land of mineral resources. To support such extraction and other economic activities conducive to the growth of the metropolis, the federal government invested large sums of money (under the Long Range Plan) to develop Hopi infrastructure. The government did not provide similar funds to support local capital accumulation and independent economic growth, even though termination of federal responsibility for the Hopis was also part of the Long Range Plan.

The economic consequences of these events are manifest. The Hopi economy in the latter part of the twentieth century remains dependent on jobs and funds that the federal government and externally controlled private corporations provide. The extraction of minerals from Hopi land provides significant income to the Tribal Council, but profits from these and other activities go largely to multinational corporations and to state and federal governments in the form of taxes. Surpluses are siphoned away from the reservation, and little capital accumulation (required for independent economic growth) is generated. The Hopis provide labor and raw materials to the metropolis. They consume the finished products furnished by the dominant sociocultural system.[12]

The modern creation of economic underdevelopment among the Hopis has affected their entire sociocultural system. Many of the changes discussed earlier are, at least in part, associated with the economic and political forces now under consideration. For example, the rise of agency towns represents the development of metropolis-satellite relationships on the reservation. Economic and political power are concentrated in these communities. A new local elite (composed of workers for federal and tribal agencies; Nagata 1970:186–187) resides in these agency towns. These individuals frequently have ties not only to the reservation community, but also to other elite groups in other (non-Hopi) metropolises. Hopi leaders have much in common with leaders from other tribes. Such leaders share some interests with the elites of other units in the pyramidal structure that Jorgensen describes. For example, since the Hopi and Navajo tribal councils require revenue from mineral leases to operate, their members have a vested interest in and are likely to support the metropolis' positions.[13]

The reservation economy is also linked to changes in Hopi social organization and structure. As noted earlier, economic underdevelopment forces many Hopis to seek employment away from the reservation. Jobs that Hopis (and other Native Americans) find in the city are usually low paying and often temporary. Native American urban unemployment is higher than for most other ethnic groups. For these and other reasons, Hopis frequently return to the reservation, only to leave again in search of other jobs. Even on the reservation, people frequently move between agency towns and their home pueblos. Such economically motivated residential instability, coupled with consumer demands fostered by the metropolis, contributed to the increased significance of nuclear family households and to the decline in significance of lineages, clans, and phratries.[14]

Finally, the political and economic power of the metropolis contributed to the secularization of political life and, perhaps, to the decline of religious ceremonies. The federal government established the Hopi Tribal Council. The federal government's needs motivated this action, not Hopi needs. The power of the Tribal Council has come at the expense of traditional leadership positions. Because traditional political leaders were also the chief priests of Hopi religion, the deterioration of their political power contributed to a decline in their religious power. Young people may now seek secular political positions and power without undergoing rigorous religious training. Because esoteric knowledge is no longer a vehicle of political and religious power, it is not reproduced and is lost.

In summary, economic and political dependency influenced the nature of Hopi culture and society during the twentieth century. Every feature of Hopi life, from traditional subsistence agriculture to ideological authority, has felt the force of unequal exchange between European-Americans and Hopis. Nevertheless, the Hopis persist as a distinct sociocultural entity despite the forces that have operated on them during this period.

Part Three
Process, Explanation, and Social History

8. Environment, Population, and Cultural Contact: The Exogenous Processes of Persistence and Change

WE BEGAN THIS BOOK by asserting that anthropology is the study of humankind and the human condition. This statement establishes the general domain of anthropology, but it does not describe what anthropologists actually do. It does not specify what they study and how they go about explaining their subject matter. We then declared that anthropologists approach their studies from widely diverging theoretical positions, asking dissimilar "why" questions about distinct aspects of the human condition. Some of the most consequential questions that anthropologists ask are about variation in knowledge and behavior, patterns in culture and society, and persistence and change of sociocultural systems. We then outlined our interests in sociocultural persistence and change. We also expressed our opinion that one useful way to approach this topic is through the presentation at social histories.

In Part Two, we partially reconstructed Hopi social history. We presented five case studies from different times, beginning in Western Pueblo prehistory and ending in the modern Hopi era. The case studies do not portray five hundred years of Hopi history in all of its detail. Rather, they focus on different concrete events that archaeologists and anthropologists consider crucial in shaping Hopi social history. In addition, our case studies portrayed some of the diversity of anthropological inquiry and explanation to which we alluded. As stated, our objective in Part Two was not merely to provide a summary of Hopi social history or of anthropological explanations for specific, concrete events that have affected Hopis. We intended also to provide a foundation from which to move to a more general level of discourse about anthropological explanation.

In this chapter, we pursue this objective further by employing the events of Hopi social history in a more extensive discussion of significant variables, processes, and anthropological explanations of sociocultural persistence and change. To do so, we begin by isolating six *broadly defined types of variables* that are critical to an understanding of Hopi social history. Six categories of variables are also fundamental to many other anthropological explanations of sociocultural persistence and change: (1) demography, (2) environment, (3) sociocultural contact, (4) social structure, (5) culture, and (6) human agency. "Demography" designates the size and density of human populations and changes in these conditions over time. "Environment" refers to the physical circumstances and conditions within which a sociocultural system is situated. "Sociocultural contact" designates communicative interaction between representatives of distinct sociocultural systems or traditions. "Social structure" refers to organization or pattern in social relationships, behavior, and institutional arrangements. "Culture" designates a conceptual framework of meaning and moral responsibility that individuals acquire as members of social groups. "Human agency" designates the meaningful and purposeful or goal-directed actions that individuals perform. Humans are "agents" capable of deliberate activity, including forbearance and the ability to "act otherwise."

The remainder of Chapter 8 and Chapter 9 are divided into sections according to the separate categories listed. In this chapter, we consider the first three types of variables: population, environment, and sociocultural contact. These factors, taken together, constitute possible *exogenous* influences on sociocultural systems. Such factors and forces for sociocultural persistence and change originate "outside" the social and cultural systems that they affect. In response to such externally induced forces, sociocultural systems may display complex internal adjustments or changes. In Chapter 9, we consider the second set of three variables: social structure, culture, and human agency. Taken together, these are possible *endogenous* forces for persistence or change.[1] An "endogenous process" denotes one that originates "within" a sociocultural system. Endogenous effects are those resulting from ". . . the structure of systems of interaction or . . . [from] the effects [outcomes] produced by these structures" (Boudon 1979:129). Endogenous effects result from human agents employing culturally based frameworks of meaning and morality in structures of social interaction.

For each of the categories listed above, we intend to (1) summarize arguments from the Hopi case studies, concerning the role of such variables and processes in sociocultural persistence and change, and (2) generalize from Hopi social history to a discussion of the wider explanatory significance of the variables and processes. The latter requires that we relate our discussion to analyses of sociocultural persistence and change that anthropologists have presented about groups other than the Hopis. Before proceeding, however, we must make four related points about the above variables and our concern with them. First, we recognize there are different ways to construct such a list. "Demographic" and "environmental" might, for example, be conjoined in a category labeled "nonsociocultural variables." This category would include variables that are not inherently social or cultural, but affect sociocultural systems. Second, some of the above categories are closely interrelated. "Culture" and "human agency," for example, are closely associated, because human agents almost inevitably employ cultural frameworks when engaging in deliberate action. Third, some of the variables and processes that we include in a single category are analytically separable. In the category "social structure," for example, we include variables that could be divided into multiple categories, using such traditional anthropological terms as "economy," "kinship," "polity," "class," and "religion." Fourth, we are aware that other anthropologists might not accept our categories and definitions. Our definition of social structure, for example, differs widely from the one that Claude Lévi-Strauss (1963) and his followers employ. In short, our list of the factors for sociocultural persistence and change has an element of arbitrariness. Nevertheless, we have reasons for using this list to organize our discussion. We make these reasons explicit as we provide more precise definitions of the categories and consider explanations of sociocultural persistence and change in the sections that follow.

Demographic Variables

As exemplified in Hopi social history, demographic variables significant to the analysis of sociocultural persistence and change include the *size and density of human populations and changes in these conditions over time*. Although demographers only rarely use these dimensions of population variability analytically in their studies of modern populations, anthropologists are interested in such dimensions. This is so primarily because population size and density are closely related to social structure. Stability in the former is often associated with (and used to explain) stability in the latter. Changes in population size and density (population growth or decline, aggregation or dispersal) is related to (and used to explain) corresponding changes in social structure. Persistence or change that demographic variables cause in one level of social structure can ramify throughout a sociocultural system.

Statements about specific relationships among demographic and sociocultural variables in Hopi social history appear throughout our case studies. The first of such statements occurs in Chapter 3, where Upham

discusses the "abandonment" of prehistoric Western Pueblo villages between 1450 and 1539. As he notes, "depopulation," involving population loss from disease, warfare, malnutrition, or other causes, has been
posited to account for various episodes of abandonment (e.g., Colton
1936; Morris 1939; Titiev 1944; Martin, Quimby, and Collier 1947).
Each of these explanations postulates a cause-effect relationship between the changing size and density of prehistoric Western Pueblo
populations and an external or exogenous factor.

After reviewing these and other explanations of the abandonment
phenomena and the evidence offered in support of each, Upham postulates that a certain type of archaeological site, the nonarchitectural artifact scatter or limited-activity site, may be important in explaining
some Southwestern regional abandonment. In current models, agricultural villages are focal points on the landscape, and some limited-
activity sites are viewed as a part of the agricultural adaptation. In this
scenario, limited-activity sites are seen as purely "logistic," meaning that
they are task-specific. Agricultural activities may, for example, require
the erection of a field house or the establishment of a temporary field
camp where a villager may reside periodically during the growing season. Similarly, fourteenth- and fifteenth-century Western Pueblo vil-
lagers continued to hunt and gather natural resources at low levels to
augment their agricultural diet. These hunting-gathering forays away
from the village may have resulted in the formation of other limited-
activity sites (e.g., hunting stands and processing sites). In this model,
permanent village residence and agricultural activities constrain the
number of limited-activity sites.

As shown in Chapter 3, limited-activity sites make up a large portion
of some regions' archaeological records. They comprise between 40 and
60 percent of all Western Pueblo-region sites. Such a high proportion of
limited-activity sites suggests that far higher rates of mobility were characteristic of some periods. In Chapter 3, Upham also examined artifact
assemblages from limited-activity sites and found them to differ from
those of village sites. On the basis of these data, he postulates that Western Pueblo and other prehistoric Southwestern groups used different
adaptive strategies at different times. He also suggests that mobile and
sedentary peoples occupied portions of the Southwest contemporaneously. The high proportion of limited-activity sites in some regions is
direct evidence of mobile hunting-gathering peoples. Upham then presents data showing that the earliest Spanish explorers of the region reported the presence of nomadic hunter-gatherers between the larger
permanent Western Pueblo settlements.

Based on this hypothesized *population structure* and on historic evidence of adaptive change, assimilation, and population amalgamation among Apache and other groups in the Rio Grande and Rio Conchos regions, Upham argues that *adaptive shifts* from sedentary agriculture to mobile hunting-gathering were responsible for some regional "abandonments." In Upham's model, the people did not disappear from the region. Their pattern of sedentary agricultural living did. As Upham argues, the Western Pueblo responded to changes in the natural and social environments, not by fleeing the area or dying in large numbers, but by changing their mode of living.

In Chapter 4, attention is focused on the highly probable sixteenth-century Western Pueblo demographic collapse. Spanish explorers and colonists unintentionally caused this collapse when they introduced smallpox and other diseases. As discussed in that case study, when archaeologists compare the Western Pueblo of A.D. 1400 to the Hopis, Zunis, and Acomas of the sixteenth and seventeenth centuries, the former are (1) significantly more in number, (2) farming more intensively (less extensively), (3) trading more frequently and intensively with groups from other regions, (4) politically more centralized and more highly integrated with other sociocultural systems, and (5) economically more stratified. To account for such momentous sociocultural changes from Western Pueblo prehistory to Hopi history, Upham assumes (based on crosscultural study) that population size and density and social structure (especially economic and political structure) are interrelated. The five social-structural features listed above are often characteristics of "large-scale" societies. Such societies have large permanent settlements, sizable populations, and economic and political specialization. As noted, early Spanish chronicles describe Hopi, Zuni, and Acoma societies as much smaller in scale. To account for this change, Upham postulates a major Western Pueblo demographic collapse during the sixteenth and seventeenth centuries. Drawing on crosscultural data from other New World areas and on quantitative epidemiological models, he assesses the likelihood of smallpox reaching the American Southwest both before Spanish contact and in the intervals between recorded history during the sixteenth and seventeenth centuries. He concludes it highly probable that Southwestern smallpox epidemics occurred during these periods. The Western Pueblo appear no different in their susceptibility to European crowd infections than other New World groups. In summary, Upham associates features of social structure with demographic structure and accounts for changes in the former by citing changes in the latter. He explains Western Pueblo demographic change by referring to the "exogenous shock" (Netting 1990:37) of diseases introduced to Native American populations through contact with European peoples.

In Chapter 5, Rushforth hypothesizes that demographic variables twice affected Hopi sociocultural persistence and change between 1680 and 1880. First, following other anthropologists, he assumes that Hopi participation in the Pueblo Revolt and Awatovi's destruction were deliberate political acts. He contends that such acts partially deterred Spanish contact during the seventeenth and eighteenth centuries. He then speculates that, as an unintended consequence of such acts, the Hopis avoided major epidemics during that time. Consequently, Hopis maintained a relatively stable population of about 7,000 through this period. Because the Hopis survived, they reproduced their social and cultural systems. More importantly, because the Hopi population was relatively stable, only insignificant changes occurred in their social structure.

The second argument from Chapter 5 associating demographic variables to sociocultural persistence and change focuses on the 1851–1853 population collapse. This catastrophe resulted from a smallpox epidemic introduced through contact with the European-Americans, who were entering the Southwest in increasing numbers at that time. The epidemic reduced the number of Hopis from around 6,720 to about 2,500, altering the scale and, most likely, the structure of Hopi society. One hypothesized effect on Hopi social structure was an increase in noncontrolling-clan membership in religious groups. The number of individuals from different descent groups participating in a ritual that a single descent group controlled probably increased. When the members of a descent group became too few to perform successfully the rituals it controlled, the step of allowing more individuals from other descent groups to participate made it possible to continue performing the ceremony. As demographic decline affected more and more descent groups, religious institutions once based on descent ideology and membership became religious sodalities. Hopis deliberately altered social institutions so their religious beliefs, values, and activities could be reproduced with minimal change. Following this transformation, Hopis rationalized the structural rearrangements by incorporating references to them in Hopi mythology.[2]

Anthropologists also employ demographic variables and arguments in their explanations of the Oraibi split, as reported in Chapter 6. Bradfield (1971), for example, refers to stress that Oraibi's large population (ca. 800) placed on that village's agricultural system because of drought conditions and Oraibi Wash's erosion around the turn of the twentieth century. In Bradfield's explanation, climatic circumstances and population pressures created economic conditions that caused the split of the pueblo. He suggests there were more people than the fields could support, so the village divided.

Demographic variables and arguments also appear in our final case study dealing with twentieth-century Hopi culture and society. Rushforth suggested, for example, that population growth and increased residence off-reservation and in agency towns, represents a major trend among Hopis. Economic pressures, heightened by Hopi population growth, motivate many individuals to seek permanent or temporary employment away from the Hopi Mesas. If people return to the reservation, they are often inclined to live in agency towns such as Polacca. Job opportunities, political power, and modern amenities are concentrated in these newer communities. These people might eventually try off-reservation life again. They might also resume residence in their home villages on the Mesa tops. In such places as Moenkopi, economically motivated residential instability has increased the significance of nuclear families. The previously more prominent lineage households have become less significant. Again, demographic forces (i.e., population mobility) led to rearrangements of patterns of social behavior and social structure.

In summary, one significant generalization emerges from arguments that anthropologists make about the effects of demographic variables on Hopi sociocultural persistence and change. Hopi population size, density, stability, and instability have, throughout Hopi social history, been causally related to different features of Hopi social structure (e.g., kinship, economic, and political structure). Stability in Hopi demography has been associated with stability in Hopi social structure. Change in the former has been related to change in the latter. We now investigate such associations by viewing them within a wider anthropological context.

Demography: A Historical Framework

Thomas Robert Malthus, Herbert Spencer, and Charles Darwin were among the first modern thinkers to recognize the effects of population size and density on biological and sociocultural systems. Malthus, the father of modern demography, argued that biological populations grow continuously at a natural rate limited only by the available food supply. In his view, populations continue to increase until their food runs out. According to Malthus, a fierce "struggle for existence" then results, with starvation and death capping population size (Malthus 1791). According to Malthus, for humans, the only solutions to this inevitable condition are found in the "prudential restraints of continence and delayed marriage" (Notestein 1960). Thus, some scholars consider the "Malthusian Theorem" to be a pessimistic view of the human condition. This theorem sees population growth as the "prime mover" of biological and sociocultural change and human restraint as the only path to sociocultural persistence.[3] As seen in our case studies, this view is simplistic when applied to the Hopis. Hopi social history is not the mere reflection of Hopi demographics.

Today in anthropology and other social sciences, Malthusian thinking is viewed as "deterministic." It places too great an emphasis on population increase as fuel for the engine of sociocultural change. Nevertheless, Malthus' arguments are influential because they have stimulated the thinking of many other social philosophers.

One such philosopher was Herbert Spencer, who saw wisdom in Malthus' extreme views, although he disdained the inherent pessimism of strict Malthusianism. Like Malthus, Spencer postulated a direct relationship between population increase and food supply. He tempered his views of this relationship, however, by discussing systems of population regulation that function at the level of village, town, or city. He also recognized that variation in the natural environment makes deterministic views unfeasible.[4] Spencer's formulation is meaningful for two reasons. First, it recognizes the importance of social-organizational variables as mediating the relationship between food supply and population. Second, it recognizes that environmental variation must be considered when discussing changes in any population's demographic parameters. These two themes continue to dominate thinking about the role of demographic variables in explanations of sociocultural persistence and change. Further, these two themes are relevant to explanations offered in the Hopi case studies. They are especially pertinent to arguments about adaptive diversity and abandonment and arguments about the Oraibi split.

Malthus contended that only continence and human restraint could prevent unchecked population increase. Barring these, population size would increase geometrically, while food supply would only increase arithmetically. Studies of hunter-gatherers and other groups, however, suggest that many factors are influential in regulating group size (Eckstein, Stein, and Wolpin 1988). In the western desert region of the United States, for example, ethnographically known Western Shoshoni groups (who speak a Uto-Aztecan language belonging to the same language family as the Hopis) used a variety of practices to regulate their fertility and mortality. Shoshoni regularly used restraint (coitus interruptus) and continence (ritual sexual abstinence) (Thomas 1979:124; Steward 1938; Fowler and Fowler 1971). The Shoshoni also used abortion, infanticide, and senilicide to control the size of their groups. The Shoshoni did not, however, employ the latter practices routinely. Instead, they used them only periodically. Thomas has argued that the Shoshoni made conscious decisions about whether to regulate group size through infanticide, senilicide, or abortion. They did so, however, only after carefully considering probable resource productivity in a given year (cf. Thomas 1979:125–126). So, the Shoshoni appear to have regulated their birth and death rates to avoid depletion of their critical natural resources.

Some anthropologists have claimed that all hunter-gatherers regulate their populations below the level that would deplete their vital subsistence resources (e.g., Birdsell 1968). While this might be descriptively accurate for some groups, like the Shoshoni, anthropologists know that population regulation is not universal among hunter-gatherers. Many anthropologists believe, for example, that unchecked *population growth* among hunter-gatherers in certain late Pleistocene environments (ca. twelve thousand years ago) led to the development of food producing techniques and the "agricultural arts" (White 1959; Binford 1968; Cohen 1977). Archaeologists have made similar arguments about the Western Pueblo region. They suggest that unchecked population growth partially explains the adoption of agriculture, formation of villages, and intensification of both local and extralocal economic activities.[5]

These views of population regulation and unchecked population growth represent extreme positions regarding the importance of demographic variables in models of sociocultural persistence and change. On the one hand, reference to conscious decisions about population regulation emphasizes individual intentions to maintain the sociocultural status quo without changing modes of subsistence or settlement. In the Shoshoni case, their sociocultural strategies to regulate population appear to have operated for hundreds of years until the late 1800s (cf. Thomas 1979). In this scenario, if a group's population increases beyond some perceived level, *individuals* follow certain practices to limit further growth. If their efforts are successful, they may continue in their traditional hunting and gathering. On the other hand, unchecked population growth in this scenario conforms to the Malthusian notion of *natural population increase*. If population growth remains unchecked, a group will increase faster than its food supply. If group size expands beyond the level of resource depletion, hunter-gatherers would be faced with several alternatives. First, they could split into smaller groups and move into different environments. Second, they could intensify their food procurement activities to compensate for their increased numbers. Third, they could use advances in technology to change their mode of subsistence. According to Malthusian theory, barring these alternatives, the hunter-gatherers would face poverty, misery, and death.[6]

Following this scenario further, we might suggest that during the last twelve thousand years, New World hunting-gathering groups regulated their group size through (1) birth and death practices, (2) group fissioning or amalgamation, and (3) subsistence intensification or deintensification. These alternatives would be extremely effective solutions to problems that population growth engenders. These solutions, however, are short-term resolutions to the chronic predicament of unchecked population growth. Eventually, all environments would be filled with hunting-gathering groups whose populations were in equilibrium with the available resources. Further, these peoples' efforts to intensify their subsistence activities would inevitably produce diminishing returns on labor investment. Archaeologists concerned with the Western Pueblo region have made this point repeatedly about Southwestern hunter-gatherers (see Cordell 1984:181–188).

Leslie White recognized the problem of diminishing returns for hunter-gatherers (1959:290). He also contended that such peoples could solve this problem through technological innovation; specifically, through agriculture. Moreover, he linked the adoption of new technology to the demographic and organizational features of society and culture. He suggested that, when a region becomes filled with groups of hunter-gatherers who have intensified wild-food procurement as much as possible, the only real alternatives are found in conscious decision-making to regulate population size *or* in the adoption of a new (agricultural) technology. As White notes (1959:290), selection of this latter alternative has profound implications for every facet of a group's culture and society. With this knowledge, we may use the two idealized alternatives to discuss the evolutionary significance of demographic variables in explanations of culture change and persistence. Groups that opted to regulate their populations below the level of resource depletion continued to gather and hunt. Their hunting-gathering lifeway was reproduced and persisted. Groups that opted for or were forced to adopt new agricultural technology entered the era of food production. Their lifeway changed.

Simply to say that a group persisted or changed is no explanation. We must address the relevant "why" questions. We must explain, for example, why peoples selected certain alternatives from among the many available. In the present discussion of demographic variables, we have examined the relationship between population size and density in a general way. We have made use of social theory and ethnological generalizations to illustrate how group size and population growth are related to subsistence technology and to variation in social structure. We have also examined these issues by focusing on the extreme positions social scientists have taken. On a more specific level, we expect individual cases to vary depending on the exigencies of local conditions. At this level, the social histories of individual groups become critical. Thus, we contrast our more general discussion of demographic variables in this chapter with the specific explanations offered in our Hopi case studies.

Two axes of demographic variability are properties of all human populations: population size and population density. Population size and density, as indicated earlier, have profound influences on a group's social structure. Upham (1990) has argued that particular social systems are really nothing more than solutions to specific problems of labor management and subsistence production. He has also argued that the size and density of human populations are associated with the complexity of group decision-making. We adopt this view here. We suggest that social-structural complexity and institutional decision-making complexity are related to variation in the size and density of populations, although such relationships may vary from case to case due to historical circumstances.

Elsewhere, Upham (1987, 1990) has sought to clarify the relationship between social structural complexity and these two demographic variables by reevaluating Feinman's and Neitzel's comparative study of social and political structure (1984). Based on data they compiled for 106 ethnographically known New World groups, including the Hopis, Upham constructed a series of statistical analyses to evaluate how various indicators of political control (e.g., number of administrative levels, craft production, sumptuary rules, and burial practices) correlate with population size and density. Although his results remain tentative, overall population size was strongly correlated (correlation coefficient = 0.929779, explaining more than 86 percent of the variance) with seven variables related to centralized (and sometimes coercive) political control.

Strong positive relationships are shown to exist, for example, between the total size of a population and a leader's control of warfare or storage. Similar strong relationships hold between population size and special burials, provisioning with special food, and obeisance from followers. Feinman and Neitzel associate the latter with high status for leaders. Upham's analysis also shows that as population size increases, so do the number of institutionalized administrative levels. Feinman and Neitzel and several other anthropologists (e.g., Johnson 1978; Naroll 1956) have reached this same conclusion. The strength of these combined relationships is significant at the 0.01 level, although the predictive value of the equation is weak.

Significantly, Upham identified population threshold values for each of the variables he considered. The mean threshold value for each was approximately 10,500 people. This means that many of the attributes of political complexity that Feinman and Neitzel identify have a statistically higher probability of occurrence in *total regional populations* larger than this figure. From this analysis, it became clear that *population density* was as consequential as total population size. This finding has immediate implications for the interpretation of Western Pueblo prehistory and early Hopi history. The total Hopi population exceeded this threshold value before the demographic collapse following the introduction of European diseases. Between 1680 and 1850, Hopi population remained slightly below the threshold value. After 1851–1853, following another epidemic, the Hopi population fell even lower. When anthropologists wrote their first descriptions of Hopi culture and society during the early 1900s, the scale of this society was drastically different from what it had once been.

Other anthropologists have also explored this issue. Naroll (1956) has shown, for example, that communities larger than about 500 people generally have more centralized political leadership. This finding is not surprising because, as community size increases, the number of face-to-face interactions with different individuals also increases and the potential for disputes and conflict is therefore elevated (cf. Flannery 1972; Johnson 1983). Community populations larger than 500 must also have strategies for resource allocation and mate selection. We find Naroll's result particularly intriguing since a group of 500 is also the approximate size of the minimum local population in which regular community endogamy is feasible (Wobst 1974). Community endogamy allows individuals to use marriage as a means to gain access to or maintain control of local strategic resources. Consequently, when communities larger than approximately 500 people exist within total regional populations of 10,500, the potential for emergent social and political hierarchies is increased. In the past, many of the Hopi communities exceeded 500 people. Oraibi, for example, had more than 800 people when it disintegrated in 1906. Thus, the factional split Rushforth described in Chapter 6 may be placed in the demographic and political context developed here.

Such conclusions about demographic thresholds are neither new nor surprising (e.g., Michels 1915:26–27). Several previous researchers have explored the relationship between demographic variables and the formation of political hierarchies (Niemi and Weisberg 1972; Dahl and Tufte 1973; Noell 1974; Mayhew 1973; Mayhew and Levinger 1976). Their work indicates that centralized political bodies are more likely to evolve as the size of a system increases. "Michael's iron law of oligarchy" was originally extended only to groups whose populations had reached a critical level between 1,000 and 10,000 (Mayhew and Levinger 1976:1017).

There may, however, be an illusion of "magic numbers" in this discussion. The population figures provided here are simply estimates. Such numbers do not, by themselves, explain anything. Neither are they substitutes for empirical data. We believe, however, that threshold values in such variables do exist and when such values are met (within certain prescribed ranges), changes in the form and structure of sociocultural systems occur. Demographic variables play a necessary role in explanations of sociocultural persistence and change. This claim does not entail, however, that demographic "prime-mover" arguments are sufficient to explain the emergence and evolution (the social histories) of specific sociocultural systems. First, anthropologists must explain why the size and density of populations change. This requires reference to sociocultural factors. Second, many nondemographic forces act to promote sociocultural persistence and change. Recourse to pat prime-mover arguments is thus antithetical to the goals of explaining persistence and change.

There is actually a "chicken and egg" controversy in anthropology about the roles that population growth and changes in population density play in sociocultural persistence and change. On one side of this controversy are anthropologists who favor a strict Malthusian approach. They might argue that groups that adopt food-producing strategies do not solve their demographic problems. Instead, such groups are actually adopting a strategy that leads to increased population growth and increased population density (cf. Bee 1974:157). Archaeologists have made this argument for the Western Pueblo of A.D. 700 (see Cordell 1984). In this case, a more secure food supply is viewed as promoting additional population growth and, again, the Malthusian leveling mechanisms of misery and death are seen as social afflictions that reduce total population. On the other side of this controversy are anthropologists who endorse Ester Boserup's views (1965, 1981). Boserup contends that population increases (especially increases in the density of population [cf. Netting 1990]) lead people to adopt more intensive agricultural systems. This results in increased agricultural output. In this framework, advances in technology are critical. When a growing population threatens to outstrip agricultural output, people require new technological measures to alleviate their demographic problems. Upham (1982) has made such an argument about agricultural intensification for the fourteenth-century Western Pueblo communities. He suggests that demographic insecurity prompted Western Pueblo populations across the Colorado Plateau and Mogollon Rim regions to intensify their agricultural activities by constructing soil- and water-control devices.

Like most "which comes first" controversies, this one lacks a facile solution. Malthus and Boserup adopt positions that represent pessimistic and optimistic extremes regarding human demographic circumstances. Rather than adopt one or the other extreme, we prefer Blanton's (1975) position. He suggests it is unnecessary to assume that human populations tend to grow. Rather, he seeks explanations of population growth "by referring to the dynamics of the society in question . . . [When] explaining the dynamics of societies . . . look for causal factors other than population growth and related population processes" (Blanton 1975:180). Cordell (1984) and Upham (1982) took this approach in their work. We adopted the same approach in the Hopi case studies. When constructing our own arguments about Hopi social history, and when evaluating others' arguments, we emphasized demographic processes. Nevertheless, we explicitly eschew demographic "prime-mover" explanations for elements of Western Pueblo prehistory and Hopi social history. Upham, for example, examined changes in residence and subsistence to explain the "abandonment" of Western Pueblo areas. He offered this explanation, after rejecting the Malthusian alternative, because there is no good evidence for a population crash in the Western Pueblo during the fourteenth and fifteenth centuries. Similarly, Upham sought to explain depopulation in the Western Pueblo region during the early contact period, not by referring to the Malthusian leveling mechanisms of misery and death due to overpopulation, but by analyzing the introduction of epidemic diseases through culture contact and Spanish colonization.

Throughout this section, we have emphasized demographic variables and, especially, the way population growth and population size affect culture and society. We have also suggested, however, that a group's population size and rate of growth or decline is conditioned by the relationships between demography, environment, mode of subsistence, and unique organizational features of each society. In the following section we consider environmental variables and elaborate on this point.

Environmental Variables

We use the term "environment" to encompass the physical or material circumstances within which a sociocultural system is located. We include in this category such factors as climate, topography, soils, hydrology, flora, and fauna. Anthropologists, including those who have studied the Hopis, usually hold that factors demonstrably connected to a group's subsistence and economy are most significant (Steward 1938, 1955).

The effects of environmental variables on Hopi culture and society during the past five hundred years were discussed at various places in our case studies. The material conditions within which these people live were shown to have implications for several events in Hopi social history. In Chapter 3, we showed that early archaeological explanations of the "abandonment" (meaning depopulation and migration) of Puebloan villages during the fifteenth and sixteenth centuries focused on variation in climate and on critical drought episodes. Later archaeologists referred to the overutilization of agriculturally marginal lands or to population-resource imbalances. The latter denote stress that relatively large populations place on local resources. Still later archaeologists recycled the climatic argument and suggested that periods of drought, erosion, and arroyo cutting made agriculture difficult or impossible and led to Puebloan group migration to more favorable areas with better access to water.

In Upham's view, abandonment explanations that assume environmental catastrophe or demographic collapse are misguided. Instead, he emphasizes the "adaptive diversity" and flexibility of Western Puebloan social structure. For each group, he posits alternating periods of sedentary agriculture and mobile hunting-gathering. Nevertheless, environmental variables continue to play a central explanatory role in Upham's scheme. The resilience or flexibility he sees in Western Pueblo subsistence and social structure occurs because the Southwest is a marginal environment for agriculture. When local environmental conditions changed (for example, because of drought or overexploitation of resources), people responded by restructuring their subsistence activities and economy, not by migrating en masse to a new region. For Upham, environmental conditions partly caused the alternating periods of sedentary and mobile existence.

In Chapter 5, Rushforth discussed two explanations that incorporated environmental variables. The first was Brew's explanation of the return of Rio Grande Puebloan peoples to their homes after spending time among the Hopis following the Pueblo Revolt (1949:32). He attributes their return to drought-caused stress placed on the Hopi agricultural system. In Brew's analysis, drought conditions placed severe pressure on the Hopi economy. This created tension, even fighting, among the Rio Grande peoples and their Hopi hosts. The tension and fighting caused or motivated the former to leave. Hence, the imbalance between people and resources that generated the original stress or imbalance was reduced.

Many different anthropologists (e.g., Spicer 1962; Eggan 1970; Titiev 1944) have supported another, second explanation including environmental variables, which Rushforth also discussed in Chapter 5. This explanation suggests that geographical isolation and the agricultural marginality of Hopi territory acted throughout the Spanish period (ca. 1540 to 1850) to maintain Hopi cultural and social isolation. In the view of many anthropologists, such geographical isolation and agricultural marginality (which lessened Spanish motivation to conquer Hopi territory) reduced opportunities for Hopis to communicate with other peoples. Less frequent communication resulted in less borrowing or diffusion. Hence, less sociocultural change took place. In our hypothesis, the significance of such isolation (which was also a byproduct of deliberate Hopi political acts such as the destruction of Awatovi) was that the Hopis partially avoided severe population losses from diseases such as smallpox, measles, and influenza.

In Chapter 6, environmental variables play a crucial role in Bradfield's explanation of the Oraibi split. Environmental variables also contribute to Whiteley's and others' explanations of the same event. Bradfield's explanation of the Oraibi split is similar to Brew's explanation of the return of the New Mexican Puebloan peoples to their homes in the mid-1700's. Both theorists suggest that drought conditions, coupled with large human populations, placed critical pressure on the Hopi agricultural economy. This stress led to movements and relocations of people. In the former case, non-Hopis returned to the Rio Grande Valley. In the latter case, "Hostiles" left Oraibi to found Hotevilla and, eventually, Bacavi. Both theorists employ arguments about the relationship of human populations to their food resources. The only apparent difference in their analyses is that Bradfield contributes more particulars than does Brew concerning environmental conditions, such as soil composition, that affected traditional Hopi agriculture independently of human population pressure.

In Whiteley's explanation of the Oraibi split, deteriorating environmental conditions caused by drought contributed significantly to corrupted conditions at Oraibi. Religious leaders interpreted such conditions from the perspective of Hopi mythology. They then took the extreme religious action of destroying the village.

Finally, in Chapter 7, two more accounts of Hopi sociocultural persistence and change incorporate environmental variables. Nagata (1970) refers to Hopi geographical isolation and agricultural marginality when accounting for Hopis' delayed incorporation into the American economy. He assumes, as have others, that isolation promotes sociocultural persistence, and that contact results in change. According to Nagata, because the Hopis were isolated from American expansion until recent times, their sociocultural system retained many features from earlier historical periods. Clemmer (1978a) refers to the mineral wealth on Hopi and Navajo land when discussing episodes of directed culture change in the twentieth century. In his views, for example, the operation of the Hopi Tribal Council in the 1970s and 1980s (and everything this new form of political organization means for Hopi social structure) must be partially understood in light of the Council's role in signing leases with multinational corporations for the development of Hopi coal.

One significant generalization about the effects of environmental variables on sociocultural persistence and change emerges from our case studies of Hopi social history. The environment imposes constraints on human actors and social systems, but these constraints are neither always limiting nor always determinant. Instead, the exigencies of the material environment pose problems that people must solve through decision-making and the conscious use of technology. That Hopis have persisted in an arid and unpredictable environment is ample testament to the flexibility and resilience of their decision-making system and to the sophistication in their use of a relatively simple technology. We explore this idea and its implications further by examining them within the context of more general anthropological concerns.

Environment: A Historical Framework

As noted earlier in this chapter, Herbert Spencer was one of many social philosophers who concluded that variation in the natural environment affected the demographic parameters of human groups. Although Spencer did not explicitly formulate this idea in 1876, he was talking about the concept of "carrying capacity," or the ability of an environment "to sustain a [population] level without [environmental damage]." Carrying capacity is the population level for long term survival (Odum 1971:125). Ecologists use this term to denote the theoretical energy value that can be extracted from an environment while allowing any living population to remain in a state of balance or equilibrium. Usually, ecologists measure such energy values in terms of total biomass or usable biomass.

Anthropologists, after first flirting with this type of ecological approach to modeling human systems (Zubrow 1971; Brush 1977), have now realized that human populations are far too complex to model using concepts such as carrying capacity and biomass. Today, anthropologists use carrying capacity to denote the potential of specific environments to support human populations of different size and density following different subsistence strategies, but they do not seek to measure the specific carrying capacity of an environment for a given human group. Instead, they employ different approaches. William T. Sanders and David Webster, for example, have identified what they believe is an appropriate framework for explaining many of the key transitions in the last ten thousand years of human history. They suggest that "different evolutionary trajectories relate to variations in the natural environment, such as degree of . . . risk, diversity, productivity . . . and size and character of the environment" (1978:250). In Sanders' and Websters' approach, the variables of environmental risk, environmental diversity, and environmental productivity, as well as the size, character, and location of the specific environment are viewed as determining the size and organizational complexity of human populations. In their approach, the interaction of such variables "influence . . . demographic patterns [that is, variability in size and density of population], which in turn bring about adaptive structural changes as society passes from one [evolutionary] stage to another" (1978:276).

Some anthropologists might consider such an approach deterministic because it posits a controlling role for the interaction of specific environmental variables with those of demography and organization. When deterministic roles are given to specific environmental variables, explanations that are generated fall within the school of social thought known as *environmental determinism*. As Hardesty notes (1977:1), "the most pervasive theme [of this school] is . . . that the physical environment plays the role of 'prime mover' in human affairs. Personality, morality, politics and government, religion, material culture, biology . . . [have all been explained] by environmental determinism." To this list we would add the demographic variables of population size and population growth.

Hardesty contrasts environmental determinism with another approach in anthropology, environmental possibilism. Possibilist arguments hold that the environment is a limiting, not determining, factor in human sociocultural development. Consequently, explanations in this genre may explain why some features of culture did not occur, although they may not provide an explanation of why certain traits and features are present (Hardesty 1977:4).

Betty J. Meggars provides a classic argument that illustrates the kind of thinking the possibilist approach embodies (1954). She postulates, following Julian Steward (1938, 1955), that groups (and their cultures) articulate with environments primarily through their subsistence systems. She also suggests that "the most vital aspect of environment from the point of view of culture is its suitability for food production" (1954:802). Meggars claims that, for periods before the emergence of food production, environments were "relatively equal over the major portion of the earth's surface" (1954:802) in their ability to supply humans with food. Following the development of agriculture, however, environmental differences conferred differential advantages to some groups.

From this underlying premise, Meggars developed a classification of environments based on agricultural potential. She sought correlations between cultural development and environmental potential. To accomplish this task, she surveyed available ethnographic and archaeological data from South America and Europe and constructed a developmental scheme that links levels of cultural development with generalized characterizations of the environment. Meggars argues that strong positive correlations exist between marginal environments and the presence of simple sociocultural systems; similar strong correlations are found between environments with "increasable" and unlimited agricultural potential and complex sociocultural systems. On the basis of these data, she concludes that "the level to which a culture can develop is dependent upon the agricultural potential of the environment it occupies" (1954:815). Meggars refers to this statement as the "law of environmental limitation on culture."

Meggars' law stirred controversy in anthropology, and, in the years following publication of her paper, spirited exchanges and counterformulations appeared in several scholarly journals.[7] Interest in Meggars' ideas stemmed from the way she characterized specific kinds of environments. She did so on the basis of soil type and identified large environmental areas as having no or limited agricultural potential. This meant that the latter areas could not support cultural developments beyond a rudimentary level. Meggars included in her Type I (areas of no agricultural potential) and Type II (areas of limited agricultural potential) environments, for example, tropical savannas, tropical forests, and *selva* regions of the world. These environments have thin soils that have high potential for waterlogging and erosion. Based on her archaeological fieldwork in the tropical forests of South America, she felt such a position was justified. As Meggars argued, no evidence of complex, highly developed archaeological cultures are found in this region.

Other archaeologists who studied the Maya took exception to Meggars' "law" (e.g., Coe 1957; Altschuler 1958). The Maya, who occupied parts of Mexico, Guatemala, and Honduras, were an advanced, prehistoric New World culture. In the tropical forests of these areas, Mayan civilization developed and flourished from A.D. 300 to 900. In Meggars' classification, however, the tropical forests of Mexico, Guatemala, and Honduras were Type II environments with limited agricultural potential. Consequently, Meggars' law predicted that these areas could not support elaborate cultural developments. Yet Mayan cultural and social complexity rivaled anything found at the time in Europe. Mayan cities with elaborate ceremonial centers and large populations dotted the tropical forests. Archaeological evidence indicates complex Mayan sociopolitical and religious systems were supported by intensive agriculture, craft specialization, and extensive exchange networks.[8] Based on these data, Meggars' law is incorrect.

Where did Meggars go wrong? She erred in two ways. First, she did not appreciate the role of technology in overcoming environmental obstacles. Today, we know that by A.D. 300 the Maya had developed extensive systems of ridged and drained fields that were based on a sophisticated understanding of soil and water management (Blanton et al. 1981). These fields were highly productive. Crops grown on them could sustain large populations. Second, Meggars underestimated variation in the environments she classified, especially local variation. We now know that the tropical rainforests and humid equatorial lowlands are not homogenous environments with redundant soils, landforms, and vegetation. Instead, elevation, topography, and facing create an environmental mosaic that human groups can exploit. The Maya, for example, appear to have capitalized on just such variation. They located sites near *bajos* and *aguadas* (natural depressions) that they could use as reservoirs (Blanton et al. 1981: 173, 179). They selected areas with specific edaphic conditions for growing different kinds of crops. Consequently, by understanding their environment and employing technology to exploit local environmental conditions, the Maya were able to develop and flourish in the tropical lowland forest. Archaeologists and anthropologists have made claims about the Southwestern arid desert environment that are similar to the ones Meggars made about tropical rainforests. Meggars included as Type I environment (areas with no agricultural potential) some of the world's desert regions. More than seventy years ago, William H. Holmes wrote of the Southwest that "it is here made manifest that it is not so much the capabilities and cultural heritage of the particular stock of people that determines the form of material culture as it is their local environment" (1919:47).

Since Holmes wrote these words, anthropologists have frequently made both deterministic and possibilistic arguments about Southwest peoples. Archaeologists have, for example, asserted that adverse Southwestern environmental conditions and droughts were responsible for many regional "abandonments." Scholars like Brew and Bradfield have suggested, for example, that adverse climatic conditions precipitated human migrations in historic times. Despite their commonality, such deterministic and possibilistic environmental arguments often fail to consider independent sociocultural events and processes that have contributed to sociocultural change and persistence among Southwestern peoples like the Hopis. Such arguments, as they pertain to the Southwest, have frequently failed to acknowledge human adaptive responses for coping with environmental risk and uncertainty. Prehistoric Western Pueblo peoples, for example, had within their cultural repertoires adaptively diverse strategies for responding to contingent environmental circumstances. Finally, and, perhaps, most importantly, local environmental variability in the Southwest makes generalizing about the Southwestern environment difficult.

An interdisciplinary team of researchers consisting of an archaeologist, dendroclimatologist, hydrologist-geomorphologist, and palynologist recently illustrated why generalizations about the Southwestern environment are problematic. The team collaborated on a reconstruction of the paleoenvironments of the central and northern Southwest (Euler et al. 1979; Dean et al. 1985; Gumerman 1988). They compiled data principally from Black Mesa, Arizona, in the heart of Hopi country, and provided relatively precise records of past climatic (as measured through effective moisture), and vegetational and erosional cycles. They then compared these cycles to sequences of sociocultural development to examine the relationship between environmental variation and sociocultural change. Their results are illuminating. First, they found it impossible to provide a single, generally applicable characterization of environmental conditions for the central and northern Southwest. Rather, they found that different local areas experienced the vagaries of climate differently depending on patterns of rainfall, wind, and erosion. Such patterns resulted from the convectional and cyclonic storm patterns common to the Southwest (see Cordell 1984:24–27). This finding is not surprising to those who live in the Southwest. The adage "it didn't rain on my side of the street" can be literally true. Richard Ford pursued the implications of this storm pattern in the northern Southwest (1972).

He showed that such weather conditions can result in significant yield differences even for *adjacent* agricultural fields. Through their reconstruction of paleoenvironments, Dean and his colleagues demonstrated that such conditions have prevailed in the Southwest for the last fourteen hundred years.

More specifically, Dean and the others showed that local Southwestern climatic conditions are highly variable. With regard to precipitation, for example, they demonstrated how variation is related not only to the timing of rainfall, but also to its spatial distribution, seasonal frequency, duration, and intensity. Because of Southwestern storm patterns, rainfall is variable within and between local valley systems. Consequently, precipitation may be more than adequate for agriculture in one place, while in adjoining areas little or no rain falls, and water resources are too meager for farming.

Dean and his colleagues characterize episodes of variation in past Southwestern environments by high and low frequency variability:

> Environmental variability can be characterized as the product of low frequency environmental processes with cycles (regular or irregular) longer than one human generation (ca. 25 years) and of high frequency environmental processes that exhibit shorter cycles. Low frequency processes are responsible for phenomena such as fluctuations in stream flow and ground water levels and episodes of erosion and deposition along stream courses, while high frequency processes are responsible for phenomena such as seasonal and annual climatic variability and fluctuations in crop yields and natural resource productivity. (Dean et al. 1985:538)

They go on to point out that low frequency environmental processes, because of their duration, would usually not be apparent to human populations. In contrast, high frequency environmental processes would be "apparent to human populations and most behavioral buffering mechanisms [would be] adaptations to expectable high frequency fluctuations" (1985:538). They then seek to correlate sequences of sociocultural development in the Western Pueblo region with episodes of low and high frequency environmental variation.

They find that no simple correlation exists between variation in environmental processes and episodes of sociocultural change or persistence. Rather, they identify seven major adaptive responses to environmental variation that prehistoric Western Pueblo people used when buffering environmental risk and uncertainty. These responses include increased residential mobility, shifts in the location of permanent settlements, changes in subsistence mix, reliance on exchange ties with other

groups, social integration through ceremonialism, agricultural intensification, and increased territoriality and warfare (Dean et al. 1985:
547–549). Behavioral responses to high and low frequency environmental processes, especially with respect to subsistence strategies, thus
vary from region to region and through time in the Western Pueblo area.

Given these conditions, it is not surprising that Southwestern peoples'
agricultural adaptations reflect their attention to regional climatic conditions. The Hopis, for example, developed an agricultural strategy that
reflects a sophisticated practical understanding of high and low frequency environmental processes. As noted, Hopi agriculture has been
described as a hedge-your-bets strategy because of the way Hopis locate
their agricultural fields. Archaeological evidence suggests that Hopis
and their ancestors have used this strategy for several centuries. In the
Hopi case, their understanding of environmental variation has allowed
them to occupy the Hopi Mesas for perhaps eight hundred years.

We may now draw some conclusions about the environment's effects
on Hopi social history. Phrased differently, we may comment on the way
that we and other anthropologists have used environmental variables to
account for features of Hopi sociocultural change and persistence. First,
many archaeologists and anthropologists that we discussed have offered
determinist or possibilist arguments. These scholars assign causal significance to environmental forces in their Hopi social histories. In
our arguments, however, we contend that the environment plays an almost passive role. In Upham's analysis of abandonments, for example,
he attributes primary significance to internal cultural and social variables. Adaptive alternations between sedentary agriculture and mobile
hunting-gathering reflect a group's strategic flexibility, not a mechanical
response to environmental conditions. Similarly, the Oraibi split represents a deliberate response to environmental and political-economic
conditions, not automatic behavior due to environmental stimuli. This
reasoning reveals a bias in our interpretations that the reader should
recognize. This bias views purely environmental explanations as mecha-
nistic. Many environmental explanations fail to attend adequately to internal sociocultural processes and human agency. This is, of course, different from saying that the environment is unimportant in explanations
of sociocultural change or persistence.

To illustrate this difference, we again consider the work of Dean and
his colleagues. They have shown that prehistoric Western Pueblo groups
used different adaptive responses when facing environmental diversity,
risk, and uncertainty (their high and low frequency processes). A close
examination of the archaeological data shows that Western Puebloan
peoples responded differently on separate occasions to similar patterns

of climatic and environmental variation (see Plog 1978; Cordell and Plog 1979; Braun and Plog 1982; Upham 1982; Cordell 1984). This suggests that their cultural strategies or decision heuristics selected different behavioral responses depending on cultural and social, as well as environmental conditions. Cultural and social conditions relevant to such decision making appear to have included (1) group size and demographic composition; (2) neighboring groups' size and composition; and (3) the nature of social, economic, and political ties within and between groups. Consequently, we would argue that environment is profitably viewed as the "setting" for sociocultural systems. Barring catastrophic environmental events that eliminate entire social groups and transform the landscape rapidly (e.g., earthquakes, vulcanism, and floods), environmental variables are often (or should frequently be) of secondary importance in anthropological explanations of sociocultural persistence and change. Environmental conditions may be necessary, but they are rarely, if ever, sufficient to account for sociocultural persistence and change. We believe, therefore, that demography, sociocultural contact, social structure, culture, and human agency are more critical to an understanding of social-historical processes. Having said this, we reiterate that environmental conditions are potentially important to explanations of sociocultural phenomena. We suggest, however, that environmental variables be placed in an appropriate context, defined by the conjunction of the other variables listed here. This is what we did in our own explanations of events in Hopi social history.

Sociocultural Contact

"Sociocultural contact" denotes interaction, either direct or indirect, between individuals from different, autonomous sociocultural systems. Sociocultural contact is, by this definition, completely neutral regarding various analytical perspectives that might focus exclusively on one or another dimension of contact to the exclusion of the other dimensions. It is neutral, for example, concerning perspectives that might emphasize contact between individuals rather than groups or between cultures rather than social structures. In agreement with "acculturation theory," we see the results of contact to be influenced by (1) the form and content of the sociocultural systems which, through their individual members, are in contact; and (2) the demographic, environmental, cultural, and social-structural context within which contact occurs. Further, in our view, human agency plays a significant role in contact. Contact can be motivated by distinct purposes and, because of this, can have widely disparate results. Nevertheless, contact often or invariably results in some kind of sociocultural change.

Anthropologists have frequently explained events in Hopi social history by referring to sociocultural contact between Hopis and other peoples. We summarized several of these explanations in our case studies. In Chapter 3, we noted that earlier archaeological explanations of Southwestern abandonments refer to raiding and warfare between Puebloan peoples and non-Puebloan peoples. Some anthropologists have suggested that such aggressive contact is one possible cause of depopulation and migration. Chapter 4 is devoted almost entirely to investigating the consequences of early (indirect and direct) contact between Western Pueblo peoples and Spanish explorers and colonists. While pursuing their own ends, the Spanish unintentionally introduced epidemic diseases to the New World. Smallpox and other crowd infections reduced Southwestern populations, including that of the Hopis, to one-fourth or even one-tenth of what they had been previously. This catastrophe altered the scale of Hopi society and resulted in the changes noted earlier.

In Chapter 5, we focused on Hopi resistance and persistence from about 1680 until 1850. During this time, geographical distance and Hopi attitudes limited contact with the Spanish colonialists. Rushforth speculated that, as an unintended biological consequence of their political actions, Hopis avoided at least some epidemics that other Native Americans experienced as a result of their interactions with Europeans. Hence, the Hopi population remained relatively stable during these years. This stability possibly contributed to stability in Hopi culture and social structure. In 1851–1853, however, contact with the newly powerful European-Americans induced sociocultural changes among the Hopis. Diseases that the new immigrants brought decimated the Hopis and, as noted earlier, altered the scale of Hopi society.

Chapter 6 also notes the arrival among the Hopis of missionaries, government personnel, and European-American settlers, who brought with them new ideas and values. Hostility or friendliness toward these immigrants and their government became the focus of factional disputes and contributed, among other things, to Oraibi's split in 1906. Titiev considers contact with the American government to be the casus belli of the split, but attributes primary significance to internal sociological mechanisms. Clemmer (1978a) claims that contact with the European-Americans was the primary cause of the split. For him, contact created economic, religious, and political stress in Oraibi and other Hopi villages. According to Clemmer, this stress either led to or enhanced Hopi political factionalism. The exacerbation of political factionalism, in turn, resulted in Oraibi's disintegration. Whiteley also incorporates Hopi contact with European-Americans in his explanation of Oraibi's split. In his view, Oraibi's religious leaders interpreted conditions partially created by contact with European-Americans as fulfilling states of affairs foretold in Hopi mythology. Such conditions demanded of the leaders that they take deliberate action to destroy the village. Rushforth offers a hypothesis that acknowledges both Clemmer's and Whiteley's analyses. He contends that the Oraibi split can be viewed as a "social movement," similar to other social movements that occurred among Native Americans around 1900. Oraibi leaders initiated this social movement in response to conditions of deprivation that contact helped create. Conditions among the Hopis and other Native Americans at the turn of the century help us understand the mental states of individuals who participated in such movements as the Ghost Dance, Sun Dance, and the destruction of Oraibi. Hopi contact with European-Americans precipitated such conditions.

In Chapter 7, Rushforth focused his attention on several sociocultural trends occurring among the Hopis during the twentieth century. These included (1) an increase in population, accompanied by shifts in residential pattern; (2) a change in the economic foundation of society from subsistence agriculture to wage labor; (3) the adoption of many items of Western material culture; (4) a decline in the relevance of traditional descent-based social institutions, accompanied by the expanded significance of nuclear families; (5) a deterioration of traditional religious institutions; and (6) a secularization of the political system. These trends are largely the product of Hopi contact with European-Americans. Titiev explicitly attributes many of these changes to the construction of an all-weather road between the Hopi Reservation and surrounding communities in the 1950s. The road made travel faster and easier, and increased interaction between Hopis and outsiders. According to Titiev, many of the above changes represent diffusion, or Hopi borrowing of traits. In his view, for example, traditional Hopi religious institutions are less significant now than in the past because, through cultural diffusion, the Hopis acquired such technological innovations as irrigation. These innovations gave the Hopis enhanced understanding of and control over the natural realm. The innovations made Hopis less reliant on supernatural understandings and techniques. Accordingly, Hopi religious institutions declined.[9]

Other anthropologists also employ sociocultural contact and diffusion in their explanations of twentieth-century Hopi sociocultural changes. Nagata (1970), for example, refers to the significance of Hopi students and workers who return home after their off-reservation experiences. He contends that they are a source of change in Hopi culture and society. New beliefs, values, and items of material culture diffuse to the reservation through such individuals. Dockstader makes similar claims about off-reservation experience (1979). Whiteley acknowledges the influence of Western technological innovations that have diffused to the Hopis (1988a:147–150, 160). He also stresses the importance of schools in the acculturation of Hopi children (meaning by this their assimilation of non-Hopi cultural traits) (1988a:221–223). Kennard, like Titiev, stresses the breakdown of Hopi isolation that resulted from paved roads and the arrival of cars and trucks (1965:27).

For us, twentieth-century Hopi contact with the outside world (the breakdown of isolation, the diffusion of cultural traits, and the increasing experience of Hopis with non-Native Americans) is reasonably understood within the context of the political-economic structure within which such contact occurs. As noted in Chapter 7, the most prominent fact about twentieth-century Hopis is their incorporation into the U.S. and world political economies. This incorporation (which is contact characterized by a distinctive kind of relationship between the interacting groups) helps explain many of the trends listed above and discussed in Chapter 7. Specifically, this relationship entails one group's political and economic domination of another. One group or society (a metropolis) develops economically and politically by exploiting the resources and labor of the other (a satellite). While the former grows, the latter becomes or remains underdeveloped politically and economically. In Chapter 7, Rushforth discussed the subordination of Hopi interests to those of the metropolis. He illustrated such subordination in different ways and suggested that it is related to the sociocultural changes noted. The growth of agency towns such as Polacca, for example, is not simply the movement of people to locations where modern amenities are available. Polacca's growth is not explained simply as the diffusion of Western demand patterns. Rather, this new settlement pattern reflects a concentration of economic and political power on the reservation in ways predicted by the metropolis-satellite model of economic development. Individuals employed by the federal government or a corporation in agency towns appear to possess more economic and political power than other Hopis who continue to reside in pueblos established earlier in Hopi history. Such empowered Hopis, accordingly, develop shared interests with the metropolis and may support some of its positions concerning, for example, economic development on the reservation.

We now offer a summary of the significance of sociocultural contact to Hopi social history. First, contact between Hopis and other groups frequently, if not inevitably, resulted in Hopi sociocultural change. Second, such change was sometimes relatively direct and uncomplicated;

involving, for example, the diffusion of material-cultural items. In other instances, it was more indirect and complicated. The consequences of contact-induced disease and population for Hopi social history, for example, became apparent only through later, intricate social-structural realignments. Third, the form and content of Hopi culture and society influenced the outcome of contact. "Cultural conservatism" acted for many years to restrict outside influence. Fourth, the structure of Hopi contact situations influenced the resulting persistence and change in Hopi culture and society. The unequal exchange characteristic of twentieth-century Hopi contact with European-Americans, for example, has led to several changes in Hopi culture and society. Had domination and subordination not been characteristic of this contact, economic underdevelopment and everything this entails might not have been created on the reservation. Or, for that matter, the reservation system itself might not have been established.

Sociocultural Contact: A Historical Framework

Anthropologists have been interested in the social and cultural effects of contact since Franz Boas' time. For Boas and other "historical particularists," an understanding of any cultural system (or of persistence and change therein) could only be acquired through historical analysis. Contact played a central role in such analysis because "diffusion" (the intercultural transmission of traits; cultural borrowing) was considered a basic source for new cultural features ("independent invention" was the other). To understand an institution such as the Plains Indian Sun Dance as it occurred in one specific culture (e.g., the Lakota), an anthropologist needed to discover from which group the Lakota borrowed the ceremony, under what conditions the diffusion occurred, and how the Sun Dance was then integrated into Lakota culture. Such diffusion studies led naturally to the idea of "culture areas," geographical areas within which many traits had diffused from one group to another and within which groups shared many cultural features.[10]

Between the 1930s and 1960s "acculturation theory" played a dominant role in American anthropology. This school of thought, which concentrated on sociocultural change, emerged from earlier Boasian historical particularism. For acculturation theorists, the description of contact-induced change was a major part of the modern anthropologist's job. They also felt that sociocultural change provided one of the best opportunities for the study of "cultural dynamics" (Barnett et al. 1954:973). Much of acculturation theory has been summarized in two papers. The first was written in the 1930s (Redfield, Linton, and Herskovits 1936). Participants in the 1953 Social Science Research Council Summer Seminar on Acculturation wrote the second (Barnett et al. 1954). The latter paper defines the concept of acculturation "as culture change that is initiated by the conjunction of two or more autonomous cultural systems" (Barnett et al. 1954:974). According to these anthropologists,

> Acculturative change may be the consequence of direct cultural transmission; it may be derived from noncultural causes, such as ecological or demographic modifications induced by an impinging culture; it may be delayed, as with internal adjustments following upon the acceptance of alien traits or patterns; or it may be a reactive adaptation of traditional modes of life. (1954:974–975)

Barnett and his coauthors differentiate culture from both the individual and society. They restrict the concept of acculturation to contact-induced changes in cultural systems ("habits of doing and believing"). They also explicitly define four "facets" of acculturation. These are features of contact and acculturation that require empirical consideration in any study of this subject matter: (1) the properties of the "cultural systems" that come into contact, (2) the nature of the "contact situation," (3) the "conjunctive relations" between the cultural systems in contact, and (4) the "cultural processes" that result or emerge from the conjunctive relations (1954:975). The properties of cultural systems significant to acculturation processes include, minimally, boundary-maintaining mechanisms, the relative rigidity or flexibility of internal cultural structure, and the presence of self-maintaining mechanisms.[11] Hopi conservatism would be one such property of Hopi culture that affected their contact with other peoples and contributed to Hopi resistance to acculturation.

The nature of the contact situation refers to ". . . those noncultural and nonsocial phenomena that provide the contact setting and establish limits of cultural adaptation" (Barnett et al. 1954:979). The most critical features of the contact situation are the "ecological context" and the "demographic characteristics" of the peoples involved. For the Hopis, geographical separation and the small number of Spanish who contacted them during the sixteenth, seventeenth, and eighteenth centuries influenced the outcome of such contact.

Conjunctive relations refer to the "intercultural role networks that not only establish the framework of contact but also provide the channels through which the content of one cultural system must be commu-

nicated and transmitted to the other" (Barnett et al. 1954:980). The social statuses and roles of individuals from separate cultural traditions
who come into contact, as well as the new statuses and roles established
through contact influence the nature of communication between the
contacting cultures. Hence, they influence the results of contact. Because Spanish military personnel and priests provided the channel
through which most contact between the Hopis and Europeans was accomplished between 1540 and 1800, for example, the results of contact
were probably different from what they would have been if individuals
with different occupations had been more involved. Military leaders and
priests challenged Hopi political and religious autonomy in ways that
might not have occurred had contact been achieved through individuals
occupying different status positions.

Barnett and his collaborators claimed that cultural processes associated with contact between two or more cultural systems are "numerous,
varied, and complex." Nevertheless, they list four "fairly specific, recur-
ring sequences of events in acculturation." These include: (1) "intercultural transmission" (or diffusion), (2) "cultural creativity," (3) "cultural disintegration," and (4) "reactive adaptations" (Barnett et al. 1954:
984). Diffusion and integration are defined in the Boasian sense. "Cultural creativity" refers to "reorganizations," "reinterpretations," and "syn-
cretisms" that occur with the incorporation of foreign features into a
cultural system. New forms with new meanings are generated through
such creativity. "Cultural disintegration" denotes the "destructive consequences" of contact for the acculturated system. A previously autonomous cultural system, for example, might become politically dependent
on some other group and lose cultural traits that were associated with
their previous autonomy. "Reactive adaptations" entail a withdrawal and
entrenchment of native values in response to threats that a contacting
group pose. Hopi actions at Awatovi might be classified as this type of
process.

Barnett and his coauthors also discuss conjunctive relations through
time as displaying either "progressive adjustment" or "stabilized plu-
ralism." The former normally leads either to "cultural fusion" (generation of a "genuine third sociocultural system") or "assimilation" (one
group's complete absorption of another). The latter results from "the
failure of two cultures in contact to lose completely their autonomy"
(1954:990). The authors finally discuss several topics, for example,
differential rates of change found in different features of culture and
sequential developments in acculturation over long periods of time
(1954:990ff.).

Barnett et al. do not explicitly define one last concept that is, nevertheless, part of their acculturation theory, and which they use in their discussion. The concept is expressed as a distinction between "directed" and "non-directed situations." According to Spicer, this distinction is basic because "it makes clear the two most general classes of contact situation" (1961:519–520, citing Linton 1940:501). Spicer continues by explicitly establishing the social-interactional differences between the two types of contact situation. In directed contact, the members of one contacting group sanction the behavior of individuals from the other contacting group. The members of a superordinate group control the actions of individuals from the subordinate group. According to Spicer, it "is highly misleading to think of what happens [in this situation] in terms of the metaphor 'borrowing', unless we remind ourselves that true borrowing requires the borrower to act in terms of another's interests and values" (1961:520).

Following Spicer, Richard Clemmer incorporated directed contact into his account of twentieth-century Hopi sociocultural change. As discussed below, this concept partially anticipates at least one of the criticisms that anthropologists sometimes make of acculturation theory.

Many anthropologists have used acculturation theory, as Barnett et al. summarize it, as a framework for their studies. Through the 1970s and 1980s, however, a consensus emerged among anthropologists that such studies were misguided in fundamental ways. Jorgensen provides a useful summary of these criticisms as they apply specifically to acculturation studies of Native American peoples (1978:1, 70–73). For him, acculturation theory and explanations of change within that framework failed for at least four reasons. First, they are often tautological. Anthropologists might classify real-world events as one "process" or another (e.g., syncretism) and then assume that they have explained the phenomena solely by having classified them. In the example of syncretism, however, establishing that elements from separate cultural traditions have been "fused," forming some new cultural trait, does not explain how and why this fusion occurred. Second, acculturation studies are frequently ad hoc. Anthropologists have often based their generalizations on the study of a single group, and their explanations are frequently intended to account for acculturation in that group only. Hence, they do not employ proper comparisons and controls. Third, acculturation studies are often ex post facto. Anthropologists have frequently generalized only after having completed their studies. They frequently make no attempt to test and reject hypotheses. Fourth, and most telling, the acculturation framework is "obfuscating because it confuses the important issues about domination-subjugation, and the causes and persistence of oppression and deprivation, and because it directs our attention toward the politics of assimilation, progress, and integration which have rationalized American political and economic dealings with Indians for two centuries" (Jorgensen 1978:71).

Anthropologists like Linton (1940) and Spicer (1961) seemingly tried to anticipate Jorgensen's last criticism by distinguishing directed from non-directed contact situations. In directed situations, the interests and power of dominant sociocultural systems generate different results than occur in non-directed situations. As noted in Chapter 7, Clemmer uses the concept of directed contact to connect acculturation theory and the metropolis-satellite model of economic underdevelopment (1978a).

We believe that Jorgensen's criticisms are well placed. In our view, many acculturation studies and the acculturation framework in general did not adequately explain contact-induced sociocultural change. Acculturation scholars did not fail, however, because they *necessarily* excluded the concept of power or dominance in contact situations, but because they frequently confused a list of the factors potentially influencing culture change and a typology of change events or kinds of culture change with an explanation of the processes involved. Knowing that the structure of contact situations and the nature of the sociocultural systems involved in the contact, among other things, can affect the results of contact does not explain how and why a particular outcome occurred. Further, knowing (after the fact) the consequences of some contact situation and having a reasonable scheme for classifying such results does not itself explain how and why the events occurred as they did.

In our view, the acculturation framework failed because it lacked a general theory of human action in social groups. It lacked a theory of the relationships among human agents, conceptual systems, and social structures. Other schools of thought in anthropology, however, share this deficiency. Perhaps acculturation theory should not be criticized any more than other approaches for this shortcoming. Acculturation theorists did recognize many of the significant factors and events surrounding contact-induced culture change and contributed significantly to our understanding of potentially significant variables.

As noted earlier, the metropolis-satellite model of economic development is directly relevant to considerations of sociocultural contact. In Chapter 7, we suggested that political economists are interested in economic development and the loci of control over the resources and surpluses central to this process. Dependency theory focuses on exploitative external relationships between societies or nations. This focus, by definition, raises issues of culture contact. The metropolis-satellite model suggests that in unrestrained capitalistic growth, economic and political power tend to be concentrated. "Metropolises," the loci of such concentrations, expand at the expense of their "satellites." The latter are areas peripheral to concentrated power and from which metropolises expropriate land, resources, and labor. Metropolises grow to serve the needs of their ruling classes by expropriating from satellites both capital and surpluses.

In the modern world, much culture contact has occurred within a political-economic framework that the metropolis-satellite model reasonably describes. In North America, for example, contact between European-Americans and Native Americans has generally been structured such that the interests of the former have dominated the interests of the latter (Jorgensen 1978). European-American society has expanded economically, politically, and militarily, at the expense of Native American satellites, to serve the needs of the ruling class. The ruling class is represented, for example, by the owners of railroads and lumber and mining interests. Jorgensen has cogently summarized the results of such exploitation over the last century of contact between European-Americans and Native Americans (1978).

9. Social Structure, Culture, and Human Agency: The Endogenous Processes of Persistence and Change

IN CHAPTER 8, we considered exogenous factors and processes. These originate outside autonomous sociocultural systems. We now focus on endogenous factors influencing persistence and change. These include social structure, culture, and human agency. Taken interactively, these variables constitute the central components of autonomous systems of structured human interaction. Endogenous processes involving or incorporating these variables originate *within* sociocultural systems.

Social Structure

Social structure designates enduring patterns in personal relationships, individual or group behavior, and institutional arrangements. As we use this term, social structure explicitly incorporates patterns in (1) economy, (2) kinship, descent, and marriage, (3) polity, (4) class, and (5) religion. Social structure, thus, includes both economic infrastructure and social and political superstructure. For us, social structure is relational, transcends individual behavior, and is organized into levels that imply explanatory priority.

Social-structural variables appear in many different arguments about events in Hopi social history. In several instances, as reported in our case studies, archaeologists and anthropologists have sought to explain features of Hopi social structure. These scholars have addressed "why" questions about the form, content, stability, and transformation of Hopi social institutions and arrangements. In Chapter 5, for example, we hypothesized that cross-clan membership in Hopi religious sodalities became more prevalent because of the demographic collapse of 1851–1853. We posited that the structure of Hopi religious institutions varied in response to change in Hopi demographic contingencies. After smallpox devastated the Hopi population, individual clans were unable to fulfill their religious duties. Because of this inability, the members of descent-based religious groups allowed more individuals from other descent groups to participate in their rituals. The original descent groups, however, retained control and leadership of their religious organizations.

In parallel analyses of Hopi sociocultural persistence and change, other anthropologists assert that some features or levels of Hopi social structure are dependent on others. Titiev's explanation of the Oraibi split illustrates such an argument. For him, the Oraibi split belongs to a class of similar events consisting of the disintegration of descent-based societies. In Titiev's view, Oraibi's split exemplifies processes related to individual and group responses to stress in descent-based societies with feeble political structures. As reported in Chapter 6, he suggests that Oraibi's fissioning resulted from inherent weakness in Hopi social and political structure. This weakness manifested itself through the split, in response to pressures that contact with European-Americans generated. Oraibi disintegrated, according to Titiev, because the pueblo lacked strong leaders who could overcome the divisive tendencies of Hopi descent groups when external pressures intensified such tendencies. In this explanation, Titiev gives explanatory priority to internal social structural variables. He also acknowledges, however, the effects of external contact between groups, individual personalities, and personal loyalties. This type of explanation implies there are necessary and sufficient conditions for the maintenance of social groups. Such explanations imply, for instance, that social institutions must exist to overcome opposition between descent groups. Such opposition is based on the contrasting interests of individuals from the groups. If institutions do not exist that act to overcome such conflicting interests, or if existing institutions are inadequate to overcome opposing interests, communities composed of multiple corporate descent groups will divide when stressed. Such communities will not endure.

Other explanations from our case studies also refer to causal relationships between different levels of social structure. In several of these explanations, anthropologists gave priority to economic structures, institutions, and arrangements. These scholars considered economic structure to be causally more influential than other social-structural levels. Some of these anthropologists have posited that when Hopi economic arrangements persist, other social arrangements also endure. When Hopi economic structure changes, other levels of social structure also change. Bradfield's account of the Oraibi split illustrates such arguments. In his analysis, environmental pressures eroded Oraibi agriculture's productive potential. Environmental degradation, thus, generated pressure on Hopi economic structure. There were more people than Oraibi farming could feed. When Oraibi economic arrangements were undermined, people were obliged to move. The village was forced to divide.

Nagata's study of Moenkopi social-structural change is another analysis that assigns causal priority to economic arrangements. He suggests that Moenkopi lineage solidarity collapsed in the modern world partly because people increased their participation in wage labor and the cash economy (1970:250). For him, Hopi descent-group solidarity in the past was intimately tied to their agricultural system. Descent group interests were focused on agriculture and on rituals that supported the agricultural system. When wage labor and the cash economy replaced older Hopi economic practices, new and more flexible residential patterns were favored, and cooperation outside the immediate family was discouraged. Descent-group solidarity was undermined because people farmed less and practiced Hopi religion less. Hence, the importance of nuclear family households expanded at the expense of traditional, more inclusive groupings such as lineages, clans, and phratries. Changes in economic structure caused changes in household and kinship structure.

The twentieth century creation of Hopi economic underdevelopment provides a third example of such argumentation. In Chapter 7, Rushforth contended that Hopi satellite status in the U.S. political-economic system has partly determined the structure of their modern economy. He also suggested that contemporary Hopi economic structure has affected other features of their social system. Rushforth suggested that the development of agency towns, the increased significance of nuclear family households in some pueblos, the secularization of political institutions, and the decline of traditional religious institutions are all related to economic conditions created by unequal economic exchange between European-Americans and Hopis.

Social Structure: A Historical Framework

Anthropologists use the term "social structure" in different ways. Various definitions of social structure are derived from the specific subjects that these scholars investigate. Included among such subjects are: (1) patterned relations among groups and individuals, (2) patterns in individual and group behavior, (3) complexity or differentiation in social structures, (4) the division of labor, (5) institutional subsystems, (6) statuses and roles, (7) interrelations between environment, population, and social structure, (8) class structure, (9) communicative face-to-face interaction and associated emergent interactional structures, (10) the social construction of reality, and (11) the structural analysis of kinship and myths (see Blau 1975b:2). Different conceptions of social structure are associated with each of these diverse subjects.

A basic distinction exists between definitions of social structure as "actually existing relationships" among the differing elements of society and definitions that view social structure as an abstract model consisting of logical relationships. The former is represented in the work of A. R. Radcliffe-Brown and other British structural-functionalists (e.g., Radcliffe-Brown 1952:190). The latter is embodied in the studies of Claude Lévi-Strauss and the French structuralists. Lévi-Strauss suggests that "social structure has nothing to do with empirical reality but with models which are built up after it" (Lévi-Strauss 1963:279).

As indicated earlier, we adopt a view of social structure philosophically similar to Radcliffe-Brown's. We do not, however, commit ourselves to a functionalist conception of social structure or deny the significance of social structural models that may or may not be "real." Most anthropologists who have studied Hopi social life, including Titiev and Eggan, have employed similar ideas. Because of this similarity, despite the interesting and provocative nature of Lévi-Strauss' ideas about structure, persistence, and change, we devote most of our attention in this chapter to "realist" conceptions of social structure. We are concerned with elements interrelated in social structures. We are also interested in ideas about persistence and change in such structures. We thus attend primarily to two schools of anthropological thought, British structural-functionalism and Marxist anthropology.

British Structural-Functionalism

British structural-functionalism derives historically from Emile Durkheim's sociology (e.g., Durkheim 1958, 1960, 1963). Radcliffe-Brown cites the French scholar when discussing, for example, the desirability of a natural science of society, the irreducibility of social phenomena, social function, collective representations (common sentiments and beliefs, or "culture," as Radcliffe-Brown defines this term), and mechanical and organic solidarity.

As indicated above, Radcliffe-Brown envisioned social structure to be a system of actually existing "institutionally controlled or defined relationships" among individuals. From this perspective, individuals are viewed, not as organisms, but as human beings occupying positions in a social structure (1952:10). For Radcliffe-Brown, social systems, structures, institutions, and organizations required explanation. Radcliffe-Brown and his followers asked "why" questions about such social phenomena. They answered such questions about social facts by referring to other social facts. They used social features as independent variables in answers to more inclusive "why" questions. In Chapter 1, we provided an example of the first type of explanation. Radcliffe-Brown explained institutionalized mother-in-law avoidance by referring to the role it plays in maintaining harmony or order in social systems (Radcliffe-Brown 1952). This explanation points to a critical theoretical issue in the sociology Radcliffe-Brown envisioned, namely, the nature and source of "social continuity" (1952:10). As in Durkheim's sociology, social equilibrium, order, and harmony were crucial to Radcliffe-Brown. For him, the persistence of social systems across generations was surprising and required explanation.[1]

Radcliffe-Brown and other structural-functionalists achieve their understanding of social continuity by metaphorically viewing societies as biological organisms. They employ an "organic analogy" in their analyses. Radcliffe-Brown argues, for example, that for "forms of social life" to persist, structural continuity is required. For structural continuity to be achieved, conflict must be "restrained or regulated." Social institutions ("established norms of conduct"), like the components of biological systems, can be understood through their contribution to continued functioning or survival of the system. In biological life, the heart may be understood through an analysis of its role in regulating the flow of blood throughout a body. In social life, the institution of mother-in-law avoidance might be understood in terms of its role in regulating or reducing conflict within a social system. For biological systems to persist, blood must flow. For social systems to persist, conflict must be restrained. According to Radcliffe-Brown, the latter is a "law of social physiology" (1952:186). Obviously, functional explanation plays a major part in such analyses. "The function of any recurrent activity . . . is the contribution it makes to the maintenance of the structural continuity" (Radcliffe-Brown 1952:180). For Radcliffe-Brown, various social institutions "function" to reduce conflict within social systems (to maintain internal harmony or consistency) and may be explained by their contribution to the functional unity of the total system.[2]

Within Radcliffe-Brown's sociology, there is conceptual room for explanations of both social persistence and change. Nevertheless, his ideas emphasize social harmony and continuity from a static or synchronic perspective. He assumed that if a social system existed, it was functioning adequately. If a social system persisted, disruptive forces were being restrained. Values and attitudes necessary for harmony within the system were being inculcated in individuals.

Many anthropologists now feel that Radcliffe-Brown's ideas and ex-

planations were misguided. Even within British structural-functionalism, several anthropologists eventually doubted the validity of the organic analogy, the assumption of harmony, functional explanation, and
synchronic studies. Max Gluckman's work provides an example. Early
in his career (during the 1940s), as represented in "Rituals of Rebellion
in Southeast Africa," Gluckman viewed conflicts and rebellions among
Eastern Bantu peoples to be *supportive* of social harmony. He suggested
that acting out conflict either directly or indirectly emphasizes "the social cohesion within which the conflict exists" (1963:127) and "in complex ways *renews the unity of the system*" (1963:112, emphasis added).
Conflict was seen to achieve or function to promote unity. Conflict was
thought to be *necessary for social harmony.*

In 1963 Gluckman adopted a new position on conflict and rebellion
in Africa (1963:35–38). At that time, he denied the appropriateness of
the organic analogy, stressed the existence of "discrepant and conflicting
motives" for individuals in African social systems, emphasized the "discrepant processes" that are part of any social structure and culture, and
suggested that social systems are "open" to influences from environment
and from other societies. He concluded by suggesting that social institutions and processes are never perfectly adjusted: "The institutions, and
the values and laws they [the social processes] embody, are often independent, discrepant, and even conflicting" (1963:38). Gluckman's reanalysis of African civil wars and ritual rebellions reflects how many of
the tenets of British structural-functionalism have been revised.

Claims that Gluckman made about conflict simultaneously represent
the way such scholars handled social change. Structural-functionalists
conceptualized social change primarily as an *endogenous process.* For
them, social change usually resulted from *conflict* between individuals,
groups, or institutions. They further assumed that such conflict was
generated by processes originating in social structure. In Gluckman's
analysis, leaders and followers in Eastern Bantu states develop conflicting motives *because of their positions in social structures.* Their structurally generated motives led to both social continuity and change.

Victor Turner analyzed Ndembu ritual in a manner that exemplifies
structural-functionalist concerns with conflict as well as their concern
with symbol systems. In this school, symbol systems can help to overcome endogenous stress and strain. Turner suggests, for example, that
norms governing behavior can overlap and conflict. For him, ritual
often helps to overcome such conflict by emphasizing a single norm or
closely and "harmoniously" interrelated set of norms (Turner 1967:40).
At one point, Turner discusses the *nkula,* a Ndembu women's fertility
ritual, in terms that could easily be modified to fit Marxist conceptions

of "ideology." Through this ritual, he suggests, rebellious women are "induced and coerced by means of precept and symbol to accept . . . [their] culturally prescribed destiny" (1967:43). Rather than discuss the "functions" of symbol systems further here, we return to them later after reviewing ideas from a second approach that also emphasizes endogenous social-structural variables in analyses of sociocultural persistence and change.

Marxist Anthropology

Historians and social scientists have subjected Karl Marx's sociological theories to hundreds of interpretations and reinterpretations since the 1860s. Scholars have intensively analyzed the development of Marx's thought, different claims that he made, and contradictions among some of his theoretical positions. Our intention is not to duplicate these discussions, but to review the central tenets of his approach to sociocultural persistence and change.

According to Eric Wolf (1982:73ff.), Marx began with two "axiomatic understandings of the human condition." Contemporary anthropologists largely share these opinions. The first is that humans are part of nature. When humans confront and transform nature through production, they change their own character. The second is that *Homo sapiens* is a social species. The way that humans organize socially partially determines how they confront and transform nature. The way that humans confront and transform nature partially determines how they organize socially. Given these axioms, Marx developed a view of social history summarized in the preface to his *Contribution to the Critique of Political Economy* (1904). For Marx, "legal relations" and "forms of state" are grounded in material conditions. "The mode of production of material life determines the general characters of the social, political and spiritual processes of life" (1904:11). Further, when the "material forces of production" come into conflict with the social "relations of production," social revolution ensues. When the economic foundation of society changes, the "superstructure" of social, legal, political, spiritual, and aesthetic forms is also transformed. Neither group nor individual consciousness explains such transformations. Rather, "conditions of material life" explain consciousness (1904:12).

Means of production include land, raw materials, other resources, tools, and technology. Means of production along with labor processes (work, energy expenditure) constitute the *forces of production*. Development of the forces of production is largely a historical process. Such development includes, for example, the invention of tools and technology, changes in the labor process, creation of new sources of energy, and education of social classes. Within Marxist theory, these are major factors and forces for social change.

The labor process is a necessary condition of human existence. It is common to all sociocultural systems. Nevertheless, labor and labor processes exist only within historically determined social conditions. They exist only as part of a more inclusive *production process*. The latter, by definition, consists of a "complex set of mutually dependent relations among nature, work, social labor, and social organization" (Wolf 1982: 74). Such *relations of production* are socially established, defined, and constituted connections among laborers and associations of all the forces of production to each other. Among the most fundamental of these relations are economic ownership or control of productive forces, labor, and surpluses.

Marx sometimes equates *mode of production* with economic structure. He emphasizes the significance of relations of production to economic structure and suggests that mode of production "determines the general character of the social, political and spiritual processes of life." He also argues that "the direct relationship of the owners of the conditions of production to the direct producers . . . reveals the innermost secret, the hidden basis of the entire social structure" (1967:3:791). Marx adds to his view of mode of production by stressing the importance of the way in which *surplus* is produced and controlled. With such ideas in mind, Emmanual Terray suggests that an analysis of the mode of production is not simply a description of economic arrangements. In Terray's view, mode of production refers to a three-part system: (1) the economic base (consisting of characteristic forces and relations of production); (2) juridico-political superstructure; and (3) ideological superstructure (1972:97).

Within Marx's sociology, each stage of human history can be classified according to its characteristic mode of production. As suggested, mode of production influences or determines the nature of social, legal, political, and religious institutions. Mode of production also determines the aesthetic and philosophical bases of social life. Economic structure determines the nature of the "state" (other levels of social structure) and the character of social consciousness (culture). That is, the economic "base" determines the nature of "superstructure."

Marx's economic interpretation of society and history must be conjoined with his theory of *social class*. Although Marx never systematically elaborated the latter, his definition of and ideas about social class are implicit in various of his writings (e.g., 1963). Classes are social groups that emerge as the product of economic structures. They are groups whose members share economic conditions and, because of this, come to share permanent economic interests. The basis for classes lies in the production process. Shared interests and purposes derive from common relations of production. Within Marx's analysis of the "capitalist mode of production," for example, two great classes emerge, the proletariat and the bourgeoisie. The former is the working class of laborers. The members of this class create and add to use-values. The latter is the class of modern capitalists. The members of this class own the means of production and employ wage labor. Within the capitalist mode of production, workers share objective, economically based interests because of their common position within the economic structure. As the mass of workers unites, it develops a common "class consciousness." Workers develop a subjective awareness of their objectively shared interests. The proletariat becomes a "class for itself." Its interests then transcend those of individual workers and are in direct conflict with those of the bourgeoisie. Conflicting interests lead to a broad struggle between classes and to working-class movements designed to overthrow the capitalist system. Such conflicting interests and their results are *inherent to the capitalist mode of production.* Conflicting interests are endogenous to the system. From the Marxist perspective, members of social classes pursuing common interests (that conflict with those of other classes) become central *agents of social change.* Struggles between classes originating in conflicting interests that arise from relations of production help account for social change.

The conflicting interests of social classes constitute one of two types of contradiction inherent to capitalism and other modes of production. Such contradictions are driving forces for social change. *Contradictions* occur when: (1) the attainment of one goal comes at the expense of another or (2) the pursuit of an end (within a particular socioeconomic context or mode of production) results in circumstances that undermine the attainment of that end. In the case of conflicting classes, the satisfaction of bourgeois interests comes at the expense of working-class interests. Such conflict represents the first type of contradiction.

The second type occurs between the forces of production (land, raw materials, technology, scientific knowledge, sources of energy) and relations of production. Marx exemplifies such contradictions in his discussions of the capitalist mode of production. He begins with the assumption that labor is the source of use-value and of surplus-value, and that profit is generated by extracting surplus-value from labor. For Marx, the second type of contradiction becomes evident in the following sequence of events. First, competition among capitalists leads them to seek to reduce labor expenses by introducing labor-saving technological innovations. Second, these innovations increase productivity. However, they also displace workers and reduce profit margins. Third, the reduction of profit margins forces marginal capitalists out of business and into the working class. This concentrates control over the means of production in the hands of fewer bourgeoisie. Fourth, as the working class grows and as unemployment and displacement among workers increases, production exceeds consumer demand. Fifth, as a result, economic collapse occurs, workers unite, the class struggle expands, working-class movements develop, and political revolution ensues. Sixth, the demise of private property and the loss of capitalist control over production forces is the final consequence (Marx and Engels 1967a:93–94). According to Marx, the development of capitalism and capitalist pursuit of profits result in circumstances that undermine the attainment of those ends. This pursuit acts to unite workers. The united workers then overthrow the bourgeoisie's monopoly over capital. Contradictions inherent in or endogenous to capitalism create conflict and incompatibilities that result in transformation of the system.

Marx's concept of *ideology* is crucial to an understanding of conflict, contradiction, and change. For Marx, ideology constitutes part of social consciousness. The latter is part of the superstructure that forces and relations of production create. More precisely, ideology refers to distorted forms of thought or consciousness that stem from and conceal the existence and nature of conflict and contradictions such as those discussed above. Ideology is a "false" or "inverted" form of consciousness that conceals structural contradictions and thereby contributes to their reproduction. Thus, ideology performs two "functions" in Marxist thought. First, it promotes sociocultural persistence or cohesion by *concealing conflicts and contradictions* that might otherwise cause the development of class consciousness, working-class movements, and social revolution. Second, ideology *serves and perpetuates the interests of ruling classes*. Ideology may accomplish both functions when individuals are disposed or convinced to accept their position within the system of social classes and relations of production (see Althusser 1971).[3]

Within anthropology, Marxist thought assumes a variety of forms, for example, Hegelian Marxism, phenomenological Marxism, Marxist structuralism, structural Marxism, Marxist feminism, and mechanical Marxism (see Diamond 1979:1). We make two observations about differences among these approaches. First, Marxist anthropologists differ in their conceptions of social structure. Structural Marxists like Maurice Godelier (1977), for example, borrow their definition of social structure from Lévi-Strauss. Other Marxists adopt "realist" views of social structure (e.g., Terray 1972; Scott 1985). Second, Marxist anthropologists differ in the explanatory priority they assign to infrastructure and superstructure and even their separation or lack of separation into levels. Structural Marxists, for example, are critical of "vulgar materialism" (simplistic economic determinism or utilitarianism). They also commonly invert the traditional Marxist relationship between economic base and superstructure by assigning explanatory priority to the latter. They partially explain persistence or change in mode of production by reference to ideology. Other Marxist anthropologists insist on maintaining the view that allocates causal priority to the economic base.

Despite such differences, Marxist anthropologists are interested in the extension of Marx's ideas to noncapitalistic (precapitalist) modes of production such as hunting-gathering, nomadic pastoralism, and self-sustaining agricultural systems. They seek to extend his ideas to societies "dominated" by kinship, tradition, and cultural reason. In their studies of precapitalist modes of production, Marxist anthropologists often begin by investigating labor processes and focusing on factors and relations of production (e.g., Scott 1985:68). Given knowledge of infrastructure, Marxists proceed by analyzing the way that forces and relations of production articulate with the derivative sociopolitical and ideological superstructures (Terray 1972:97–105).

Marxist anthropologists handle sociocultural persistence and change in familiar ways. First, they emphasize the contradictions discussed earlier. Second, these scholars acknowledge the role of *external* sources of change such as the environment, population, and sociocultural contact (including conquest) (e.g., Godelier 1977; Taussig 1980; Wolf 1971; Worsley 1957; Kahn and Llobera 1981b:289). Third, they recognize the influence of technological innovation and invention on change processes. For them, technological innovation constitutes change in the *forces of production.* Innovation must be understood within the context of existing *relations of production.* As noted earlier, Marxist anthropologists, especially structural Marxists, stress the need to avoid vulgar materialism or economic determinism. One of the ways they do so is by emphasizing the part that relations of production and ideology play in filtering the results of technological change (and also in filtering the impact of environment, population, and culture contact). For Marxist anthropologists, technological innovation might also create contradictions between the forces and relations of production. These contradictions might then result in social revolution and transformation. Fourth, Marxist anthropologists underscore ideology's role in sociocultural persistence and change (e.g., Taussig 1980).

Marxist anthropology and structural-functionalism may now be compared and contrasted, beginning with apparent differences between the two schools. The first of these differences pertains to their conceptions of social structure. As indicated, structural-functionalists often define social structure as actually existing relationships among social actors. To the contrary, many Marxist anthropologists employ a concept of social structure inspired by Lévi-Strauss' idealism. Further, to many Marxists, structural-functional conceptions of social relations are themselves distortions and "self-concealing ideological constructs" (Taussig 1980:9). For these Marxists, "reified" views of social structure can conceal objective relations of production. Second, the two schools assign different explanatory priority in their studies of social systems. For the structural-functionalists, the "point of entry" is usually social structure (excluding economic structure). Economic arrangements and symbolic systems are derivative and secondary in their analyses. Marxists (excepting structural Marxists) assign explanatory priority to the economic base. Other levels of social structure and superstructure are secondary. Finally, structural-functionalist studies have been largely synchronic. Studies in Marxist anthropology, in principle, incorporate historical change.[4]

Despite these differences, structural-functionalists and Marxist anthropologists often approach sociocultural change in similar ways. In both schools of thought, social systems are seen to possess *inherent characteristics that can create stress, tension, or pressure that leads to systemic transformation.* Structural-functionalists emphasize corporate descent groups in their studies of social structure. They have used the term "dysfunction" to label social stresses and strains. Marxists emphasize infrastructure and social classes. They employ the term "contradiction" when studying modes of production. Despite these terminological differences, however, scholars from the two schools frequently analyze dysfunctions and contradictions in similar ways. Both groups assume that social-structural parameters create differences in interests and values among the members of social systems. Both begin their studies by attempting to discover and describe such structurally rooted differences. Structural-functionalists might, for example, assume that the members of one descent group have interests in competition with those of other descent groups in the same society. Marxists might assume that members of the working class possess interests opposing those of capitalists. For both schools of thought, oppositions or contradictions between such structurally rooted interests and values lead to conflict between the members of the different groups. Members of different descent groups might come into conflict over scarce land. Members of different social classes might struggle over access to life's necessities. For structural-functionalists and Marxists, such *conflict is a fundamental source of social change.*

Within the context of such analyses, structural-functionalists and Marxists also assign similar roles to culture or social consciousness. Structural-functionalists often conceive of symbolic systems as being derivative of social structure. Many Marxists view ideological super-structure to be derivative of the economic base.[5] Nevertheless, the former discuss the contribution that beliefs and values make to social harmony or cohesion. The latter discuss ideology's significance in concealing conflict between classes and in supporting or perpetuating the upper class's privileges. Further, at least some Marxist anthropologists emphasize ideology's role in cultural resistance to domination (e.g., Taussig 1980; Wessman 1981:264–319). For both schools of thought, symbolic systems that mitigate contradiction and conflict are factors for social persistence.

Several anthropologists have analyzed Hopi sociocultural persistence and change using ideas from structural-functionalism.[6] Others have employed concepts reminiscent of those associated with Marxist anthropology. Titiev's description of Hopi social structure and explanation of the Oraibi split, for example, derive from his training in structural-functionalism. His ideas are also similar in some respects to those of Marxist anthropologists. In this regard, we find it interesting to compare Marx's image of capitalist society with Titiev's image of Hopi society. For Marx, the "capitalist integument . . . is burst asunder" when means and relations of production become incompatible (Marx 1967:1:715). For Titiev, because of the strength of Hopis' ties to clans and the weakness of their ties to villages, a "Hopi pueblo is like an object with a thin outer shell which holds together a number of firm, distinct segments— should the shell be cracked, the segments would fall apart" (Titiev 1944:69). For both Marx and Titiev, pressures that result in a "bursting" or "cracking" of the social integument come from internal conflict and contradiction among the components of social structure. Upham has made claims similar to Marx's and Titiev's. In an earlier work (1982), he discussed the presence of "systemic hypercoherence" in the late-prehistoric Western Pueblo regional system. He then suggested that the collapse of this system derived, in part, from its highly integrated nature. In this case, the productive failure of a few component communities ramified throughout the regional system and tore apart its social, economic, and political fabric. Internal conflict and contradiction is also evident in Awatovi's destruction.

Other analyses of Hopi sociocultural persistence and change have made claims related to structural-functionalist conceptions of symbol systems and Marxist notions of ideology (e.g., Whiteley 1988a, 1988b). This topic raises issues concerning the role of cultural variables in sociocultural persistence and change.

Cultural Variables

Culture is, for us, a conceptual system. It is a framework of meaning and moral responsibility that individuals acquire as members of social groups (Rushforth with Chisholm 1991). Cultural systems define the meaning of acts, objects, and events. They determine what is good and bad, and define worthy goals. They also establish the appropriate means for pursuing those ends. Cultural systems are separate from but intimately related to individual mental states and human agency and action. Further, cultural systems: (1) are largely, but not completely shared by the members of social groups, (2) transcend the beliefs and values of individuals, (3) sometimes endure, and (4) sometimes change.

Cultural variables were central to many of the anthropological explanations that we considered in the Hopi case studies. Several anthropologists whose work we reviewed actually attempted to explain persistence or change of Hopi culture. The most frequently invoked of such explanations attributed the persistence of traditional Hopi culture (as a system) to their geographical and social isolation. As noted in Chapter 5 Titiev (1944), Eggan (1950), Spicer (1962), Nagata (1970), and Dockstader (1979) have all made this claim. Their common argument is that culture change derives from culture contact. If a group remains isolated through geographical, social, or other means, its members have fewer opportunities to borrow and assimilate new ideas and concepts. Therefore, that group's culture is less likely to change. Presumably, such persistence would be enhanced in a small-scale, culturally homogenous society. Groups with less cultural diversity have fewer "raw materials" from which to fashion culture change.

A second explanation that concentrates on cultural variables suggests that Hopi *cultural conservatism* has contributed since first Spanish contact to Hopi sociocultural persistence. Anthropologists have defined cultural conservatism, roughly, as Hopis' uncommon appreciation for their own beliefs, values, and customs, coupled with their willingness to assume the responsibility of actively perpetuating Hopi cultural traditions (cf. Clemmer 1978a:39). Anthropologists have maintained that this value is a core feature of the Hopi cultural system. They have also asserted that this value contributes to persistence of the entire Hopi sociocultural system (e.g., Titiev 1944; Spicer 1962; Clemmer 1978a; Whiteley 1988a). When Hopis with conservative values confront new conditions (for example, when they encounter new ideas from Spanish priests or European-American bureaucrats), they reject or resist change. If new conditions present problems that they must solve, conservative Hopis seek solutions from among their own cultural resources. Conservative Hopis refuse to adopt new beliefs and values from foreign sources.

Rushforth's explanation (following historians and other anthropologists) of Awatovi Pueblo's destruction illustrates the part that cultural conservatism plays in some explanations of Hopi sociocultural persistence and change. Rushforth suggested that the Hopis who destroyed Awatovi were partially motivated by their desire to end corrupt conditions that Awatovi's acceptance of Spanish priests had engendered. He also suggested that this extreme action displayed and reinforced Hopi religious leaders' power to negatively sanction deviant behavior. Hopi leaders used this power to effectively restrict Spanish presence at the Mesas for 175 years. This restricted presence partially limited sociocultural change during that period. Hence, conservative values motivated or led to actions that supported sociocultural persistence.

Whiteley's analysis (1988a) of the Oraibi split provides another example of such explanations. In his view, culturally conservative Oraibi priests faced extraordinarily corrupt conditions around 1900. The priests interpreted those circumstances using Hopi religious texts. They then sought to solve their problems through religious actions. Myth told the priests that Oraibi corruption signaled the pueblo's end and the beginning of a new phase of Hopi history. Accordingly, the priests deliberately divided the village and destroyed the Oraibi religious system as it had been constituted. Ironically, Whiteley's explanation both incorporates and then inverts the significance of Hopi cultural conservatism. Cultural conservatism led to the destruction of Oraibi. Hopi leaders intended this action to revolutionize Hopi religious and political institutions.

Clemmer's study of twentieth-century Hopi revitalization and resistance also incorporates Hopi cultural conservatism. He suggests that such values motivate some Hopis to resist external political-economic domination. Such Hopis remain less than fully integrated in European-American society.

Cultural variables also entered into our hypothesis about a possible post-1850 increase in cross-clan membership in Hopi religious sodalities. We speculated that demographic collapse during the 1850s changed membership patterns in Hopi religious institutions. If this causal relationship holds, Hopis might have reinterpreted the cultural bases of

those institutions to rationalize or explain the new forms of membership. They might have assigned new meanings to the compositions of
religious societies. These modifications might have been accomplished
in ways that Clemmer describes as the "Hopi mythic process." Hopi mythology changed to explain the arrival of Spanish, European-Americans,
and Mormons. Hopi mythology might also have changed to account for
increased participation by members of noncontrolling clans in religious
ceremonies. If this were true, Hopi culture changed in response to
changes in social-structural variables. The latter had been transformed
in response to modifications in Hopi demographic structure.

We can now summarize cultural variables as both consequence and
cause of sociocultural persistence and change in Hopi social history.
First, Hopi cultural frameworks of meaning and moral responsibility
have persisted or changed, in part, as a consequence of the stability
or instability of Hopi social arrangements. Second, Hopi cultural beliefs
and values have, perhaps, contributed to Hopi sociocultural stability.
This stability was partially accomplished through individual and group
actions. Hopi culture provided such individuals and groups with motivations and directions.

Cultural Variables: A Historical Framework

During our considerations of culture contact and of social structure, we
reviewed the part that knowledge, belief, and value systems play in sociocultural persistence and change. In the next section of this chapter,
we discuss selected cultural variables while reviewing human agency
and action. Accordingly, we limit our discussion here to two issues. The
first concerns the part that cultural values play in sociocultural persistence and change. The second concerns ideology's role in the same
processes.

In their analyses of Hopi social history, anthropologists have almost
inevitably incorporated some cultural variables. Scholars referring to
the Hopi value of "conservatism" employ arguments related to those
that the German sociologist, Max Weber, developed in his analysis of
Western socioeconomic history (1927, 1958). Weber was interested in
the part that Calvinist ideas and values played in Western capitalism's
development. For him, Calvinism encouraged in individuals certain attitudes and actions (a "specific and peculiar rationalism . . . [a certain
type] of rational conduct" [1958:26]) that resulted in capitalism's development. Ideas and values, rather than material conditions and economic structures, led to the relevant sociocultural changes. For Weber,

an explanation of capitalism's rise was obtained by "understanding" forces that motivated actors to behave in distinctive entrepreneurial ways. Those ways of behaving resulted in economic changes.

In Weber's account of Western socioeconomic history, he also discussed a serious obstacle to capitalism, namely, "economic" or "primitive traditionalism." For Weber, "At the beginning of all ethics and the economic relations . . . is traditionalism, the sanctity of tradition." According to Weber, the "incapacity and indisposition to depart from the beaten paths is the motive for the maintenance of tradition" (Weber 1927:354). Traditionalism may be tied to material interests. It may also be supported through supernatural sanctions (Weber 1927:355).

Weber's traditionalism seems closely related to cultural conservatism. It is an "attachment to tradition and to the pietistic relations of fellow members of tribe, clan, and house-community . . . [that represents] a tempering of the unrestricted quest of gain" (Weber 1927:356). Hopi ethnographers, as noted, have referred to such cultural values when explaining Hopi resistance to change during the Spanish, Mexican, and European-American historical periods. Acculturation theorists concerned with boundary-maintaining features of cultural systems discuss the implications of such values for contact situations. Similarly, anthropologists who have studied peasant cultures and societies often refer to "peasant conservatism" (or its equivalent) when accounting for peasant economic organization or the ties between peasants and more inclusive political-economic systems (e.g., Redfield 1941; Foster 1965; Scott 1976). Marshall Sahlins differentiates "cultural reason" from "practical reason" in ways that seem to equate the former with primitive conservatism and the latter with utilitarian rationality (1976). Marxist anthropologists are also interested in such values. They seek to extend Marx's ideas to precapitalist modes of production within which kinship and primitive traditionalism "dominate." By doing so, these anthropologists seemingly accept traditionalism's significance without adopting its explanatory implications.

In summary, various anthropologists assume that ideas, beliefs, and values are causally involved in sociocultural persistence and change. They sometimes refer to cultural conservatism or traditionalism when trying to understand social actors' behavior, especially in non-Western societies. They assume that conservatism ensures maintenance of traditional forms of thought and behavior. They believe that transformation of this value or set of values will lead to other cultural and social changes.

Scholars have frequently criticized these ideas (e.g., Boudon 1986: 145ff.). First, analyses like Weber's *oversimplify* the events and causes of social history. Using the above concepts and explanatory scheme to explain large-scale revolutionary or evolutionary social transformations, for example, is "metaphysical." It is not empirical or rational (Boudon 1986:122). Second, such explanations overemphasize the autonomy of ideas and values. Cultural variables might help explain selected cases of sociocultural persistence or change. In other circumstances, however, cultural variables themselves persist or change in response to exogenous or other endogenous factors. In the latter cases, giving explanatory priority to values and other cultural phenomena is incorrect. Third, studies incorporating reference to the causal effects of ideas and values seem often to assume that the mere presence of the values establishes their significance for accounts of sociocultural persistence or change. If, for example, Hopis value tradition, and if their sociocultural system remained unchanged through time, the former must account for the latter. Correlation, however, does not establish causation.

As discussed earlier, cultural variables are also significant in structural-functional and Marxist accounts of sociocultural persistence and change. Theorists from both schools of thought stress the role that social consciousness plays in perpetuating social structure. Of particular interest to us is the Marxist concept of ideology. As noted, social scientists use this term in different ways. We are concerned with its meaning as "false consciousness" and with the effects of "ideological domination" on sociocultural persistence and change. According to Marx and Engels, ruling classes have control not only over means of material production, but also over the "means of mental production" (1967b:61). For them, "The ruling ideas are nothing more than the ideal expression of the dominant material relationships . . . grasped as ideas" (Marx and Engels 1967b:61). Such ideological domination is termed, following Gramsci (1971), *hegemony*. Marxists suggest that beliefs and values produced and controlled by dominant classes replicate their control over material production and promote their own interests. Members of subordinate classes, through their acceptance of such beliefs and values, are *mystified* about (unaware of) their own interests and circumstances. Since dominant classes control beliefs and values, and since subordinate classes accept such ideology as "natural" (Bourdieu 1977a:164), *mystification through ideological domination* inhibits development of class consciousness and, hence, social movements. Accordingly, ideological domination promotes sociocultural persistence. Values and ideas constitute an elemental, sometimes insurmountable obstacle to change. This argument explains, for some Marxists, why capitalism thrives despite social structural contradictions and class conflicts. James Scott summarizes this view by suggesting that ideological hegemony is frequently sufficient to guarantee "spontaneous consent" and "social peace" (1985:316). Only when ideological hegemony fails, do ruling classes resort to violence.

Scott continues, however, by questioning the explanatory usefulness of ideological hegemony (1985:318ff.). He suggests there are five reasons why hegemony and related concepts are likely to mislead investigators in their analyses of class conflict. First, members of subordinate classes are frequently aware of their situation and of the mystifying nature of a dominant ideology. Second, members of subordinate classes rarely see ideology as inevitable, natural, and just. "So far as the realm of ideology is concerned, no social order seems inevitable . . . to all of its subjects" (1985:331). Third, the concept of hegemony overestimates the extent of consensus and coherence, while underestimating the amount of conflict within ideological systems. Fourth, ideological subordination does not preclude revolutionary change, since the objectives of most social movements are "limited and even reformist in tone" (1985:318). Individuals with merely reformist demands may employ revolutionary methods. Fifth, "breaking of the norms and rules of a dominant ideology is typically the work of the bearers of a new mode of production—for example, capitalists—and *not* of subordinate classes such as peasants and workers" (1985:318). Dominant ideologies are not frequently "shattered" by the development of counterhegemonies among the members of subordinate classes (1985:346).

Scott develops his criticisms using ethnographic data from his analysis of agriculture and class relations in a Malaysian peasant village. Residents of "Sedaka," although engaged in a well-described class struggle, do not act and talk in ways consistent with the conventional view of hegemony. Rather, Scott suggests that Sedaka poor are not mystified about their situation. They reject characterizations that the rich use against them. They view agricultural innovation in ways that differ from the rich. The poor contest the rich's version of social reality. They "penetrate" the rich's self-serving discourse. They understand economic reality. They manipulate values serving their own class interests. Within economic and political limits, the poor defend their interest through "boycotts, quiet strikes, theft, and malicious gossip" (Scott 1985:304).

Scott makes two critical points. First, Sedaka class ideology emerges from the *practical activity* of real social actors who pursue their own "material and symbolic interests" (1985:310). Hence, Sedaka rich and poor have "divergent constructions" of social norms that are based on their respective class interests (1985:198ff.). Second, Sedaka poor are not mystified about or by their circumstances. They understand their situation, reject ideological domination, and engage in a myriad of "everyday forms of peasant resistance" to defend their interests. For us,

Scott's ethnographic documentation of these claims represents a welcome addition to anthropological literature. Moreover, Scott's concept of everyday forms of peasant resistance is a significant contribution to our understanding of sociocultural persistence and change. He defines this idea by contrasting everyday resistance to more overt, confrontational resistance. In contradistinction to the anticipated quiet acquiescence of ideologically dominated poor, Scott found peasants who stubbornly struggle to resist exploitation and ideological domination.

The origins of this struggle, in Scott's analysis, derive not only from objective circumstances, but also from actors' interpretations and understandings of those situations. Scott does not ignore actors' social consciousness. He suggests that the meanings actors assign their acts, "the symbols, the norms, the ideological forms they create constitute the indispensable background to their behavior" (1985:38). Scott also stresses that actors' intentions are not "unmoved movers." Rather, there is constant communication between acts and meanings. Nevertheless, for Scott, actors' conscious meanings, understandings, and values play a crucial part in the explanation of everyday resistance. Acts of resistance to claims and appropriations are agents' intentional acts. Such agents are frequently motivated by self-interest.

If Malaysian peasants do not acquiesce to their subordinate status, and if this case is representative of other peasant systems, what provides for peace and stability? According to Scott, one possible answer might be that stability is provided through real or threatened force and "*not by peasant values and beliefs*" (1985:40, emphasis added).

Scott explicitly addresses issues concerning sociocultural change in two contexts. First, the Malaysian peasants he describes were in the midst of significant socioeconomic change. Scott's discussion of the sources of such change attends primarily to *externally induced transformations* in the forces of production. He focuses on the green revolution's implications for Malaysian rice agriculture. The application of new technology (e.g., new strains of rice, double cropping, tractors, and combine harvesters) to Sedaka agriculture has altered relations of production and class structure. Further, under these contact conditions, local peasant elites have themselves become dependent on external forces such as foreign buyers. This dependence has created *ideological contradictions* that help explain the form of Malaysian peasant resistance (1985:311–312).

The second context within which change enters Scott's analysis concerns the *cumulative effects of everyday acts* of resistance. The resistance Scott discusses is individual, informal, anonymous, silent, flexible, persistent, and coordinated through "networks of understanding and prac-

tice" (1985:297–298). It is not formal, public, obtrusive, openly confrontational, and coordinated by formal or central leadership. Scott's
analysis suggests that the *aggregation of individual acts* can lead to either
sociocultural persistence or change. On the one hand, individual resistance may successfully defend peasant material interests in a manner
that allows peasants as a group to reproduce themselves (1985:307).
On the other hand, the cumulative result of individual resistance may
be establishment of a "climate of opinion" (1985:300) or a "long-run
war of attrition" (1985:298), both of which cause or contribute to systemic transformation.

Scott's ideas are intriguing for the perspective they give on events in
Hopi social history. The Pueblo Revolt, the destruction of Awatovi, and
Oraibi's split represent active, even violent resistance to domination by
external sociopolitical forces. Social-movement theory might account
for some of these events. Hopis also responded to potential domination
by engaging in numerous acts of "everyday resistance." Whiteley (1988a)
and Clemmer (1978a) discuss such actions. They included (1) Hopi leaders' use of verbal and behavioral strategies that were intended to delay
and confuse negotiations with foreign religious and political representatives, (2) Hopis' refusal to send children to European schools, (3)
their refusal on several occasions to be immunized, (4) their refusal to
participate in allotment and their disruption of the allotment process by
removing survey stakes, (5) their refusal to participate in IRA tribal referenda, and (6) the refusal of some villages to participate in Tribal
Council politics and developmental schemes. The nature and effects of
such Hopi resistance raise issues about relationships between sociocultural systems and individual agency and action.

Human Agency and Action

Human agency entails meaningful, purposeful, or goal-directed actions.
Human beings are agents capable of conscious deliberation and intentional activity, including deliberate forbearance. Agents are capable of
intervening in the world through their actions. These interventions
have empirical implications for events and objects in the world. Much of
human behavior is "considered action" (Fodor 1975; Rushforth 1985;
Rushforth with Chisholm 1991). As argued in Chapter 1, people act in
specific ways partly because of their beliefs and values. Among the
beliefs and values significant to such actions are those that categorize:
(1) the situations within which people act, (2) the behavioral alternatives
available to individuals and groups within those situations, (3) the goals

motivating action, and (4) the probable effects of behaving in one way or another.

Human agency appears implicitly or explicitly in several explanations of events in Hopi social history. Before discussing these, however, we must deal with explanations that give the impression of incorporating agency, but actually deny agency an explanatory role. We refer here to some of the accounts that include cultural conservatism among the explanatory variables (e.g., Dozier 1970; Spicer 1962). On close analysis, individual agents play only a tangential role in these accounts. These explanations assume implicitly that individuals: (1) internalize beliefs, values, and norms as part of their cultural tradition; (2) enact or follow these cultural principles; and (3) inevitably perpetuate their sociocultural system through their behavior. In such arguments, individuals are not credited with consciousness or volition. Once enculturated, people have few options. Hence, human agency is omitted from the explanation. These anthropologists account for behavior by describing culture. Culture simply duplicates and perpetuates itself through a human medium.[7]

In opposition to such analyses, Whiteley's account of the Oraibi split demonstrates explicit explanatory use of human agency. In his explanation, Oraibi's division resulted from conscious actions that the pueblo's religious elite undertook. The priests evaluated natural and social events, determined a course of action to correct the problems that they perceived, and then purposefully divided the village. Whiteley does not, however, deny the explanatory significance of environmental, economic, and acculturative stresses. To the contrary, he asserts that these forces are a necessary part of a complete explanation of the split. He simply maintains that conscious agents interpreted their empirical circumstances, and that environmental, economic, and acculturative effects partially depended on the interpretations. Agents' actions are necessary, but not sufficient, to explain the split.

Our proposed elaboration of Whiteley's analysis similarly incorporates human agency. Our suggestion that the split be understood within the explanatory context of social movement theory, however, also includes an attempted explanation of why Oraibi leaders had the beliefs, values, and motives they did. To account for the mental states of Oraibi religious leaders, we referred to the political-economic deprivation that Hopis experienced during the late 1800s and early 1900s. We hypothesized that such deprivation gave rise not only to the Oraibi split, but also to the Ghost Dance, Sun Dance, and other religious movements. The form and content of these social movements varied depending on the cultural background of specific peoples.

In summary, we make three points about human agency in Hopi social history. First, the demographic, environmental, cultural, and social structure of several situations seem to have constrained and possibly determined individual actions.[8] For these events, it might be reasonable for an anthropologist to deny the explanatory significance of human agency. Second, many incidents in Hopi social history appear to have been loosely enough structured that human agency significantly influenced the course of events. In these cases, individual Hopis possessed behavioral options from which they deliberately chose. Their choices or the consequences of their choices affected later Hopi social history. Third, anthropologists have disagreed tacitly about which events were which. Bradfield's analysis of the Oraibi split, for example, suggests that it was the first type of event (wherein human agency was insignificant and individual actions determined by other forces). Whiteley's analysis suggests that it was the second type of event.

Human Agency and Action: A Historical Framework

We begin this discussion by reiterating that agency must be distinguished from mere "enactment" or "execution" of cultural rules and social norms (Ortner 1984:150; Bourdieu 1977a:24, 96) and from the mechanical "working out of an established order" (Sahlins 1981:6). Agency entails that agents think and that their mental states influence or determine features of their behavior. Agents are capable of conscious, deliberate, and meaningful acts, including forbearance. Agents make decisions. They have reasons for acting the way they do. Their acts convey meaning. An opposing view of humans envisions their behavior to be the result of an automatic execution of cultural and social rules. In this perspective, people respond mechanically to situations. They follow scripts, perform scores, implement plans, or follow ground rules (see Bourdieu 1977a:96). In the parlance of computer science, people execute programs. Within this latter framework, culture either provides or consists of the scripts, scores, plans, rules, or programs. Given this perspective, an anthropologist might explain individual and group behavior by explicit or implicit reference to rules and to native actors' dispositions to enact the rules. As noted, various anthropologists who refer to Hopi conservatism when explaining individual behavior and resistance to foreign influence exemplify this view. We are concerned, however, with anthropological positions that acknowledge a more "active" social agent and the explanatory significance of human agency.

Anthropologists often hold one of two positions concerning relationships among individuals, cultures, and societies. Many of the anthropologists discussed earlier understand culture and society to be largely independent of individuals, to have an existence separate from that of individuals, and to require explanation "in their own terms." American anthropology's concern with the "superorganic" (White 1959) and British anthropology's assumption of the "irreducibility" of social phenomena are examples. Anthropologists concerned with human agency, however, usually adopt a form of "methodological individualism."[9] This position suggests that all social phenomena be understood and explained through analyses of individual motivations, thoughts, and actions. In one of its strongest forms, methodological individualism contends that social phenomena be "reduced" to individual phenomena.

In anthropology's history, various scholars have embraced methodological individualism in their studies of sociocultural persistence and change. Among such anthropologists are Homer Barnett (1953, 1954), Anthony F. C. Wallace (1956), and Fredrik Barth (1966, 1967). Barnett advocated the position he labeled "nominalism," and distinguished it from "realism." The former acknowledges "only the individual, not the species or the genus" (1954:1002). Accordingly, for Barnett, the acculturation processes of modification and incorporation were mental processes occurring in individuals' minds in contact situations. Wallace referred to the concept of "mazeway" when explaining revitalization movements. "The mazeway is nature, society, culture, personality, and body image, as seen by one person" (Wallace 1956:266). When individuals' mazeways become severely stressed and traditional stress-reducing strategies prove ineffective, a radical change in some individual's mazeway might result. This individual (or these individuals) might become the source and motivating agent(s) of a revitalization movement. Barth is concerned with individual motivations and decision-making processes that motivate individual actions and lead to social change. Persons willing to assume risk and pursue new courses of action that might provide larger rewards are termed "entrepreneurs." Social change occurs when entrepreneurial behavior is institutionalized because of its increased payoffs.

More recent anthropological and sociological analyses adopt modified versions of methodological individualism. We refer here to different versions of praxis theory (e.g., Bourdieu 1977a; Sahlins 1981; Giddens 1976, 1979, 1984; Boudon 1979, 1982, 1986; Fabian 1983). Practice theorists, as well as others who emphasize, for example, "cultural decision-making" (Goodenough 1956; Keesing 1967; Rushforth 1984, 1985) or "transactionalism" (Barth 1966; Kapferer 1976), share several broad philosophical and empirical interests, while varying in their specific concerns. Practice theorists are broadly interested in a question that we also raise. How do sociocultural systems (cultures, societies, social systems, cultural structures, or social structures) persist? Practice theorists often approach this question by focusing on the conceptual systems and activities of individuals and groups. They suggest that cultural systems persist when individuals or groups transmit their conceptual frameworks, beliefs, and values from one generation to the next. They contend that social systems persist when patterns of activity and interaction are stable through time and across space. Practice theorists often explain such cultural and social persistence by referring to the actions and activities of individuals and groups. They focus on human *practices* and suggest that sociocultural systems persist *because the practices of individuals and groups persist.* Mechanisms for the persistence of practices are ipso facto mechanisms for the persistence of sociocultural systems. Further, factors that alter the organization of human activities or practices are forces for sociocultural change. How anthropologists and sociologists give substance to these statements occupies the remainder of this chapter.

To begin, contemporary scholars frequently trace the concept of *praxis* and discussions of its significance to Marx. For Marx, praxis consisted of ("free, universal, creative, and self-creative") actions and activities through which humans produce and, as a consequence, through which they shape their social worlds. Marx emphasized the *practical actions of production* and the social ramifications of such activities. Practice theorists in anthropology and sociology share these interests. They are concerned with: (1) the nature of human action and agency; (2) the relationship of human agency and individual and group actions to sociocultural processes and structures; (3) how social processes are realized or instantiated in everyday (practical) social activities, interactions, or practices; (4) both the intended and unintended consequences of such human activities; and (5) how "social production and reproduction" are related to or constitutive of sociocultural persistence and change.

Practice theorists are concerned with human actions and activities. They are also interested in the relationships of practices to sociocultural systems and structures. They are, therefore, also frequently interested in human agency.[10] As noted earlier, scholars frequently identify human agency with intention, purpose, goal direction, will, and motivation. From the perspective defined by the conjunction of these ideas, human agents are said to engage in intentional or purposeful behavior. Agents act the way they do because they intend to achieve certain ends. Agents often justify their actions by citing their *reasons* for having behaved in some manner. Assuming this perspective, scholars contend that human behavior is meaningful, communicative, and symbolic. These statements, however, beg several questions about intentions, purposes, motivations, and meanings, and about the relationships of such phenomena to individuals, cultures, and social structures. Practice theorists usually agree on at least two points about these concepts: (1) that human agency and action can not be described or explained as "mere enactment" and (2) that groups or social systems do not exhibit agency or possess intentions. Nevertheless, different anthropologists and sociologists provide distinct answers to more specific questions about these concepts. Consequently, such scholars have different theories of human agency and action.

Similarly, practice theorists commit themselves to one or another position about the nature of culture and social structure. Although many practice theorists consider culture and social structure to be real, they frequently employ different definitions of these phenomena. Practice theorists define culture in ways ranging from systems of knowledge and rules to conceptual structures in the Lévi-Straussian sense. They define social structure in terms varying from class structure to the "rules and resources" that organize social systems. Because of their competing views about agency, action, culture, and society, practice theorists have distinct ideas about the relationship of individuals to systems and structures. Despite their shared focus on everyday practical activities, interactions, and practices, their explanations of individual actions and of sociocultural systems are not unified.

Practice theorists often use the term "social reproduction" in their explanations. This concept is central to their accounts of the extension of cultural and social systems through time and across space. They attribute this idea to Marx's sociology (Marx 1967). For Marx, modes of production require reproduction. Labor and relations of production must be recreated for a mode of production to persist. This need constrains superstructure. Within contemporary practice theory, social reproductive processes renew or recreate cultural and social structures. Such reproductive processes are located primarily in individual and group everyday activities. For these scholars, individuals' actions are both *constrained by and creative of* cultural and social structures. However, since practice theorists differ in their views of human agency and action and in their definitions of cultural and social systems, they also differ in their conceptions of social reproduction.

To make these concepts more concrete, we now review the work of three different theorists, Anthony Giddens (1976, 1979, 1984), Pierre Bourdieu (1977a, 1977b), and Marshall Sahlins (1976, 1981). Anthony Giddens refers to his approach in sociology as the theory of "structuration." Giddens begins with the notion that "The production of society is a skilled performance, sustained and 'made to happen' by human beings" (1976:15). For Giddens, it is necessary to begin by distinguishing three concepts: structure, system, and structuration (1979:62ff.; 1984: 25ff.). Structures consist of "rules and resources, organized as properties of social systems. Structure only exists as 'structural properties'" (1979: 66). Social systems are "reproduced relations between actors or collectivities, organized as regular social practices" (1979:66). Structuration consists of "conditions governing the continuity or transformation of structures, and therefore the reproduction of systems" (1979:66). For Giddens, social systems are patterns of social relationships, "reproduced interdependence[ies] of action," or recurrent, "regularized practices" that exist only in and through the activities and interactions of human agents. When activities and interactions cease, social systems cease. For Giddens (1979:66), social systems are reproduced through the reproduction of structural principles (rules and resources). Structures are reproduced through their use by knowledgeable agents in regularized practices.

Giddens links his theory of structuration directly to human agency. Accordingly, Giddens attends to the "acting self." He develops a concept of agency and action that incorporates intentionality, but emphasizes other characteristics (1976, 1979, 1984). His reasons for not reducing agency to intention are related to his conception of human action as "a continuous flow of conduct" (rather than a series or aggregate of independent, intentionally based acts) and to the importance he places on the "unintended consequences of intentional activity" (1984:3–14). According to Giddens, an agents' actions are "interventions in events in the world." The world would be different were it not for such interventions. In addition, agents intend some of the outcomes of their interventions. They do not intend some of the other outcomes. Such unintended consequences are based in, but related differently to, intentions than are the intended consequences. In Chapter 5, we suggested that Hopi leaders achieved one of their intended effects, isolation from Spanish contact, by destroying Awatovi Pueblo. Awatovi's destruction may also have had an unintended consequence: partial Hopi avoidance of epidemic diseases. The two effects would have had different relations to Hopi leaders' intentions. Because of such complications, Giddens stresses the significance to agency and action of "reflexive monitoring," "knowledgeability," "practical consciousness," "interpretive schemes," "rationalization," "accountability," "power," and the "ability to have acted otherwise" (1976, 1979, 1984). Using such concepts, Giddens constructs a model of agents who know what they are doing, are able to attend reflexively to their actions, and are able to account for, justify, or give reasons for their actions. They often do the latter by referring to or using the same stocks of knowledge that they employed when acting (1979:57). During these processes, agents use the "rules and resources" constituting the structuring principles of their sociocultural system. Such rules are "codes and norms" (1979:104). Codes are "interpretive schemes" that actors draw on and reproduce during their communicative interactions (1979:97–100; 1984:29). Agents employ such interpretive schemes to comprehend and assign meanings to their own and others' actions during interaction. This process, as well as the normative establishment of rights, duties, and responsibilities, is accomplished through accommodation, adjustment, and negotiation between agents while they interact (1979:85–87).

Giddens divides resources into two major types: authorization and allocation. These two types of resources constitute structures of domination "which are drawn upon and reproduced as power relations in interaction" (1979:100). Authorization consists of capabilities to generate power over persons, while allocation consists of capabilities to do so over material phenomena. For Giddens, power is critical to agents and social life. To act, agents must have power in the form of "will," and also in the form of institutional access to authorization and allocation. Without power, agents are incapable of action.

For Giddens, legitimation is a theory of normative regulation. In his view, normative regulation and sanction can not be explained by referring to the "internalization of values as need-dispositions." Moral obligation does not imply internalized moral commitment and "moral claims do not operate with the mechanical inevitability of events in nature" (1976:109). Rather, moral claims (regarding rights, duties, and responsibilities) involve the *reactions of others* and must be "negotiated." The participants in social interaction must interpret and legitimize the norms. Agents must make the norms "count" (1976:110).

Within Giddens' theory of structuration, social reproduction is the *reproduction through interaction and practice* of structures of signification, domination, and legitimation, and of the social systems that such structures organize. For him, social systems are produced and reproduced in interaction. He emphasizes that social reproduction is an unintended consequence of individuals' intended acts and that "any explanation of social reproduction which imputes teleology to social systems must be declared invalid" (1979:7). For Giddens, acts of communication, power, and sanction that are accomplished using structural principles simultaneously reproduce those structures. Communicative practices that deeply embed interpretive schemes in "practical consciousness" are central to processes reproductive of structures of signification. Language and linguistic codes, for example, are reproduced by the process of speaking. Structures of domination are reproduced through the exercise of power in social interaction. Structures of legitimation are reproduced by agents using normative sanctions in social practices. For all of these practices and processes, Giddens stresses the significance of socialization, routine, and tradition.

Pierre Bourdieu develops different notions of human agency, action, practice, social structure, and cultural and social reproduction. His views are heavily influenced by Marxist thought (1977a). Like Giddens and Sahlins, Bourdieu believes that human actions cannot be explained as enactment, that practice cannot be reduced to "mechanical reaction" or "mechanical necessity," and that processes embedded in everyday practices are central to the production and reproduction of conceptual and social systems (1977a:73, 97). From this common position, however, Bourdieu moves in a separate direction. He develops a specific concept of human agency and action that he labels "habitus."[11] This concept is pivotal, not only to his view of individual action, but also to his explanations of the relationship between individuals and social structures and of social production and reproduction. Bourdieu defines habitus as "systems of durable, transposable *dispositions,* structured structures predisposed to function as structuring structures . . ." (1977a: 72, emphasis in original). Habitus is a system of dispositions. "It designates a *way of being, a habitual state* (especially of the body) and, in particular, a *predisposition, tendency, propensity, or inclination*" (Bourdieu 1977a:214 n.1). Habitus consists of structured, durable dispositions that are not to be confused with, described, or explained as "legalistic" rules. Rule formulations are, for Bourdieu, always secondary rationalizations. For Bourdieu, agents do not mechanically follow rules, however much they might rationalize their behavior by referring to rules (1977a:20, 36–37, 76). Habitus (socially acquired and structured dispositions consisting of both cognitive and motivational structures) is the basis for actors' "regulated improvisations" that, in turn, constitute social practices. An actor acquires his or her habitus from the "objective conditions" within which he or she exists. In Bourdieu's vision, objective structures establish social conditions that tend to reproduce the habitus that created those conditions. Objective conditions, for Bourdieu, consist of class and group structures: ". . . science apprehends (objective conditions) through statistical regularities as the probabilities objectively attached to a group or class . . ." (1977a:77). Such social structures, according to Bourdieu, create habitus ("aspirations and practices," "cognitive and motivational structures"). Habitus, through its influence on the organization of practice, tends to reproduce those objective conditions (1977a: 77, 83, 97, 163–165, 166). Habitus links through time the two sets of objective conditions. It reproduces conditions at time (T_2) in the form of conditions at time (T_1). Objective class conditions (measured, for example, by access to jobs, education, and political office) create dispositions in human agents that, when enacted, tend to reproduce the structures that originally engendered those dispositions. Social reproduction occurs unintentionally (as "intentionless invention") through the practices that class or group dispositions produce.

Marshall Sahlins provides the third and final version of practice theory that we consider (1976, 1981). Sahlins develops his ideas most clearly in his book, *Historical Metaphors and Mythical Realities* (1981). He focuses in that work on events during and after Captain James Cook's 1778 arrival in the Hawaiian Islands. Sahlins examines issues concerning the relationship between structure and history (events in the world) by concentrating on practice, "human action in the world" (1981:6). Like other practice theorists, Sahlins disclaims the view of human action as mere enactment or the mechanical "working out of an established order" (1981:6) and carefully delineates an alternate view. This alternate view conceptualizes human action as intentional, meaningful, and motivated by culturally constituted interests and values (1981). His understanding of these closely related concepts is influenced by the conjunction of structural linguistics, structural anthropology, and semiotics. In the introduction to his book, Sahlins sets out a view of the relationship of structure (*la langue*) and practice (*la parole*) upon which he eventually builds a more general model of practice (1981:5–6). He suggests that the history of a language is made in speech. In speech (action), linguistic signs take on contingent relationships and values depending partially on people's socially constituted and individually variable instrumental purposes. Signs are thus subjected to reanalysis and recombination. "Unprecedented forms and meanings" can result. People employ systems of signs to experience the world. The contingent world, however, can cause revaluation of systems of signs.

Agents, in Sahlins' analysis, are idealized social actors who occupy positions in social systems. The latter are organized as "schemes of social distinctions." They are composed of groups and social classes. Culturally defined positions in social systems establish for "acting subjects" their pertinent, socially constituted (but individually variable) interests, intentions, and motivations (1981:35–36, 50). Agents' intentional, purposeful actions are motivated by interests pertinent to culturally constituted conceptual systems or "received structures." Agents do not pursue some universal "utilitarian" logic (Sahlins 1976; 1981:68). They accomplish their *intentional actions* by means of *signs*. Hence, the semiotic concepts of "interest and value" are key to Sahlins' view of the acting subject (1981:68–69). For Sahlins, the conventional meanings of signs may be analyzed through the Saussurean idea of "the conceptual value of the sign." The sense, conceptual meaning, or conventional value of a sign is determined by its relationship to other signs in the "collective symbolic scheme" (1981:68–69). However, agents use signs to accomplish their own socially constituted and, perhaps, individually variable purposes. Through their use in real circumstances, signs are brought into (unique) contact with their referents. In and through such practice (constituting an "objectification of signs"), signs acquire "contingent," "contextual," "intentional," or instrumental value" (1981:69). Signs are connected to symbolic structures through their conventional value. They are connected to socially constituted individuals through their instrumental value. The latter are, in Sahlins' view, equivalent to the "interests" that motivate intentional acts. An "interest in something is the difference it makes for someone." It is a social fact because it is derivative from the socially constituted conventional values of signs. Agents are motivated by the interests derivative of conceptual structures: "The intentional value, of course, derives from the conventional value—also in history, vice versa—but the latter is an intersubjective relationship of signs, different in quality and mode of existence from personal experience" (1981:69).

Praxis, for Sahlins, is social actors' enactment of signs in contingent circumstances. It is the interaction of system and event, the "structure of the conjuncture" (1981). Practice is informed or organized by cultural conceptions, culturally constituted interests and values, or "received structures" (1981). Events tend to be "encompassed" within the system as constituted (1981:50). However, practice takes place in the contingent real world. There is no guarantee that the real world will match received structures. Nor is there any guarantee that individuals interacting in the same event operate with the same conceptual systems. As a result, practice has "*sui generis* developments" or emergent properties that themselves are amenable to structural analysis (1981:33, 77). Sahlins' book provides examples of such emergent properties from contact between British sailors and Hawaiian peoples during the late 1700s. According to Sahlins, an analysis of the events that took place shows that English captains and seamen and Hawaiian chiefs and commoners (including both men and women) approached contact events with distinct, socially determined interests and motivations. Not only did they fail on many occasions to understand each others' actions, but the effects of ambiguities and contradictions in such interactions led to Hawaiian culture change.

Social or cultural reproduction, for Sahlins, is reproduction of "received structures." These are cultural or conceptual systems, systems of social distinctions, or symbolic schemes (1981). Social or cultural reproduction takes place when such cultural systems or conceptual schemes "encompass" real world events. Such encompassment is accomplished when actors organize their intentional activities according to received conceptual systems. When actors interpret and understand contingent events through received categories, and when they pursue interests derivative of the conventional values of those systems, social or cultural reproduction occurs. As a result, conceptual systems are reproduced in and through such activities.

In addition to cultural and social reproduction, Sahlins is also interested in change. According to Sahlins, events and real-world circumstances do not always (perhaps rarely, if ever) match received structures. When signs (the constituent elements of symbolic structures) are "objectified" in the real world, they receive contingent meanings that might vary from their conventional meanings. These contingent meanings may "work back" into conceptual structures and initiate change in those systems. Instrumental values affect conventional values and, depending on their relationship to other elements of the symbolic system, may cause change throughout that structure (1981:67). Sahlins illustrates the processes of "failed" reproduction, of "defeated intention and convention" using examples taken from Hawaiian contact history (1981: 50). In this analysis, Sahlins is concerned with the "clash of cultural understandings and interpretations" within the context of culture contact (1981:68). The "historical stress" (1981:38, 43), the "structure of conjunction," of such situations creates *contradictions and ambiguities* (1981:34) in actors' understandings of events. This generates mutual *conflicts and criticisms* among the individuals involved. These forces lead to a pragmatic reevaluation of received categories. New conceptual content is "picked up" in experience and conventional values are changed by contingent interests. Although such forces are most clearly seen in culture contact, Sahlins explicitly acknowledges their presence in all societies and all practice: "one may question whether the continuity of a system ever occurs without its alteration, or alteration without continuity" (1981:67).

Other practice theorists, including Giddens and Bourdieu, also address the issues Sahlins raises concerning cultural and social change. In agreement with Sahlins, these scholars frequently adopt a view of change that incorporates several basic points. First, they believe that the forces and factors for change (as well as reproduction) are located in the organization of interactions in real-world activities and interactions, in practice. They often suggest that the potential for change "is inherent in every circumstance of social reproduction" (Giddens 1979:210ff.; 1984:244ff.). Second, many of them contend that sociocultural change is, in some sense, *failed reproduction* (e.g., Bourdieu 1977a:211 n.92). An understanding of change, then, requires an understanding of cultural and social reproduction. Third, many of them emphasize that events in the real world are contingent, and that change (and reproduction) represent *a conjunction of multiple factors and forces* (see Giddens 1984:245, 251). Sahlins is not alone in his emphasis, for example, on the importance of culture contact on processes of change (e.g., Scott 1985). Fourth, various practice theorists stress that both reproduction and change are "unintended consequences" of acting subjects' intentional activities (Giddens 1979:210ff.). Actors rarely intend change. They rarely understand the implications of their actions for sociocultural systems. Fifth, practice theorists frequently suggest that *contradictions* in the organization of practice can lead to failed reproduction and, hence, to systemic transformations (Giddens 1984:245). This emphasis represents continuity with the Marxist origins of practice theory.

In summary, we make four observations about practice theory and its contribution to the analysis of sociocultural persistence and change. First, there is no single practice theory. Rather, there are multiple theories, each of which is based on a distinct conception of human action and agency and of cultural and social structures. Second, despite the differences in their approaches, practice theorists agree that the study of human action, interaction, and practice enhances our understanding of sociocultural persistence and change. We agree and suggest that practice theory's eventual contribution to anthropological theory will be determined by the extent to which it clarifies the organization of individual and group activities. Third, concerning sociocultural persistence and change, practice theorists frequently acknowledge many of the factors and forces for change and persistence that we discussed earlier. Conflict and contradiction, for example, are as consequential to Sahlins' analysis of Hawaiian contact history as they are to Titiev's analysis of the Oraibi split.

10. Explanation and Hopi Social History

IN CHAPTER 1, we raised several significant anthropological issues. The most basic of these concerned human behavior, sociocultural systems, and relationships among individual action, culture, and society. We then focused attention on sociocultural persistence and change by asking two questions. Why do sociocultural systems sometimes persist through time with little variation? Why do they sometimes change? We devoted the remainder of the book to investigating some of the different answers that anthropologists have provided to these questions.

We initiated our investigation of sociocultural persistence and change by reconstructing a Hopi social history. We began our reconstruction by describing the Western Pueblo before first contact with Spanish explorers and colonialists. We then dealt with the Spanish, Mexican, and early European-American periods between 1540 and 1909. We concluded by characterizing twentieth-century Hopi culture and society. Throughout our case studies, we concentrated on features of Hopi culture and society that demonstrated either extraordinary persistence or fundamental change during a given era. At every point, we were interested not only in discovering, describing, and documenting events in Hopi social history, but also in using accounts of those events to examine anthropological explanations of sociocultural persistence and change. In some instances, features of our reconstruction were frankly conjectural. In such cases, as exemplified by our proposal that cross-clan membership in Hopi religious societies increased following the 1851–1853 smallpox epidemic, we based our accounts primarily on indirect evidence. We were willing to do so for two reasons. First, we felt that the indirect evidence was strong enough to warrant our hypotheses. Second, by so speculating we were able to introduce and discuss additional critical issues concerning anthropological approaches to sociocultural persistence and change.

Our reconstruction of Hopi social history was also intended to address the question, "Why does the contemporary Hopi sociocultural system possess its particular formal and substantive characteristics?" Generalizing from our Hopi social history and review of anthropological approaches to sociocultural persistence and change, the answer we provided can be divided into two parts. The first part referred to our assumptions about the initial state, configuration, or condition of the Hopi sociocultural system. The second part of our answer (to which we devoted most of our attention) focused on processes that affected the Hopi sociocultural system once it existed.

Our social history began with the assumption that Hopi ancestors were present at First, Second, and Third Mesas around A.D. 1100, when Hopis first occupied Oraibi. Thus, we assumed that the contemporary Hopi sociocultural system developed from the prehistoric Western Pueblo sociocultural system and that features of the former must be explained by referring to features of the latter. The form and content of present-day Hopi culture and society are partly determined by the configuration of Western Pueblo culture and society. As Sahlins pointed out in his discussion of structuralism, "Change begins with culture, not culture with change . . . history begins with a culture already there" (Sahlins 1976:22–23). For us, Upham's and other archaeologists' reconstruction of the Western Pueblo defined the Hopi sociocultural system's initial state. As chaos theorists emphasize, complex systems are extremely sensitive to their initial conditions. The smallest difference in a system's initial conditions can affect its intermediate and final states. This sensitivity to initial conditions, sometimes known as the "butterfly effect," is symbolized by the hypothetical influence on weather patterns of an insect's fluttering wings. We are convinced that equally complex causal connections are found in sociocultural systems. The beliefs and values that a few individuals held at one point in a sociocultural system's history, for example, might lead those people to act in a certain manner. Their actions might have momentous intended and unintended consequences for events and processes that occur later in their group's social history. These later events and processes might, in turn, result in significant sociocultural change that otherwise would not have occurred. An example of this effect is seen in Oraibi's leaders' actions of 6 and 7 September 1906. Later in this chapter, we report another sociocultural example of the butterfly effect taken from Hawaiian history (Sahlins 1981).

Given the original state of the Hopi (Western Pueblo) sociocultural system, we then focused on specific social and cultural features, established their persistence or change through a specified period, and investigated anthropological accounts of the processes underlying such stability or transformation. An expected but critical point emerged from our analysis. Persistence and change in the Hopi sociocultural system since the prehistoric period has been the result of *multiple and complex processes*. There are three separate but related senses in which this statement is justified. First, Hopi social history is the *cumulative result* of many events that, when taken together, have produced the contemporary form and content of Hopi culture and society. Phrased differently, persistence and change in the Hopi sociocultural system have resulted from the *historic concatenation or accumulation* of multiple episodes of change and persistence. Contemporary Third Mesa Hopi individuals' participation in traditional ceremonies, for example, is partly determined by their residence in particular Third Mesa pueblos. People from Hotevilla, for instance, are more likely to participate in traditional religious ceremonies than people from Kykotsmovi. The reasons for this lie partially in circumstances that resulted from Oraibi's disintegration. The Oraibi split was influenced by contact with European-Americans. Such contact was affected by conditions created by the 1851–1853 smallpox epidemic. The results of this epidemic were affected by political-economic conditions going back to Awatovi's destruction and the Pueblo Revolt. And so on. The accumulation of such effects reflects the sensitivity of historical processes to the initial and intermediate states of sociocultural systems. Because of this sensitivity, Hopi social history and the social histories of all peoples are highly particularistic. This does not imply, however, that sociocultural processes cannot be isolated, treated locally and partially (Boudon 1986), and eventually used as the bases for generalization to and explanation of other cases of sociocultural persistence and change. Such generalization is a central goal of anthropology.

The second sense in which Hopi social history is the result of multiple and complex processes involves the *conjunction and interaction* in specific events and circumstances of many different variables and processes. Historic events crucial to Hopi sociocultural persistence and change have resulted from complex interactive processes involving many different types of variables and processes. Such variables and processes have included those we discussed in the case studies and examined in Chapters 8 and 9. The Oraibi split, for example, was not caused by any single factor. No single exogenous process (e.g., culture contact, population pressure, or environmental change through drought and erosion) and no single endogenous process (e.g., weak political organization, conflicting descent-group interests, or deliberate actions, including social movements) accounts for the pueblo's disintegration. Rather, several of these variables and processes operated *simultaneously and in-*

teractively to bring about that result. As Whiteley suggests, "ecological and social near-chaos" dominated Oraibi before the split. Oraibi priests interpreted those circumstances and then followed a course of action designed to remedy the culturally perceived problems. The intersection of these *separate fields of causation* led to the split.[1] The conjunction of environmental, social, cultural, and intentional processes caused Oraibi's disintegration. Several theorists whose ideas we reviewed in Chapter 9 (e.g., Gluckman 1963; Sahlins 1981; Giddens 1984; Boudon 1986) share the view that sociocultural change and persistence result from such intersections. Sahlins' discussion of what happened to European-Hawaiian relations because Captain Cook's ship, the *Resolution,* sprung its foremast is germane. Ruin of the mast occurred a few days after Cook had embarked from Kealakekua on his way to Kahiki in January 1779. Because his ship's mast broke, Cook returned to Kealakekua. From the perspectives of both the British and the Hawaiian sociocultural systems, the breaking of the mast was an exogenous event that disrupted a serendipitous correlation between Cook's prior activities and the traditional Hawaiian ritual calendar. This disruption led the Hawaiians to reinterpret Cook's presence in terms different from their previous understanding. The new Hawaiian interpretations led them to interact with Cook and his men in more aggressive ways. Such interactions contributed directly and immediately to events that culminated in Cook's death. Because of Cook's death, the course of European-Hawaiian contact history changed (Sahlins 1981:22ff.).

The intersection of different fields of causation, as exemplified in Sahlins' Hawaiian case, not only raises the issue of the multiplicity and interaction of processes in sociocultural persistence and change, but also the issue of *chance* or *contingency* (see Gould 1989:284–284). Is it reasonable to label the effects of the *Resolution*'s broken foremast on Hawaiian history as due to chance or the contingent conjunction of events? The explanatory situation is as follows. Intelligible physical forces caused the mast's destruction (the fluttering of a butterfly's wings). Cook's return to the island for repairs is understandable. Later interactions between the British and Hawaiians are comprehensible and easily explained (given a knowledge of Hawaiian conceptual structures, specifically, of Hawaiian mythological and ritual structures). The effects of Cook's death on ensuing European-Hawaiian relations are discernible. However, the breaking of the foremast and Hawaiian conceptual structures are not themselves causally related. They were not previously linked. They were completely independent, belonging to separate fields of causation. Nevertheless, the chance (contingent) synchronic intersection of these otherwise unrelated causal chains affected later historic events and resulted in a transformed Hawaiian sociocultural system.[2] For us, following Boudon (1986), contingency or chance consists of such "Cournot effects." Chance is not a "substance." Rather, it is a "structure which is characteristic of certain sets of causal chains as perceived by an outside observer" (Boudon 1986:179). When used to label such causal chains, chance or contingency plays a crucial role in sociocultural persistence and change. Anthropologists must attempt to discover and describe such causal structures and distinguish them from other, more frequently discussed, causal structures where one action or object is seen to be the cause of another.[3]

The third sense in which Hopi social history must be viewed as the result of multiple and complex processes concerns the *changing nature of causal relationships* among variables involved in different episodes of persistence and change. Potentially significant exogenous and endogenous factors were not equally influential in each episode of Hopi history. On one occasion, an exogenous factor such as sociocultural contact might have been determining. In another situation, an endogenous factor such as conservative Hopi values might have been crucial. On other occasions, undoubtedly representing the majority of cases, multiple factors and processes (e.g., contact, population change, economic pressure, and agency) might have operated interactively to pattern historic events. Which of these situations existed depended on the structure of the event and the nature of the processes involved. Further, the roles that different factors played and the relationships among factors changed in different situations and processes. On one occasion, changes in Hopi population structure might have affected Hopi social arrangements. In other circumstances, Hopi social institutions might have had important implications for Hopi demography. Again, which situation was which depended on the circumstances and processes involved.

Adding to the complexity and multiplicity of sociocultural processes in social history (and specifically to the changing nature of causal relationships in sociocultural processes) is a fundamental feature of human consciousness and intentional behavior, namely, "reflexivity." Reflexivity denotes the ability of knowledgeable agents to monitor their own behavior, interpret those actions (evaluate their meaning and effectiveness), and modify, when necessary, future goals and actions. As Giddens says, agents "have, as an inherent aspect of what they do, the capacity to understand what they do while they do it" (1984:xxii). Agents are capable of self-regulation. They can (1) interpret past and present events and their responses to specific circumstances, (2) interpret the meaning and effectiveness of their responses to those circumstances, and (3) respond differently if those circumstances appear again. Human agents can respond differently to the same configuration of events on different occasions. Those behavioral responses can have different intended and unintended consequences for the sociocultural systems in which the actors are members. The same factors, forces, and processes might affect sociocultural systems differently and uniquely on separate occasions. History never repeats itself, in part, because people remember. Because people remember, they may act in new ways when situations similar or identical to past circumstances appear. There is at least one additional reason that history never repeats itself. Sociocultural events and processes are complex and contingent in the ways discussed above. It is unlikely that specific configurations of events and processes could ever be duplicated (cf. Gould 1989).

In summary, monistic determination is inappropriate to an understanding of Hopi social history, or of any other group's social history. Hopi sociocultural persistence and change have been the result of multiple and complex processes. Hopi social history represents an accumulation of causal processes through time. Specific episodes in Hopi social history have resulted from the intersection of multiple processes and separate causal fields.

Our analysis of Hopi social history and consideration of anthropological approaches to the study of sociocultural persistence and change have led us to several conclusions about sociocultural persistence and change and about explanations of these phenomena. First, we are convinced that studies in social history represent a productive way to approach the topics of sociocultural persistence and change. Asking questions about real events or episodes, focusing on *local and partial processes* (Boudon 1986), provides an empirical base for constructing rational, if incomplete, explanations of persistence and change. From such limited explanations it might be possible to move toward a more general and inclusive theory of persistence and change. Further, we feel that social history represents an auspicious meeting place for archaeology and sociocultural anthropology. Both archaeologists and sociocultural anthropologists (as well as other social scientists and historians) can contribute to the understanding of any people's social history. As noted earlier, social history is an accumulation of historic events representing episodes of persistence and change. The initial states of sociocultural systems help determine the outcome of such episodes. Archaeologists contribute to our understanding of those initial conditions.

Second, we suggest that certain variables and processes are likely to be significant to explanations of sociocultural persistence and change. These include: (1) the exogenous factors of population, environment, and culture contact; and (2) the endogenous factors of social structure, culture, and human agency. We consider several specific factors and processes as being especially significant to analyses of sociocultural persistence and change. Among these are conflict, contradiction, and scale. The first two of these, as noted in Chapter 9, appear in different forms in various schools of anthropological thought. They have been most important to anthropologists investigating endogenous processes of change. We suggest that conflict and contradiction may be equally important to investigations of exogenous processes. Sociocultural contact, for example, might create internal conflict that leads to change. Hopi disputes between Hostiles and Friendlies at the turn of the twentieth century provide an example. Further, we stress that conflicts and contradictions might be found in or shown to affect any of the components of structured systems of human interaction: culture, social structure, and agency. Scale is especially important to investigations of the effects of demographic structure on sociocultural systems.

Our claims in the previous paragraph should not be taken to imply that the variables and processes we listed will be equally important in all events or that these variables will play the same role in any event with which they are associated. To the contrary, as indicated earlier, the significance of these variables and the roles that they play are likely to vary depending on the events and processes involved.

Second, we have stressed the complexity (accumulation, interaction, conjunction, and synchronization) of processes involved in sociocultural persistence and change. We also suggested that the role of specific variables in the relevant processes may change depending on the circumstances involved. We conclude from these points that there is currently no single, general, and acceptable theory of sociocultural persistence and change (cf. Boudon 1986). Presently, the most satisfactory anthropological accounts of sociocultural persistence and change are local and partial. They are constructed from the partial social histories of specific groups. Such accounts establish precisely which sociocultural features have persisted or changed within a well-defined set of temporal, environmental, and sociocultural conditions. They then provide evidence suggesting that specific processes operated under those conditions and led to precisely defined sociocultural results. They make limited claims about the general nature of the processes and the relationships among relevant variables. They make limited claims about a general science of society and recognize that history is not and will not be deducible or predictable.

Third, despite our conclusion that a universal theory of sociocultural persistence and change is yet to be developed, we emphasize the importance of maintaining nomothetic goals in the anthropological investigation of this topic. Although it might be impossible to predict specific historical events (for all of the reasons mentioned), it might be feasible to account for and predict the *general direction* of historical trends. In Hopi social history, for example, it might be impossible for an anthropologist to predict the specific effects of a hypothetical Hopi population increase during the initial period of the twenty-first century. It might be possible, however, to anticipate changes in scale-related social phenomena as the Hopi population expands hypothetically to twice its current size. It would be reasonable, for example, to expect changes in social institutions that are tied to the managerial needs that a large population engenders. It might be impossible to predict specific new social configurations after population increase. It might, however, be possible to predict some characteristics of such social configurations. In Hopi prehistory, Western Pueblo institutions associated with prehistoric long-distance trade and political complexity probably constitute examples of such scale-related institutions.

To conclude our discussion, we offer a summary of the view of sociocultural persistence and change that emerged from our efforts in writing this book. First, we continue to believe that it is profitable to distinguish culture, society, and human agents as the endogenous components of autonomous sociocultural systems. We feel that our definitions of these phenomena are useful. Culture consists of conceptual structures (knowledge, beliefs, and values). Society consists of interactional structures (patterns of behavior, institutions, and arrangements). Human agents engage in intentional actions that have both intended and unintended consequences. The three components combine in structured systems of human interaction. They combine in practice. We suggest that any descriptive or explanatory account of sociocultural systems or of human practice must incorporate references to and analysis of these components.

Second, we believe that forces for sociocultural persistence and change may "enter" through any one of the major components of sociocultural systems of human interaction. Sociocultural persistence and change may be the result of forces operating on cultural, social, or intentional (mental) systems. Forces that act, for example, to modify cultural beliefs might lead to changes in social and intentional structures. Forces that independently affect the structure of interaction might result in changes in the form and content of cultural systems.

Third, we suggest that forces affecting sociocultural systems may originate from within autonomous systems of interaction (e.g., as the result of contradictions in the goals of actors within those systems). They may also originate outside autonomous systems of interaction (e.g., as a consequence of population changes that alter the objective conditions within which interactions take place). Accordingly, we find the endogenous-exogenous distinction to be a valuable idealization. We are, nevertheless, aware that definitions of endogenous and exogenous processes depend on the scope of systems being considered.

Fourth, as implied above, we concur with practice theorists that the interactions of cultural, social, and intentional structures in practice often provide the key to understanding sociocultural persistence and change. The forces and factors that act on such structures (individually or conjunctively) do so within the context of structured interaction.

Fifth, as discussed above, we feel that any investigation of sociocultural persistence and change within the framework sketched here must begin by focusing on partial and local processes. Theoretical generalizations are difficult to achieve. If mental structures, for example, were shown to be determinant in one episode of social history, they might be partially or completely derivative in another. If population increase is established as the cause of sociocultural change in one situation, it might be the result of sociocultural change in another. We suggest that anthropologists acknowledge this possibility regardless of which forces and factors they emphasize when investigating specific cases.

Sixth, although we suggest that social scientists recognize the importance of cultural, social, and intentional structures in their explanations of sociocultural persistence and change, we realize that anthropologists and archaeologists will normally focus on different components of structured systems of human interaction. Archaeologists, in particular, must concentrate on societal (material or behavioral), rather than cultural and intentional, structures. The reasons for this are manifest. Because archaeologists focus on material culture, they usually lack direct (and sometimes indirect) evidence of cultural and intentional systems. In general, the archaeological record (that is, material cultural remains and their contexts and associations) is an *unintentional or unintended consequence* of the intentional actions of human individuals, as well as other forces. It is, in principle, impossible to infer or deduce actors' intentionality from such unintended consequences. Does this mean that archaeologists have little to contribute to our understanding of sociocultural persistence and change? No. It simply means that paleopsychology is not possible. Archaeologists' contributions will be determined primarily by the extent to which they discover and describe processes affecting patterns in group behavior *independent* of cultural and intentional structures.

We now conclude Chapter 10 by restating our original goals. Our aims were to (1) reasonably reconstruct Hopi social history, making clear various interpretations of events; (2) make explicit either others' or our own answers to "why" questions about sociocultural persistence and change in Hopi social history; and (3) clarify the nature of anthropological argumentation about the relevant processes. Despite the qualifications and limitations emphasized above, did we succeed in accomplishing our stated goals through the presentation of Hopi case studies and later discussions? We leave it to the reader to judge. Concerning number (2), saying that we (or others) have answered "why" questions about Hopi social history is materially different from saying that we (or others) are correct. Answers to questions about the correctness or truth of explanations raise issues concerning the nature of scientific (including anthropological) investigation. Some researchers might claim that their explanations are general and true. They might refer to universal laws. Other scholars might assert that their explanations are valid only within or assuming a specific explanatory framework. Others might claim that their explanations are accurate for only a few specified cases. Our position concerning the Hopi case studies approximates the weaker two of these claims. We acknowledge that for any of the specific events and processes discussed, there may be different analyses. We realize there may be significant processes operating in particular events that we did not consider. We are aware that the acquisition of new data pertaining to the variables we or others used in specific cases may change the way anthropologists now think about the relevant events and processes. We know that, as more data are acquired, support may be found that is presently lacking for one of the explanations that we discounted. Consequently, our and others' explanations of events in Hopi social history must be viewed with healthy skepticism until more data are obtained that bear on the relvant questions. Even after this, uncertainty remains.

If this seems unusual, the reader should remember that the scientific method demands that all descriptions, postulates, and theories be considered provisional, in anticipation of new data and, possibly, new explanatory frameworks. All knowledge within the scientific world view is, by definition, tentative because researchers continually test and refine or reject their hypotheses and theories. Thus, a new explanation might temporarily replace an old explanation, but the former, like the latter, is only valid until another still more parsimonious, elegant, or general explanation appears. We believe that this argument holds for all explanations in anthropology.

Notes

1. Perspectives on Persistence and Change

1. We base some of these ideas on explanations of in-law avoidance provided by Tylor (1889), Radcliffe-Brown (1952), Murdock (1949), and Driver (1966).

2. We use the term "sociocultural" from this point forward to emphasize the conjunction of conceptual and behavioral domains.

3. This is related to what has become known among chaos theorists as the "butterfly effect," or a sensitive dependence on initial conditions. We discuss this idea briefly in Chapter 10.

4. See Mera (1935) and Hawley (1937) for earlier versions of this kind of approach.

5. In this and related discussions, we are influenced by Michel Foucault's work (e.g., 1972).

6. For discussions of different definitions of culture, see Keesing (1974) and Ortner (1984).

2. The Western Pueblo and the Hopis

1. In the discussion that follows, we employ past tense forms of verbs. We do not intend, at this point, to convey anything about change or persistence of Hopi culture and society through time and into the modern world. In this chapter, we are simply describing earlier periods of Hopi history.

2. For comments on the interpretation of Spanish documents, see Chapter 1 and Whiteley (1988a).

3. These are middle and lower Rio Grande regions of New Mexico.

4. Peter Whiteley suggests that anthropologists significantly underestimate the extent of Hopi trade from this period (personal communication, n.d.). He points out, for example, that Hopis acquired salt from Zunis, horses from Mormons, and wool, mutton, and coal from Navajos.

5. In the discussion that follows, we ignore certain differences between the descriptions of Hopi culture and society that Titiev and Eggan provide. One such area of difference pertains to the definition of Hopi households and their role in Hopi social life. Anticipating further discussion, we point out here that the nature of

households (and other features of social structure) has been one of many contentious issues in anthropological studies of the Hopis. Anthropologists debate over the "reality" of such levels and institutions, the rights, duties, and responsibilities associated with them, whether they are named, and other issues. We address some of these points later.

6. For a more complete discussion of Hopi political organization, see Whiteley (1987).

3. Regional Abandonments and the Western Pueblo

1. Cordell (1984:122–152) provides a summary of these and related ideas.

2. In some cases, more particularistic traits are used (e.g., Wheat 1955).

3. See Amsden (1932:194) and Schroeder (1952:140) for discussions concerning the Spanish use of these terms.

4. Colonial Contact, Disease, and Population Decline

1. Recall here that Hopi of the ethnographic present period neither imported significant quantities of food nor engaged in intensive agriculture.

2. See Whittlesey (1978) for a different interpretation of the burial record.

3. We refer here to estimates and reconstructions that anthropologists attempted between 1900 and 1960.

4. See Upham (1986) for a rather complete listing of pertinent references.

5. See Milner (1980) and Ramenofsky (1982) for a graphic portrayal of a deterministic model for general epidemics.

6. See also MacCallum and McDonald (1957:248) for a description of this experiment.

5. Hopi Resistance to Subjugation and Change

1. Peter Whiteley points out that the impression of stability may be due primarily to our lack of accurate historical records before the 1850s (personal communication).

2. See summaries by Bartlett (1934), Spicer (1962), and Simmons (1979a).

3. See Hieb (1972) and Ortiz (1972b:158–161) for discussions of Hopi sacred clowns.

4. See Wiget (1982) for an evaluation of the accuracy of this and other versions of the revolt at Oraibi.

5. Peter Whiteley pointed out to us that the "relocation" of Walpi from a point midway to the top of First Mesa was actually a "reoccupation" of a traditional village site (personal communication).

6. Peter Whiteley discusses such political actions in depth (1988a). We review some of his work in Chapter 6.

7. Whiteley feels strongly that Awatovi's destruction occurred in November

1700, at a time when Awatovi men were in their kivas performing sacred ceremonies (personal communication).

8. We are conscious of the difficulties involved in interpreting historical documents. We know that population estimates from such sources must be questioned at every turn. We acknowledge the speculative nature of assigning numbers and figures to prehistoric and early historic puebloan populations. Nevertheless, we believe that the figures we present are reasonable. Further, by addressing population, we are able to introduce important points about the relationship of population size and stability to sociocultural persistence and change. We acknowledge the speculative basis for such claims as they pertain to the Hopi.

9. Whiteley disagrees with this characterization. He suggests that anthropologists have underemphasized the extent of extralocal Hopi trade during the early historic and ethnographic present periods (personal communication).

10. Whiteley suggests that by the 1870s other Native American groups began to encroach on traditional Hopi territories (personal communication).

11. Whiteley points out that this description is more accurate for Second Mesa than for First and Third Mesas. On Third Mesa, the relationships are more fixed (personal communication).

12. We fully acknowledge the speculative nature of the ensuing discussion. We know that many anthropologists will disagree with our suggestions. The suggestion that cross-clan membership in religious sodalities intensified post 1851–1853 will go against many of their intuitions. Nevertheless, we offer this hypothesis because there is some evidence that it occurred and because the hypothesis allows us to discuss relationships between demography and sociocultural institutions. Cross-clan memberships in sodalities might have become central far earlier in Hopi social history. If it did, the mechanisms we discuss were probably important to the process.

13. We emphasize that this description pertains to Second Mesa, not to villages from other Mesas. We merely raise the possibility that the historically recorded events at Second Mesa might have occurred elsewhere, if not following the 1851–1853 epidemic, then sometime before.

6. Village Fission at Old Oraibi

1. We base much of our historical reconstruction on Titiev (1944) and Whiteley (1988a, 1988b). There are some contradictions between Titiev's and Whiteley's versions of Hopi history. More specifically, through a careful combination of archival and ethnographic work, Whiteley has been able to correct certain errors in Titiev's reconstruction. We are convinced about most points by Whiteley's documentation. When discrepancies appear, we accept Whiteley's account over Titiev's.

2. See Whiteley (1985, 1986, 1988a) for a different version of Hopi land tenure. We discuss Whiteley's analysis of Hopi land tenure later in this chapter.

3. Whiteley feels that this and other claims made below about Oraibi ceremonies at the turn of the century might be exaggerations (personal communication). He suggests that there was more ceremonial cooperation and less competition among the Oraibi factions during these years than previously thought. This suggestion fits well with his interpretation of the Oraibi split.

4. Whiteley explicitly challenges this date. Historical records imply that Hopis had burros and other livestock much earlier than Bradfield suggests (personal communication).

5. Compare Bradfield's arguments to Brew's explanation of the return of Rio Grande peoples to New Mexico after their stay at the Hopi Mesas (Chap. 5).

6. We point out, however, that Clemmer is critical of these explanations of the Oraibi split. Such explanations require reference to actors' internal motivations.

7. Also see Krutz on *diingavi*, acts "designed in deliberation" (1973).

8. See Titiev for corroboration (1944:62).

9. Parenthetically, Clemmer discusses the Oraibi split within the context of Hopis' historical resistance to acculturation. He never labels the split a revitalization movement, however, or fully develops this explanation (see Clemmer 1978a: 55–58, 70, 77).

10. Aberle cites Swanson (1960), Burridge (1969), and Jorgensen (1972) as the sources of his concept of power.

11. These visitors were probably not Oraibi Hopi. They were likely from First Mesa (Mooney 1896:813–814).

7. Accommodation to the Modern World

1. Whiteley disputes vigorously this account. He suggests that: (1) Navajos encroached on traditional Hopi lands much earlier than this; (2) Hopis never restricted their activities to the Mesas as strictly as anthropologists have implied; and (3) the origins of the Navajo-Hopi land dispute go back at least to the 1890s (personal communication). He has evidence that the Hopis have protested Navajo presence on their traditional lands in every decade since the 1890s.

2. In 1965 a survey of District 6 determined the district actually consisted of 650,013 acres (Kammer 1980:641).

3. These events occurred with La Farge's "mixture of threat and cajolery" (Whiteley 1988a:234). See also Clemmer (1978b:25).

4. Whiteley disputes Clemmer's claim. Based on his own research, Whiteley suggests that the Council was abolished when it was unsuccessful in getting Hopi lands back (personal communication).

5. The trip between Moenkopi and Flagstaff now took two hours, rather than three days.

6. We take all Bacavi figures from Whiteley (1988a:130–136).

7. For a discussion of these trends at Bacavi, see Whiteley (1988a:142–145; 1988b:130).

8. Parenthetically, we discussed the marginality of Hopi agricultural land in Chapter 5. This marginality possibly contributed to Hopi isolation during the Spanish period.

9. According to Whiteley, clan membership identity supersedes "Hopi" and village identity among contemporary Hopis (1988a).

10. Whiteley actually limits many of his claims to Bacavi Pueblo.

11. Again, Whiteley disputes this view (personal communication).

12. We are aware of exceptions, such as the Hopi Electronics Corporation and

craft production, like painting, silver smithing, and *katchina* carving. We feel, however, that our general characterization of the underdeveloped Hopi economy is accurate.

13. We know that this may be an exaggeration. Nevertheless, it is a defensible position.

14. For similar arguments about other Native Americans, see Jorgensen (1978, 1972), Munsell (1967), Robbins (1971), Knack (1975), and Callaway and Henderson (n.d.).

8. Environment, Population, and Cultural Contact

1. We are aware of the idealization implicit in distinguishing exogenous from endogenous factors.

2. See Clemmer (1978a) on the Hopi "mythic process." We discuss this topic in Chapter 5.

3. See Hollander (1986) or Eckstein, Stein, and Wolpin (1988) for a different view.

4. See Spencer (1873) as cited in Carniero (1967:10) and Bee (1974:44).

5. See Cordell (1984) for a summary of these views.

6. Kleinman (1980) provides a convincing rejection of this conclusion.

7. See, for example, Coe (1957), Meggars (1957), Hirschberg and Hirschberg (1957), Altschuler (1958), Ferdon (1959).

8. For a recent summary of Maya civilization, see Blanton et al. (1981).

9. See White (1949) for similar arguments concerning the relation of religious beliefs to technology.

10. For a more extended discussion of historical particularism and sociocultural change, see Bee (1974:67ff.).

11. See Chapter 3 concerning flexibility and adaptive shifts.

9. Social Structure, Culture, and Human Agency

1. Some historians of the social sciences argue that Durkheim's intellectual descendants view humankind as fundamentally competitive or antagonistic. For Durkheim's descendants, questions about social persistence are fundamental. Social persistence, for these scholars, occurs despite inherently destructive human qualities.

2. See Robert Brown (1963:Chap. 9) for a more complete account of functionalist explanation.

3. Parenthetically, followers of Marx have reinterpreted ideology in at least two ways that differ from the definition provided here. The first reinterpretation equates ideology with social consciousness or "ideological superstructure"; the second with political ideas connected to the interests of a class (Bottomore et al. 1983:221; see Williams 1977:55 for a slightly different list of three definitions of ideology).

4. Some anthropologists, however, criticize structural Marxists for their Lévi-Straussian model of social structure and for treating societies as though they had no history (see Kahn and Llobera 1981b:298).

5. See Sahlins (1976) for a clear discussion of this issue.

6. For criticisms of these studies, see Whiteley (1985, 1986).

7. See below concerning "enactment" and the "working out of an established order."

8. See Boudon's related discussion of "open" and "closed" situations (1986:181).

9. See Giddens (1984:213ff.) for different versions of methodological individualism.

10. We are aware of potential conflicts between Marxist theory (emphasizing social classes and group consciousness) and bourgeois theories of agency that stress individual interests and decision making. The views can be reconciled, although we will not sketch the arguments here.

11. We could argue that Bourdieu's concept of habitus actually denies the significance of agency.

10. Explanation and Hopi Social History

1. We borrow the phrase "fields of causation" from Sahlins (1981:22).

2. Boudon uses the term "synchronization" to discuss these ideas (1986:178).

3. For a valuable discussion of these and such related matters as the distinction between "open" and "closed" processes and the indeterminate nature of innovation, see Boudon (1986:154–189).

References

Aberle, David F.
1982   *The peyote religion among the Navajo.* Viking Fund Publications in Anthropology, vol. 42. Chicago: Univ. of Chicago Press.
1983   Navajo economic development. In *New perspectives on the pueblos,* ed. Alfonso Ortiz, 641–658. Albuquerque: Univ. of New Mexico Press.
Aberle, David F., and Omar C. Stewart
1957   *Navajo and Ute peyotism: A chronological and distributional study.* University of Colorado Studies, Series in Anthropology, no. 6. Boulder: Univ. of Colorado Press.
Adams, Robert McCormick
1980   Strategies of maximization, stability, and resilience in Mesopotamian society, settlement, and agriculture. *Proceedings of the American Philosophical Society* 122(5):329–335.
Adams, W. Y., D. P. Van Gerven, and R. S. Levy
1978   The retreat from migration. *Annual Review of Anthropology* 7:483–532.
Aikens, C. Melvin
1966   *Virgin-Kayenta cultural relationships.* Univ. of Utah Anthropological Papers, no. 79. Salt Lake City: Univ. of Utah Press.
Althusser, Louis
1971   *Lenin and philosophy and other essays.* New York: Monthly Review Press.
Altschuler, Milton
1958   On the environmental limitations of Mayan cultural development. *Southwestern Journal of Anthropology* 14:189–198.
Amsden, Charles A.
1932   Navajo origins. *New Mexico Historical Review* 7:193–209.
Bailey, Norman T. S.
1975   *The mathematical theory of infectious diseases and its applications.* New York: Hafner Press.
Bancroft, H. H.
1889   *Arizona and New Mexico, 1530–1888.* San Francisco: History Co.
Baran, Paul
1957   *The Political Economy of Growth.* New York: Monthly Review Press.

Barber, Bernard
1941   Acculturation and messianic movements. *American Sociological Review*
          6:663–669.
Barnett, Homer
1953   *Innovation: The basis of culture change.* New York: McGraw-Hill.
Barnett, Homer G., Leonard Broom, Bernard J. Segel, Evon Z. Voght, and James B.
     Watson
1954   Acculturation: An exploratory formulation. *American Anthropologist*
          56(6):973–1002.
Barth, Fredrik
1966   *Models of social organization.* Royal Anthropological Institute of Great Brit-
          ain and Ireland Occasional Papers, no. 23. Oxford.
1967   On the study of social change. *American Anthropologist* 69(6):661–669.
Barth, Fredrik, ed.
1963   *The role of the entrepreneur in social change in northern Norway.* Bergen:
          Scandinavian Univ. Books.
1978   *Scale and social organization.* New York: Columbia Univ. Press.
Bartlett, Katharine
1934   Spanish contacts with the Hopi, 1540–1823. *Museum Notes* 6:1–12.
          Flagstaff: Museum of Northern Arizona.
1936   Hopi history, no. 2: The Navajo wars, 1823–1870. *Museum Notes* 8:33–37.
          Flagstaff: Museum of Northern Arizona.
Basso, Keith H.
1979   *Portraits of "the Whiteman": Linguistic play and cultural symbols among the
          Western Apache.* New York: Cambridge Univ. Press.
Beaglehole, Ernest
1937   *Notes on Hopi economic life.* Yale University Publications in Anthropology,
          no. 15. New Haven: Yale Univ. Press.
Beaglehole, Ernest, and Pearle Beaglehole
1935   *Hopi of the Second Mesa.* American Anthropological Association Memoir,
          no. 44. Menasha, Wis.
Beal, John D.
1987   *Foundations of the Rio Grande classic: The lower Chama River* A.D. *1300–
          1500.* Southwest Project, no. 137. Southwest Archaeological Consultants,
          Inc. Santa Fe.
Becker, Niels
1979   Vaccination programs for rare infectious diseases. *Biometrika* 52(2):
          443–453.
Beckett, Patrick
1981   *An archaeological survey and assessment of Gran Quivera National Monu-
          ment, New Mexico.* Report prepared for the National Park Service, South-
          western Region, Cultural Resources Management Division. Las Cruces:
          New Mexico State Univ.
Bee, Robert L.
1974   *Patterns and processes: An introduction to anthropological strategies for the
          study of sociocultural change.* New York: Free Press.

Benedict, Ruth
1934   *Patterns of culture.* Boston: Houghton, Mifflin.
Beneson, Abram S.
1972   Smallpox. In *Communicable and infectious diseases,* ed. F. H. Top and P. F. Wehrle, 592–607. St. Louis: C. V. Mosby Company.
Biella, J. V., and Richard C. Chapman
1980   *Archaeological research and mitigation at the Star Lake Mine: A mitigation plan and research design.* Santa Fe: School of American Research, Contract Archaeology Program.
Binford, Lewis R.
1962   Archaeology as anthropology. *American Antiquity* 28:217–225.
1964   A consideration of archaeological research design. *American Antiquity* 29:425–441.
1967   Smudge pits and hide smoking: The use of analogy in archaeological reasoning. *American Antiquity* 52(1):1–12.
1968   Post-pleistocene adaptations. In *New perspectives in archaeology,* ed. Lewis Binford and Sally Binford, 313–342. Chicago: Aldine.
Birdsell, Joseph B.
1968   Some predictions for the pleistocene based on equilibrium systems among recent hunter-gatherers. In *Man the hunter,* ed. Richard B. Lee and Irven DeVore, 229–240. Chicago: Aldine.
Bishop, Ronald L., Valetta Canouts, Suzanne P. De Atley, Alfred Qoyawayma, and C. W. Aikens
1988   The formations of ceramic analytic groups: Hopi pottery production and exchange, A.D. 1300–1600. Manuscript in the authors' possession.
Black, Stephen L.
1977   Archaeological background. In *An archaeological survey of the Radium Springs area, southern New Mexico,* ed. T. R. Hester, 19–28. Archaeological Survey Report, no. 26. San Antonio: Univ. of Texas Center for Archaeological Research.
Blanton, Richard
1975   The cybernetic analysis of human population growth. In *Studies in archaeology and biological anthropology: A symposium,* ed. A. C. Swedlund, 116–126. Memoirs of the Society for American Archaeology 30. Washington, D.C.
Blanton, Richard, S. A. Kowalewski, G. Feinman, and J. Appel
1981   *Ancient Mesoamerica: A comparison of change in three regions.* New York: Cambridge Univ. Press.
Blau, Peter M.
1975b   Introduction: Parallels and contrasts in structural inquiries. In *Approaches to the study of social structure,* ed. Peter M. Blau, 1–20. New York: Free Press.
1975c   Parameters of social structure. In *Approaches to the study of social structure,* ed. Peter M. Blau, 220–253. New York: Free Press.
Blau, Peter M., ed.
1975a   *Approaches to the study of social structure.* New York: Free Press.

Bloch, W.
1982   An archaeological clearance survey of a proposed natural gas pipeline, Dona
        Ana County, New Mexico. Cultural Resources Management Division Report,
        no. 520. Las Cruces: New Mexico State Univ.
Bodine, John J.
1972   Acculturation processes and population dynamics. In New perspectives on
        the pueblos, ed. Alfonso Ortiz, 257–285. Albuquerque: Univ. of New Mex-
        ico Press.
Bolton, Herbert E., ed.
1930   Spanish exploration in the Southwest, 1542–1706. New York: Charles
        Scribner's Sons.
1949   Coronado: Knight of pueblos and plains. Albuquerque: Univ. of New Mexico
        Press.
Boserup, Ester
1965   The conditions of agricultural growth. Chicago: Aldine.
1981   Population and technological change: A study of long-term trends. Chicago:
        Univ. of Chicago Press.
Bottomore, Tom, Lawrence Harris, V. G. Kiernan, and Ralph Miliband, eds.
1983   A dictionary of Marxist thought. Cambridge, Mass.: Harvard Univ. Press.
Boudon, Raymond
1979   The logic of social action: An introduction to sociological analysis. Trans.
        David Silverman. London: Routledge & Kegan Paul.
1982   The unintended consequences of social action. London: Macmillan.
1986   Theories of social change: A critical appraisal. Berkeley: Univ. of California
        Press.
Bourdieu, Pierre
1977a   Outline of a theory of practice. Cambridge: Cambridge Univ. Press.
1977b   Cultural reproduction and social reproduction. In Power and ideology in
        education, ed. Jerome Karabel and A. H. Halsey, 487–511. New York: Ox-
        ford Univ. Press.
Brachman, P. S.
1970   Nosocomial infection: Airborne or not? Paper presented at conference,
        Center for Disease Control, Atlanta.
Bradfield, Richard M.
1971   The changing pattern of Hopi agriculture. Occasional Papers, no. 30. Lon-
        don: Royal Anthropological Institute.
1973   A natural history of associations. 2 vols. London: Duckworth.
Brandt, Elizabeth A.
1976   On secrecy and the control of knowledge through speech. Paper presented
        at the Southwest Anthropological Association Meeting, San Francisco.
1979   Sandia pueblo. In Handbook of North American Indians. Vol. 9, The South-
        west, ed. Alfonso Ortiz, 343–350. Washington, D.C.: U.S. Government
        Printing Office.
Braun, David P., and Stephen Plog
1982   Evolution of "tribal" social networks: Theory and prehistoric North Ameri-
        can evidence. American Antiquity 47:504–525.

Brew, James Otis

1946   *Archaeology of Alkali Ridge, southeastern Utah.* Papers of the Peabody Museum of American Ethnology, vol. 21. Cambridge, Mass.: Harvard Univ. Press.

1949   Part I: The history of Awatovi. In *Franciscan Awatovi: The excavation and conjectural reconstruction of a 17th-century Spanish mission establishment at a Hopi town in northeastern Arizona,* ed. Ross Gordon Montgomery, Watson Smith, and James Otis Brew, 2–43. Peabody Museum of American Archaeology and Ethnology Papers, vol. 36. Cambridge, Mass.: Harvard Univ. Press.

1979   Hopi prehistory and history to 1850. In *Handbook of North American Indians.* Vol. 9, *The Southwest,* ed. Alfonso Ortiz, 514–523. Washington, D.C.: U.S. Government Printing Office.

Brockman, F.

1982   *An archaeological clearance survey of a seismic testing line in south-central Dona Ana County, New Mexico.* Cultural Resources Management Division Report, no. 534. Las Cruces: New Mexico State Univ.

Brown, David E.

1971   *Approaches in the social dimensions of mortuary practices.* Memoirs of the Society for American Archaeology, no. 25. Washington, D.C.

Brown, Gary M.

1982   *Preliminary report on archaeological research during 1981 at Nuvakwewtaqa (Chavez Pass).* Interim report prepared for the National Science Foundation and the U.S.D.A. Forest Service, Southwestern Regional Office. Albuquerque, N.M.

Brown, Kaye

1976   Quantitative testing and revitalization behavior: On Carroll's explanation of the ghost dance. *American Sociological Review* 41:741–744.

Brown, Robert

1963   *Explanation in social science.* Chicago: Aldine.

Brush, Stephen B.

1977   *Mountain, field and family: The economy and human ecology of an Andean valley.* Philadelphia: Univ. of Pennsylvania Press.

Bryan, Kirk

1941   Pre-Columbian agriculture in the Southwest as conditioned by periods of alluviation. *Annals of the Association of American Geographers* 31:219–242.

Burridge, Kenelm

1969   *New heaven, new earth: A study of millenarian activities.* New York: Schocken Books.

Callaway, Donald G., and Eric Henderson

n.d.   Industrial development, income, and household composition: The Navajo case. Manuscript.

Carmichael, David

1982   *Archaeological survey of the southern Tularosa Basin, New Mexico.* Report prepared for the Environmental Office, Directorate of Facilities Engineering, Fort Bliss Air Defense Center. Fort Bliss, Tex.

Carniero, Robert, ed.
1967   Introduction. In *The evolution of society: Selections from Herbert Spencer's principles of sociology,* ix—lvii. Chicago: Univ. of Chicago Press.

Carroll, Michael
1975   Revitalization movements and social structure: Some quantitative tests. *American Sociological Review* 40:389–401.
1976   Reply to Brown. *American Sociological Review* 41:744–746.
1979   Rejoinder to Landsman. *American Sociological Review* 44:166–168.

Chapin, F. H.
1892   *The land of the cliffdwellers.* Boston: W. D. Clark and Co.

Chase, J. E.
1976   Deviance in the Gallina: A report on a small series of Gallina human skeletal remains. In *Archaeological investigations in the Llaves Area, Santa Fe National Forest, New Mexico, 1972–1974,* ed. H. W. Dick, 66–106. Archaeological Report no. 13. Albuquerque: U.S.D.A. Forest Service, Southwestern Region.

Christie, A. B.
1980   *Infectious diseases: Epidemiology and clinical practice.* Edinburgh: Churchill Livingstone.

Cibola National Forest
n.d.   Archaeological site files. Cibola National Forest, U.S.D.A. Forest Service, Region 3, Albuquerque.

Clark, G. A.
1967   A preliminary analysis of burial clusters at the Grasshopper site, east-central Arizona. Master's thesis, Univ. of Arizona.

Clemmer, Richard O.
1978a   *Continuities of Hopi culture change.* Ramona, Calif.: Acoma Books.
1978b   Black Mesa and the Hopi. In *Native Americans and energy development,* ed. Joseph G. Jorgensen, 17–34. Cambridge, Mass.: Anthropology Research Center.
1979   Hopi history, 1940–1970. In *Handbook of North American Indians.* Vol. 9, *The Southwest,* ed. Alfonso Ortiz, 533–538. Washington, D.C.: U.S. Government Printing Office.

Coe, William R.
1957   Environmental limitations on Mayan culture: A re-examination. *American Anthropologist* 59:328–335.

Cohen, Mark Nathan
1977   *The food crisis in prehistory: Overpopulation and the origins of agriculture.* New Haven: Yale Univ. Press.

Collins, John J.
1968   A descriptive introduction to the Taos peyote ceremony. *Ethnology* 7:427–449.

Colton, Harold S.
1932   *A survey of prehistoric sites in the region of Flagstaff, Arizona.* Bureau of American Ethnology Bulletin, no. 104. Washington, D.C.: Smithsonian Institution.

1936   The rise and fall of the prehistoric population of Northern Arizona. *Science* 84:337–343.

1939   *Prehistoric culture events and their relationship in Northern Arizona.* Museum of Northern Arizona Bulletin, no. 17. Flagstaff.

1946   *The Sinagua, a summary of the archaeology of the region of Flagstaff, Arizona.* Museum of Northern Arizona Bulletin, no. 22. Flagstaff.

Colton, Harold S., and Frank C. Baxter

1932   *Days in the Painted Desert and the San Francisco Mountains: A guide.* Northern Arizona Society of Science and Art Bulletin, no. 2. Flagstaff.

Connelly, John C.

1979   Hopi social organization. In *Handbook of North American Indians.* Vol. 9, *The Southwest,* ed. Alfonso Ortiz, 539–553. Washington, D.C.: U.S. Government Printing Office.

Cordell, Linda S.

1984   *Prehistory of the Southwest.* San Diego: Academic Press.

1986   *Rowe archaeological research project final report.* Submitted to the National Science Foundation. Washington, D.C.

1989   Hopi prehistory: Overview and issues. In *Seasons of the Katchin,* ed. Sylvia Brakke Vane, 1–16. Ballena Press Anthropological Papers, no. 34. Hayward: Ballena Press and California State Univ.

Cordell, Linda S., and Fred Plog

1979   Escaping the confines of normative thought: A reevaluation of Puebloan prehistory. *American Antiquity* 44:405–429.

Cordell, Linda S., and Steadman Upham

1983   Agriculture in the Southwest. In *Theory and model building: Refining survey strategies for locating prehistoric heritage resources,* ed. Linda Cordell and Dee F. Green, 38–58. Cultural Resources Document, no. 3. Albuquerque: U.S.D.A. Forest Service, Southwest Region.

Courlander, Harold

1971   *The fourth world of the Hopis.* New York: Crown Publishers, Inc.

1982   *Hopi voices: Recollections, traditions, and narratives of the Hopi Indians.* Albuquerque: Univ. of New Mexico Press.

Crosby, A. W.

1972   *The Columbian exchange: Biological and cultural consequences of 1492.* Westport, Conn.: Greenwood.

Cummings, Byron

1910   The ancient inhabitants of the San Juan Valley. *Bulletin of the University of Utah,* no. 3(3):part 2. Salt Lake City.

1915   Kivas of the San Juan drainage. *American Anthropologist* 17(2):272–282.

Cushing, Frank H.

1922   Oraibi in 1883. In *Contributions to Hopi history,* ed. Elsie C. Parsons, 253–268. *American Anthropologist* 24(3):253–298.

Dahl, R. A., and E. R. Tufte

1973   *Size and democracy.* Stanford: Stanford Univ. Press.

Davis, Emma Lou

1965   Small pressures and cultural drift as explanations for abandonment of the San Juan area, New Mexico, and Arizona. *American Antiquity* 30:353–355.

Davis, Irvine
1979   The Kiowa-Tanoan, Keresan, and Zuni languages. In *The languages of Native America,* ed. Lyle Campbell and Marianne Mithun, 390–443. Austin: Univ. of Texas Press.

Dean, Jeffrey S.
1970   Aspects of Tesgi phase social organization. In *Reconstructing prehistoric pueblo societies,* ed. W. A. Longacre, 140–174. Albuquerque: University of New Mexico Press.

Dean, Jeffrey, Robert C. Evier, George J. Gumerman, Fred Plog, Richard H. Hevly, and Thor N. V. Karlstrom
1985   Human behavior, demography, and paleoenvironment on the Colorado Plateau. *American Antiquity* 50:537–554.

Deloria, Vine, Jr., and Clifford M. Lytle
1983   *American Indians, American justice.* Austin: Univ. of Texas Press.

Diamond, Stanley, ed.
1979   *Toward a Marxist anthropology: Problems and perspectives.* The Hague: Mouton.

DiPeso, Charles
1956   *The Upper Pima of San Cayetano del Tumacacori: An archaeo-historical reconstruction of the Ootam of Pimeria Alta.* The Amerind Foundation, no. 7. Dragoon, Ariz.

Dixon, C. W.
1962   *Smallpox.* London: J. & A. Churchill.

Dobyns, Henry F.
1966   Estimating aboriginal American population: An appraisal of techniques with a new hemispheric estimate. *Current Anthropology* 7(4):395–416.
1983   *Their numbers became thinned: Native American population dynamics in eastern North America.* Knoxville: Univ. of Tennessee Press.

Dobyns, Henry F., and Robert C. Euler
1967   *The Ghost Dance of 1889 among the Pai Indians of Northwestern Arizona.* Prescott: Prescott College Press.

Dockstader, Frederick J.
1979   Hopi history, 1850–1940. In *Handbook of North American Indians.* Vol. 9, *The Southwest,* ed. Alfonso Ortiz, 524–532. Washington, D.C.: U.S. Government Printing Office.
1985   *The Kachina and the White Man: The influences of white culture on the Hopi Kachina cult.* Albuquerque: Univ. of New Mexico Press.

Donaldson, Thomas
1893   *Moqui Pueblo Indians of Arizona and Pueblo Indians of New Mexico.* Eleventh U.S. Census. Extra Census Bulletin, no. 15. Washington, D.C.: U.S. Census Office.

Dorsey, George A., and Henry R. Voth
1901   *The Oraibi Soyar ceremony.* Field Columbian Museum Publication, no. 55. Anthropological Series, no. 3(1). Chicago.

Downie, Allan W.
1965   Poxvirus group. In *Viral and rickettsial infections of man,* ed. F. L. Horasfall and I. Tamm, 932–993. Philadelphia: J. B. Lippencott Co.

Downie, Allan W., and K. R. Dumbell
1947   Survival of variola virus in dried exudate and crusts from smallpox patients. *Lancet* 1:550.
Dozier, Edward P.
1961   Rio Grande pueblos. In *Perspectives in American Indian culture change,* ed. Edward H. Spicer. Chicago: Univ. of Chicago Press.
1970   *The Pueblo Indians of North America.* New York: Holt, Rinehart and Winston.
Driver, Harold E.
1966   Geographical-historical versus psycho-functional explanations of kin avoidances. *Current Anthropology* 7:131–182.
Duran, Meliha S.
1982a   *Patterns of prehistoric land use in Dona Ana County, New Mexico.* Cultural Resources Management Division Report, no. 471. Las Cruces: New Mexico State Univ.
1982b   *An archaeological clearance survey of an electrical transmission line for the medium security prison, Dona Ana County, New Mexico.* Cultural Resources Management Division Report, no. 490. Las Cruces: New Mexico State Univ.
Durkheim, Emile
1958   *The rules of sociological method.* Trans. Sarah A. Solovay and John H. Mueller. New York: Free Press.
1960   *The division of labor in society.* Trans. George Simpson. New York: Free Press.
1963   *Suicide: A study in sociology.* Trans. John A. Spaulding and George Simpson. New York: Free Press.
Earls, A.
1987   *An archaeological assessment of Las Huertas, Soccorro.* Papers of the Maxwell Museum, no. 3. Albuquerque.
Eckstein, Zui, Steven Stein, and Kenneth I. Wolpin
1988   Fertility choice, land, and the Malthusian hypothesis. *International Economic Review* 29(2):353–361.
Eddy, Frank W.
1966   *Prehistory in the Navajo Reservoir District, Northwestern New Mexico.* Museum of New Mexico Papers in Anthropology, no. 15, parts 1 and 2. Santa Fe.
Eggan, Fred
1950   *Social organization of the Western Pueblos.* Chicago: Univ. of Chicago Press.
1964   Alliance and descent in Western Pueblo society. In *Process and pattern in culture,* ed. Robert A. Manners, 175–184. Chicago: Aldine.
1970   Foreword. In *Modern Transformations of Moenkopi Pueblo,* by Shuichi Nagata, i–x. Urbana: Univ. of Illinois Press.
Eisenberg, Leonard A.
1968   Oraibi: An example of Pueblo fission. Master's thesis, Univ. of Arizona.
Elliot, Michael L.
1982   *Large pueblo sites near Jemez Springs, New Mexico.* Cultural Resources Report, no. 3. Santa Fe National Forest. Santa Fe.
Ellis, Florence, and H. S. Colton
1974   *Hopi Indians.* Garland: New York.

Espinosa, J. Manuel, trans. and ed.
1988   The Pueblo Indian Revolt of 1696 and the Franciscan missions in New Mexico:
        Letters of the missionaries and related documents. Norman: Univ. of Okla-
        homa Press.

Euler, Robert C., and S. M. Chandler
1978   Aspects of prehistoric settlement patterns in Grand Canyon. In Investi-
        gations of the Southwestern Anthropological Research Group, ed. Robert C.
        Euler and George J. Gumerman, 73–86. Flagstaff: Museum of Northern
        Arizona.

Euler, Robert C., George J. Gumerman, Thor N. V. Karlstrom, Jeffrey S. Dean, and
     Richard H. Henly
1979   The Colorado Plateau: Cultural dynamics and paleoenvironment. Science
        205:1089–1101.

Fabian, Johannes
1983   Time and the other: How anthropology makes its object. New York: Columbia
        Univ. Press.

Feinman, Gary, and J. Neitzel
1984   Too many types: An overview of sedentary prestate societies in the Amer-
        icas. In Advances in archaeological method and theory. Vol. 7, ed. Michael
        Schiffer, 39–102. New York: Academic Press.

Fenner, Frank, and Donald O. White
1976   Medical virology. New York: Academic Press.

Ferdon, Edwin N., Jr.
1959   Agricultural potential and the development of cultures. Southwestern Jour-
        nal of Anthropology 15(1):1–19.

Fewkes, Jesse Walter
1893   A-wá-to-bi: An archaeological verification of a Tusayan legend. American
        Anthropologist (o.s.) 6:363–375.
1902   Minor Hopi festivals. American Anthropologist 4(3).
1922   Oraibi in 1890. In Contributions to Hopi history, ed. Elsie C. Parson, 268–
        283. American Anthropologist 24(3):253–298.

Fish, Paul, P. Pilles, and S. K. Fish
1980   Colonies, traders, and traits: The Hohokam in the north. In Current issues
        in Hohokam prehistory, ed. David Doyel and Fred Plog, 151–175. Anthro-
        pological Research Papers, no. 23. Tempe: Arizona State Univ.

Flannery, Kent V.
1972   The cultural evolution of civilizations. Annual Review of Ecology and Sys-
        tematics 3:399–426.

Fodor, J. A.
1975   The language of thought. New York: Crowell.

Ford, Richard I.
1972   An ecological perspective on the eastern pueblos. In New Perspectives
        on the pueblos, ed. Alfonso Ortiz, 1–18. Albuquerque: Univ. of New Mex-
        ico Press.

Forde, C. Daryll
1931   Hopi agriculture and land ownership. Journal of the Royal Anthropological
        Institute 41(4):357–405.

Forrest, Earle R.
1961   *The Snake Dance of the Hopi Indians.* Los Angeles: Westernlore Press.

Forrestal, Peter P., trans.
1954   *Benavides' memorial of 1630.* Washington, D.C.: Academy of American Franciscan History.

Fortes, Meyer
1945   *The dynamics of clanship among the Tallensi.* London: Cambridge Univ. Press.
1949   *The web of kinship among the Tallensi.* London: Cambridge Univ. Press.

Foster, George M.
1965   Peasant society and the image of limited good. *American Anthropologist* 67:293–315.

Foucault, Michel
1972   *The archaeology of knowledge.* New York: Pantheon Books.

Frank, André Gunder
1967   *Capitalism and underdevelopment in Latin America.* New York: Monthly Review Press.
1979   *Dependent accumulation and underdevelopment.* New York: Monthly Review Press.
1984   The development of underdevelopment. In *The political economy of development and underdevelopment,* ed. Charles K. Wilber, 99–108. New York: Random House.

Fried, Morton
1967   *The evolution of political society: An essay in political anthropology.* New York: Random House.

Frigout, Arlette
1979   Hopi ceremonial organization. In *Handbook of North American Indians.* Vol. 9, *The Southwest,* ed. Alfonso Ortiz, 564–576. Washington, D.C.: U.S. Government Printing Office.

Fowler, D. D., and C. S. Fowler, eds.
1971   *Anthropology of the Numa: John Wesley Powell's manuscripts on the Numic peoples of Western North America, 1868–1880.* Smithsonian Contributions to Anthropology, no. 14. Washington, D.C.

Geertz, Armin
1984   A reed pierced the sky: Hopi Indian cosmography on Third Mesa, Arizona. *Numen* 31(2):216–241.

Geertz, Clifford
1973   *The interpretation of cultures.* New York: Basic Books.
1976   "From the native's point of view": On the nature of anthropological understanding. In *Meaning in anthropology,* ed. Keith H. Basso and Henry A. Selby, 221–238. Albuquerque: Univ. of New Mexico Press.

Gibson, Charles
1964   *The Aztecs under Spanish rule: A history of the Indians of the Valley of Mexico, 1519–1810.* Stanford: Stanford Univ. Press.

Giddens, Anthony
1976   *New rules of sociological method: A positive critique of interpretive sociologies.* New York: Basic Books.

1979   *Central problems in social theory: Action, structure, and contradiction in social analysis.* Berkeley: Univ. of California Press.
1984   *The constitution of society: Outline of the theory of structuration.* Berkeley: Univ. of California Press.

Gluckman, Max
1963   *Order and rebellion in tribal Africa.* New York: Free Press.

Godelier, Maurice
1977   *Perspectives in Marxist anthropology.* Cambridge: Cambridge Univ. Press.

Goodenough, Ward
1956   Residence rules. *Southwestern Journal of Anthropology* 12:22–37.

Gould, Stephen J.
1989   *Wonderful life: The Burgess Shale and the nature of history.* New York: W. W. Norton & Company.

Gramsci, Antonio
1971   *Selections from the Prison notebooks.* Trans. and ed. Quinten Hoare and Geoffrey Nowell Smith. London: Lawrence & Wishart.

Graves, Michael
1978   White Mountain redware design variability. Paper presented at the 77th annual meetings of the American Anthropological Association, Los Angeles.

Gregory, David A.
1981   Western Apache archaeology: Problems and approaches. In *The Protohistoric period in the North American Southwest,* A.D. *1450–1700,* ed. David R. Wilcox and W. B. Masse, 257–274. Anthropological Research Papers, no. 24. Tempe: Arizona State Univ.

Gregory, Herbert E.
1917   *Geology of the Navajo country.* United States Geological Survey Professional Paper, no. 93.

Griffen, P. B.
1967   A high status burial from Grasshopper Ruin, Arizona. *The Kiva* 33:37–53.

Guernsey, Samuel J., and Alfred V. Kidder
1921   *Basket-maker caves of northeastern Arizona.* Papers of the Peabody Museum of American Archaeology and Ethnology, vol. 8(2). Cambridge, Mass.: Harvard Univ.

Gulliver, P. H.
1955   *The family herds: A study of two pastoral peoples in East Africa, the Jie and the Turkana.* London: Routledge and Kegan Paul.

Gumerman, George J.
1968   The archaeology of the Hopi Buttes District, Arizona. Ph.D. dissertation, Univ. of Arizona.
1970   *Black Mesa: Survey and excavation in northeastern Arizona, 1968.* Prescott: Prescott College Press.

Gumerman, George J., ed.
1988   *The Anasazi in a changing environment.* Cambridge: Cambridge Univ. Press.

Gumerman, George, and Robert C. Euler
1976   *Papers on the archaeology of Black Mesa, Arizona.* Carbondale: Southern Illinois Univ. Press.

Gumerman, George J., and Alan S. Skinner
1968   A synthesis of the prehistory of the central Little Colorado Valley, Arizona. *American Antiquity* 33:185–199.

Gumerman, George, Deborah Westfall, and Carol S. Weed
1972   *Archaeological investigations on Black Mesa: The 1969–1970 seasons.* Prescott: Prescott College Press.

Hack, John T.
1942   *The changing physical environment of the Hopi Indians of Arizona.* Papers of the Peabody Museum of American Archaeology and Ethnology, vol. 35. Cambridge, Mass.: Harvard Univ. Press.

Hackett, Charles Wilson
1937   *Historical documents relating to New Mexico, Nueva Vizcaya, and approaches thereto, to 1773, collected by Adolph Bandelier and Fanny R. Bandelier.* Publication no. 330, part 3. Washington, D.C.: Carnegie Institution of Washington.

Hackett, Charles Wilson, and Charmion Clair Shelby
1942   *Revolt of the Pueblo Indians of New Mexico and Otermin's attempted reconquest, 1680–1682.* Albuquerque: Univ. of New Mexico Press.

Haggett, P.
1966   *Locational analysis in human geography.* New York: St. Martin's Press.

Haggett, P., and J. Chorley
1969   *Network analysis and geography.* London: Arnold.

Hakken, David, and Hanna Lessinger, eds.
1987   *Perspectives in U.S. Marxist anthropology.* Boulder: Westview Press.

Hale, Kenneth, and David Harris
1979   Historical linguistics and archaeology. In *Handbook of North American Indians.* Vol. 9, *The Southwest,* ed. Alfonso Ortiz, 170–177. Washington, D.C.: U.S. Government Printing Office.

Hamer, W. H.
1906   Epidemic disease in England: The evidence of variability and persistence of type. *Lancet* 1:596–574, 655–662, 733–739.

Hammond, George P.
1926–27   Don Juan de Onate, and the founding of New Mexico. *New Mexico Historical Review,* vols. 1 and 2. Santa Fe.

Hammond, R., and P. D. McCullough
1974   *Quantitative techniques in geography.* Oxford: Clarendon Press.

Hammond, George P., and Agapito Rey, trans.
1928   *Obregon's history of 16th century explorations in Western America.* Los Angeles: Wetzel Publishing Co.
1929   *Expedition into New Mexico made by Antonio de Espejo, 1582–1583; as revealed by the journal of Diego Perez de Luxan.* Quivira Society Publication, no. 1. Los Angeles.

Hantman, Jeffrey L.
1979   Environmental fluctuation and migration: An historical study. Paper presented at the 23rd annual meeting of the Arizona-Nevada Academy of Sciences. Tempe.

1984   Regional organization of the northern Mogollon. *American Archaeology* 4:171–180.

Hardesty, Donald L.
1977   *Ecological anthropology.* New York: Alfred A. Knopf.

Harkey, M.
1981   *An archaeological clearance survey of nine seismic testing transects in Dona Ana and Sierra counties, New Mexico.* Cultural Resources Management Division Report, no. 470. Las Cruces: New Mexico State Univ.

Harris, Marvin
1959   The economy has no surplus? *American Anthropologist* 61(2):185–199.

Haury, Emil
1936   *The Mogollon culture of southwestern New Mexico.* Medallion Papers, no. 20. Globe, Ariz.: Gila Pueblo.
1958   Evidence at Point of Pines for a prehistoric migration from northeastern Arizona. In *Migrations in New World culture history,* ed. R. H. Thompson, 1—6. Social Science Bulletin, no. 27. Tucson: Univ. of Arizona.
1976   *The Hohokam: Desert farmers and craftsmen.* Tucson: Univ. of Arizona Press.

Hawley, Florence M.
1934   *The significance of the dated prehistory of Chetro Ketl, Chacao Canyon, New Mexico.* Univ. of New Mexico Bulletin, Monograph Series, no. 1. Albuquerque.
1937   Pueblo social organization as a lead to pueblo history. *American Anthropologist* 39:504–522.
1946   The role of Pueblo social organization in the dissemination of Catholicism. *American Anthropologist* 48:407–415.

Hayes, Alden C.
1981   *Contributions to Gran Quivera archaeology, Gran Quivera Monument, New Mexico.* Publications in Archaeology, no. 17. Washington, D.C.: National Park Service.

Heindreich, Charles Adrian
1967   A review of the Ghost Dance religion of 1889–90 among the North American Indians and comparison of eight societies which accepted or rejected the dance. Master's thesis, Univ. of Oregon.

Herskovits, Melville J.
1938   *Acculturation: The study of culture contact.* New York: J. J. Augustin.

Hester, Thomas R., ed.
1977   *An archaeological survey of the Radium Springs area, southern New Mexico.* Archaeological Survey Report, no. 26. San Antonio: Univ. of Texas Center for Archaeological Research.

Hewett, Edgar L., J. Henderson, and W. W. Robbins
1913   *The physiography of the Rio Grande Valley, New Mexico, in relation to pueblo culture.* Bureau of American Ethnology Bulletin, no. 54. Washington, D.C.: Smithsonian Institution.

Hieb, Louis A.
1972   The Hopi ritual clown: Life as it should not be. Ph.D. dissertation, Princeton Univ.

1979   Hopi world view. In *Handbook of North American Indians.* Vol. 9, *The South-west,* ed. Alfonso Ortiz, 577–580. Washington, D.C.: U.S. Government Printing Office.

Hibben, Frank
1975   *Kiva art of the Anasazi at Pottery Mound.* Las Vegas: K. C. Publications.

Hill, James N.
1968   Broken K Pueblo: Patterns of form and function. In *New perspectives in archaeology,* ed. Lewis Binford and Sally Binford, 103–142. Chicago: Aldine.
1970   *Broken K Pueblo: Prehistoric social organization in the American Southwest.* Anthropological Papers of the Univ. of Arizona, no. 18. Tucson: Univ. of Arizona.

Hill, W. W.
1944   The Navajo Indians and the Ghost Dance of 1890. *American Anthropologist* 46:523–527.

Hilley, G.
1983   *An archaeological clearance survey of ten seismic testing transects in Sierra, Luna and Dona Ana counties, New Mexico.* Cultural Resources Management Division Report, no. 542. Las Cruces: New Mexico State Univ.

Hilley, John
1982   *407 miles of archaeological transect sampling in the basins of southern New Mexico.* Cultural Resources Management Division Report, no. 475. Las Cruces: New Mexico State Univ.

Hirschberg, Richard I., and Joan F. Hirschberg
1957   Meggar's law of environmental limitation on culture. *American Anthropologist* 59:890–891.

Hodge, Frederick W.
1912   *Handbook of American Indians north of Mexico.* Bureau of American Ethnology Bulletin, no. 30, parts 1 and 2. Washington, D.C.: Smithsonian Institution.

Hoebel, E. Adamson
1935   The Sun Dance of the Hekandika Shoshone. *American Anthropologist* 37:570–581.

Hollander, Samuel
1986   On Malthus's population principle of social reform. *History of Public Economy* 18(2):187–235.

Hohman, D.
1982   Sinaqua social organization: Inferences based on prehistoric mortuary practices. Master's thesis, Northern Arizona Univ.

Holmes, N.
1919   *The handbook of aboriginal American antiquities.* Bureau of American Ethnology Bulletin, no. 60, part 1. Washington, D.C.: Smithsonian Institution.

Horsfall, F. L., and I. Tamm, eds.
1965   *Viral and rickettsial infections of man.* Philadelphia: J. B. Lippencott Co.

Huntington, Ellsworth
1914   *The climatic factor.* Publication no. 192. Washington, D.C.: Carnegie Institution of Washington.

Huq, Farida
1976   Effects of temperature and relative humidity on variola virus in crusts. *Bulletin of the World Health Organization* 54:710–712.
Irwin-Williams, Cynthia
1967   Picosa, the elementary southwestern culture. *American Antiquity* 32: 441–457.
1968a   Configurations of preceramic development in the southwestern United States. *Eastern New Mexico University Contributions in Anthropology* 1(1): 1–9.
1968b   Archaic culture history in the southwestern United States. *Eastern New Mexico University Contributions in Anthropology* 1(4):48–54.
1968c   The reconstruction of Archaic culture in the southwestern United States. *Eastern New Mexico University Contribution in Anthropology* 1(3):19–23.
1973   The Oshara tradition: Origins of Anasazi culture. *Eastern New Mexico University Contributions in Anthropology* 5(1).
James, Harry
1974   *Pages from Hopi history.* Tucson: Univ. of Arizona Press.
Jennings, Jesse D.
1957   *Danger Cave.* Univ. of Utah Anthropological Papers, no. 27. Salt Lake City: Univ. of Utah Press.
1964   The desert west. In *Prehistoric man in the New World,* ed. J. D. Jennings and E. Norbeck, 149–174. Chicago: Univ. of Chicago Press.
Jett, Stephen C.
1964   Pueblo Indian migrations: An evaluation of the possible physical and cultural determinants. *American Antiquity* 29(3):281–300.
Jewett, Roberta
1989   Distance, interaction, and complexity: A pan-regional comparison of the spatial organization of fourteenth century settlement clusters in the American Southwest. In *The sociopolitical structure of prehistoric Southwestern society,* ed. Steadman Upham, Kent Lightfoot, and Roberta Jewett, 363–388. Boulder: Westview Press.
Johnson, Gregory A.
1978   Information sources and the development of decision-making organizations. In *Social archaeology,* ed. Charles Redman et al. New York: Academic Press.
1983   Decision-making organization and pastoral nomad camp size. *Human Ecology* 11:175–199.
Jorgensen, Joseph G.
1971   Indians and the metropolis. In *The American Indian in urban society,* ed. Jack O. Waddell and O. Michael Watson, 66–113. Boston: Little, Brown.
1972   *The Sun Dance religion.* Chicago: Univ. of Chicago Press.
1978   A century of political economic effects on American Indian society, 1880–1980. *Journal of Ethnic Studies* 6(3):1–79.
1980   *Western Indians: Comparative environments, languages, and cultures of 172 western American tribes.* San Francisco: W. H. Freeman and Co.
Kahn, Joel S., and Josep R. Llobera, eds.
1981a   *The anthropology of pre-capitalist societies.* London: Macmillan.

Kahn, Joel S., and Josep R. Llobera
1981b   Towards a new Marxism or a new anthropology? In *The anthropology of pre-capitalist societies,* ed. Joel S. Kahn and Josep R. Llobera, 263–329. London: Macmillan.

Kammer, Jerry
1980   *The second Long Walk: The Navajo-Hopi land dispute.* Albuquerque: Univ. of New Mexico Press.

Kapferer, Bruce, ed.
1976   *Transaction and meaning: Directions in the anthropology of exchange and human behavior.* Philadelphia: ISHI Publications.

Keesing, Roger
1967   Statistical models and decision models of social structure: A Kwaio case. *Ethnology* 6:1–16.
1974   Theories of culture. *Annual Review of Anthropology* 3:73–97.
1987   Anthropology as interpretive quest. *Current Anthropology* 28(2):161–176.
1989   Exotic readings of cultural texts. *Current Anthropology* 30(4):459–479.

Kelley, J. Charles
1952a   Factors involved in the abandonment of certain peripheral southwestern settlements. *American Anthropologist* 54:356–387.
1952b   The historic Indian pueblos of La Junta de los Rios. *New Mexico Historical Review* 27(4):257–295; (5):21–51.

Kelly, William H.
1953   *Indians of the Southwest: A survey of Indian tribes and Indian administration in Arizona.* Tucson: Univ. of Arizona Press.

Kennard, Edward A.
1965   Post-war economic changes among the Hopi. In *Essays in economic anthropology, proceedings of the 1965 annual spring meeting of the American Ethnological Society,* ed. June Helm, 24–32. Seattle: Univ. of Washington Press.
1972   Metaphor and magic: Key concepts in Hopi culture and their linguistic forms. In *Studies in linguistics in honor of George L. Trager,* ed. M. Estelle Smith, 468–473. The Hague: Mouton.
1979   Hopi economy and subsistence. In *Handbook of North American Indians.* Vol. 9, *The Southwest,* ed. Alfonso Ortiz, 554–563. Washington, D.C.: U.S. Government Printing Office.

Kessel, William B.
1976   White Mountain Apache religious cult movements: A study in ethno-history. Ph.D. dissertation, Univ. of Arizona.

Kidder, Alfred V.
1915   Pottery of the Pajarito Plateau and of some adjacent regions in New Mexico. *Memoirs of the American Anthropological Association,* no. 2(6), pp. 407–462. Menasha, Wisc.
1924   *An introduction to the study of southwestern archaeology.* Smithsonian Miscellaneous Collections, no. 146(1). Washington, D.C.: Smithsonian Institution.

Kidder, Alfred V., and Anna O. Shepard
1936   *The pottery of Pecos, vol. 2.* Papers of the Phillips Academy Southwest Expedition, no. 7. New Haven: Yale Univ. Press.

Kirkpatrick, D. T., and Meliha S. Duran
1982   *An archaeological clearance survey of eight seismic testing transects in Sierra, Luna, and Dona Ana counties, New Mexico.* Cultural Resources Management Division Report, no. 498. Las Cruces: New Mexico State Univ.

Kleinman, D. S.
1980   *Human adaptation and population growth: A non-Malthusian approach.* New York: Universe Books.

Knack, Martha C.
1975   Contemporary southern Paiute household structure and bilateral kinship clusters. Ph.D. dissertation, Univ. of Michigan.

Krutz, Gordon V.
1973   The native's point of view as an important factor in understanding the dynamics of the Oraibi split. *Ethnohistory* 20(1):77–89.

Kunitz, Stephen J.
1973   *Demographic change among the Hopi and Navajo Indians.* Lake Powell Research Project Bulletin, no. 2. Washington, D.C.: National Science Foundation.

La Barre, Weston
1938   *The Peyote Cult.* Yale Univ. Publications in Anthropology, no. 19. New Haven: Yale Univ. Press.
1969   *The Peyote Cult.* Enlarged ed. Hamden: Shoestring Press.
1972   *The Ghost Dance: Origins of religion.* New York: Dell.

Laird, W. David
1977   *Hopi bibliography: Comprehensive and annotated.* Tucson: Univ. of Arizona Press.

Landsman, Gail
1979   The Ghost Dance and the policy of allotment: Comment on Carrol, ASR June, 1975. *American Sociological Review* 44:162–166.

Lange, Charles H.
1979   Relations of the Southwest with the Plains and Great Basin. In *Handbook of North American Indians.* Vol. 9, *The Southwest,* ed. Alfonso Ortiz, 201–205. Washington, D.C.: Smithsonian Institution.

Laumbach, K.
1981a   *An archaeological survey of the Plains Electric transmission line from Las Cruces to Alamogordo, New Mexico.* Cultural Resources Management Division Report, no. 446. Las Cruces: New Mexico State Univ.
1981b   *An archaeological survey of a portion of a Petty-Ray geophysical seismic testing line in Sierra County, New Mexico.* Cultural Resources Management Division Report, no. 484. Las Cruces: New Mexico State Univ.
1982   *An archaeological survey of 150 miles of seismic testing transects in Sierra and Dona Ana counties, New Mexico.* Cultural Resources Management Division Report, no. 518. Las Cruces: New Mexico State Univ.

Leach, Edmund R.
1954   *Political systems of highland Burma.* Boston: Beacon Press.

Leathers, Nezzie Lee
1937   The Hopi Indians and their relations with the United States government to 1906. Master's thesis, Univ. of Oklahoma.

Lehmer, D. J.
1948   *The Jornada branch of the Mogollon.* Social Science Bulletin, no. 17. Tucson: Univ. of Arizona.

Lesser, Alexander
1933   Cultural significance of the Ghost Dance. *American Anthropologist* 35: 108–115.

Lévi-Strauss, Claude
1963   *Structural anthropology.* New York: Basic Books.

Lightfoot, Kent G.
1984   *Prehistoric political dynamics: A case study from the American Southwest.* Dekalb: Northern Illinois Univ. Press.

Lindsey, A. J., Jr.
1969   The Tsegi phase of the Kayenta cultural tradition in northeastern Arizona. Ph.D. dissertation, Univ. of Arizona.

Linton, Ralph
1940   *Acculturation in seven American Indian tribes.* New York: D. Appleton-Century.
1943   Nativistic movements. *American Anthropologist* 45:230–240.

Lloyd, Christopher
1986   *Explanation in social history.* Oxford: Basil Blackwell.

Logan, M. H., and William Sanders
1976   The model. In *The valley of Mexico: Studies in prehispanic ecology and society,* ed. Eric R. Wolf, 31–58. Albuquerque: Univ. of New Mexico Press.

Longacre, William A.
1964   Sociological implication of the ceramic analysis. In *Chapters in the prehistory of Arizona,* II, ed. Paul S. Martin et al., 155–167. Fieldiana: Anthropology 55. Chicago Natural History Museum.
1970a   *Archaeology as anthropology: A case study.* Anthropological Papers of the University of Arizona, no. 17. Tucson: Univ. of Arizona Press.
1970b   A historical review. In *Reconstructing prehistoric pueblo societies,* ed. William A. Longacre, 1–10. Albuquerque: Univ. of New Mexico Press.

Lowie, Robert H.
1929   *Notes on Hopi clans.* Anthropological Papers of the American Museum of Natural History, no. 30(6), pp. 303–360. New York.

Lycett, Mark T.
1984   Social and economic consequences of aboriginal population decline from introduced disease. Paper presented at the 49th Annual Meetings of the Society for American Archaeology, Portland.

MacCallum, F. O., and J. R. McDonald
1957   Survival of variola virus in raw cotton. *Bulletin of the World Health Organization* 16:247–254.

Macquet, J. J.
1961   *The premise of inequality in Ruanda.* London: Oxford University Press.

Malthus, Thomas R.
1971   *An essay on the principle of population.* New York: Augustus M. Kelley.

Marshall, M. P., and H. J. Wait
1984   *Rio Abajo: Prehistory and history of a Rio Grande province.* Santa Fe: New
         Mexico Historical Program.
Martin, Paul S., and Fred Plog
1973   *The archaeology of Arizona: A study of the Southwest region.* Garden City,
         N.J.: Doubleday/Natural History Press.
Martin, Paul S., J. B. Ruialdo, E. Bluhm, H. C. Cutler, and R. Grange, Jr.
1952   *Mogollon cultural continuity and change: The stratigraphic analysis of Tularosa
         and Cordova Caves.* Fieldiana: Anthropology 40. Chicago Natural History
         Museum.
Martin, Paul S., G. I. Quimby, and D. Collier
1947   *Indians before Columbus.* Chicago: Univ. of Chicago Press.
Marx, Karl
1904   *A contribution to the critique of political economy.* Trans. I. N. Stone. Chi-
         cago: International Library Publishing Co.
1963   *The poverty of philosophy.* New York: International Publishers.
1967   *Capital.* 3 vols. New York: International Publishers.
Marx, Karl, and Friedrich Engels
1967a   *The communist manifesto.* London: Penguin.
1967b   *The German Ideology.* London: Lawrence & Wishart.
Matson, R. G., and W. D. Lipe
1978   Settlement patterns on Cedar Mesa: Boom or bust on the northern periph-
         ery. In *Investigations of the Southwestern Anthropological Research Group,*
         ed. Robert C. Euler and George J. Gumerman, 1–12. Flagstaff: Museum of
         Northern Arizona.
Mayhew, B. H.
1973   System size and ruling elites. *American Sociological Review* 38:468–475.
Mayhew, B. H., and R. L. Levinger
1976   On the emergence of oligarchy in human interaction. *American Journal of
         Sociology* 81:1017–1049.
McAllister, Stephen P., and Fred Plog
1979   Small sites in the Chevelon drainage. In *Limited activity and occupation
         sites,* ed. Albert E. Ward, 17–23. Contributions to Anthropological Studies
         1. Albuquerque: Center for Anthropological Studies.
McGregor, John C.
1941   *Winona and Ridge Ruin, I: Architecture and material culture.* Museum of
         Northern Arizona Bulletin, no. 18, part 1. Flagstaff.
McGuire, Randall H.
1983   Review of Polities and power: An economic and political history of the
         Western Pueblo by Steadman Upham. *American Antiquity* 48:651–652.
Meggars, Betty J.
1954   Environmental limitation on the development of culture. *American Anthro-
         pologist* 56:801–824.
1957   Environmental limitation on Maya culture: A reply to Coe. *American An-
         thropologist* 59:888–890.

Mendenhall, W., and J. E. Reinmuth
1978   *Statistics for management and economics.* North Scituate, Mass.: Duxbury Press.

Mera, Harry P.
1935   *Ceramic clues to the prehistory of north central New Mexico.* Technical Series Bulletin, no. 8. Santa Fe: Laboratory of Anthropology.

Meriam, Lewis
1928   *The problem of Indian administration.* Baltimore: Johns Hopkins Univ. Press.

Merton, Robert K.
1936   The unanticipated consequences of purposive social action. *American Sociological Review* 1.
1975   Structural analysis in sociology. In *Approaches to the study of social structure,* ed. Peter M. Blau, 21–52. New York: Free Press.

Michels, R.
1915   *Political parties.* Trans. F. Paul and C. Paul. New York: Hearst's International Library.

Milner, George R.
1980   Epidemic disease in the post-contact Southeast: A reappraisal. *Mid-Continent Journal of Archaeology* 5(1):39–56.

Mitra, A. C., J. K. Sarker, and M. K. Mukherjee
1974   Virus content of smallpox scabs. *Bulletin of the World Health Organization* 51:106–107.

Montgomery, Ross Gordon, Watson Smith, and John Otis Brew
1949   *Franciscan Awatovi: The excavation and conjectural reconstruction of a 17th-century Spanish mission establishment at a Hopi town in northeastern Arizona.* Peabody Museum of American Archaeology and Ethnology Papers, vol. 36. Cambridge, Mass.: Harvard Univ. Press.

Mooney, James
1896   *The Ghost Dance religion and the Sioux outbreak of 1890.* Annual Report of the United States Bureau of Ethnology, no. 14, part 2, pp. 641–1136. Washington, D.C.: Smithsonian Institution.

Morgan, Lewis Henry
1877   *Ancient society.* New York: Holt, Rinehart and Winston.

Morris, Earl H.
1919a   *Preliminary account of the antiquities of the region between the Mancos and La Plata rivers in southwestern Colorado.* Annual Report of the Bureau of American Ethnology, no. 33, pp. 155–206. Washington, D.C.: Smithsonian Institution.
1919b   *The Aztec ruin.* Anthropological Papers of the American Museum of Natural History, no. 26, part 1. New York.
1921   Chronology of the San Juan area. *Proceedings of the National Academy of Sciences* 7:18–22.
1939   *Archaeological studies in the La Plata district, southwestern Colorado and northwest New Mexico.* Publication no. 519. Washington, D.C.: Carnegie Institution of Washington.

Morris, L., A. L. de Lamos, and O. J. da Silva
1970   Investigations of hospital associated smallpox in Vitoria, Espirito Santo. *American Journal of Public Health* 60:2231.
Munsell, M.
1967   Land and labor at Salt River: Household organization in a changing economy. Ph.D. dissertation, Univ. of Oregon.
Murdock, George P.
1949   *Social structure.* New York: Free Press.
Nagata, Shuichi
1970   *Modern transformations of Moenkopi pueblo.* Urbana: Univ. of Illinois Press.
1971   The reservation community and the urban community: Hopi Indians of Moenkopi. In *The American Indian in urban society,* ed. Jack O. Waddell and O. Michael Watson, 114–159. Boston: Little, Brown.
Naroll, Rodney
1956   A preliminary index of social development. *American Anthropologist* 56: 687–715.
Nelson, Nels C.
1914   *Pueblo ruins of the Galisteo Basin, New Mexico.* Anthropological Papers of the American Museum of Natural History, no. 15(1). New York.
1919   The archaeology of the southwest: A preliminary report. *Proceedings of the National Academy of Sciences* 5:114–120.
Nequatewa, Edmund
1936   *Truth of a Hopi: Stories relating to the origin, myths, and clan histories of a Hopi.* Flagstaff: Northland Press.
Netting, Robert McC.
1990   Population, permanent agriculture, and polities: Unpacking the evolutionary portmanteau. In *The evolution of political systems: Sociopolitics in small-scale sedentary societies,* ed. Steadman Upham. Oxford: Oxford University Press.
Newman, Stanley
1964   A comparison of Zuni and Californian Penutian. *International Journal of American Linguistics* 30(1):1–13.
Niemi, R. G., and H. F. Weisberg
1972   The effects of group size on collective decision-making. In *Probability models of collective decision-making,* ed. R. G. Niemi and H. F. Weisberg, 125–148. Columbus, Ohio: Merrill.
Noell, J. J.
1974   On the administrative sector of social systems. *Social Forces* 52:549–558.
Nordenskiold, Gustof
1893   *The cliff dwellers of the Mesa Verde, southwestern Colorado: Their pottery and implements.* Trans. D. Lloyd Morgan. Chicago: P. A. Norstedt and Soner.
Notestein, F. E.
1960   *Essays on population: Malthus, Huxley and Osborn.* New York: New American Library.
Odum, Howard T.
1971   *Environment, power, and society.* New York: Wiley.

Opler, Morris E., and H. Opler
1950   Mescalero Apache history in the Southwest. *New Mexico Historical Review* 25(1):1–36.
Opler, Marvin K.
1940   The character and history of the Southern Ute Peyote Rite. *American Anthropologist* 42(3):463–478.
Ortiz, Alfonso
1972b   Ritual drama and the Pueblo world view. In *New perspectives on the pueblos,* ed. Alfonso Ortiz, 135–161. Albuquerque: Univ. of New Mexico Press.
Ortiz, Alfonso, ed.
1972a   *New perspectives on the pueblos.* Albuquerque: Univ. of New Mexico Press.
1979   *Handbook of North American Indians.* Vol. 9, *The Southwest.* Washington, D.C.: U.S. Government Printing Office.
Ortner, Sherry B.
1984   Theory in anthropology since the sixties. *Society for Comparative Study of Society and History* 26(1):126–166.
Overholt, Thomas W.
1974   The Ghost Dance of 1890 and the nature of the prophetic process. *Ethnohistory* 21:37–63.
Paige, Jeffrey M.
1975   *Agrarian revolution: Social movements and export agriculture in the underdeveloped world.* New York: Free Press.
Parsons, Elsie Clews
1922   Oraibi in 1920. In *Contributions to Hopi history,* ed. Elsie C. Parsons, 283–298. *American Anthropologist* 24(3):253–298.
1933   *Hopi and Zuni ceremonialism.* American Anthropological Association Memoirs, no. 39. Menasha, Wis.
1939   *Pueblo Indian religion.* 2 vols. Chicago: Univ. of Chicago Press.
1940   Relations between ethnology and archaeology in the Southwest. *American Antiquity* 5:214–220.
Pepper, George H.
1920   *Pueblo Bonito.* Anthropological Papers of the American Museum of Natural History, no. 27. New York.
Plog, Fred
1974a   *The study of prehistoric change.* New York: Academic Press.
1974b   Settlement patterns and social history. In *Frontiers of anthropology,* ed. Murray J. Leaf, 68–93. New York: D. Van Nostrand Co.
1978   The Keresan bridge: An ecological and archaeological account. In *Social archaeology,* ed. Charles Redman, Mary Jane Berman, Edward V. Curtin, William T. Longhorn, Jr., Nina M. Versaggi, and Jeffrey C. Wanser, 349–372. New York: Academic Press.
1981   *Managing archaeology: A background for cultural resource management on the Apache-Sitgreaves National Forest, Arizona.* Cultural Resources Management Report, no. 1. Albuquerque: U.S.D.A. Forest Service, Southwestern Region.
1983   Political and economic alliances on the Colorado Plateau, A.D. 400–1450.

In *Advances in world archaeology.* Vol. 2, pp. 289–330. New York: Academic Press.

1985   Status and death at Grasshopper: The homogenization of reality. In *Status, structure, and stratification: Current archaeological reconstructions,* ed. M. Thompson, M. T. Garcia, and F. J. Kense, 161–166. Calgary: Archaeological Association of the University of Calgary.

Plog, Fred, ed.
1974a   *The study of prehistoric change.* New York: Academic Press.

Plog, Fred, R. Effland, and Dee Green
1978   Inferences using the SARG data bank. In *Investigations of the Southwestern Anthropological Research Group,* ed. Robert C. Euler and George J. Gumerman, 139–148. Flagstaff: Museum of Northern Arizona.

Plog, Stephen
1969   Prehistoric population movements: Measurement and explanation. Manuscript on file at the Field Museum of Natural History, Chicago.

Popper, Karl
1966   *The open society and its enemies.* Vol. 2. London: Routledge.

Powell, Shirley
1980   Material culture and behavior: A prehistoric example for the American Southwest. Ph.D. dissertation, Arizona State Univ.

Prudden, T. Mitchell
1918   A further study of prehistoric small house ruins in the San Juan watershed. *Memoirs of the American Anthropological Association,* no. 5, pp. 1–50. Lancaster, Penn.

Radcliffe-Brown, A. R.
1952   *Structure and function in primitive society.* New York: Free Press.

Ramenofsky, A. F.
1982   The archaeology of population collapse: Native American response to the introduction of infectious disease. Ph.D. dissertation, Univ. of Washington.

Redfield, Robert
1941   *Folk cultures of the Yucatan.* Chicago: Univ. of Chicago Press.

Redfield, Robert, Ralph Linton, and Melvin J. Herskovits
1936   Memorandum for the study of acculturation. *American Anthropologist* 38: 149–152.

Reed, Erik K.
1946   The distinctive features and distribution of the San Juan Anasazi culture. *Southwestern Journal of Anthropology* 2(3):295–305.

1948   The Western Pueblo archaeological complex. *El Palacio* 55(1):9–15.

1949   Sources of upper Rio Grande culture and population. *El Palacio* 56(6): 163–184.

1955   Trends in Southwestern archaeology. In *New interpretations of aboriginal American culture history,* 46–58. 75th Anniversary Volume of the Anthropological Society of Washington. Washington, D.C.

1958   Comment. In *Migration in New World culture history,* ed. Raymond H. Thompson, 7–8. Social Science Bulletin, no. 27. Tucson: Univ. of Arizona.

Rhodes, A. J., and C. E. Van Rooyen
1962   *Textbook of virology for students and practitioners of medicine.* Baltimore: Williams and Wilkens Co.
Riley, Carroll L.
1974   Mesoamerican Indians in the early Southwest. *Ethnohistory* 19(3):247–260.
1980   Mesoamerica and the Hohokam: A view from the 16th century. In *Current issues in Hohokam prehistory: Proceedings of a symposium,* ed. David Doyel and Fred Plog, 41–48. Anthropological Research Papers, no. 23. Tempe: Arizona State Univ.
1987   *The frontier people: The greater Southwest in the protohistoric period.* Albuquerque: Univ. of New Mexico Press.
Robbins, Lynn
1971   Blackfeet families and households. Ph.D. dissertation, Univ. of Oregon.
Roberts, Frank, Jr.
1929   *Shabik'eshchee Village, a late Basketmaker site.* Bureau of American Ethnology Bulletin, no. 92. Washington, D.C.: Smithsonian Institution.
1930   *Early pueblo ruins in the Piedra district, southwest Colorado.* Bureau of American Ethnology Bulletin, no. 96. Washington, D.C.: Smithsonian Institution.
1939   *Archaeological remains in the Winterwater district, eastern Arizona: Part I, house types.* Bureau of American Ethnology Bulletin, no. 121. Washington, D.C.: Smithsonian Institution.
Rogers, Sir Leonard
1926   *Smallpox and climate in India: Forecasting of epidemics.* Medical Research Council Special Report, no. 106. London: His Majesty's Stationary Office.
Rouse, I.
1958   The inference of migration from anthropological evidence. In *Migrations in New World culture history,* ed. R. H. Thompson, 63–68. Social Science Bulletin, no. 27. Tucson: Univ. of Arizona.
Rushforth, Scott
1984   *Bear Lake Athapaskan kinship and task group formation.* Canadian Ethnology Service Paper, no. 96. Ottawa: National Museums of Canada.
1985   Some directive illocutionary acts among the Bear Lake Athapaskans. *Anthropological Linguistics* 27(4):387–411.
Rushforth, Scott, with James S. Chisholm
1991   *Culture persistence: Continuity in meaning and moral responsibility among the Bearlake Athapaskans.* Tucson: Univ. of Arizona Press.
Sahlins, Marshall
1976   *Culture and practical reason.* Chicago: Univ. of Chicago Press.
1981   *Historical metaphors and mythical realities: Structure in the early history of the Sandwich Islands Kingdom.* Ann Arbor: Univ. of Michigan Press.
Sanders, William T., and Barbara J. Price
1968   *Mesoamerica: The evolution of a civilization.* New York: Random House.
Sanders, William T., and David Webster
1978   Unilinealism, multilinealism, and the evolution of complex societies. In *So-*

       cial archaeology, ed. Charles Redman et al., 249–302. New York: Academic
       Press.

Sando, Joe S.

1979   The pueblo revolt. In *Handbook of North American Indians.* Vol. 9, *The*
       Southwest, ed. Alfonso Ortiz, 194–197. Washington, D.C.: U.S. Govern-
       ment Printing Office.

Sartwell, P. E.

1976   Memoir of the Reed-Frost epidemic theory. *American Journal of Epidemi-*
       ology 103:138–140.

Sauer, Carl O.

1935   *Aboriginal population of northwestern Mexico.* Ibero Americana, no. 10.

Schiffer, Michael B., A. P. Sullivan, and T. C. Klinger

1978   The design of archaeological surveys. *World Archaeology* 10:1–29.

Schoenwetter, James, and Alfred E. Dittert, Jr.

1968   An ecological interpretation of Anasazi settlement patterns. In *Anthropolog-*
       ical archaeology in the Americas, ed. Betty Meggars, 41–66. Washington,
       D.C.: Anthropological Society of Washington.

Scholes, France V.

1937   Troublous times in New Mexico, 1659–1670. *New Mexico Historical Re-*
       view 12(2):134–174.

1942   *Troublous times in New Mexico.* Publications in History, vol. 7. Albuquer-
       que: New Mexico Historical Society.

Schroeder, Albert H.

1952   Documentary evidence pertaining to the early historic period of southern
       Arizona. *New Mexico Historical Review* 27:137–167.

1960   *The Hohokam, Sinagua, and Hakataya.* Archives of Archaeology, no. 5.
       Madison.

1972   Rio Grande ethnohistory. In *New perspectives on the pueblos,* ed. Alfonso
       Ortiz, 41–70. Albuquerque: Univ. of New Mexico Press.

1973   The Mescalero Apaches. In *Human systems research, technical manual,*
       124–144. Tularosa, N.M.: Human Systems Research Corporation.

1979a   Pueblos abandoned in historic times. In *Handbook of North American In-*
       dians. Vol. 9, *The Southwest,* ed. Alfonso Ortiz, 236–254. Washington,
       D.C.: U.S. Government Printing Office.

1979b   History of archaeological research. In *Handbook of North American Indians.*
       Vol. 9, *The Southwest,* ed. Alfonso Ortiz, 5–13. Washington, D.C.: U.S.
       Government Printing Office.

Schwartz, Douglas W.

1956   Demographic changes in early periods of Cohonina prehistory. In *Pre-*
       historic settlement patterns in the New World, ed. G. R. Willey, 26–31. Vi-
       king Fund Publications in Anthropology, vol. 23. New York.

Scott, James C.

1976   *The moral economy of the peasant: Rebellion and subsistence in Southeast Asia.*
       New Haven: Yale Univ. Press.

1985   *Weapons of the weak: Everyday forms of peasant resistance.* New Haven: Yale
       Univ. Press.

Sekaquaptewa, Emory
1972   Preserving the good things of Hopi life. In *Plural society in the Southwest,*
        ed. Edward M. Spicer and Raymond H. Thompson, 239–260. Albuquer-
        que: University of New Mexico Press.
Sekaquaptewa, Helen
1969   *Me and mine.* Ed. Louise Udall. Tucson: Univ. of Arizona Press.
Service, Elman R.
1962   *Primitive social organization: An evolutionary perspective.* New York: Ran-
        dom House.
Shimkin, Demitri B.
1953   The Wind River Shoshone Sun Dance. *Bureau of American Ethnology Bul-
        letin,* no. 151, pp. 397–484. Washington, D.C.: Smithsonian Institution.
Shyrock, Henry S., Jacob S. Segal, and Associates
1975   *The methods and materials of demography.* Vol. 2. Washington, D.C.: U.S.
        Department of Commerce, Census Bureau.
Simmons, Leo W., ed.
1942   *Sun Chief: The autobiography of a Hopi Indian.* New Haven: Yale Univ. Press.
Simmons, Marc
1979a   History of Pueblo-Spanish relations to 1821. In *Handbook of North Ameri-
        can Indians.* Vol. 9, *The Southwest,* ed. Alfonso Ortiz, 178–193. Washing-
        ton, D.C.: U.S. Government Printing Office.
1979b   History of Pueblos since 1821. In *Handbook of North American Indians.*
        Vol. 9, *The Southwest,* ed. Alfonso Ortiz, 206–223. Washington, D.C.: U.S.
        Government Printing Office.
Sipes, Richard Grey
1980   *Population growth, society and culture: An inventory of cross-culturally tested
        causal hypotheses.* New Haven: HRAF Press.
Slotkin, J. Sidney
1955   Peyotism, 1521–1891. *American Anthropologist* 57:202–230.
1956   *The Peyote religion: A study in Indian-White relations.* Glencoe, Ill.: Free
        Press.
Snow, Dean R., and Kim M. Lamphear
1988   European contact and Indian depopulation in the Northeast: The timing of
        the first epidemics. *Ethnohistory* 35(1):15–33.
Snow, Dean R., and W. A. Starna
1984   Sixteenth century depopulation: A preliminary view from the Mohawk Val-
        ley. Paper presented at the 49th Annual Meetings of the Society for Ameri-
        can Archaeology, Portland.
Soper, H. E.
1929   Interpretations of periodicity in disease prevalence. *Journal of the Royal Sta-
        tistical Society,* series A, 139:468–500.
Spencer, Herbert
1866   *The principles of biology.* New York: D. Appleton.
1873   *The study of sociology.* New York: D. Appleton.
Spicer, Edward H.
1961   Types of contact and processes of culture change. In *Perspectives in Ameri-*

can Indian culture change, ed. Edward H. Spicer. Chicago: Univ. of Chicago Press.

1962   *Cycles of conquest: The impact of Spain, Mexico, and the United States on the Indians of the Southwest, 1533–1960.* Tucson: Univ. of Arizona Press.

Spier, Leslie

1935   *The Prophet Dance of the Northwest and its derivatives: The source of the Ghost Dance.* General Series in Anthropology, no. 1. Menasha, Wis.: George Banta Publishing Co.

Stanislawski, Michael B.

1979   Hopi-Tewa. In *Handbook of North American Indians.* Vol. 9, *The Southwest,* ed. Alfonso Ortiz, 587–602. Washington, D.C.: U.S. Government Printing Office.

Stearn, E. W., and A. E. Stearn

1945   *The effects of smallpox on the destiny of the Amerindian.* Boston: Bruce Humphries.

Steele, Susan

1979   Uto-Aztecan: An assessment for historical and comparative linguistics. In *The languages of native America,* ed. Lyle Campbell and Marianne Mithun, 444–544. Austin: Univ. of Texas Press.

Steward, Julian H.

1937   Ecological aspects of Southwestern society. *Anthropos* 32:87–104.

1938   *Basin-Plateau aboriginal sociopolitical groups.* Bureau of American Ethnology Bulletin, no. 120. Washington, D.C.: Smithsonian.

1955   *Theory of culture change.* Urbana: Univ. of Illinois Press.

Stewart, Omar C.

1987   *Peyote religion: A history.* Norman: Univ. of Oklahoma Press.

Stone, Jane

1975   An application of a systems theoretic approach to artifact analysis. Master's thesis, State Univ. of New York, Binghamton.

Stuart, David E., and R. P. Gauthier

1981   *Prehistoric New Mexico: Background for survey.* Santa Fe: Historic Preservation Bureau.

Swanson, Guy E.

1960   *The birth of the gods: The origin of primitive beliefs.* Ann Arbor: Univ. of Michigan Press.

Tainter, Joseph A.

1981   Perspectives on the abandonment of the northern Tularosa Basin. Paper presented at the Second Jornada Mogollon Conference, Eastern New Mexico Univ., Portales.

Taussig, Michael T.

1980   *The devil and commodity fetishism in South America.* Chapel Hill: Univ. of North Carolina Press.

Taylor, M. R., and D. Brethauer

1980   *An archaeological survey of five geophysical testing transects in southeastern Dona Ana County, New Mexico.* Cultural Resources Management Division Report, no. 416. Las Cruces: New Mexico State Univ.

Taylor, Walter W.
1954   Southwestern archaeology: Its history and theory. *American Anthropologist* 56:561–575.
Terray, Emmanuel
1972   *Marxism and 'primitive' societies.* New York: Monthly Review Press.
Thomas, David Hurst
1979   *Archaeology.* New York: Holt, Rinehart and Winston.
Thomas, G.
1974   Air sampling of smallpox virus. *Journal of Hygiene* 73:1.
Thornton, Russell
1981   Demographic antecedents of a revitalization movement: Population change, population size, and the 1890 Ghost Dance. *American Sociological Review* 46:88–96.
1986   *We shall live again: The 1870 and 1890 Ghost Dance movements as demographic revitalization.* New York: Cambridge Univ. Press.
Titiev, Mischa
1944   *Old Oraibi: A study of the Hopi Indians of Third Mesa.* Peabody Museum of American Archaeology and Ethnology Papers, vol. 22. Cambridge, Mass.
1972   *The Hopi Indians of Old Oraibi: Change and continuity.* Ann Arbor: Univ. of Michigan Press.
Top, F. H., and P. F. Wehrle, eds.
1972   *Communicable and infectious diseases.* St. Louis: C. V. Mosby Company.
Turner, Christy, and Nancy T. Morris
1970   A massacre at Hopi. *American Antiquity* 35(3):320–331.
Turner, Victor
1967   *The forest of symbols: Aspects of Ndembu ritual.* Ithaca: Cornell Univ. Press.
Tylor, Edward B.
1889   On a method of investigating the development of institutions: Applied to laws of marriage and descent. *Journal of the Royal Anthropological Institute* 18:245–269.
Ubelaker, Douglas H.
1988   North American Indian population size, A.D. 1500 to 1985. *American Journal of Physical Anthropology* 77:289–294.
Upham, Steadman
1978   Final report on archaeological excavations at Chavez Pass Ruin, Coconino National Forest, Arizona: The 1978 field season. Manuscript on file at the U.S.D.A. Forest Service, Coconino National Forest. Flagstaff.
1982   *Polities and power: An economic and political history of the Western Pueblo.* New York: Academic Press.
1984   Adaptive diversity and Southwest abandonment. *Journal of Anthropological Research* 40(2):235–256.
1986   Smallpox and climate in the American Southwest. *American Anthropologist* 88(1):115–127.
1987   A theoretical consideration of middle range societies. In *Chiefdoms in the Americas,* ed. Robert D. Drennen and Carlos A. Uribe, 345–367. New York: Univ. Press of America.

1989   East meets west: Hierarchies and elites in Pueblo society. In *The socio-political structure of prehistoric southwestern societies,* ed. Steadman Upham, Kent Lightfoot, and Roberta Jewett, 77–102. Boulder: Westview Press.

Upham, Steadman, ed.
1990   *The evolution of political systems: Sociopolitics in small-scale sedentary societies.* Cambridge: Cambridge Univ. Press.

Upham, Steadman, and Gail M. Bockley
1989   The chronologies of Nuvakwewtaqa: Implications for social processes. In *The sociopolitical structure of prehistoric Southwestern societies,* ed. Steadman Upham, Kent G. Lightfoot, and Roberta A. Jewett, 447–490. Boulder: Westview Press.

Upham, Steadman, and Lori Stevens Reed
1989   Regional systems in the central and northern southwest: Demography, economy, and sociopolitics preceding contact. In *Archaeological and historical perspectives on the Spanish borderlands west.* Vol. 1, *Columbian Consequences,* ed. David Hurst Thomas, Washington, D.C.: Smithsonian Institution.

Upham, Steadman, and Glen E. Rice
1980   Up the canal without a pattern: Modeling Hohokam interaction and exchange. In *Current issues in Hohokam prehistory,* ed. David Doyel and Fred Plog, 78–106. Anthropological Research Papers, no. 23. Tempe: Arizona State University.

Upham, Steadman, Kent Lightfoot, and Roberta Jewett, eds.
1989   *The sociopolitical structure of prehistoric southwestern societies.* Boulder: Westview Press.

Van Rooyen, C. E., and A. J. Rhodes
1948   *Viral diseases of man.* New York: Thomas Nelson and Sons.

Vane, Sylvia Brakke, ed.
1989   *Seasons of the Katchin.* Ballena Press Anthropological Papers, no. 34. Hayward: Ballena Press and California State Univ.

Vivian, Gordan, and T. W. Mathews
1965   *Kin Kletso, a Pueblo III community in Chaco Canyon, New Mexico.* Southwestern Monuments Association Technical Series 6: parts 1 and 2. Coolidge, Ariz.

Voth, Henry R.
1901a   *The Oraibi Powamu ceremony.* Field Columbian Museum Publication, no. 61. Anthropological Series, no. 3(2). Chicago.
1901b   *The Oraibi Summer Snake ceremony.* Field Columbian Museum Publication, no. 83. Anthropological Series, no. 3(4). Chicago.
1903a   *The Oraibi Marau ceremony.* Field Columbian Museum Publication, no. 156. Anthropological Series, no. 11(1). Chicago.
1903b   *The Oraibi Oáqol ceremony.* Field Columbian Museum Publication, no. 84. Anthropological Series, no. 6(1). Chicago.
1905a   *The traditions of the Hopi.* Field Columbian Museum Publication, no. 96. Anthropological Series, no. 8. Chicago.
1905b   *Oraibi natal customs and ceremonies.* Field Columbian Museum Publication, no. 97. Anthropological Series, no. 6(2). Chicago.

Wallace, Anthony F. C.

1956 Revitalization movements. *American Anthropologist* 58:264–281.

Wallerstein, Immanuel

1974 *Capitalist agriculture and the origins of the European World-Economy in the sixteenth Century.* Modern World-System, vol. 1. New York: Academic Press.

1980 *Mercantilism and consolidation of the European world-economy, 1600–1750.* Modern World-System, vol. 2. New York: Academic Press.

Ward, Albert E., ed.

1979 *Limited activity and occupation sites.* Contributions to Anthropological Studies, no. 1. Albuquerque: Center for Anthropological Studies.

Waters, Frank

1963 *Book of the Hopi.* New York: Viking Press.

Watkins, J. W. N.

1973 Ideal types and historical explanation. In *Modes of individualism and collectivism,* ed. J. O'Neill. London: Heinemann.

Weaver, Donald E., Jr.

1972 A cultural-ecological model for the Classic Hohokam period in the lower Salt River Valley, Arizona. *The Kiva* 38(1):43–52.

Weber, Max

1927 *General economic history.* Trans. Frank H. Knight. New York: Greenberg.

1958 *The Protestant ethic and the spirit of capitalism.* Trans. Talcott Parsons. London: George Allen and Unwin.

1968 *Economy and society.* New York: Bedminster Press.

Wehrle, P. F., J. Posch, K. H. Richter, and D. A. Henderson

1970 An airborne outbreak of smallpox in a German hospital and its significance with respect to other recent outbreaks in Europe. *Bulletin of the World Health Organization* 43:669.

Wendorf, Fred, and Eric K. Reed

1955 An alternative reconstruction of northern Rio Grande prehistory. *El Palacio* 62(5–6):131–173.

Wessman, James W.

1981 *Anthropology and Marxism.* Cambridge, Mass.: Schenkman Publishing Company.

Whalen, Michael E.

1977 *Settlement patterns of the eastern Hueco Bolson.* Centennial Museum Anthropological Paper, no. 4. El Paso: Univ. of Texas at El Paso.

1978 *Settlement patterns of the Western Hueco Bolson.* Centennial Museum Anthropological Paper, no. 6. El Paso: Univ. of Texas at El Paso.

Wheat, Joe Ben

1955 *Mogollon culture prior to* A.D. *1000.* Memoirs of the Society for American Archaeology, no. 10.

Whipple, Amiel W.

1855 *Report upon the Indian tribes: Explorations and surveys for a railroad route from the Mississippi River to the Pacific Ocean.* Vol. 3. Washington, D.C.: U.S. Government Printing Office.

White, Leslie
1949   *The science of culture.* New York: Farrer, Straus.
1959   *The evolution of culture.* New York: McGraw-Hill.
Whiteley, Peter M.
1985   Unpacking Hopi "clans": Another vintage model out of Africa? *Journal of Anthropological Research* 41(4):359–374.
1986   Unpacking Hopi "clans": Further questions about Hopi descent groups. *Journal of Anthropological Research* 42(1):69–79.
1987   The interpretation of politics: A Hopi conundrum. *Man* (n.s.) 22:696–714.
1988a   *Deliberate acts: Changing Hopi culture through the Oraibi split.* Tucson: Univ. of Arizona Press.
1988b   *Bacavi: Journey to Reed Springs.* Flagstaff: Northland Press.
1989   Hopitutskwa: An historical and cultural interpretation of the Hopi traditional land claim. Manuscript on file with the authors.
Whittlesey, Stephanie M.
1978   Status and death at Grasshopper Pueblo: Experiments toward an archaeological theory of correlates. Ph.D. dissertation, Univ. of Arizona.
Wiget, Andrew O.
1982   Truth and the Hopi: An historiographic study of documented oral tradition concerning the coming of the Spanish. *Ethnohistory* 29(3):181–199.
Wilber, Charles K., ed.
1984   *The political economy of development and underdevelopment.* New York: Random House.
Wilcox, David R.
1979   The theoretical significance of fieldhouses. In *Limited activity and occupation sites,* ed. Albert Ward, 25–31. Contributions to Anthropological Studies, no. 1. Albuquerque: Center for Anthropological Studies.
1981   The entry of Athapaskans into the American Southwest: The problem today. In *The protohistoric period in the North American Southwest, A.D. 1450–1700,* ed. David R. Wilcox and W. B. Masse, 213–256. Anthropological Research Papers, no. 24. Tempe: Arizona State Univ.
Williams, Raymond
1977   *Marxism and literature.* New York: Oxford Univ. Press.
Wimberly, M., and A. Rogers
1977   Archaeological survey, Three Rivers drainage, New Mexico. *The Artifact* 15.
Wiseman, Regge N.
1986   *An initial study of the origins of chupadero black-on-white.* Archaeological Society Technical Note, no. 2. Albuquerque.
Wittfogel, Karl
1957   *Oriental despotism.* New Haven: Yale Univ. Press.
Wobst, H. Martin
1974   Boundary conditions for Paleolithic social systems: A simulation approach. *American Antiquity* 39:142–178.
Wolf, Eric R.
1971   On peasant rebellions. In *Peasants and peasant societies,* ed. Teodor Shanin. Baltimore: Penguin.

1982   *Europe and the people without history.* Berkeley: Univ. of California Press.
Wormington, H. Marie
1957   *Ancient man in North America.* Popular Series, no. 4. Denver: Denver Museum of Natural History.
Worsley, Peter
1956   The kinship system of the Tallensi: A reevaluation. *Journal of the Royal Anthropological Institute* 86 : 37–75.
1957   *The trumpet shall sound.* London: MacGibbon and Kee.
Yoffee, Norman
1979   The decline and rise of Mesopotamian civilization: An ethnoarchaeological perspective on the evolution of social complexity. *American Antiquity* 44 : 3–35.
Zubrow, Ezra B. W.
1971   Carrying capacity and dynamic equilibrium in the prehistoric Southwest. *American Antiquity* 36 : 127–138.

Index

Abandonments, prehistoric southwestern, 15, 43; and adaptive diversity, 52, 54–56, 63, 64, 68, 69, 117, 183, 193, 201; theories of, 47–51, 66, 182, 192, 199, 203

Aberle, David F., 142–148, 153, 258 n.10

Abiquiu-Chama, 33

Abortion, 187

Acculturation: at Oraibi Pueblo, 130, 136, 137; theories about, 202, 205, 206, 207–210, 228, 233, 235, 258 n.9; among twentieth-century Hopis, 165, 169, 171, 173

Acoma Pueblo, 10, 15, 29, 30, 33, 36, 65, 68, 74, 108; population and disease among, 94, 95, 108, 183

Adams, Robert McCormick, 52–54

Adams, W. Y., 50

Adaptation, 62–64, 68, 186, 193, 196, 199–201, 207, 229 n.11; archaeologists' questions about, 47

Adaptive diversity, 15, 48, 52–56, 59, 63, 69, 186, 193, 201. See also Abandonments

Adaptive strategies, 62, 64, 66, 68, 182, 183

Agencies, U.S. government, 151–153, 156, 165

Agency: and endogenous processes in sociocultural persistence and change, 232–244, 249, 251, 260 n.11; and human action, 7, 25, 26, 163, 180, 181, 201, 202, 225, 227; and power, 238–240. See also Behavior; Consciousness; Deliberation; Endogenous processes; Exogenous processes; Intentionality; Rationalization; Unintended consequences

Agency towns, 159, 162, 175, 185, 205, 212, 214

Aggregation: of individual actions, 232, 238; of southwestern Native populations, 36, 54, 68, 69, 181

Agriculture: and adaptive shifts, 49, 68; and control of Hopi fields, 39, 121, 124, 139, 168; and ecological explanation, 197, 198, 200, 201; and hedge-your-bets Hopi strategy, 34, 38, 112, 132, 201; and Hopi economy (1680–1879), 100, 106, 110, 112; and Hopi religion, 117; and Malaysian peasants, 230, 231; Marxist interest in, 222; at Oraibi Pueblo, 24, 131–137, 213; and population, 63, 187, 188, 192; and prehistoric Western Pueblos, 30, 34–36,

Gran Quivira, 33
Grasshopper Pueblo, Ariz., 51
Graves, Michael, 73
Gregory, Herbert E., 47, 49
Griffen, P. B., 36, 73
Gulliver, P. H., 66
Gumerman, George J., 48, 199

Habitus, 240, 241, 260 n.11. *See also*
      Bourdieu, Pierre
Hack, John T., 34, 49
Hackett, Charles Wilson, 104
Haggett, P., 32
Hale, Kenneth, 10
Hamblin, Jacob, 107
Hammond, George P., 32, 65
Hanley, Theresa, viii
Hano Pueblo, 10, 102, 110, 113
Hantman, Jeffrey L., 32, 51
Hardesty, Donald L., 196, 197
Harkey, M., 62
Harris, David, 10
Harris, Marvin, 72
Havasupai Indians, 125, 147
Hawaiian social history, 241–244, 246,
      248, 249. *See also* Sahlins,
      Marshall
Hawley, Florence M., 19, 49, 255 n.5
Heevi'ima, 150
Hegelian Marxism, 221
Hegemony, 229, 230. *See also* Ideology
Herskovits, Melvin, 8, 143, 144, 207
Hester, Thomas R., 62
Hewett, Edgar L., 47, 49
Hibben, Frank, 33
Hieb, Louis A., 42, 256 n.3
Hill, James, 20, 61
Hill, W. W., 143, 147
Hilley, G., 62
Hirschberg, Richard I., 269 n.7
Historical particularism, 5, 8, 206
Hodge, Frederick W., 129
Hohman, D., 36, 73, 74
Holbrook, Ariz., 152, 161
Hollander, Samuel, 259 n.3
Holmes, N., 198, 199
Hostiles, 125–129, 135, 136, 138, 146,
      150, 151, 159, 194, 251

Hotevilla Pueblo, 10, 129, 135, 150, 151,
      155, 167, 169, 170, 194, 247
Hueco Phase, 61
Hunter-gatherers, 30, 38, 47, 164, 186–
      188, 222; and adaptive diver-
      sity, 15, 49, 53, 54–57, 61,
      63–66, 68, 69, 182, 183, 193,
      201. *See also* Abandonments;
      Mobility
Huntington, Ellsworth, 47, 49
Huq, Farida, 83, 84
Hypercoherence, 74, 224

Ideology: foreign to Hopis, 98, 106;
      Ghost Dance, 125, 143, 147;
      Hopi descent, 184; Hopi po-
      litical, 127, 136, 159, 176;
      Hopi religious, 119–123;
      Marxist definitions and views
      of, 172, 184, 218–225, 227,
      229–231
Imbalance between people and re-
      sources, 194
Immigration, 108
Improvisations, 240. *See also* Habitus
Incarceration, 126, 127, 136, 151, 153
Indios Rayados, 30. *See also* Chichi-
      mecos; Querechos
Infanticide, 53, 187
Influenza, 15, 37, 74, 75, 194. *See also*
      Disease; Epidemics; Smallpox
Infrastructure: Hopi, 121, 156, 174; in
      Marxist analyses, 212, 222,
      223
Initiate, 149, 243
Innovation: in anthropological theory,
      7, 260 n.3; technological, 134,
      188, 222, 230
Instability, 6, 227; economically moti-
      vated residential 164, 169,
      175, 185; population 122
Integration of levels, 72
Intensification: and ecological regula-
      tion, 54, 188; of subsistence
      and population growth, 187,
      188, 192, 201; in Western
      Pueblo agriculture, 35, 36,
      54, 56, 63, 192, 201. *See also*